D1259463

Drink and British Politics since 1830

A Study in Policy-Making

John Greenaway
Senior Lecturer in Politics
School of Economic and Social Studies
The University of East Anglia

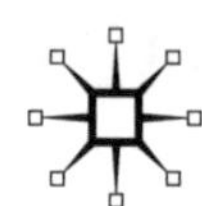

First published 2003 by
PALGRAVE MACMILLAN
Houndmills, Basingstoke, Hampshire RG21 6XS and
175 Fifth Avenue, New York, N.Y. 10010
Companies and representatives throughout the world

PALGRAVE MACMILLAN is the global academic imprint of the Palgrave Macmillan division of St. Martin's Press, LLC and of Palgrave Macmillan Ltd. Macmillan® is a registered trademark in the United States, United Kingdom and other countries. Palgrave is a registered trademark in the European Union and other countries.

ISBN 0–333–91782–0

This book is printed on paper suitable for recycling and made from fully managed and sustained forest sources.

A catalogue record for this book is available from the British Library.

Library of Congress Cataloging-in-Publication Data

Greenaway, J. R.
Drink and British politics since 1830 : a study in policy-making / John Greenaway.
p. cm.
Includes bibliographical references and index.
ISBN 0-333-91782-0 (cloth)
1. Drinking of alcoholic beverages–Government policy–Great Britain–History. I. Title.

HV5446G74 2003
363.4′1′0941–dc21 2003040515

10 9 8 7 6 5 4 3 2 1
12 11 10 09 08 07 06 05 04 03

Printed and bound in Great Britain by
Antony Rowe Ltd, Chippenham and Eastbourne

This book is dedicated to my late parents

George William and Joyce Mary Greenaway

both fine historians

Contents

List of Abbreviations

AA	Alcoholics Anonymous
BMA	British Medical Association
BTL	British Temperance League
CAMRA	Campaign for Real Ale
CCB	Central Control Board (Liquor Traffic)
CETS	Church of England Temperance Society
CPRS	Central Policy Review Staff
DHSS	Department of Health and Social Security
DORA	Defence of the Realm Act
MoH	Ministry of Health
MoT	Ministry of Transport
MRC	Medical Research Council
MTCP	Ministry of Town and Country Planning
NCA	National council on Alcoholism
NHS	National Health Service
NTDA	National Trade Defence Association
NTL	National Temperance League
PA	Pedestrians' Association
PP	*Parliamentary Papers*
PRO	Public Record Office
RoSPA	Royal Society for the Prevention of Accidents
TLL	Temperance Legislation League
UKA	United Kingdom Alliance
W.C.	War Cabinet Papers
WHO	World Health Organisation

Acknowledgements

This book has been long in gestation. My interest in the politics of Drink began back in the 1970s when, as a Ph.D student at the Politics Department of the University of Leeds, I researched the Local Option Question and British Politics, 1864–1914. I then moved on to completely different areas of research, including the theory and practice of policy-making. Some ten years ago, it struck me that the politics and policy-making regarding alcohol in Britain remained underresearched, particularly in the period after 1900, and that this might prove a fruitful area for an interdisciplinary study that drew upon the approaches of both History and Political Science. A visit to the Public Record Office confirmed the existence of vast quantities of largely unexplored archival material. Such indeed was the richness of this material that I decided to curtail my original plan and to limit my original researches to the period prior to 1970, which was when the government papers ceased to be available to me.

In the lengthy process of researching the book, I have therefore become indebted to many persons and institutions. I wish to express my gratitude to the staff of numerous libraries and archives where I have worked, who have met my needs and requests for information with unfailing cheerfulness and helpfulness.

I must give special thanks to the staff of the Library of the University of East Anglia, who have helped me in my work over a long period of time. I should particularly like to mention the staff of the Public Record Office whose ability to conjure up obscure files in as little as a quarter of an hour has never ceased to amaze me.

I should like to thank Mr T. Garth Waite and the staff of the United Kingdom Alliance for allowing me access to the documents in their care. My thanks are due to the following for permission to consult and quote from unpublished material: the Marquess of Salisbury in respect of the papers of the Third Marquess of Salisbury; the Clerk of Records, the House of Lords Record Office in respect of the Viscount Davidson Papers and, on behalf of the Beaverbrook Foundation, in respect of the Bonar Law and Lloyd George Papers; Lambeth Palace Library in respect of the Randall Davidson Papers; the Syndics of Cambridge University Library in respect of the Lord Randolph Churchill Papers; the trustees of the W. H. Smith Trust in respect of the Hambleden Papers.

I am grateful to the University of East Anglia for allowing me two periods of semester-long study leave to research and write this book. The School of Economic and Social Studies at UEA has provided me with a stimulating intellectual environment in which to research. I should particularly like to thank those attending the staff/postgraduate seminar of the Politics and Sociology Sector, who provided helpful comments on two draft papers on Drink and politics. I have also greatly benefited over the years from exchanges with my students studying policy-making at UEA, both at a postgraduate and undergraduate level.

On a personal note I owe a lasting debt to my former Ph.D superviser, Owen Hartley, for giving me invaluable and stimulating insights into how historical study could be enriched by political science. Many colleagues over the years have shown an encouraging interest in my work, for which I am grateful. In particular, I should like to take this opportunity of thanking Richard Chapman and John Street for general support at various stages of my academic life. David Fahey and David Gutzke kindly offered me advice on the location of sources at various times.

I am grateful to Albert Weale for reading a section of the book and for providing some very useful reflections on the nature of the policy process. Geoff Searle found time in a busy schedule to read almost all the draft typescript and I am very grateful to him for numerous suggestions and advice. I should also like to thank my friend Terence Ioan for providing the cartoon drawing for the cover of this books.

My wife, Denise Carlo, has helped me immeasurably over the years, at times by distracting me from my work and at other times driving me on to complete it.

Finally, my greatest debt is to my late parents, to whom this book is dedicated, who not only encouraged me to take up an academic career but also, in the early years, provided me with much support along the way.

I remain, of course, solely responsible for any errors or shortcomings that this work may contain.

JOHN GREENAWAY

1
Introduction

The aim of this book

This is a study of the high politics of social policy-making. This book looks at how elite politicians and decision-makers reacted to and wrestled with one particular social issue, 'Drink', in Britain over a long historical period. The Drink issue does not loom very large in general, secondary histories of the period, in contrast to other social policy areas such as housing, poverty, or education. Nevertheless, between 1830 and 1970 Drink attracted considerable excitement and interest in a variety of quarters. The Victorian temperance movement, at first the object of suspicion, came to be seen by most elites as a remarkable and commendable expression of grass roots popular enlightenment. Both J. S. Mill and T. H. Green used Drink legislation as key examples in their attempts to define the role of the state in a liberal polity. A royal commission in the 1890s spoke of a 'gigantic evil', and in 1901 'temperance reform' was seen to merit a whole chapter to itself in C. F. G. Masterman's influential volume of essays on social reform.[1] Demonstrations on either side in favour of or against the liquor licensing bills of 1904 and 1908 were enormous, on a scale comparable to those of the Campaign for Nuclear Disarmament or the Countryside Alliance three generations later. The First World War saw widespread hysteria on the impact of drinking on national efficiency, along with serious moves to take the whole alcohol industry under state control. After 1945, both drink and driving and the health implications of alcohol consumption attracted interest and controversy among pressure groups and officials within Whitehall and, in the former case, considerable popular interest.

One reason for the relative lack of interest on the part of historians and political scientists in Drink is the changeable and elastic nature of the issue. The terms in which it was debated have varied widely from one generation to another. The very definition of the 'problem' – and, indeed, whether it was a problem at all – was contested. It was an area where there was little consensus and one that interacted with a plethora of other policy areas in complex ways. Yet, for precisely these reasons, Drink as a social policy question has attractions for the political scientist. It prompts a range of interesting general questions about the (changing) nature of British politics and of the policy process in general. What light does it shed on the changing nature of the political system over this period (including behaviour of parties, pressure groups and civil servants)? How insulated is the world of high politics from the pressures of popular agitation or mobilised opinion from 'below'? Why does an issue come in and go off the political agenda? What determines the discourse with which an issue is debated and how do dramatic changes in this discourse affect the substance of policy-making? What is the role of ideas and dominant policy paradigms in determining policy outputs? How is 'scientific' or statistical evidence used and manipulated by policy makers? How elastic are more general political ideologies and what is their relationship to particular policy ideas? How far do bureaucratic structures shape the nature of the policy process? How much leeway do individual politicians have to take initiatives on the issue? This is a wide enough range of questions to address. The focus of the book is therefore limited to the high politics of the Westminster and Whitehall arenas and the interplay between them and outside groups or influences. Areas such as the changing role that alcohol played in British society during this period, the issue of alcohol in relation to social control, the inner workings of various pressure groups, and comparisons with other countries – all interesting and important questions worthy of study – are not my prime concern.

Such a self-imposed limitation is in any case necessary, given that I have chosen to cover such a wide span of years. This in itself brings advantages as well as dangers. Historians have a tendency to compartmentalise themselves into periods: so that, for example, one finds rather few detailed policy studies spanning both the turning points of 1914 or 1945, to the possible distortion of the historical process. Political scientists, for their part, being interested in theoretical approaches, are often impatient of historical detail or concentrate too narrowly on the contemporary. Yet, if one is studying the impact of ideas in bringing about policy change, then it is necessary to look over several decades. On the debit side, a long chronology means that depth of historical detail has to be sacrificed. Several of the individual historical chapters that follow could well warrant a book in their own right; for example, on Drink and the First World War. There is room for more attention to the politics of Drink in Scotland and Wales. In examining the period 1945–70, I have concentrated on three detailed case studies, but there are many other subjects, such as the tied house question, or the regulation of hours of work or wages in the Trade, which could have illuminated the workings of government and the policy process at this time. My original intention had been to continue the story up to the present, but such was the richness of the documentary and archival material available, that it seemed best to stop in 1970, at the time when, under the thirty-year rule, the government records ceased to be available to me. Research beyond that point would have had to rely on interviews and thus use a different methodology. I have, however, supplied a short epilogue, which reflects on some of the salient developments of more recent years, but which does not claim to be based on original research. As this is a study of high politics, I have based it upon extensive primary sources, including politicians' papers and Public Record Office material. However, I have also had the benefit of being able to draw upon some fine historical scholarship. Foremost here are Brian Harrison's comprehensive and pioneering analysis of Drink in Victorian society and politics in the period up till 1874 and Wilson and Gourvish's economic history of the brewing industry throughout the period.[2] For the late-Victorian period, there are scholarly monographs by A. E. Dingle, D. A. Hamer, Lilian Shiman, David Gutzke, and a series of articles by David Fahey.[3] For the period after 1900, scholarly material, other than that on the economic and the medical history aspects, becomes decidedly thin on the ground. Apart from a handful of articles on the First World War, one has to move on to Betsy Thom's recent, well researched study of policy towards alcoholism and alcohol problems in the 1950s and after.[4] Rob Baggott provides some sensitive analysis of government policies towards alcohol in the period 1945–85, but without the benefit of access to Public Record Office material.[5]

The intangible nature of the Drink question

A persistent feature of the Drink issue throughout our period is the lack of any consensus among contemporaries at any time about the values of Britain's 'oldest drug', alcohol. Attitudes towards other substances may have changed over the years but have rarely elicited such prolonged and heated disputation. The use of tobacco (by men), for example, was generally viewed in positive terms right up until the 1950s, but thereafter it rapidly came to be seen as a major health problem.[6] Attitudes and policy towards opiates have shifted in more complex ways, but it is possible to categorise dominant policy paradigms at different periods.[7] However, from the 1830s to the present, Drink has been a bone of contention. In the Victorian period many saw it as essential to civilised life, with beer being as English as roast beef. Many others saw it as the 'devil in solution', the harbinger of disease, destitution and dissolution. Yet others approved its moderate use, whilst recognising its dangers. But, in our own day, we find equally varied assessments. Thus, the claim by the Institute for Alcohol Studies in 1988 that more than 40,000 people a year in Britain died from alcohol related diseases was challenged by the wine writer, Jancis Robinson, who claimed that the only reliable figure was the 3,000 deaths directly attributed to drinking and that judicious use of alcohol was socially beneficial.[8] In 1990, we find views long held in some medical circles that problem drinking was a 'disease' challenged by the director of the government sponsored charity, Alcohol Concern, who stressed that most problems stemmed from 'moderate, not dependent' drinkers.[9] At the same time, other government departments viewed existing restrictions on sales as anachronistic and harmful to the tourist trade.

Assessments of the nature Drink as a political issue have been as varied as judgements about the virtues of alcohol itself. In the nineteenth century, it came to be widely accepted that intemperance, especially among the working class, was a major social problem. But was Drink the causal factor in evils such as crime, disorder, poverty and prostitution, or was drunkenness or intemperance the symptom of an impoverished and inadequate environment? Unlike education, for example, Drink was not an issue that, notwithstanding broader ramifications, could be contained as a discrete policy area centring upon a bureaucratic and administrative nexus. A remarkable feature of the whole period covered by this book is that Drink is redefined again and again. In the 1830s, we see the problems debated in terms of restrictive practices and political economy. Soon after, Drink essentially becomes a moralist issue of temperance and individual purity. In the mid-Victorian period, it is being debated in terms of a social evil. By the 1880s, it is being analysed in terms of social reform and collectivist state action. At the turn of the century, it slots into the debates on supposed national and racial degeneration and also on political corruption. In the First World War, it essentially becomes an issue of efficiency and national security. After 1919, the dominant discourse revolves around the nature of drinking as a leisure activity and the means to achieve the 'improved pub'. From 1950, the terms of reference have changed again, with a focus on Drink as a health issue. However, it is also seen as an economic question; indeed by the 1990s we have come full circle and we find a rigorous discussion of monopolies and the free market once again. All the various discourses overlap and this complicates the politics of particular policy proposals. We find Drink becoming entangled along the way with an amazing array of other legislative and policy concerns. Thus, at various times, we find it embroiled with fiscal policy, sabbatarianism, local government reform, political corruption, food control, nationalisation, town planning, health policies, road safety, tourism, health, and football hooliganism. The broader political aspirations of parties and individual political leaders, as well as the bureaucratic interests of various departments or agencies, also impinge on the story.

Those who took part in the debates on the Drink question often held strong beliefs, but it is an area into which the mainstream political ideologies of nineteenth- and twentieth-century Britain do not easily fit. Liberals, conservatives and socialists were divided on the issue again and again. The result was that Drink tended to generate its own ideological schools. Yet, often the debate became bogged down in technicalities and what, from the perspective of a later generation, seem extremely narrow terms of debate. Thus, from 1880–1908, there is excessive concentration on the technicalities of how to reduce numbers of public houses; from 1908–30, it is the concept of 'disinterested management' that generates most attention; after 1945 specialist debates about the 'disease' concept of alcoholism swamp more general discussion of the effects of drinking on health and social problems. Yet, from time to time, the policy arena is affected or even transformed by external events or developments. The most remarkable example of this is the impact of the First World War which completely recasts the terms of the debate and brings in new personnel and institutions that shape policy. But we can point to other exogenous factors, such as the urban planning and rebuilding schemes after 1945 or the development of the European Community after 1970. Then there are changes in the broader cultural or social developments of modern Britain, such as the development of new leisure pursuits after 1900, the changing position of women in society, or the decline of nonconformity. Britain was not the only country where policies towards alcohol were hotly debated and, from time to time, we find policy exponents searching for models from abroad, notably the USA, Sweden and France. The result is a complex story of policy adaptation and, at times policy experimentation, where both administrative and political forces interact with ideas and intellectual aspirations.

For many years the focus of those political scientists outside the Marxist tradition studying the policy process was on the institutional forces that shaped policy in different 'stages': gestation, formulation and implementation. Traditional liberal democratic interpretations that placed most emphasis on political parties and allied pressure groups as the battering rams of change were challenged by explanations in terms of competing bureaucratic politics. Latterly, policy networks have been seen as the core forces. All such approaches were appropriate to the dominant, pluralist perspectives of the postwar period. However, more recently the focus has shifted to policy change that encompasses broader dynamics involving such concepts of policy innovation, policy learning, policy mutation and policy agendas.[10] These allow a wider intellectual scope. Particularly pertinent to our study is the interest in the role of ideas or general intellectual paradigms in policy-making and the way in which they interact with political and bureaucratic forces. My object is to relate the history of the high politics of Drink to some of these concepts. In the chapters that follow, I tell the story of the politics of Drink from 1830 to 1970 in the form of an analytical narrative and then, in the final chapter, I reflect on what it reveals about both the changing nature of the British political system and current theories of the policy-making process.

2
The Drink Problem in Early Victorian Britain, 1830–70

Governments had been concerned about the dangers of intoxicants as far back as Tudor times. The link to public disorder or crime was the main issue. Hence, the very first reference in England to liquor licensing came in a statute of 1494 that dealt with the problem of 'vagabonds' and gave the justices of the peace power to 'reject and put away common ale selling' where they deemed necessary.[1] From time to time, moralists also waxed lyrical about the effects of overindulgence among the masses. This was especially marked in the celebrated 'gin mania' in London in the eighteenth century, so vividly satirised and illustrated by Hogarth. However, there had been no systematic policy or attitude towards alcohol or its abuse. Indeed, the gin problem had been the unintended result of the landed interest in Parliament desiring to dispose of a glut of corn and to raise money for a war with France.[2] By the early nineteenth century, however, the issue of the excess consumption of alcohol began to be defined as a social problem, one of intemperance or excessive drinking.

Several factors explain this shift. In the first place, changes in agrarian practices at the time of the industrial revolution, by facilitating the production of alcohol, made 'new and potentially disruptive patterns of alcohol consumption feasible'.[3] Secondly, the processes of industrialisation and urbanisation actually encouraged excessive drinking. Intemperance was frequently the response to a truly wretched and debilitating environment by men and women who were enjoying a fluctuating, but on occasions high, cash income. The popular adage that drink was the quickest and easiest way out of the slums of Manchester was borne out by Engel's lurid account of the resort of the working class to alcohol.[4] In the early part of the nineteenth century the public house, for all its deficiencies, was often the one oasis of recreational activity, open to all, at little cost, in a desert of drabness and squalor. Here were centred so many of the things that made life tolerable: warmth, bright lights, music, singing, simple games, newspapers and good company. The *per capita* figures show that alcohol consumption was actually rising at this period, peaking in the period 1875–79.[5] At all events, drunkenness was far more visible in an urban society than in the rural communities of the past. This ties in with a third factor: excessive drinking was rapidly becoming dysfunctional in an industrial society. The toper weaving at home could afford periodic bouts of inebriety, but working in a large factory he might throw a whole workforce out of gear. The occasional drunkard might safely be employed in a coaching inn, but in a railway signal box he became a deadly liability. The more precise ordering of society, together with its increasing fluidity, encouraged new virtues of thrift, self-discipline and temperance. Moreover, the new urban elite of iron masters, factory owners and the like had a direct social and economic interest in increasing the efficiency and security of their workmen.[6] These were to form the backbone of the temperance movement. As society became more mobile and fluid, and as the effect of industrialisation and urbanisation was to multiply the opportunities for the fulfilment of individual desire, so the response was to promote new measures for regulating those passions by the governing classes.[7]

A fourth factor behind the shift in attitudes was the rapid growth of alternatives to drink. Before 1830, there had been few safe alternative beverages and few opportunities for recreation not linked to the consumption of alcohol. In Victorian Britain, this rapidly changed. Nonalcoholic beverages and alternative forms of 'rational' recreation multiplied. This was the backcloth against which an organised temperance movement emerged from the grass roots that sought to challenge existing *mores* with competing values and lifestyles closely linked to evangelical religion.[8] For the first time, it became possible to articulate a challenge to the position of Drink in British society. Finally, attitudes towards drinking markedly changed among social elites. In part, this was an aspect of the change in manners from Regency to Victorian Britain. Heavy drinking, once condoned in the public schools and among the professions, by 1870 was distinctly frowned upon.[9] Intemperance, moreover, was increasingly seen to be linked, whether causally or otherwise, with other social evils such as poverty, crime, gambling and prostitution. It was also increasingly regarded as perverting the political process by debasing man's rational and higher moral faculties.[10]

As a consequence, many expressed a fear that intemperance might prove to be the Achilles heel of Victorian society. At first, such pronouncements emerged from the organised teetotal or temperance movement, but later they were to be found coming from the mouths of leading clerics, social thinkers or politicians, or in the reports of influential committees of inquiry. Thus, Cobden claimed that temperance reform 'lay at the root of all social and political progression in the country'.[11] A committee of the Convocation of Canterbury in 1869 concluded that intemperance was a 'terrible vice', an evil of 'gigantic dimensions and disastrous results', and a select committee of the Lords in 1879 found drunkenness to be one of the chief causes of disorder and distress.[12] H. A. Bruce, Home Secretary in 1871, believed the evil 'was so great as to be a blot upon our social system, and a disgrace to our civilization'.[13] A decade later, Gladstone sonorously declared that in Britain 'greater is the calamity and curse inflicted upon mankind by intemperance than by the three great curses war, pestilence and famine', although his private views were very much more relaxed.[14] The fact that such utterances may sometimes have been made under a measure of political constraint in no way diminishes their significance. By 1870, popular concern at the temperance problem had become so widespread that politicians felt bound to be seen to be concerned. In short, Drink had become a political, as well as a social and moral, issue.

Little substantial legislation was passed between 1830 and 1870, apart from the Beer Act of 1830, but the period was important for crystallising attitudes. It was one thing for contemporaries to agree that there was a problem, but quite another to decide the lines of a solution. Two questions here were pertinent: What should be the correct relationship between legislative and non-legislative agencies; and What form should any government controls take? It is possible to distinguish six broad approaches.

Six Victorian solutions to the problem

(i) 'Moral suasion'

Fundamental to this position was the belief that it was neither legitimate nor effective for the state to use its power to attack intemperance. Various schools of thought can be found under this banner. Most forceful and influential was J. S. Mill. Mill took the example of temperance legislation to argue that the state might legitimately control or limit the actions of its subjects only insofar as they infringed the rights of others or hindered the discharge of their responsibilities or obligations to their fellows. 'No person ought to be punished simply for being drunk; but a soldier or a policeman should be punished for being drunk on duty.'[15] Moreover, attempts by the state to step beyond its rightful sphere would be self-defeating. He conceded it was possible that a man 'might be guided in some good path, and kept out of harm's way . . . But what will be his comparative worth as a human being?'.[16] The path of true progress lay through moral enlightenment. These views appealed to many Liberals in the mid-century who saw the way forward through progressive education. But some aspects of his teaching also attracted many Conservatives, such as the third Marquess of Salisbury, who believed that man could not hope for moral regeneration through political action and that temperance should be a matter for the churches not Parliament. This opinion was echoed by all those less philosophical MPs and others who disliked the idea of temperance legislation or were concerned to defend the position of the Trade. These found in Mill's ideas a useful justification for their own opinions. It was, they stoutly maintained, 'impossible to make men sober by act of Parliament' and that there was no need for 'grand-maternal Government which ties night caps on a grown-up nation by act of Parliament'.[17]

The period after 1830 saw the rapid rise of a teetotal temperance movement.[18] But, initially, the temperance movement shared Mill's aversion to legislation on the issue. The early teetotal movement was a crusade directed at reforming the lives of individuals. Alcohol was not merely harmful, but positively evil; men and women must be persuaded to abandon it. 'Conversion' was at once the beginning and the end of teetotal moral suasionist ambitions: in the conversion of the individual to total abstinence lay the regeneration of society as a whole. 'We must never forget', declared the revered teetotal pioneer Joseph Livesey, 'that our proper mission, is *moral suasion*, and that without success in this all legislation will be fleeting and baseless.'[19] The intemperance of society was thus the sum total of the intemperance of individuals. However, in practice temperance enthusiasts were rarely averse to welcoming government legislation, which Livesey himself conceded might provide 'powerful *auxiliaries*' for the moral battle.[20]

There thus existed a strong body of opinion in Victorian Britain, drawn from various quarters, which doubted whether action on the part of the government could ever remove the scourge of intemperance or even do much to alleviate it. Rather, the solution lay in the long-term operation of non-legislative agencies. Such a position could be held by conservatives, liberals and socialists, as well as temperance fieldworkers. However, during a period when state intervention in public health, education, railway safety and hours or conditions of labour became increasingly the norm, it became more difficult to insist that government had no responsibility on the matter whatsoever.[21] The issue was rather more one of the degree and timing of useful 'auxiliary' measures. Many Liberal politicians presented this in terms of legislation moving alongside, but not ahead of, public opinion. John Bright, the most famous teetotal politician of the period and the very incarnation of progressive Liberal opinion, provides a good example. There were, he was convinced, no short cuts. Only 'the general education of the people' could help advance temperance; 'this is a slow process, but other means seem for the most part to have failed. I am sorry to say this, but my experience brings me to this conclusion.'[22] The 'friends of temperance should leave Parliament, and form *opinion*, trusting that when opinion is formed whatever is judicious in legislation will naturally and easily follow'.[23] Hence, it was not legislation *per se* but legislation in 'advance' of public opinion which he found distasteful. By 1870, few Liberals took a purely libertarian attitude towards Drink, this had become the preserve of some Conservatives and apologists for the Trade.

(ii) Intemperance a product of a faulty social order

Many who stressed the environmental causes of drunkenness were just as hostile to, or sceptical about, restrictive temperance legislation as moral suasionists. Here, intemperance was seen as part of the 'Condition of England' question which so exercised thinkers in the period. 'Gin-drinking', Dickens wrote in 1836, 'is a great vice in England, but wretchedness and dirt are a greater; and until you improve the homes of the poor, or persuade a half-famished wretch not to seek relief in the temporary oblivion of his own misery, with the pittance which divided among his family, would furnish a morsel of bread for each, gin-shops will increase in number and splendour.'[24] Early socialists, such as Robert Owen and Friedrich Engels, endorsed these sentiments. It was a position taken by many radicals as well. A line from Francis Place, through G. J. Holyoake, J. A. Roebuck and Robert Blatchford to Horatio Bottomley, often with secularist associations, protested against both the paternal attitudes of teetotallers and the efforts of legislators to restrict drinking. As with the temperance movement, this lobby group was often populist and emotional. It appealed unashamedly to the great majority of British artisans and workmen, who saw no harm in a glass of beer or spirits and resented attempts by elites at Westminster or the local town hall to regulate their lives.

Nevertheless, as Brian Harrison has shown, not all early radical working-class leaders took this position. Many welcomed both the temperance movement and temperance legislation. The movement could be seen as helping working men achieve a measure of independence and free thinking. Drink, moreover, was portrayed by some socialists and radicals as an instrument used by the governing class to deprave and undermine the workers and to deaden their radicalism. Public houses were a means of manipulating elections, and the taxes on liquor a way of foisting the tax burden on the working rather than the propertied classes.[25] Throughout the century, working-class political movements were therefore split on the temperance issue. In practice, most socialists who placed their main faith in social and economic progress usually accepted that some form of legislation or restriction on Drink might also have a beneficial effect. Similarly model employers, like Titus Salt or the Quaker cocoa manufacturers, who recognised the environmental causes of poverty, made sure that their model villages were also strictly dry.

(iii) The 'traditional' system of regulation

The starting place for legislation was not one of *laissez faire*. Sales of alcohol were already hemmed about by regulations far greater than those applying to other trades. It is perhaps misleading to describe as a 'system' what was scarcely systematic and which had been developed in response to a variety of pressures and needs. In England and Wales over the years since 1552, it had become established that only the local justices of the peace could issue licences for the 'on' sales of liquor. Licensing legislation was consolidated in 1828.[26] Conditions were endorsed on licensees, who were not to adulterate their liquor, serve it in fraudulent measure, wilfully permit gaming or drunkenness, or allow notoriously bad characters to assemble in the house. The only restriction on opening hours was a prohibition on sales during the usual hours of divine service on Sundays, Good Fridays and Christmas Day. The retail sale of spirits for 'off' consumption was prohibited except from public houses, though wholesale wine dealers and brewers-for-sale were able to vend wine and beer respectively. In 1828, there were about 50,000 licences in England for the sale of alcohol on the premises. Of these, 45,000 held a spirit licence, 18,000 a wine licence and 700 a sweet licence.[27] Liquor licensing had a much shorter history in Scotland, given the difficulty of controlling the predominant drink, whisky. But the English system of magisterial control was extended to Scotland in 1756, and the law strengthened and consolidated in 1828.[28]

By this date, the government also possessed an enormous financial interest in the proper relation of intoxicants, with £17,836,000 being raised from taxes on sales and a further £681,000 from the licences themselves.[29]

Licensing legislation was not designed to promote the temperance of individuals or, indeed, of society as a whole. Its purpose was to regulate the Trade in the interests of the 'public good', namely by preventing disorder, curbing adulteration and by raising taxation. As one MP typically declared in 1874: 'When the House had restricted the number of houses and the number of hours during which drink should be sold, and had placed the trade under the supervision of the police, it would have done all it ought to do, and all that could be legitimately expected of it.'[30] Regulation was designed to protect the public from the results of excess drinking, but no attempt was made to influence drinking habits directly. Drunkenness *per se* was no offence. However, this traditional pattern of minimal restriction had various ambiguities. One such centred on the question of defining the 'public good'. As popular feelings changed it became possible to broaden the scope. It might be argued, for example, that there was no meaningful distinction between regulation for the maintenance of public order and regulation for the temperance health of the nation. Traditional control could be tightened up, so that the licensing laws offered a useful mechanism for social good, while stopping short of a temperance policy that was designed to impose a new morality upon the people. Further ambiguity lay in the position of the magistrates and in the relationship between central and local government jurisdiction. The licensing statutes were the creations of central government and were applied on a national scale, but their application and interpretation on a local level depended upon the local magistracy. The magistrates were responsible for assessing the wants and needs of the neighbourhood within their jurisdiction. But as both the role of the magistrates in local government and temperance opinion in the localities changed, the whole operation and *raison d'être* of the licensing process was laid open to question. As British local government moved in the direction of representative democracy, the licensing position of the magistrates became increasingly uncomfortable, and even anomalous. Yet crucial questions were left unresolved. Was liquor licensing an administrative or a judicial matter, or both? What form of authority other than the magistrates would be best able to determine the wants and requirements of the community? How was a 'community' to be defined, and how localised should liquor licensing be? Such questions sprang from the dichotomy inherent in liquor licensing being both an instrument of central government control and a means of catering for the wants and requirements of local communities. It was not clear whether the coherence of the traditional approach of licensing regulation depended upon the maintenance of the traditional structure of control, the magistrates, or whether regulation could be safely entrusted to some more democratic body.

(iv) Free licensing

Notwithstanding the modest impact of the traditional licensing law, it came under sharp attack in the early part of the nineteenth century. Many argued for freer sales rather than more restriction. The movement for free licensing had various components. One was an attack on the arbitrary powers of the licensing justices, who were sometimes erratic and capricious in their decisions. In places, this descended into jobbery and corruption, as magistrates' clerks could line their pockets. The 'trading justices' of Middlesex were particularly notorious.[31] Any two justices, by issuing a licence, could substantially increase the value of a property on account of the monopoly value: in parts of London this could be as much as £1,000, an enormous sum.[32] A broader political point was made by radicals, already smarting under the administration of public order, the game laws and the poor laws. For them, the justices' discretionary power was yet another example of the oppression of the people by a privileged and corrupt oligarchy, who, secure with their own well-stocked cellars, limited the poor man to the choice of a handful of houses, where he would be exposed to the caprices of a fraudulent publican or a monopolistic brewer. Moreover, since public houses were of such obvious electoral significance, it was natural that justices should have weighed carefully the 'colours' of prospective applicants. Conditions varied from place to place and from year to year, but the case of Norwich in 1836 was probably not untypical. Here, the local Whigs, after capturing the magisterial bench, promptly granted licences to those of their supporters who had been persistently refused them by the previous Tory bench.[33] Radicals, who rarely benefited from the system, had every interest in sweeping it aside.

Free licensing also represented an attempt to apply ideas of *laissez faire* economic theory to the process of liquor licensing.[34] Free licensing supporters argued that once the licensed trade was opened to all men of good character, the labouring classes would be able to discriminate between good and bad liquor. The superior product would oust the inferior, and the efficient, energetic and enterprising vendor would dispossess his inefficient, idle and unimaginative competitor. Limitation on the number of retail outlets was therefore unnecessary. In a free licensing system, the number of retail outlets would automatically be adjusted according to the laws of supply and demand. The requirements of the neighbourhood, which the justices were supposed to assess, would be automatically met. For the arbitrary decisions of the magistracy and the baneful effects of tied houses would be substituted the 'rational' forces of consumer demand.[35] When restrictions were removed, 'the result would be under the auspices of free trade, the sale of better articles in our public-houses, and the provision of better accommodation for the labouring classes'.[36] The large London brewers were suspected of fixing prices and purveying an inferior product to their tied houses. Furthermore, free traders maintained that a free market would actually promote temperance since the worst drunkenness was caused by the adulteration of liquor.[37] They pointed to the examples of France and other Latin countries where, although there were scarcely any restrictions on sales, the population was far more sober than in Britain. Undue interference on the part of the government was portrayed as leading to monopoly, to the corruption of police and local officials, to a high level of adulteration, and to the herding together of customers in cramped and unhealthy premises.

(v) Prohibition

In 1846 General Neal Dow had passed a law prohibiting the sale of intoxicants in Maine, New England, and in 1853 a Manchester-based pressure group, the United Kingdom Alliance (UKA), was founded to work for prohibition in the UK.[38] Of all the approaches to the temperance question, that of the prohibitionists was the most logical, clear cut and rigidly uncompromising. Prohibitionists believed that the consumption of alcohol was not merely dangerous or undesirable, but wholly evil and unjustifiable. Alcohol was just like any other addictive drug. The state therefore had a duty to suppress traffic in it, and no 'consideration of private gain or public revenue' should be allowed to stand in the way. 'Drink was therefore a problem which required specifically public and political, rather than private and personal reforms.'[39] The existing licensing laws themselves implied alcohol was a dangerous substance. Despite objections from some of the teetotal pioneers, prohibitionists denied any inconsistency between teetotal moral suasion and state prohibition. 'Temperance societies appeal to us to use our individual and persuasive influence for the removal of this vice – [prohibitionist bodies] appeal to us to use our influence as citizens and electors for the attainment of the same great end.'[40] The agitation for a prohibitory law 'must not be regarded, therefore, either as coincident with or as superseding the abstinence agitation, but as an ancillary and thoroughly sympathetic movement'.[41] Prohibition might be seen as the transposition of teetotal doctrines from the context of an individual to the context of society as a whole: for the individual was substituted the state; for the consumption of drink, the sale of alcohol; and for the exercise of the individual will, the enactment of prohibitory legislation. Just as an individual might foreswear the use of alcohol for the good of his physical condition, so society might renounce it for the sake of the health of the body politic. Just as total abstinence would ensure the individual of a healthy and happy future existence (in this world and the next), so prohibition would grant the race and the nation a safe and fruitful posterity. Just as teetotal orators, when taunted at their meetings with the offer of a glass of beer, rejoiced to pour the hated liquid on the ground, so prohibitionists scorned any suggestion of compromise with a traffic which they considered to be so deadly. Absolute prohibition, backed by teetotal moral suasion, could alone provide the answer to the problem of intemperance in society.

Prohibitionist ideas fell on fertile soil in the 1850s and 1860s as many teetotallers felt disappointment at the impact of purely moral suasionist messages.[42] This was the period of self-confidence for middle-class radical reforming bodies that modelled themselves on the Anti-Corn Law League and that sought to remove social evils through the mobilisation of enlightened opinion. By 1857, the UKA had secured a membership of 4,500 and its annual subscriptions had topped the £3,000 mark. Approximately one quarter of all the UKA's income came from small donations of sums of £5 and under, though on occasions in the 1860s large sums were raised in the form of guarantee funds.[43] As a pressure group, the objective of the UKA was openly political. Membership was open to teetotallers and drinkers alike. Its members were to rise above class, sectarian or party considerations to influence government. Its leaders were dogmatic, dedicated, energetic and sincere. So far as their attitude to the political process was concerned, they combined a somewhat naive belief that, since political progress was inevitable, their cause would triumph, with a somewhat populist distrust of the institutions and processes of government. Principle was placed at a premium, expediency at a discount. 'We never feel crushed when we know we are right' was the constant refrain of the UKA's chief public spokesman, Sir Wilfrid Lawson.[44]

Prohibitionists nonetheless faced some serious dilemmas. Firstly, it was not clear what their attitude should be towards efforts at liquor restriction that fell short of total prohibition. All too often they rejected any such attempts out of hand.[45] But it was not always easy to hold the line on this position, and repeatedly the prohibitionist movement would be divided over the feasibility and desirability of 'interim' attempts to alleviate the law. A second dilemma lay in reconciling the liberal democratic outlook of the potential supporters of prohibition with what was essentially an authoritarian policy.

(vi) Progressive temperance restriction

After 1830, politicians began to suggest that the law ought not merely to regulate conditions of trading, but should also be used to change the habits and behaviour of the people. Such a view was first put forward by James Silk Buckingham, MP, an oriental traveller and an extreme and voluble radical reformer, whose views on most social questions were wildly at odds with the accepted opinions of his day. He persuaded his fellow MPs to appoint a select committee in 1834 'to inquire into the extent, causes and consequences of the prevailing vice of intoxication among the labouring classes . . . in order to ascertain whether any legislative measures can be devised to prevent the further spread of so great a national evil'. Buckingham's committee, which was dominated by Evangelicals, painted a gloomy picture of the 'vice of intoxication' among the labouring classes increasing to the detriment of the 'public weal'. It proposed a bold programme of restrictive licensing reform, limitations of the sales of spirits and legislation to promote counter-attractions to the public house. Such proposals were too extreme for the time and met with considerable ridicule.[46] However, over the next forty years this restrictionist position appealed to a growing body of opinion that sought some halfway house between the passivity of traditional regulation and the absolute and impractical dogmas of prohibitionists. Difficulties arose, however, when such would-be reformers tried to translate their general ideas into practical proposals for licensing reform. Many questions were left unresolved. What form of restriction would be most suitable? What degree of restriction should be imposed? To what extent should the law move in advance of 'public opinion', and to what extent should it follow it? What was the correct relationship between legislative restriction and agencies of moral suasion? Was prohibition the logical culmination of restrictive policies, or was there a limit to the effectiveness of restrictive legislation?

Various mechanisms were suggested. One was to impose heavier taxation or differential taxation against the stronger liquors. Despite some support in political circles – for example, Gladstone in 1864[47] – there were political difficulties here. Such taxation was likely to be regressive and would stimulate public unrest. This would be aggravated by the Trade, which was never more sensitive than when it was hit directly in the pocket. Also, the saturation point on liquor taxation was thought to be low, and there was also a danger of illicit distillation and illegal trading. Finally, there was the vested interest of Chancellors of the Exchequer, whose main concern was to balance the budget and not to promote temperance. During the nineteenth century, no less than 30–40 per cent of the nation's revenue was raised from excise and licence duties: in 1940, the figure was 12.5 per cent and in 1960, 6.9 per cent.[48] 'The habitual drunkard', declared Sir Wilfrid Lawson, the prohibitionist leader in Parliament, 'was the sheet anchor of the British Constitution'.[49]

An alternative path was to reduce hours of sale. Here, there were problems about shift workers, but earlier closing on weekday nights was certainly one option canvassed to reduce drunkenness. Sunday closing had more political force behind it, as it was the point at which sabbatarianism and temperance reform met. All those perverted tastes and wasteful pursuits that were undesirable on a weekday were, on the Lord's Day, nothing less than sinful. Therefore, Evangelical groups and societies in Britain worked hard after 1834 to shorten the hours of Sunday sales or to impose Sunday closing altogether. Complete Sunday closing was passed for Scotland in 1853 after a vigorous five-year campaign headed by leaders of the Scottish kirk and Lord Kinnaird of Rossie Priory, a Privy Councillor and Lord Lieutenant of his county.[50] There were powerful historical precedents for Sunday closing in Scotland, and the reform aroused only muted opposition. In England, moves to restrict hours were far more controversial, both because feeling on the question was more libertarian and because the national drink, beer, could not be kept open in flasks in the same way as whisky in Scotland. Nevertheless, the English licensing laws treated Sunday opening as a special case, with restrictions on opening to ensure no clashes with church services. However, the disastrous attempts in 1854–55 to introduce severe restrictions on Sunday trading in general, including public houses, which led to serious rioting in Hyde Park, was an object lesson in the dangers of social elites imposing measures which were too far 'in advance' of working class opinion.[51] Henceforth, legislators generally considered it best to err on the side of caution.

A third possible path to achieve restriction was to limit the number of retail outlets selling drink. The argument here was that a superfluity of competing licences encouraged men to drink to excess. If there were fewer gin-palaces and alehouses, the weak-minded would incur less temptation. But the practical difficulties here were obvious. How was the licensing authority to determine an appropriate degree of reduction? The magistrates had already been criticised for the way in which they performed the much simpler task of deciding whether any new licences were to be issued. It would be far more invidious to decide which licensees were to lose their livelihood, and compensation might have to be paid.

Restrictionist reformers lacked any means by which they might gauge public opinion or provide for local variation according to regional needs or requirements. As temperance sentiment grew, the restrictionist approach was bound to find increasing favour. Restrictionists began with the assumption that the drinking of alcohol was more or less undesirable, and as an objective they recommended progressive restriction on the facilities for the sale of intoxicants. The state was regarded as having both the right and the duty to restrict and limit the consumption of strong drink wherever possible, and to wean consumers away from it. But there was little agreement as to how that restriction could best be achieved, or what techniques of reform were the most suitable.

Table 2.1 summarises the six approaches to Drink that had emerged during the early years of our period. However, contemporaries themselves did not always view the issue in such clear cut terms, especially when confronted with the technical details of liquor legislation. Indeed, there was room for overlap and confusion between them. Thus, both moral suasionists and socialists worked within the existing regulation; regulation itself necessarily entailed some restriction; progressive temperance restriction might be envisaged as leading ultimately to prohibition; and prohibition, if applied on a local permissive basis, might itself come to be viewed as an element of restrictionist reform. Yet, time and again, proposals for Drink legislation were to founder on the misunderstandings and mutual recriminations of reformers who started from different assumptions.

Parliament and liquor licensing, 1830–70

The period started with a bold and successful attempt to liberalise the English and Welsh Trade by removing the retail 'on' sale of beer from the control of the licensing justices. The Beer Act of 1830, passed after a hasty parliamentary inquiry, allowed anyone to sell beer (but not wines or spirits) on the mere payment of an excise fee of two guineas, thus establishing a dual pattern of licensing: full public houses and the new beerhouses. The Beer Act was motivated by political rather than temperance considerations and marked the culmination of long pressure from

Table 2.1 Six models of the Drink Question 1830–70, summarised

	Moral Suasion	*Social Conditions*	*Traditional Control*	*Free Licensing*	*Prohibition*	*Progressive Restriction*
Diagnosis of problem	Individual moral failings	Poor economic and social environment	Public Order; Excess Drinking	Monopolistic brewers; Poor product; Poor outlets; Privileged justices	Alcohol a devilish and addictive substance	Alcohol a dangerous substance
Solution	Temperance education	New social and economic order	Necessary minimum regulation	Improved products and retail outlets; Encouragement of lighter beverages	Complete prohibition	Legislation to discourage consumption
Mechanisms for reform	Exortation; Promotion of teetotalism; Ancillary legislation	Social reform in general; Economic changes	Acts of Parliament; Local magistrates	Free market; Strict policing; Discriminatory taxation	Local veto	Taxation; Shorter hours; Fewer outlets; Stricter policing; Counter-attractions

radicals to curb the power of the local justices. However, it was justified according to the free licensing arguments outlined above.

The most recent and authoritative historians of the brewing industry have described this act as 'one of the most extraordinary pieces of all nineteenth-century legislation'.[52] How was it that so significant a modification in the traditional structure of licensing was made with such ease? The answer is to be found in a complex interaction of various factors. In the first place, the Act reflected free licensing theories. A series of parliamentary inquiries and minor pieces of legislation had addressed the issue of freeing up the market in beer ever since 1815. This tied in with Lord Liverpool's government's efforts to adopt various social and economic liberalising policies to meet rapid social changes since the wars with France. Secondly, there was concern about an increase in spirit drinking and consequent drunkenness; beer at this period was widely seen as the healthier and more temperate drink (teetotalism only emerged after 1830). Thirdly, a sharp slump in the price of cereals led to widespread distress in the rural areas and agitation for a reduction in taxation on necessities, especially beer. In the face of this pressure, the Tory ministry felt obliged to take some rapid action, and they chose a policy of large-scale tax reduction. Remission of the beer duty was thought to be the most popular and effective form of concession, and it was easy to combine with this the scheme for opening up the beer trade. Popular unrest was assuaged and liberal economists rallied to support the ministry. Furthermore, the natural opposition to a measure of this kind was muted by an untoward combination of circumstances. The large porter brewers were bought off by the accompanying abolition of the beer duties, while the opposition of the agricultural high Tories was emasculated because they had long been critical of Wellington's policies on both the economy and Catholic emancipation and tended to oppose rather than support many of the Tory ministry's actions. Wellington had nothing to lose by isolating them and associating them with the self-interested publicans, while simultaneously dividing the Whigs, Canningites and Radicals. In this way, an act which rested on clearly-defined, *a priori* economic theory was ironically the work of a government whose members thought primarily of short term political advantage.[53]

The impact of the measure was immediate with 24,324 licences being taken out in the first six months, to be followed by a further 21,000 over the next eight years. The Act received harsh treatment both at the hands of contemporaries and the later temperance movement. Its operation coincided with a spate of further rural unrest in

1830–32, and a select committee in 1833 received much evidence that it had been responsible for a great increase in intemperance and disorder among the lower classes.[54] Magistrates, giving evidence before this body, luridly portrayed the new outlets as little better than disreputable hovels, associated with whoring, gambling and petty crime. They painted a particularly bleak picture 'of the male working class, rural and urban alike, being paid in the beer houses on Saturday evening, drinking themselves comatose in the following thirty hours, wrecking family life, increasing the poor rates and undermining work attitudes.'[55] Such indictments reflected the prejudices of the elite and were rarely borne out with hard evidence. Nevertheless even Goulburn, one of its sponsors, admitted disappointment.[56] Neither did the free market solution seem to have improved the quality of the outlets or products. Over the next twenty years, a series of select committees investigated the issue. The general consensus was that the new beerhouses were generally of a poor quality and had become largely tied to the brewers.[57] Nonetheless, opinion in Parliament in the 1850s was far from writing off free-licensing ideas as mistaken. Many free traders maintained that any deficiencies in the beerhouse system were due to imperfections of detail or administration, or to the unfair competition from the public houses who were able to keep open later at night. They looked at the detailed conduct of licensing to see if there were any artificial hindrances that were preventing practice from matching theory. Indeed, many MPs during the 1840s and 1850s were convinced that the licensing system needed to be opened up still further. Thus, the Villiers Committee of 1854 recommended the effective replacement of magistrates' regulation by a new body of public house inspectors and more effective policing.[58]

Gladstone's wine-retailing legislation of 1860 indicates the persistence of free-licensing ideas. As part of the commercial treaty with France of 1860, Gladstone modified the wine duties. He also took the opportunity to open up the retail side of the wine trade by allowing virtually any grocer or shopkeeper to take out an excise licence for the sale of wines in bottles for consumption off the premises, and by giving eating houses the right to serve wines with meals.[59] Gladstone was convinced that monopoly and the existence of a property value in licences 'constitutes the most formidable impediment to the exercise of police and magisterial control'.[60] His proposals would simultaneously provide 'some new, and cleaner channels for consumption' and encourage a shift away from spirits and fortified wines to lighter table wines, thereby helping temperance.[61] Free trade measures would thus inaugurate 'a very important experiment in connection with the tastes, habits, and moral and social well-being of the country'.[62]

Between 1830 and 1860, therefore, the traditional model of liquor control was sharply challenged by the champions of free licensing. This tied in with the general rise of free-trading ideas, which attacked mercantilist and other restriction on the exchange of goods. However, in the case of Drink, the power of conservative forces was greater than in other areas, given the power of the magistrates and the sensitivity of the issue as far as law and order was concerned. Only for a brief period, in Liverpool in the 1860s, was there an attempt by a magistrate's bench to pursue a free-licensing policy.[63] There were problems in ensuring the operation of a free market in alcohol sales. In purely economic terms, not all of the drink industry could respond to market forces very easily. The spirit industry in Scotland remained largely specialised, while in England and Wales the dominant demand was for cheap, draught beers or ciders where profit margins were low and the product neither kept long nor travelled well. Moreover, the manufacture of liquor was a highly specialised and expert business. As in banking, family ties were strong and it was not easy for enterprising outsiders to enter the Trade and build up prosperous businesses on the strength of commercial judgement. In most provincial areas, there was rarely scope for more than two or three medium-sized breweries to operate. Nor were brewers primarily concerned with competition. Their interests lay more in cooperation, in opposing greedy Chancellors of the Exchequer, erratic magistrates and, as the years went by, hostile temperance societies. Similarly, with the exception of the wine trade, the retail side of the Trade was no less a locational market than the wholesale. The free-licensing advocates 'exaggerated the rigidity of demand, overestimated the mobility and rationality of custom, and exaggerated the ease and rapidity with which supply would approximate to demand'.[64]

From 1850, free-licensing ideas were also undermined by the growing popularity of temperance sentiment among nonconformist radicals, who in other areas were often the bedrock supporters of free trade. Although temperance reformers shared with the free-licensing advocates a dislike of the unelected and unaccountable magistrates, they sought their solution elsewhere. Their concern was to increase restrictions while curbing the authority of the local justices, or perhaps replacing them altogether. Between 1850 and 1870, a powerful temperance lobby grew which became increasingly vociferous in favour of government action to restrict the Trade. The purely moral suasionist outlook among teetotallers was fading. The prohibitionists of the UKA made the running. The problem for the UKA was the disjuncture between prohibition, an authoritarian solution, and the democratic ethos and ideology that otherwise permeated the organisation and the movement. The prohibitionists saw themselves, in populist terms, as agents of liberation. Their goal was to free the people from the slavery of Drink, just as earlier crusaders had freed the country from slavery, the Corn Laws, child labour and so on. Theirs was a movement from the grass roots that sought to articulate the demands of ordinary men and women to be freed from the tyranny of the Trade which was 'foisted' upon them by the magistrates and the governing class. They had to meet the obvious charge that prohibition was a dictatorial solution imposed by the state that would be both morally unjustified and impractical. In 1857, the UKA hit upon a clever ' "formula" which, enforcing the whole principle, may yet neutralise . . . opposition'.[65] The device which was to square the circle was the local veto. Ironically, this had been first suggested in an article on drunkenness by the Liberal brewer, Charles Buxton, much to his later chagrin.[66] The idea behind local veto was that the local ratepayers in a parish or similar area should be given the opportunity to vote to go dry; a two-thirds majority was usually enshrined as a safeguard. The attraction of this policy of permissive prohibition was its versatility. It was prohibition and yet not prohibition. It was an idealistic objective and a practical proposal. It was an end in itself yet also a means to an end. The prohibitionist principle was preserved, yet both broadened and narrowed: broadened because it had been expanded to include elements of localism and democracy, narrowed because it had been confined into a practical and simple piece of legislation. Here was a way of combining techniques of reform with objectives of reform, and of attracting the support of practical politicians without offending the susceptibilities of the faithful stalwarts.

A bill for local veto, the Permissive Prohibition Bill, was first introduced in the Commons in 1864 and thereafter as 'a hardy annual'. Its somewhat unlikely champion was Sir Wilfrid Lawson, the nephew of Sir James Graham, but the son of a radical and teetotal Cumberland baronet, who became the parliamentary spokesman of the UKA. Throughout a long political career, Lawson espoused a raft of progressive causes with considerable verve and wit. He was the archetypal backbencher who placed conscience far above party considerations. In the words of Brian Harrison, he stood in 'a long line of independent squires who specialised in exposing the extravagance and immorality of those in authority'.[67] The UKA directed all its political energies towards securing support for this Bill. Candidates at elections and others in positions of power and influence were mercilessly lobbied and canvassed. By 1872, nearly 1.4 million signatories were presented in favour of the measure and over a hundred MPs were prepared to support the Bill's second reading, although some doubtless as a measure of expediency rather than conviction. Local veto was to become the lodestone of the prohibitionists for the next fifty years. It was a way of reconciling liberalism with prohibition. Dry areas, such as Saltaire or Bessbrook in Ulster, showed the advantages of an alcohol-free community. Now the people themselves could choose to go down that road. The local plebiscites, moreover, would be a mechanism for temperance education. Once neighbouring areas saw the advantages of going dry, they would themselves opt to follow suit. It was a little thing to ask since the Permissive Bill involved no complicated licensing reform and could easily be slipped into the existing system without disruption.[68] Quite apart from temperance arguments, the veto could be presented as something inherently democratic, a means of placing small shopkeepers and working men upon a level with the wealthy aristocracy of the land, and of liberating the people from the justices who foisted drinkshops upon helpless communities. Both permissive legislation and the idea of local democracy were fashionable in the third quarter of the nineteenth century and the UKA attracted some support on these grounds from outside teetotal circles.[69]

Nevertheless, resistance was strong. Apart from opposition from the representatives of the Trade, local veto was lambasted by many MPs on libertarian grounds, being variously described as tyrannical, unjust, capricious and a dishonest attempt to introduce prohibition by the side door. It was also pointed out that ratepayers were unrepresentative of the adult population as a whole, so that the local veto would in effect be class legislation. Equally, criticism came from quarters more friendly to temperance restriction. Here, Lawson's Permissive Bill was attacked on the grounds that it would be certainly ineffective. Salubrious suburbs would vote to go dry rather than densely packed urban areas where the real problems lay. Drinking would also be driven underground into illegal drinking dens or unregulated clubs, and there would be constant boundary problems with drinkers pouring over from dry to wet areas. Moreover, the Bill did nothing to reform the licensing laws by tackling the excess hours of drinking or reducing the number of unsuitable or insanitary public houses.

A perennial feature of the politics of the temperance movement was the internecine disputes among the activists. The UKA was far from getting its own way. In 1862, two rival national conferences were held, each of which conducted a vigorous pamphlet war with the other.[70] In part, the differences were due to personalities, especially a bitter vendetta between J. B. Gough and F. R. Lees.[71] But issues of strategy were also at stake. The UKA and allies in the British Temperance League (technically a moral suasionist body) were attacked by the Quaker-controlled National Temperance League (NTL). The latter body scorned the local veto and advocated instead a programme of temperance restriction, including closing on Saturday nights and Sundays, the repeal of the Beer Act and stricter policing. The paper given by G. C. Campbell outlining the NTL's legislative proposals was, in turn, ridiculed by the reporter for the UKA's newspaper, in typically overblown language: 'It never fell to my lot to listen to a production more pert, offensive and cynical.'[72] Differences were underpinned, however, by the gulf between prohibitionists, who were becoming devoted to local veto to the exclusion of all else, and various groupings of licensing reformers, who adopted a restrictionist position either for its own sake or as a pragmatic compromise pending prohibition.

Although radical schemes for licensing reform, involving some democratic mechanisms as opposed to mere local veto, began to be canvassed in the late 1860s, the decade ended with reform coming from the hands of traditionalists. Here, impetus came from MPs or other elitist quarters rather than popular campaigners. One such was Col Akroyd, a Liberal MP and a dominant force in Halifax politics, who became shocked at the police returns for his boroughs and formed the Beerhouse Licensing Amendment Society which worked to restore the authority of the English magistrates over the beerhouses.[73] Another was the National Union for the Suppression of Intemperance, a moderate body based in Manchester, which quarrelled incessantly with the UKA and which sought to improve the standard of public houses. Its programme was aired before the National Association for the Promotion of Social Science.[74] It was, however, a member of the landed gentry, the Conservative MP Sir Henry Selwin-Ibbetson, who succeeded in changing the law. As a Master of the Essex foxhounds and a conspicuous supporter of county charities, he was ideally placed to command the support of prudent or conservative magistrates, as well as all sections of the temperance movement in his successful repeal of the 1830 Beer Act in 1869. By virtue of this Act, the magistrates regained full licensing powers, over all *new* beerhouses as well as public houses.[75] Significantly, this private members' Bill aroused virtually no parliamentary opposition, such was the extent to which the once powerful free-licensing ideas had been discredited. Selwin-Ibbetson's own position was a conservative one. 'There was nothing he dreaded so much as that a question of this sort should be made a subject of political agitation at an election.'[76] Local elections for a Drink control board would, in his opinion, create trouble and confusion, for they would be 'fought out with an animosity and a bitterness calculated to produce the very worst consequences'. Temperance education was indeed vitally important, but it was not something that could be forced by political means. 'He believed they would act more wisely in seeking to attain the same end by a slow and gradual progress, rather than by having recourse to violent action.'[77]

By 1870, both the purely moral suasionist and the free-licensing model of liquor control had lost much of their appeal and power. Explanations in terms of social conditions were held by a minority and had yet to grow into a powerful influence. Prohibitionist ideas had been effectively articulated and refined into a clear policy objective, the local veto; but local veto, despite powerful backing from the best organised popular temperance societies, had failed as yet to win sufficient backing in parliamentary and other elite circles. Restrictionist opinions and policy positions were by contrast far more imprecise, but were achieving more attention. There was a growing recognition that a grave problem of intemperance existed in the country, and an acceptance that the state had some responsibility to diminish that problem through wise and judicious legislation. But there were doubts as to how far legislation could go, uncertainties as to the direction it should take, and a general scepticism as to how efficacious it would prove. Restrictive measures could be built into the traditional regulative mechanisms of parliamentary legislation and magisterial regulation, but many felt that some more radical overhaul was necessary. It was generally admitted that the licensing laws were not in an altogether satisfactory condition, and frequent promises were made by Home Secretaries to review the situation and consolidate or overhaul the licensing laws. But if licensing was not yet considered a politically explosive issue, it was nonetheless already regarded as a complex or technical question. Few Home Secretaries had pronounced ideas on the question and most had more pressing business to attend to.

Nevertheless, the history of the period before 1870 shows that, apart from the temperance societies, Parliament was the only really significant forum for the discussion and consideration of the licensing question. As yet, there was relatively little influence exerted by vested interest groups or the civil service. Neither factions nor parties in Parliament were greatly involved or concerned with the question. Individual MPs, like Buckingham, Wilson Patten, Ker Seymer, William Rathbone, Wilfrid Lawson and Selwin-Ibbetson took the initiative, but their interest was purely personal not party, deriving either from practical experience as licensing justices or from *a priori* theories on the question of liquor control. Parliament as a whole generally responded by setting up select committees, comprising members who were interested in the question. These, in due course, produced reports which were sometimes drafted into bills by Home Secretaries or by individual MPs or, more usually, conveniently shelved. MPs were conscious that they were passing regulations on a question that would not affect themselves or their class directly, but might bear heavily upon the lives of the labouring population. Caution was therefore the dominant note and scepticism the prevailing attitude. After 1870, the tempo was to hot up considerably.

3

Drink becomes a Party Political Issue, 1870–95

After 1870, the democratic reform of local government held centre stage.[1] Radicals favoured the creation of democratic local bodies. Joseph Chamberlain, for example, maintained that great social questions would best be settled by participation of the people in the great urban centres. Similarly, John Morley considered that local bodies might be safely entrusted with powers that would be dangerous in the hands of the central government: 'Municipal and local bodies know the conditions with which they have to deal. They understand local necessities, and they are better able to try local experiments without possible mischievous results.'[2] Even moderate Liberal leaders had come around to favouring sensible, democratic decentralisation. Thus, in 1882, Gladstone impressed on Dodson, the President of the Local Government Board, the necessity of passing not only 'a great Local Government Bill, but a great decentralisation Bill'.[3] A decade later his final ministry aimed to establish 'local parliaments' in every village by virtue of its Parish Council Act. Nor were the majority of Conservatives necessarily averse to the idea of local devolution. Many disliked the growth of the central bureaucracy and wished to strengthen local administration in order to safeguard the position of traditional institutions and values.[4]

In advocating local veto, prohibitionists had only incidentally been concerned with the virtues of localism and democracy. However, their enthusiasm for popular mobilisation and their attack on the magistrates helped reposition the Drink issue in terms of local government. Even when Lawson's Permissive Bill had been given its first airing in 1864 John Bright, that doyen of radical liberalism, had demanded some other less dangerous way in which the ratepayers might have some influence on licensing affairs.[5] By 1870, such ideas had become commonplace. The idea of a broader local control or 'local option', while avoiding all the unpleasantness and impracticalities of a simple local veto, seemed to offer all the advantages of flexibility, participation, devolution and democracy. Indeed, the Drink question might be especially suited to local treatment, given the widely differing customs and sentiments throughout the country. The existing authorities, the justices, were already meant to take account of local conditions. If a raft of other social policy areas, such as housing, education, the poor law and sanitary affairs, were to be entrusted to newly elected *ad hoc* boards or to local councils, it would be anomalous if licensing and temperance policy alone were to be retained by the magistrates. Reform of liquor licensing in the interests of temperance therefore seemed seductively simple. However, the next twenty-five years were to disprove this. A series of politicians took up the issue, with various degrees of optimism, only for their hopes and ambitions to be dashed. Various factors came into play here, including the technical difficulties of the issue, the arousal of fierce opposition from the Trade and bitter internecine differences among the temperance lobby.

A remarkable feature of this period was the narrowness of the terms of the debate about Drink, in contrast to the pre-1870 period when argument had revolved around the grand principles. Now the debate had become much narrower, reducing the question to one of *licensing* and the connection of this with local government. The emphasis was on the relatively narrow question of the control or regulation of the outputs of drinking, especially the public houses. There was no real attempt to research the broader question of the nature of alcohol in society or the role of the pub in people's lives. In the case of temperance reformers, this partly 'derived from a feeling that an institution so roundly condemned could hardly be worth investigating'.[6] It also was symptomatic of the way in which would-be reformers became excessively immersed in the means of achieving their end at the expense of the general issues of the role and nature of alcohol and drinking. Technical issues, such as the operation of local veto or the possibility of local control over licensing, thus attracted obsessive interest.

Legislation under Gladstone and Disraeli

Initially prospects for legislation seemed favourable. By 1870, teetotalism and temperance were viewed in governing circles less as wild eccentricities than as commendable moral qualities. The temperance movement still drew its strength from radical quarters in the provinces, which were removed from the seats of power, and was tinged with non-conformity or secularism. However, its message was becoming more appealing to the governing classes. In 1861, a Church of England Temperance Society (CETS) had been formed shortly after the publication of Mrs Wightman's *Haste to the Rescue*, which had drawn the link between temperance work and evangelical mission. By 1870, the CETS had the powerful backing of the Church authorities.[7] In Parliament, as Selwin-Ibbetson had shown in 1869, a consensus now existed that the existing law was slack and that better policing and restriction of licensed outlets was highly desirable. Moderate reformers, impatient to go further, were also making a mark. Clerical influence was strong in the cumbersomely titled National Association for Promoting the Amendment of Laws Relating to the Liquor Traffic which strongly supported popular, local control over licensing. This body, which enjoyed close links with the National Association for the Promotion of Social Science and possessed two able, Liberal parliamentary spokesmen, from both sides of the border, Sir Robert Anstruther and Sir Harcourt Johnstone, demanded that *ad hoc* elected boards should replace the licensing justices, an idea supported by the CETS. Such boards already administered public health, the Poor Law and (after 1870) education. Popular control was 'the backbone of the whole question' and the key to advance.[8] As Canon Ellison, the leading figure in the CETS, sonorously put it in words that would have delighted J. S. Mill, the process of election:

> would give to . . . social reformers . . . opportunities for systematically instructing the ratepayers. Public opinion would form itself around their efforts, and as it formed, not by arbitrary interference from above, not by attempts to impose a uniform and rigid system on localities the conditions of which were widely different, but by local provisions made with the fullest knowledge of local circumstances, public opinion would insist upon a diminution of the source from which temptation came.[9]

A problem with this solution, quite apart from technical issues of overlapping boundaries of petty sessions, parishes and poor law unions, was that licensing involved both judicial and policing aspects, and elected boards would be likely to be subject to pressures from vested interests. However, Gladstone's Home Secretary, H. A. Bruce, was sympathetic both to the idea of popular involvement and to a reduction in liquor licences.[10] He was encouraged by his Prime Minister with the sentiment that 'the work of a p[ubli]c house Reformer is that of a truly Xtian missionary'.[11] Bruce, however, was to show himself to be singularly inept in his treatment of the situation. He was certainly not helped by political factors. First, his fellow Cabinet ministers showed little interest in the subject and gave him little support. The brewer, M. T. Bass, reported that one Cabinet minister had assured him he was 'not responsible' for the bill that was introduced, and Bruce himself complained to his wife that 'Gladstone cares for nothing but "Free Trade", which the House [of Commons] won't have, and I cannot get him to interest himself in the subject.'[12] Secondly, he attempted legislation at the very nadir of the ministry's fortunes in 1871–72, when there was unrest among the working classes and discontent with Lowe's budget of 1871 which had alarmed propertied interests. Finally, the Home Office administration seems to have been particularly weak, with Bruce relying too much on his private secretary, Rutson, described by Algernon West as 'singularly devoid of that tact which is necessary in dealing with men'.[13] Nevertheless, Bruce compounded his difficulties. He apparently never consulted his under-secretary, Knatchbull-Hugessen, who possessed experience of the issue, and consistently showed a tendency to dream up ambitious schemes of reform without applying himself to the technical details.[14]

In his Licensing Bill of 1871, Bruce sought to retain the licensing justices but to give them imaginative new powers. They were to decide the requirements of any area and then put up all new licences to competitive tender. But where the number of licences was to exceed 1 per 1,000 inhabitants in towns and 1 per 600 in rural areas, the ratepayers were to be given the power to decrease the number of new issues by a three-fifths majority. Thus, the ratepayers would be able to help the magistrates determine the needs of the localities. Holders of existing licences were to be given a statutory right of renewal for a ten-year period. At the end of ten years, this right would lapse and then *all* licences were to be regarded as new licences. Henceforth they were to be franchised on a ten-yearly basis, so it would be possible to repeat the process of reduction every ten years. Licences were to be in the name of the owner rather than the resident manager. In addition, Bruce proposed stiffer penalties on licensees who permitted drunkenness or adulterated liquor, along with the creation of a new force of public house inspectors, organised on a regional basis but under central control. Finally, he proposed to shorten the existing hours of opening. All houses were to close on weekdays at 11.00 p.m. in London, and 10.00 p.m. in other areas. Again, he gave additional powers to local ratepayers, a majority of three-fifths of whom would be empowered to enforce total Sunday closing or even earlier weekday evening closing.[15]

Bruce must have hoped for broad support for his proposals. In a sense, there was something for everyone to applaud. Traditionalists might welcome the permanent end of the hated beerhouses; free-licensing advocates, the opening up of the monopoly value to competition; the UKA, the plebisicitory principle; and restrictionist reformers, the efforts to reduce both the number of outlets and the hours of sale. Even the brewers should have been appeased by the ten-year period during which they were to enjoy the benefits of a full monopoly value. The initial parliamentary reaction was not unfavourable, although clearly there were enormous technical problems with such a novel and complicated scheme. However, the reaction of sections of the Trade was soon vitriolic. The Bill was portrayed as a confiscation on property and the proposed inspectors as a 'French spy system'. Such propaganda was the more effective as the debate on the Bill coincided with the Commune in Paris which was terrifying the propertied classes. The *Licensed Victuallers' Guardian* spoke of 'Bruce the Communist', while the *Morning Advertiser* denounced the Bill as centralising and despotic. The Country Brewers' Society gained new members and a fighting fund of £21,000; stormy meetings were held and petitions signed throughout the land. *The Times* doubted 'if any trade or interest in the country could have got up a stronger agitation than that we now see . . . the walls and hoardings of every town in the kingdom are covered with vigorous and stirring appeals to all classes of the population in favour of universal resistance'. A Government loss at a by-election at Durham was widely attributed to the agitation, and within a month Gladstone hastily announced the withdrawal of the Bill even before its second reading.[16] For the first time, Victorian Britain was made aware of the vulgar and noisy potential of the Trade to interest itself in politics and, at least, to rival the forces of the temperance movement. Few liberal minded MPs and thinkers viewed this with equanimity.

Bruce had made the mistake of falling between two stools. He had apparently refused even to see representations from sections of the Trade before drafting his proposals, even though their leaders were quite prepared to produce workable reforms. On the other hand, the prohibitionists singularly failed to offer more than the most lukewarm support, on the grounds that they wanted nothing to do with licensing a pernicious traffic. Bruce was the first of a long line of politicians to feel let down by the UKA and described Wilfrid Lawson as a great obstructive force who 'was weakening the hands of those who wanted to carry out a practical measure'.[17] His enthusiasm for licensing reform had now evaporated, but the ministry was forced into action by initiative taken once again by the Conservative backbencher, Selwin-Ibbetson. He had consulted with the country brewers and proposed a measure that guaranteed the existing licensees security of tenure, while restricting the issue of new licences and improving policing and other temperance measures. According to Lord Kimberley, the Colonial Secretary, Bruce suddenly became 'alarmed' at this development and proposed that Kimberley should bring forward the Government's own revised proposals in the Lords. Two days before this was scheduled, Kimberley found to his horror that Bruce had 'actually not read through the bill which was merely a sketch of a measure'. Kimberley and his civil servants had to 'work like slaves' to turn 'a confused mass of absurdity' into a 'tolerable Bill'.[18] The resulting 1872 Act did little more than impose a range of regulations onto the existing law. The measure had a particularly convoluted passage through Parliament, with Bruce again showing a marked failure to control the proceedings and, as Paul Smith has pointed out, was almost as much the product of the Conservatives as the Government.[19] Even so, the Government suffered from it, particularly regarding hours of closure. The Act gave justices outside London limited discretionary powers to enforce closing at 10.00 p.m. on weekdays and 9.00 p.m. on Sundays. When enforced, it led to widespread rioting at closing time by working men in a number of English towns and cities who demonstrated outside rich men's clubs or the homes of local temperance leaders singing *Rule Britannia*. In several places, soldiers had to disperse the crowd.[20]

Gladstone attributed his defeat at the ensuing 1874 election in large measure to the liquor interest, writing to his brother that they had been 'borne down in a torrent of gin and beer';[21] however this interpretation, once popularised by Liberal inclined historians, has been qualified by more recent scholars.[22] The Trade was not that coherently organised and supported many Liberal Tradesmen and other favourable candidates. However, in general, it was Conservative candidates who benefited and the issue is likely to have swung several seats, even if it was not the decisive factor in the election as a whole. The support of the publicans was nevertheless sufficient to stir the new Home Secretary, R. A. Cross, to amend the Act of his predecessor. The first important social measure of Disraeli's ministry was to set back the hours of closing by half an hour in towns, to repeal the adulteration clauses of the 1872 Act and to reduce the powers of entry of police into licensed premises. The Conservatives, however, in their turn hardly found the licensing question a congenial one. Cross maintained that the Government's sole object was to see that the just wants of the public were supplied and to ensure that respectable persons should be encouraged to enter the licensed Trade 'by doing away with every unnecessary and unjust restriction'.[23] However, he found it impossible to concede all that the licensed victuallers wished, so that sections of the Trade were disappointed. Moreover, both he and Selwin-Ibbetson, now Under-Secretary at the Home Office, clearly felt uncomfortable when justifying an increase in hours of opening; Cross stressed that improvement in social conditions was the best mechanism for attacking intemperance. The cross-voting and confusion during the parliamentary stages of the Bill almost equalled that of the 1872 Act, and overall the Government gained little credit from the measure.[24]

The events of 1871–74 taught politicians several lessons. Firstly, it was clear that licensing reform was now not only complicated but also potentially dangerous. Licensing questions and temperance reform had become highly political issues, which not inconceivably might determine the fate of ministries. The agitations of 1871–74 led many subsequent politicians to overemphasise the electoral significance of the noisy forces on either side of the question and to be wary of initiatives. Conversely, secondly, there might be political advantage in the question. Some on the extremes would be tempted to play up solutions which were favoured by the temperance reformers or the Traders in either a restrictionist or libertarian direction. Even advocates of moderate regulation, like Selwin-Ibbetson, were acutely alive to the party political advantage of their proposals.[25] Drink and licensing might be a good issue for an Opposition to harry and thereby embarrass the Government. 'Dizzy knows well what a prodigious advantage the rage of the publicans gives the Tory Party', Kimberley had confided to his diary.[26] Thirdly, it was increasingly evident that the issue was a complex one. So far as Parliament was concerned, the consensus of opinion had moved in favour of 'moderate' reforms or licensing restriction, but the events after 1870 had shown that no clear programme had emerged upon which middle-of-the-road reformers could unite. Instead, the main lines of reform seemed to be submerged beneath a mass of technical details and a morass of practical difficulties.

One other area which aroused less heated reaction outside Parliament was the treatment of 'habitual drunkards'. During the second half of the nineteenth century, interest began to be taken in the plight of individuals whose dependance upon alcohol had become chronic, debilitating and dangerous to themselves. This approach, which saw the drunkard as victim, did not really fit into any of the mid-Victorian models of the Drink question that we have considered. It attracted the interest of some in the medical profession. Significantly, as with more general Drink issues, it was an individual, Dr Donald Dalrymple, who took the initiative. Dalrymple had been a proprietor of a Norwich lunatic asylum who had become interested in what appeared to him to be the close link between insanity and drunkenness. He embarked on a solitary campaign for government to provide inebriate asylums, researching the provision made in the United States and other countries. After being elected as a Liberal MP in 1870, he introduced a bill for the licensing by the state of the few existing private retreats and the establishment of other asylums by the state. In 1872, he managed to get a select committee appointed to investigate the issue, and this recommended the establishment of asylums for both criminal and non-criminal inebriates, the commitment of the latter to be voluntary or at the request of friends or relatives. Opposition was strong on libertarian grounds and after 1874, Cross, the Home Secretary, showed no inclination to act on the issue. However, the late 1870s, following Dalrymple's death, saw initiatives taken by elements within the British Medical Association and the Social Science Association to press for legislation on the problem of 'Habitual Drunkards'.[27] By 1878, elite opinion had become more sympathetic. *The Times*, for example, which in 1870 had viewed the prospect of detention with utmost alarm, by 1878 spoke of inebriates being 'helpless victims of a vice which they have lost the power to withstand'.[28] Nonetheless, the Habitual Drunkards Act that was eventually passed in 1878 was a timid and watered-down, permissive measure that abandoned the idea of compulsory confinement and public expenditure.[29] The supporters of asylums could only hope that this would provide a basis for further advance. Legislation in this area, like more general liquor licensing, indicated the caution of both Parliament and the political elite. Although there was a fairly general concern about the issue and a recognition that the state had a duty to take some action, there was also caution. Legislation could only be based on the lowest common denominator and there was no driving force from within the government machine itself. Initiative was taken by outside bodies together with their parliamentary champions; and in the medical area, no less than the more general temperance sphere, such pressure was undermined by divisions of opinion and outlook among the protagonists.

Party polarisation on the issue

In retrospect, it is also clear that the legislative tangles of 1871–74 marked the beginning of a marked party and electoral polarisation on the Drink issue. Henceforth, the Trade and the political wing of the temperance movement were to align themselves increasingly with the two great parties in the state. In the early 1870s, the two parties were still divided on Drink in all sorts of complicated ways; and liquor licensing, like most social reform issues, was not seen as an area for ideological conflict. Both prohibitionists and Traders maintained their respective cause or interest to be 'above' politics.[30] There were temperance reformers among the Conservatives, for example in Liverpool, and prominent brewers or other Traders among the ranks of Liberal MPs. Nor were the temperance movement or the Trade monolithic entities; on each side there were internal tensions and jealousies which made the construction of grand strategies or programmes difficult to achieve. Before 1883, the Trade 'was poorly organized, chronically underfunded and just sporadically aroused to action'.[31] However, over the next twenty-five years the process of polarisation proceeded apace. Moreover, the issue became increasingly bound up with the more general question of collectivism versus libertarianism. Attempts at state regulation of the Drink interest could be slotted into a more general 'collectivist' assault on the liberties of Britons. Thus, the Liberty and Property Defence League in the 1880s included the 1872 Licensing Act in its blacklist of 'socialistic' measures.[32]

The dynamo which drove much of this polarisation came from within radical Liberalism. The party, during this period, was a battleground in which democratic sentiment jostled for supremacy against the more cautious parliamentary leadership and the Whig elements within the party. The Liberal caucus, developed in the great urban centres of the North, saw democracy in terms of the mobilisaton of the will of the people 'from below' to formulate and generate policies which the parliamentary leadership was to implement. In 1877 came the formation of Liberal caucuses into the National Liberal Federation, which sought to draw up coherent manifestos of democratic reform to present to the electorate. Hence, radical Liberals, from outside the mainstream temperance movement, began to seize on the issue of local control or local option as a means of stimulating the political sensibilities of the dormant mass of the population. There was surely no subject more worthy of the attention of a reforming party. First off the mark was G. O. Trevelyan, a cousin of Sir W. C. Trevelyan, President of the UKA, who stumped the country with Lawson, delivering a series of speeches in urban centres on the liquor question in December 1871. Trevelyan regarded the militant temperance reformers as the true heirs of the free trade radicals of the previous generation. They were fighting against the oppressive rule of a class which trampled upon the rights and interests of the mass of the people. The working men enfranchised in 1867 'will never even begin to have their due weight in the council of the Cabinet – they will never cease to be the tools of every schemer and the customers of every charlatan – until they unite over some worthy measure, and turn themselves into motive power of some great movement which shall carry health, plenty, virtue and happiness within their doors and the doors of their neighbours'.[33] Popular control over Drink was such a measure. Joseph Cowen, the radical MP for Newcastle, beat the same drum when, in 1876, he introduced a bill to transfer all licensing authority to directly elected boards. 'Our principle as Liberals, is government for and by the people – in democratic rule, tempered by the teachings of history, embodying the highest, and the noblest, and the purest of national aspirations.'[34] Education and agitation went hand in hand. Only through the constant pressure of organised public opinion would 'earnest and incisive' speech enforce reforms on a House of Commons at present dominated by 'the typhonic rhetoric of partisans, struggling for victory rather than for truth'.[35] Even were his proposed boards to vote for an *increase* in licences, progress would be secured, for it was better to foster by democratic debate the 'moral elevation' of mankind than to rely upon 'high-toned benevolence' of the magistrates which brought about 'beggar-like subserviency'.[36]

In the same year, the theme was taken up by a more heavyweight politician, Joseph Chamberlain, who viewed the question less in terms of education than of administration. Chamberlain had already taken an initiative in Birmingham by getting a body of public house inspectors appointed.[37] Moreover, he had made his mark as mayor of Birmingham by carrying out a bold programme of municipalisation in fields such as housing and the supply of water and gas. In these undertakings, he sought to combine the advantages of profit, efficiency and the public good.[38] Recently elected to Parliament, he was now ambitious to emerge as the leader of radicalism, an ambition that might be greatly assisted by the support of those shock troops of late-Victorian nonconformity, the temperance zealots. He had appreciated the electoral significance of the UKA in his first unsuccessful electoral contest at Sheffield.[39] However, Chamberlain was anxious to redefine the very nature of radical liberalism, as D. A. Hamer has put it, 'his aim was to change the traditional

Radicalism of opposition to and suspicion of government into a Radicalism concerned primarily with acquiring and using governmental power'.[40] Accordingly, he set about exploring ways of treating the 'drink question as we have treated the gas question'.[41] His first step was to visit Sweden, where he examined the 'Gothenburg system' of liquor control. In 1865, the municipality of Gothenburg had set up a single company, consisting of a group of the most eminent and respected citizens of the town, to administer the sale of spirits. The managers of the outlets were to have no pecuniary interest in the sale of alcohol and the shareholders were to receive a 6 per cent return on capital, with any surplus profit accruing to the municipal coffers. This model of disinterested management soon became widespread in urban areas of Sweden to complement the extensive prohibition in rural areas. The Gothenburg system was characterised by extreme austerity: the bars were antiseptic with 'perpendicular drinking' in force to discourage lingering. It all fitted into the puritan and highly-regulatory culture that then prevailed in Scandinavia.[42]

After 'an immense deal of work & enquiry', Chamberlain set forth his views in a 'very dull but I think sound' article in the *Fortnightly Review* that extolled the principles of the Swedish approach.[43] Certainly, temperance was a factor in Chamberlain's approach. He spoke of the possibility of abolishing 'those enormous sheets of plate-glass, and the globe lamps, and the mirrors and the music, and the barmaids in bloomer costume, and all that kind of thing'.[44] If the watch committees of the great British cities could be given power and authority commensurate with their importance, then there would be a real opportunity for them to turn the tide of intemperance and drunkenness. However, a further aim was to use municipal control to promote civic improvements and social reform. He introduced a licensing bill that would give municipalities permissive power to abandon licences altogether, issue them to the highest bidder or – his own preference – run them directly for the benefit of the town's finances. To his disappointment, it not only faced the expected opposition from frightened Conservatives and the Trade, but also failed to attract the support of Liberals like Bright and Lowe, who opposed it largely on free trade grounds.[45] Furthermore, it only secured the most tepid support of the mainstream temperance supporters. Chamberlain felt 'stabbed in the back'.[46] Twenty years later he had still neither forgotten nor forgiven the rigidity of the prohibitionists, describing the UKA as the greatest obstacle to temperance reform which Britain had seen during the century.[47]

The decade after 1877 saw little government initiative on liquor legislation. The prohibitionists scored significant initial success in the form of Sunday closing for Ireland in 1878 (with exemptions for afternoons in the five largest cities) and Wales in 1881.[48] Sabbatarian Irish MPs had obliged the Conservative government to appoint a select committee which found opinion in Ireland generally favourable, except for the Irish Trade.[49] There was somewhat stronger opposition to the Welsh Bill, mainly from the industrial south, but Welsh temperance reformers, religious organisations and Liberal MPs lobbied hard.[50] Both Gladstone and John Bright, although strongly opposed to prohibition, were happy to support a measure that seemed to embody the aspirations of the Welsh people. Indeed subsequently, the Act, which was the first to mark any legislative distinction between England and Wales, was hailed as marking an important step in the rebirth of the Welsh national identity.[51]

England was quite another matter and both prohibitionists and other advanced restrictionist reformers found it much more difficult to make headway there. The UKA and Lawson changed tack in 1879 by dropping the annual introduction of the local veto Permissive Bill in favour of a parliamentary resolution in favour of 'local option'. This followed secret negotiations with John Bright, whose support the prohibitionists were desperate to secure.[52] Lawson hoped that 'earnest reformers would see with great satisfaction that a move was on foot calculated to secure a union amongst us all which we have not hitherto been able to secure'.[53] Superficially, the new tactic worked brilliantly: the 1880 resolution was passed by the House of Commons and, by 1883, Harcourt and Gladstone even endorsed the resolution on behalf of the Liberal government as a whole.[54] However, a price was paid for masking the demand for local veto in favour of a broader issue of 'local option'. In the first place, the vagueness of the concept of local control allowed Liberal politicians a lot of leeway. By 1883, Gladstone's third ministry faced much discontent from the backbenchers, as a result of parliamentary congestion caused by Irish matters. A plethora of 'sectional' causes such as land reform, Scottish church disestablishment, the repeal of the Contagious Diseases Act were pressing for attention. Temperance was one of these, albeit with a vociferous lobby behind it. Harcourt warned Gladstone of 'great dissatisfaction' in the party if the ministry failed to support Lawson's resolution. It was, in fact, an easy way out, being a substitute for a licensing bill that would be bound to be controversial, time consuming and unprofitable. 'The whole question', Harcourt reflected, 'appears to me to be simply a chapter in the volume of local government.' The licensing question 'is a social question on which the needs & the sentiments of the locality should prevail. That is in fact all

Lawson's resolution asserts.'[55] So tepid indeed was Gladstone's support, that two years later he could not even recall having voted for the resolution.[56]

Furthermore, the whole issue of general local control led to incessant efforts among both prohibitionist and restrictionist reformers to dream up elaborate schemes of local option. The result was internecine divisions and tensions. At one extreme, some prohibitionist militants, led by Axel Gustafson, even rejected the UKA's stance of being non-party political and its policy of local veto as unsatisfactory compromises, and set about founding a National Prohibition Party in 1887.[57] For its part, UKA leadership stood by local veto but rejected the need for any licensing reform initiative. Lawson's 'answer to those who said "Bring in a good Licensing Bill" was "Let those bring it in who believe in it." The Alliance went for the overthrow of the trade and no such Utopian scheme as would tinker with it.'[58] But some UKA supporters wanted to be less passive. W. S. Caine, a wealthy, Liverpool, metal merchant who was a vice-president of the UKA, believed a more comprehensive reform to be in order. 'Let Lawson keep pegging away at his bill', he wrote to Alexander Balfour, another Liverpool self-made merchant prince, '*we* will bring in a better someday, and get the whole weight of the Alliance in its favour.'[59] Balfour's own unhappy efforts a few years later to construct a compromise proposal that both the UKA and the CETS could support collapsed dismally amid recriminations and conflict.[60] The restrictionist supporters of local option by means of representative authorities were themselves divided. Some wished licensing powers to be handed over to town councils or representative county boards, while others insisted that special *ad hoc* boards, comparable with the education boards, should be elected. Beyond that, there was endless debate about the extent of any local powers and whether options should be given for local veto or even Gothenburg-style disinterested management.

Reformers had, however, made some positive progress during these years. They had largely succeeded in their first objective of impressing legislators with the gravity of the temperance problem. The climate of opinion among establishment circles at the time of the Home Rule crisis in 1886 was far more favourable to the idea of temperance legislation than had been the case when Bruce and Cross had wrestled with the problem. This was partly due to general social and intellectual changes, but it also owed much to the influence of moderate temperance sympathisers among the social elite, many of whom were influenced by the CETS. Not all these sympathisers became teetotallers or joined societies or pressure groups, but their indirect influence upon government was potentially great. The more militant temperance enthusiasts had made their mark too. 'Advanced' reformers, especially in Scotland and Wales, had impressed politicians with their dedication and influence. The Liberal leaders were conscious that keen reformers might carry a large number of votes and were capable of making an electoral or political nuisance of themselves if not properly handled. Indeed, there was considerable evidence that the temperance vote could be a crucial factor in swinging individual electoral contests.[61]

Although most political leaders and MPs viewed the licensing issue as tedious, technically difficult and potentially politically embarrassing, many nevertheless still shared a common interest in introducing sensible and useful measures with the minimum of dislocation and upheaval. On the other hand, this feeling was tempered by a scepticism about the efficacy of legislation. W. E. Forster's position was typical of most front bench opinion when, in 1880, he expressed doubts whether 'law could do much in the matter' but nevertheless conceded that some reform should be introduced 'so that there would be less temptation to drink than there has been'.[62] Many temperance zealots explained politicians' continued parliamentary inaction by claiming that Westminster was dominated or corrupted by the Trade. There is little evidence to support this somewhat paranoiac explanation. Certainly, political leaders had not forgotten the events of 1871–74 and were for this reason chary of supporting ill-considered or extreme measures. Few, however, had much sympathy with the Trade's dogmatic opposition to minor reforms and many were prepared to oppose the Trade when occasion demanded. Gladstone braved the displeasure of many brewers when he commuted the malt tax for a beer duty in 1880, and again in 1881 when he raised licence fees. Childers risked fiercer opposition when he tried to raise the liquor taxes in his budget of 1885. Sunday closing was passed for Ireland and Wales in the face of fierce Trade resistance. In general, Conservatives showed no sign of positively building on the embryonic alliance with the Trade that had been a feature of the 1874 election.[63] They were anxious to avoid being stigmatised as the 'Beer and Bible' party, and hardly welcomed the publicans as respectable supporters. Moreover, they secretly admired the Liberals' fiscal policy of these years, and realised that when they regained office, they would scarcely be in a position to offer tax concessions to Tradesmen. Dogmatic opponents of all temperance legislation, such as Lord Salisbury, did not dominate the party, though they were more commonly to be found on Tory than on Liberal benches. W. H. Smith summed up the Conservative parliamentary mood in 1884 in a private communication as follows: 'The majority of our men would be very glad indeed to go as far as it is really practicable in the way of Temperance legislation, – and individually I am quite prepared to support anything which experience shows will really forward the object we have in view.'[64]

Licensing and high politics, 1888–95

After 1886, the Conservatives had their chance. The Home Rule split within the Liberal Party had given the temperance lobby extra leverage since many of the new Liberal Unionist supporters of Lord Salisbury were sympathetic to local option and other temperance reforms.[65] In 1888, Ritchie, the Unionist President of the Local Government Board, radically reformed the whole structure of English local government. He established a system of elected county councils which were to take over the administrative duties of the justices in Quarter Sessions. Since local government reform was a highly technical and complicated matter, there was considerable discussion and controversy over the Bill's detailed provisions, but the majority of MPs accepted the broad principle of the measure without much qualification. Controversy centred around those areas where there was no clear demarcation between judicial and administrative matters, in particular over the administration of the police and of liquor licensing. From the first Ritchie, who appears to have had a genuine interest in social and temperance reform,[66] recognised that licensing was a 'thorny question', but he maintained that it would not be practicable to allow justices to retain their authority on this question, once they had been relieved of their other administrative functions.[67] Ritchie's proposals resembled those which Chamberlain had drafted when President of the Local Government Board in the previous Liberal government.

Ritchie's problems stemmed from his attempt to combine the transfer of local licensing authority with a scheme for the reduction in the number of licences. Whereas twenty years before, it had been the hours of sale that attracted most attention, by the latter part of the century it was the perceived excess public houses and 'ante-69' beerhouses that had become a preoccupation. A widely held view was that the sheer number of outlets tempted the working man to overindulgence. In England and Wales as a whole at this period, the average number of persons per 'on' licences was 251, but some areas were notorious for apparent over-provision. In the Addison area of Liverpool, for example, licensed properties accounted for one seventh of the total shop frontage, while in the Hard district of Portsmouth, known popularly as 'the Devil's Acre', 13 out of the 27 premises held a licence.[68] The legal powers of the existing magistrates to refuse a renewal, other than on grounds of misconduct, were a grey area. It had been widely assumed that licences had a right of renewal, but the case of *Sharp* v. *Wakefield*, which was subject to appeal at the very time when Ritchie's bill was being prepared, suggested this might not be the case.[69] Ritchie proposed to separate the judicial from the administrative aspects of licensing. The new county councils would henceforth exercise the latter in the form of local licensing committees for local licensing districts. These committees would be composed largely of councillors elected for the areas, and were to have powers to order Sunday closing and reduction in the number of licences. Licence fees were to be increased by 20 per cent to allow for the creation of a compensation fund, and all existing revenues from drink licences would go to the new councils to provide nearly half their total income.[70]

These proposals pleased few. Predictably, the UKA slated both the practicality and the principle behind the compensation scheme. Local communities would be saddled with the accursed Trade forever and their sole hope of ridding themselves from their misery was to provide massive sums out of their own local taxation.[71] The UKA set about energetically organising a mass protest campaign in the country, with over 5,000 petitions containing over a quarter of a million signatures being presented to Parliament and memorials being sent to the Local Government Board.[72] The moderate CETS, which enjoyed many links with the Conservatives, became deeply divided on the policy. Its preferred option was directly elected boards and it urged a time limit for the compensation. Some within the society wished to cooperate with the prohibitionists in an assault on the government proposals, whereas others, haunted by the lost opportunity of 1871, strove for a compromise.[73] Outside the temperance movement, many MPs questioned the wisdom of linking the new councils with the drink issue in such a way, opening the door to corruption or the domination of elections by drink or temperance issues.[74]

Popular demonstrations, however edifying to the participants, would not in themselves have caused the Government undue concern. Matters became more serious when they found echoes within Parliament itself. The licensing clauses provided the Liberal opposition in the Commons with the ideal weapon with which to torment the Government. Here, Harcourt enthusiastically took the lead in dissuading Gladstone from a policy of merely amending the offending clauses and going instead for one of outright opposition. He was convinced this would bring 'a great convergence of support . . . from various quarters'.[75] Ever the master tactician, he urged his colleagues to consider the merits of spinning the issue out. 'In the long run', he wrote to Morley, 'it is better for us that the clauses should go by their hands than ours with regard to the future. As it is the entire cause of Temperance will have been wrecked by their blundering. In the other case we might have been accused of being enemies of local option.'[76] A further factor that added spice for the Gladstonian Liberals was the strains which the issue placed upon the still uncertain alliance of Conservatives and Liberal Unionists. Although Chamberlain urged the ministry to press ahead with the clauses,[77] W. S. Caine, then a Liberal Unionist whip, and several of his fellow Liberal Unionists declared that they could under no circumstances support the proposals.[78] Caine, indeed, spent some £600 of his own money in opposing the clauses.[79] The loss of a by-election at Southampton on 23 May was widely attributed to the divisions among local Liberal Unionists on the licensing clauses[80] and, by 8 June, 26 Metropolitan Conservative MPs urged the clauses be dropped in the interests of the party.[81] Ritchie by this stage was reported to be 'disgusted with the whole affair' and was only too pleased to abandon licensing reform, spurning some desperate last minute efforts by Caine and others to hammer out some alternative compromise.[82]

Extraordinarily, a near carbon copy of the crisis occurred a mere two years later. Temperance reform continued to attract attention as an element of social reform, even among Conservatives. One such unlikely figure was Lord Randolph Churchill who, posing as the champion of Tory Democracy and the inheritor of Disraeli's mantle, had, after 1885, pushed forward social questions and, in 1889, went so far as to describe the drink trade as 'destructive and devilish'.[83] In 1886, he had been manoeuvred out of Salisbury's ministry and his short lived interest in the temperance question was, at least in part, a ploy to embarrass the government and strengthen his position as a statesman above party. He prepared and introduced a licensing bill in 1890 that sought to transfer licensing to elected councils, but which also provided for local veto but with fair compensation.[84] Churchill's successor as Chancellor of the Exchequer, Goschen – the man he famously 'forgot' during his strategic resignation in 1886 – then proceeded to blunder into the morasses of licensing reform. Ironically, it was the success of Goschen's fiscal policy that was responsible. The Chancellor had a surplus in hand of £3,250,000, largely due to an 'extraordinary rush to alcohol'. Goschen felt that this increase in the consumption of intoxicants 'must be deplored by all', and that it placed upon the Government 'an increasing liability to deal with the question of the consumption of alcoholic liquors'.[85] Goschen's financial proposals, however, were more intellectually adroit than they were politically astute. Because of his need to find money to defray the high costs of police and other county expenditure and to appease restive, Tory rural ratepayers, he calculated that he required to raise more money from the Trade. He convinced himself that it might be possible to square the brewers by giving them a measure of security for their public house property in return for additional taxation.[86] He was encouraged in this by overtures from John Danvers Power of the Country Brewers' Society, a relative of W. H. Smith, Leader of the House, who was at this time busy trying to weld the various brewers into a more cohesive protection body.[87] Power proposed a measure of reduction that, he believed, would be acceptable both to the county councils and to the brewers. He pointed out that the vast majority of the 'most objectionable' houses were unprofitable and were only retained because of the unsettled condition of the law; he proposed first, a ban on the issue of all new licences and secondly, that county councils should be empowered to buy the unprofitable houses, paying only for fixtures and for the goodwill of the business. Such a settlement would offer 'every inducement to brewers to meet the county councils' in order to make the scheme work smoothly and, in addition, would 'disarm' those who might otherwise press for a more drastic measure in the near future.[88]

W. H. Smith was impressed by Power's ideas, and the Government's proposals of the following year closely resembled them. Goschen proposed to give the county councils a power of veto over the issue of all new licences by the magistrates, with exceptions for certain classes of refreshment licences. The councils would, in addition, be able to buy out any existing 'on' licences and so reduce the total number of licences in the county. On the other hand, the magistrates' full discretionary powers over all matters of licensing were to remain unchanged, including the existing power to refuse renewal. The proposals, unlike those of 1888, applied to Scotland as well as to England and Wales. Where they differed markedly from Power's suggestions was in the field of finance. Rather than raise money on the rates, Goschen proposed to raise a levy of 3d. per barrel on beer and 6d. per gallon on spirits (in all, a sum of about £1,304,000) to the local taxation fund.[89] This was to be divided between England, Scotland and Wales in the ratio 80:11:9. Approximately one-third of the money was to go towards defraying the general expenses of county government, a little under one-third towards the cost of policing – an appropriate destination, he considered, for drink taxes – and a little over one-third (£350,000 for England and Wales) was to be shared out between councils for the purchase of liquor licences. A council would also be able to borrow an amount not exceeding three times its share of the grant to hasten the process of immediate reduction. As an extra fillip to temperance, he also proposed to reduce the tea duty.[90]

Events followed an uncannily similar pattern to those two years previously. Ministers seem, naively, to have hoped that such a scheme would win the support of temperance societies.[91] Initially, reaction in general was not unfavourable, but the temperance militants were quick to mount a sustained protest.[92] Goschen was soon complaining about a 'vast avalanche of letters, and . . . a yellow fog of telegrams'.[93] Once again, the UKA campaign culminated in a massive demonstration in Hyde Park.[94] As in 1888, however, ministers took most alarm when public protest was reflected in the political balance at Westminster, as high politics came into play. Chamberlain, despite disliking the scheme, considered that the ministry should press ahead regardless.[95] But other Liberal Unionists were far less happy. Once again, Caine was to the fore, cooperating with the UKA to mobilise opposition among Liberal Unionist rank and file, and urging his fellow MPs to oppose the clauses of the Supply Bill in committee. Ultimately, he returned to the Gladstonian fold over the issue.[96] Many leading Liberals felt little hostility to Goschen's plans. But the opportunity for attacking and embarrassing the Government was too good to miss. Once again, the redoubtable Harcourt seized it. From the start, he was 'pegging away at the "Compensation clauses"' and working to get Gladstone 'up to the mark'. He was uncertain, as yet, 'how much *real grit* there is in the Teetotal Party' but was convinced that 'if they are determined they ought to be able to wear out the Bill'.[97] As the Ministry got into difficulties over other legislation, the Conservative backbenchers became extremely restive. 'There was', recalled one, 'a gloom in our Party such as I have never before witnessed.'[98] 'The members are generally in a rather rabid state & have to be tenderly dealt with', mused another.[99] 'I think the Government have never had so disagreeable [a] meeting as today's at the Carlton', reported George Curzon to Churchill, after Salisbury had vainly tried to rally support at a discontented party meeting on 13 June.[100] Faced with the prospect of the session stretching into August, backbenchers were only too willing to visit 'the sins of the Govt. mainly on the head of Goschen'.[101] On 19 June, the attractions of Ascot proved too much and the Ministry only scraped through the first clause of the temperance legislation by a majority of four. Harcourt was ebullient at the success of his strategy, likening it to 'a well managed siege, and the garrison are being defeated yard by yard'.[102] Four days later, the licence purchase clauses were abandoned. Even this was not quite the end of the humiliation, since the Government's proposal to hold over the money being raised from the Trade in a special fund for use in a future session was deemed inadmissible by the Speaker and in the end the funds, popularly known as the 'whisky money', were diverted to the promotion of technical education, much to the disgust of Tradesmen and the satisfaction of temperance reformers.

The compensation battles of 1888–90 were, in effect, a triumph for the prohibitionists. The success seemed to fit their ideological vision that political progress was generated by the mobilisation of popular pressure 'from below'. This period also marked the apogee of their influence within the Liberal Party. At the local level, prohibitionists began to dominate the local caucuses, and the demand for a direct popular veto on liquor licences was included in the programme of the National Liberal Federation.[103] Despite large sums expended by the Trade, the Liberals comfortably won the 1892 election. Caine, now returned as a Liberal, estimated the number of electors in sympathy with the temperance movement to be at least 700,000. If prohibitionists needed government help in passing their legislation, the government in turn depended upon their support at the polls. 'We know we can secure nothing without their help. We are equally sure they cannot carry the constituencies without ours. Our interests are therefore identical', crowed Caine.[104] There were signs that some Liberal leaders had indeed taken these lessons to heart. G. O. Trevelyan, for example, was 'impressed' and 'disgusted' by the power of the Trade. 'They *are* Toryism, and where the enemy is, there you should go for him', he wrote encouragingly to Caine. The Trade would do everything in its power to prevent the Liberals winning a big majority and 'we shall never get a big majority unless we face them pluckily while we have a small one'.[105] John Morley, more interested in the intellectual aspects of democratic liberalism, seemed no less enthusiastic. By 1889, he declared that the temperance movement was 'the greatest movement, the most far-reaching and deep-seated movement, since the great antislavery time'.[106] In 1891, he appeared on a UKA platform and declared his support for the local veto.[107]

The prohibitionists, therefore, now possessed the advantage. However, they showed themselves singularly inept in adjusting to the new situation of working with senior politicians who were at last willing to accede to the local veto, even if their motives were mixed. Initially, matters went well. Harcourt, the Chancellor of the Exchequer, set about forcing the pace by setting up a Cabinet Committee on direct veto. After some fruitless attempts to gain support from the CETS, the Committee elected to introduce a simple English and Welsh local veto bill with a time limit in lieu of compensation of three years. The bill was introduced in February 1893. However, Harcourt in his turn soon became exasperated at the quibbling nature of the support he received. First of all, Lawson refused to have any prior input into the legislation, still maintaining his view that it was up to governments to legislate on Drink. Channels of communication were, therefore, difficult and Harcourt found himself rather in the dark as to what compromises the UKA would accept on the time limit.[108] Then there was trouble over Sunday closing, with Sunday closing enthusiasts wanting universal Sunday closure with an option out, and hence declining to support Harcourt.[109] Next, the UKA and other extremists were by no means satisfied with the 'obvious defects and shortcomings in the measure'. As the UKA annual report coyly put it: there was even 'some doubt and hesitation as to whether the measure ought to be supported . . . Hence the agitation was not as promptly, alertly, vigorously, and generally undertaken as might have been the case.'[110] Finally, to Harcourt's intense annoyance, Welsh temperance Liberals insisted on pushing ahead with their own veto bill, even though it cut across Harcourt's own measure.[111] The bill failed to find sufficient legislative time in the session but, in the meantime, there was the usual paraphernalia of demonstrations, public meetings and petitions on both sides. Of the latter, the Trade organisations managed to obtain 1,163,259 signatories as opposed to 610,769 by the temperance groupings.[112] It was small wonder that the irascible Harcourt felt frustrated at the constant carping from his supposed allies. 'If the Temperance people are not satisfied of the good faith of the Govt. . . . the remedy is in their own hands & they can as soon as they please find another Govt. in whom they have more confidence. I am dead sick myself of all this constant distrust & menace on the part of rival sections, & the sooner I find myself delivered from the odious & impossible task of reconciling & satisfying them the better I shall be pleased', he lectured Lawson the following year as he set about introducing a follow up bill for the next session.[113]

We may draw several interesting conclusions from studying the local veto episode of the 1892–95 Liberal government. Firstly, the Drink question was now played out in highly political terms. As A. E. Dingle has put it, whereas in the 1880s the Liberals had been concerned to formulate a measure of practical social reform, now they increasingly saw it as a political measure for their own advantage, hence legislation had to be acceptable to the UKA, who alone seemed to possess the electoral clout, to secure this political benefit, and hence it had to take the form of the local veto.[114] But the converse of this was that, secondly, politicians used political criteria to calculate their manoeuvrings. Harcourt is the prime example. His motives were doubtless mixed and complicated. Back in the 1870s, he had been a staunch opponent of temperance legislation or what he then termed 'grandmotherly legislation'. It is conceivable that he simply became converted to the temperance cause: this was the view taken by one of his contemporaries, Sir Charles Dilke, who described Harcourt's 'conversion' as 'a curious intellectual phenomenon, this development of a belated conviction in a mind hitherto essentially opportunistic'.[115] But equally, Harcourt was now convinced that the temperance forces – 'the backbone of the Liberal Party' – were an electoral advantage that his party could not do without, and that the 'Drink Question would be very powerful in attracting many who are not upon ordinary political questions strongly with us.'[116] Moreover, the radical sectional elements in the party after Home Rule were forcing the pace with 'accumulated ferocity' and 'in a big storm safety is sometimes to be found in "cracking on" and we "run" the ship, she can't "lay to".'[117]

Even this does not explain Harcourt's continued persistence with his local veto bill. Dilke spoke of him in 1892 as 'forcing' it on a 'reluctant Cabinet'. [118] Similarly, in 1895 Sir Edward Hamilton, a senior civil servant, confided to his diary that Harcourt received minimal support for his policy from the Cabinet: 'The fact is nobody wants & still less likes his Bill.'[119] His championship of the issue may also be partly explained in the context of the internal politics of the Government. This was unusually bedevilled by mistrust, jealousy and divisions.[120] The local option question took its place in a complex power struggle that was waged throughout 1894–95 between the Prime Minister, Rosebery, and his Chancellor of the Exchequer, Harcourt. Cabinet unity had completely fragmented and ministers followed their own devices. By 1894, all political questions were tending to be viewed by members of the Cabinet less in terms of their own intrinsic merits than in terms of their likely effect upon the balance of power inside the Cabinet. The liquor question had been adopted by Harcourt as his own, and he viewed criticism of it, or interference with it, as a reflection upon his own political standing. By November 1894, relations between him and Rosebery were so bad that the latter's cool comments on local veto in a public speech at Glasgow were probably just the incentive that Harcourt needed to press ahead yet more energetically with his bill.[121] Such an interpretation is borne out by the observations of the Liberal Unionist, Sir Henry James, in December 1894 that Harcourt 'does not want to carry' his bill but had determined to 'die fighting heroically in the breach' and as a result 'his obstinacy will make his colleagues not unwilling to accept their fate at an early period in the session'.[122] Sir Edward Hamilton similarly found Harcourt expressing a willingness to fall on the issue and speculated that he might even wish to bring the Government down, so that he could dominate the Liberal Party from the front bench in the Commons and so effectively end the leadership of Rosebery.[123]

A feature of this period is the leeway which leading politicians had to take initiatives on the subject. There was no particular reason why either Goschen in 1890 or Harcourt in 1893 should have taken up temperance legislation when in the post of Chancellor of the Exchequer. Drink legislation or initiatives were very much the initiative of the individual minister. The prime minister of the day was not involved, and very often they and their Cabinet colleagues were quite opposed to the line of legislation pursued. There was also opportunity for leading political figures outside the government – Chamberlain in 1876 and Churchill in 1890 – to make their mark for whatever motives. Nor was there any bureaucratic or departmental initiative on the question. The records of the Home Office for the period are conspicuously lacking in evidence for any proactive policy initiatives from civil servants, and are wholly concerned with the technical aspects of the administration of liquor licensing. Ministers seemed often to have to make their own arrangements. Thus, Kimberley from the Colonial Office suddenly had to rescue Bruce in 1872 and work up a bill. Similarly, Harcourt and his son, Lewis, (his close political confidant) are to be found in 1895 'sitting up till nearly 3 this morning looking out various plans of local option. We devised many of great ingenuity . . . and found conclusive and unanswerable arguments against each – after which we went to bed.'[124] Just as there was little input from the civil servants, so also the pressure groups proved unable to muster any sustained influence. Partly, this was because they were on both sides endemically divided. The Trade in particular was riven with economic tensions and divisions which made cooperation difficult, whereas the fissiparousness of the temperance movement was notorious. Nevertheless, the UKA proved particularly inept in adapting to the situation where government ministers were favourable to its platform. Party polarisation was, for each side, both an opportunity and a danger, and both temperance leaders and Tradesmen could see dangers as well as opportunities in the new situation. Nor were all politicians or other figures in public life enamoured of the way in which electoral politics seemed to revolve around the Drink and temperance issue. After 1895, there was an opportunity to step back from the intense partisanship that had developed over the last two decades.

4

New Departures and Old Orthodoxies, 1895–1902

Party political polarisation had been the *leitmotif* of the Drink question in the two decades before 1895. The prohibitionists had, to a large extent, been able to shape the discourse of the question by redefining local veto in terms of a broader 'local option'. However, this had clouded the issue somewhat by masking the ideological divisions between prohibitionists and restrictionist reformers. The identification of temperance reform with local government reform had pushed the issue to the fore as ambitious politicians sought credit from taking up such an apparently popular cause. However, by 1895, the reform of English local government had come and gone. This meant that the liquor question could be viewed from a fresh perspective. Hitherto, the moderate restrictionist reformers had been frustrated both by technical complexities of the licensing issue and the obstreperousness of the interested parties on either side. Several factors after 1895 suggested the possibility of a new approach to the issue, based around moderate opinion.

New thinking on the Drink issue

At this time, elite circles outside Parliament had become more exercised at the harm to the nation's social fabric and well-being caused by excess drinking. Teetotalism made rapid headway among the ministers of the nonconformist churches after 1880.[1] More significantly, by 1900, temperance work had become extremely fashionable in the Church of England with no less than half its bishops being teetotallers.[2] The CETS, which was closely directed by the clergy, had become the most prestigious and extensive anti-drink organisation in England.[3] Similarly, licensing magistrates and leading police officers began to press for reforms in liquor licensing. Hitherto, the magistracy had been largely passive in the exercise of their duties, with the exception of the free-licensing Liverpool experiment in the mid-century and the notoriously harsh attitude of the Bradford bench. However, interest in issues such as the sale of alcohol to children, the insanitary conditions of many licensed premises, lax enforcement of the law and the excess number of licensed houses sparked a more proactive interest. Licence reduction, indeed, became something of an obsession in some quarters. The *Sharp* v. *Wakefield* case of 1891 had clearly established the authority of the magistrates to refuse a licence other than on grounds of misconduct. That few benches had done so reflected less a lack of interest in the question, than the assumption that a government would introduce a nationwide scheme. When this failed to materialise, some benches became irritated and restive.[4] For decades, temperance workers had routinely castigated the magistracy for 'foisting drinkshops on the poor'; now they suddenly found many benches to be a 'progressive' force on the issue.

A further factor was a general shift in the intellectual climate at the turn of the century. As M. J. Wiener has argued, by the later Victorian period concern at the moral anarchism and deficiencies of the individual deviant had been replaced by anxiety about the people as victims of social wreckage. The emphasis had moved from moralist preaching or repressive control to therapeutic intervention.[5] The Drink problem began to be viewed in a new light and became linked to new concerns. One such was the moral panic about national efficiency and racial degeneration at a time when social Darwinist ideas were to the fore. It became fashionable to see Britain's imperial destiny as dependent upon the health of the working class in the great urban centres: arguments which appealed to Unionist tariff reformers, Liberal Unionists and Fabian socialists alike.[6] Social problems caused by poor housing and inadequate diet would undermine the nation's position. Alcohol was soon cited as a factor in working-class decrepitude and infant mortality.[7] The argument that expenditure on alcohol caused urban squalor was an old one, but now medical opinion attributed the poor health and mortality of working-class children more directly to female intemperance. This conclusion was upheld by the influential Report of the Inter-Departmental Committee on Physical Deterioration of 1904, set up in the aftermath of the revelations of poor physique during the Boer War; and the findings of this body were seized upon and disseminated by anti-drink doctors.[8]

Medical opinion on Drink was particularly interesting at this period. A distinct 'medical temperance movement' had emerged since 1875, with links to both the secular NTL and the CETS. By 1898, no less than 900 medical practitioners and students belonged to the British Medical Temperance Association that had been formed in 1876.[9] This medical temperance lobby sought to challenge the dominant assumptions that alcohol, if not taken to excess, was a beneficial agent and that alcohol had a significant part to play in medical treatment.[10] The temperance societies themselves eagerly embraced the opportunity to bolster their cause with support from 'scientific' sources, publicising work done by doctors on the harmful effects of alcohol on the body. Many temperance doctors were motivated by general humanitarian, moralistic or religious considerations; however, as Joanne Woiak has pointed out, they also had the incentive of using the temperance issue to advance their own professional claims and position in society. 'Temperance doctors claimed the "physical basis" of abstinence principles as their special territory, distinct from the moral and legal domains, which were already well covered by others.'[11] The medical lobby could be influential in areas such as compulsory temperance education in schools, supported by the medical profession as a body in 1903. However, the force of medical lobbying, as with that of the more general temperance movement, was gravely weakened by complex internal divisions. The effect of alcohol on the human body remained hotly disputed, with teetotal doctors clashing fiercely with their 'moderationist' colleagues. Then there was division over Lamarkian ideas that either physical and mental degeneration or the craving for alcohol might be inherited. Some medical opinion believed alcoholism or chronic intemperance to be a hereditary condition and not susceptible to social reform measures.[12] Further disputes arose concerning the causal relationship between inebriety and insanity.[13] Finally, the position of the teetotal, medical temperance movement was challenged by some in the Society for the Study of Inebriety, founded in 1884, which had been continuing the campaign for a more radical policy of state asylums for inebriates.[14] Particularly after 1900, some members, including high office holders, opposed the temperance colleagues as 'unscientific' and motivated by 'extravagance and fanatical zeal'. In their view, alcoholism was a disease which required scientific research.[15] Even among those supporting the concept of alcoholism as a disease, there was little unanimity. Some saw hereditary factors as the chief cause, while others stressed environmental and behavioural factors.[16] This striking lack of consensus among 'expert' medical opinion served to weaken any pressures for legislation.[17]

By the 1890s, social scientists, no less than their medical counterparts, had turned their attention to Drink, seeing it increasingly in the context of social reform in general. The previous generation of reformers had tended to isolate Drink: the debate revolved around the extent to which it caused poverty, prostitution, wife beating and other social evils, with somewhat simplistic attitudes being struck on both sides of the debate.[18] The impact of socialist theories, the growth of sociological investigation and analysis, and the popular contemporary concern with eugenics all focused attention on the interrelation of social problems. Under the impact of these ideas, it no longer made a great deal of sense rigidly to isolate particular problems, such as temperance, housing or labour difficulties, from the general 'condition of England' question. Instead, it was tempting to regard them all in some measure as part of the broader question of poverty in an industrial society.[19] Although alcohol was obviously responsible for turning particular individuals into paupers, it was less obviously the factor which caused society as a whole to suffer from the existence of poverty and depression. The work and writings of Charles Booth during the 1880s and 1890s were particularly important in this respect. The independence and disinterestedness of Booth's motives added to the value of his work. He began his mammoth investigations into the life and work of the people of London, not in order to discover 'what made people poor', but to quantify and assess the numbers of those living in poverty. Through his painstaking researches, Booth showed the futility of attempting to isolate or compartmentalise the component aspects of working-class life. The leisure activities of the people of London simply could not be separated from their work, their physical environment or their religious beliefs. All these factors together made up a coherent cultural pattern. Above all, he was able to show that men did not become poor simply because of individual failings, for example, idleness, improvidence or drunkenness. In this view, there was no separate 'drink problem' as such: there was a problem of excess drinking which was part of the larger question of working-class poverty.[20] Others built upon Booth's work. During the 1890s, the Webbs, Seebohm Rowntree and many other students of urban society agreed that poverty was a social condition rather than an affliction of individuals, and that a 'solution' to the temperance problem could scarcely be separated from other remedial social and economic reforms.[21]

The growing popularity of socialist ideas during this period pointed in the same direction. Socialists of all persuasions believed the root cause of all social problems to lie in a faulty economic and social order. The way to eliminate social alienation was to change society and the economic order. On the other hand, in practice, few British socialists or labour leaders totally despised temperance legislation. For one thing, they shared with radical Liberals an admiration for the puritan virtues of self-help and abstinence, and they saw in strong drink one of the instruments by which the governing classes successfully exploited the toiling masses. The 'Beerage' was the ally of the capitalist manufacturers and bankers. Thus, John Burns, for example, believed that trade unions 'would have been larger, more powerful, and of greater influence, but for the drain on their members and their resources, which the drinking habits of the people inflict upon them'.[22] Burns, Arthur Henderson, J. H. Roberts, Tom Mann, Keir Hardie, George Lansbury and Philip Snowden were all at some time or other active in temperance work or supporters of legislative temperance reform.[23] However, not many socialists at this period were prepared to leave everything to social and economic change. Snowden's lengthy book, *Socialism and the Drink Question*, of 1908, portrayed Drink as but one element of the evils caused by capitalism: it was 'a selecting agent'. Prohibition by itself was not enough; however, teetotalism was to be commended as a useful 'auxiliary' weapon in the battle against poverty. Moreover, in order to achieve a socialist society, it was necessary to regulate and control all trades in the public interest. In this respect the drink trade was no different from other private business, for example railways, textile industries, coal, and gas: every one of these trades 'if left uncontrolled, is capable of becoming as great a public danger as an unregulated Drink Traffic'. Thus, restriction of the Trade was supported not as an end in itself, but as a necessary part of a socialist policy.[24] The Fabian position was a little different. They certainly believed that licensing laws ought to diminish drunkenness, but they were equally concerned to see that, in future, the law would 'interfere with the private ownership of a monopoly created by law yielding enormous profits which are now used for the encouragement of excess and the corruption of politics'.[25] The Fabians were as much interested in the industrial reorganisation of the Trade as in furthering temperance reform. They certainly accepted the claim that the people had a right to control the drink traffic, but the 'control we contemplate is wholly different from that which the teetotallers demand'.[26] The answer lay in the collective control by the people of this dangerous, but lucrative, traffic. The answer here, as in other fields, lay in municipalisation.

Thus, by 1895, an influential body of opinion had grown up, outside political parties and the temperance pressure groups, that stressed the importance of tackling the Drink question in the national interest. The problem was the lack of consensus concerning both the diagnosis and the solution of the 'problem'. For their part, leading politicians in both parties, by 1895, had grown wary of the issue and no longer saw so much opportunity for political advantage in licensing reform. Licensing was, the Liberal Chief Whip warned Campbell-Bannerman, 'a veritable hornet's nest – in truth one of the knottiest and thorniest of subjects to be touched', sentiments which were echoed by a large number of elite politicians.[27] It was elements within the Liberal Party after the 1895 election that felt this the most strongly. A mere 177 Gladstonian Liberals survived, as 411 Unionists swept into the Commons. Wilfrid Lawson himself admitted this was 'about the most complete smash that the Liberal Party ever experienced' but – rather in the manner of left wing Labour activists explaining the 1983 defeat of their party – claimed it was the 'spinelessness' of the Rosebery Government and the lukewarmness of moderate temperance people that was to blame.[28] Others in the party took a different view. The electoral defeat galvanised those who opposed nonconformist 'faddists' in general and teetotal 'fanatics' in particular, and these now mounted a campaign to reposition their party.[29] The *Westminster Gazette* surveyed all the Liberal candidates and found only a tiny proportion considered the veto bills to have been 'helpful'.[30] Kay-Shuttleworth went further: he believed the poor result reflected a deeper malaise in the Liberal leadership. The Party needed firmer guidance and had suffered because so many of the issues of the Newcastle programme, especially local veto, had been brought to the fore to fill the vacuum left by poor leadership.[31] This view was endorsed by the former Chief Whip, Arnold Morley, who believed the Trade to have been the 'most potent' of the factors working against the Party.[32]

The Trade, of course, had every interest in magnifying its 'triumph' at the election. Certainly, in England, it acted with a cohesion and a determination never before experienced, and never again equalled. The organ of the Licensed Victuallers boasted that 'the electoral forces of the Board [of the Central Protection Society], raised to their highest strength, occupied the field, and simply pervaded every constituency . . . in fine, all that experience could suggest, or energy realise, was done to crush the enemies and secure victory'.[33] The Lancashire and Yorkshire brewers claimed to have decided the fate of 40 constituencies, while in the Metropolis opposition was organised against every anti-Unionist candidate except the wine merchant, Mark Beaufoy. Indeed, in only three English and Welsh seats did the Liberals secure Trade neutrality. The election marked the culmination of the Trade's alignment to the Conservative or Unionist cause which had begun in 1874. Nevertheless,

Unionist leaders, for whom such issues as Home Rule, imperial defence or the rise of socialism were seen as pivotal, were reluctant to ascribe their acquisition and subsequent hold over office to the power of the beer barrel. 'We have not', sonorously declared Balfour, 'in this country sunk so low that our constituencies are to be manipulated at the will of any interest, however powerful, and depend upon it it does not rest with publicans and brewers . . . to determine who it is shall govern the destinies of this Empire.'[34] As the climate of elite opinion became increasingly less tolerant of the *ils ne passeront pas* position of the Trade, so Unionists came to feel more uncomfortable at a purely negative position. Moreover, the pressure of alliance with the Liberal Unionists, and the increasing interest of Joseph Chamberlain and others in Unionist schemes for social reform, meant that a totally negative policy was inappropriate. Many were, therefore, more amenable to the idea of a less politicised approach and were potentially open to new approaches, around which non-partisan opinion might rally.

The Royal Commission

Notwithstanding these new influences and outlooks, mainstream temperance reformers remained committed to the more narrow path of reform through the licensing system. There was little attempt to take on board the new approaches. After the failures of local government reform to solve the question, various attempts were made to overcome the disunity among temperance reformers by producing compromise formulae of varying degrees of complexity. A common goal was to unite the CETS, the UKA and the various other groups like the BTL. The CETS by this date had quietly abandoned its long-standing policy of elected licensing boards in favour of a programme of licence reduction, compensation, Sunday closing and stricter magisterial control. One scheme, the Manchester Bill, was promoted at a conference in Manchester in 1891 presided over by the bishop and subsequently championed by MPs from that city.[35] Two years later, the wealthy Unionist shipbuilder, Arnold Hills, who lavished a fortune on both temperance and vegetarianism and who unusually supported both the CETS and UKA, tried his hand at a series of United Temperance conferences to work out a reduction scheme. Far from creating unity, this merely spawned another reform plan, the United Bill.[36] A similar fate befell a group of Liberal Unionists in Parliament who, feeling some responsibility for the failures of 1888 and 1890, produced a particularly elaborate scheme, known as the Westminster Bill.[37] Even more acrimony was caused in Scotland by attempts of Scottish Gothenburg enthusiasts to offer electors a triple choice between limitations of licences, local municipal management, or local veto.[38] All these well-meaning attempts at cementing the unity of the temperance movement simply gave rise to further tension and dissension.[39] The gulf between prohibitionists, who wanted to abolish the drink traffic, and restrictionists, who wished to reform its operation, was made plain, despite the common endeavour to close many liquor outlets and restrict sales, which was a prime feature of these schemes.

Although Salisbury's government seemed in no mood to listen to any of these freelance proposals, pressure from a variety of sources began to be exerted on the government. Representatives of temperance opinion in all the churches met in 1895 at a conference in London, when it was agreed that the CETS, which had most links with the Unionist parties, should take the lead in pressing for reforms.[40] Accordingly, in February 1896, a deputation of the CETS, led by Frederick Temple, soon to become Archbishop of Canterbury, met Salisbury and Balfour in order to urge some action, at least along the lines of non-controversial useful reforms, such as tightening up the law on sales to children. The response was not encouraging with Salisbury declaring he was inclined to make an 'idol of individual liberty'.[41] Meanwhile, Francis Fox and other Unionist temperance reformers (especially Liberal Unionists) were trying to achieve the same ends behind the scenes. They believed that the only hope for a settlement of the licensing question lay in cooperation with the more responsible sections of the Trade, and urged a parliamentary inquiry that might lead to some moderate programme of reform. Fox and his associates calculated that the way of settling the question was to take it out of party politics and to remove it from the sterile battles between fanatical temperance reformers and obdurate publicans.[42] Simultaneously, elements in the Trade were urging the government to settle the uncertain state of the law as they were alarmed at the threat to money locked up in tied-house property. As early as 1892, the Liberal brewer, Edward Buxton, had complained to Harcourt that 'The purgatory of hot water in which the trade is kept is worse than the furnace to which some would consign them.'[43] Although the licensed victuallers still tended to resist the idea of legislation, the large London and Burton brewers were now willing to accept some licence reduction and minor reforms in return for a measure of security for their property.[44] The licensed victuallers sponsored a bill in the House of Lords along these lines in early 1896.[45] Immediately after the 1895 election, H. Cosmo Bonsor MP, of the umbrella National Trade Defence Association (NTDA), wrote to Salisbury asking for an opportunity for the Trade to put forward its views, and over the next few months he publicly expressed the Trade's willingness to consider reasonable reforms.[46] It was then that the Unionist leaders began to examine the possibility of setting up a royal commission and, by the end of January 1896, Salisbury had received from Bonsor an assurance that 'the appointment of a Royal Commission with a limited reference would I believe give general satisfaction to both the Brewers and the Licensed Victuallers'.[47] By the end of February, the Cabinet agreed to the appointment of a royal commission and its terms of reference and membership were settled over the next few months, Fox conveniently undertaking most of the detailed work.[48]

Fox could represent the granting of the Commission as a concession secured from the government. But such was not the view of ministers themselves. There can be little doubt that Balfour's main aim was simply to use the Commission as a convenient way of shelving a potentially troublesome and unrewarding question until after the next election, keeping the Trade in suspense and so more likely to assist the Unionists again.[49] The composition of the Commission, which included eight temperance reformers (including the prohibitionist MPs Caine and Whittaker), eight representatives of various sections of the Trade, and, sandwiched in the middle, eight neutrals, seems calculated to have produced a deadlock. The chairman was Viscount Peel, a former Liberal Unionist MP and Speaker of the House of Commons, and the vice-chairman Sir Algernon West, a prominent former civil servant at the Inland Revenue who had also served as Gladstone's chief of staff in his last administration.[50] Prohibitionists did not expect any joy from the Commission, but since they had persistently maintained that any airings of the evils of Drink could only be beneficial: they had (reluctantly) to go along with it.[51] The terms of reference were extremely narrow, confining the Commissioners to looking at the operation and administration of the licensing laws.

In the event, the Royal Commission sat for nearly three years, interviewed 259 witnesses, asked 74,451 oral questions, produced eight volumes of evidence, cost £7,880 17s. 10d. and ended with its members split in two factions, meeting in separate rooms and producing two divergent and partially contradictory reports. The behaviour of the chairman, Peel, exacerbated the inevitable internal tensions. His appointment had been widely welcomed in 1896, not least by representatives of the Trade.[52] However, his service on the Commission converted him into an ardent temperance reformer, to the dismay of the Traders and his fellow neutrals. As early as November 1898, the Trade representatives, fearing that Peel and the neutral Commissioners would put forward unacceptable proposals, drafted their own secret report. This, significantly, took its cue not from the evidence before the Commission but from a speech of Hicks Beach, the Chancellor of the Exchequer, at a brewers' dinner.[53] The Trade draft report was to be kept from public knowledge 'until Peel has shown his hand', but in the meantime its authors sought the assistance of Salisbury in interesting some of their neutral colleagues.[54] However, in February 1899, Peel showed the contents of his hand to be more startling than his fellow Commissioners had supposed when he had set about drafting a report very favourable to the temperance interests. The Commission then effectively dissolved into two acrimonious factions with Sir Algernon West drafting a majority report and Peel a minority one.[55]

Peel's minority report proposed a radical measure of licence reduction. Over a seven-year period in England and a five-year period in Scotland, these licences were to be reduced to the levels of 1:750 in towns and 1:400 in the country. A small measure of compensation, diminishing as the time limit wore on, was to be given, based on the annual licence rental levied or the rateable value of the house, purely as a matter of 'grace and expediency'. All claim for compensation was to cease at the end of the time limit, opening the way for additional local reduction or for 'further legislation, experimental or otherwise' which Parliament might sanction. Local veto was seen to be appropriate for Scotland and Wales at the end of the time limit. Another radical proposal was the abolition of grocers' licences; henceforth 'off' sales should be confined to special licensed retailers and not linked to general food commodities. His support received the backing of the temperance representatives on the Commission, albeit with some reservations. By contrast, West's majority report was signed by all the 'neutral' Commissioners (except Peel), by all eight Tradesmen (with reservations) and by two of the temperance Commissioners, Dean Dickinson and W. Allen, who signed both reports.[56] The latter's credentials as a temperance reformer, however, were destroyed when it became known in 1899 that he was linked with a group of MPs who were floating a brewery company. His constituency Liberals at Newcastle-under-Lyme were 'shocked beyond measure', and Allen had to 'expiate' his guilt by volunteering for service in the Boer War![57] The majority report proposed extending control by the licensing authority over both grocers' 'off' licences and the 'ante-69' beerhouses, and the addition of county councillors to the licensing body. It also called for licence reductions but compensations should be based on the market value of the house, including goodwill, and was to be raised by taxation on the Trade itself.

There was to be no time limit for existing houses, but any completely new licences were to be issued for non-renewable seven-year periods.

Reaction to the Royal Commission

The divided report caused difficulties for the Trade, the Liberal party and the advanced temperance reformers alike. Even at this time of maximum party political polarisation of the Drink issue, complex internal divisions continued to exist. The picture of a united Trade opposed by a coherent, if unrealistic, temperance grouping, each allied to a political party, is a simplification of what had become complex alignments. For the Trade, the majority report was tolerable, but even here there were problems. Many with an interest in the retail side of the Trade were unhappy with the idea of compensation coming from taxes on the Trade itself. Edward Buxton, a leading London brewer and a prominent member of the Brewers' Society, worked hard to persuade his fellow brewers to accept some degree of compromise in the form of the taxation proposed by the majority report, since the alternative minority report failed to recognise any claim for compensation in the licence itself.[58] Another critical point was the attack of the minority report upon the licensed grocers, brought into being by Gladstone in 1860 and who still ranked among the strongest supporters of the Liberals. Certainly the Peel Report had the effect of driving many of the leading off-licence holders not into the ranks of the Unionists but into a rapprochement with the mainstream Trade bodies, dominated by the on-sale market. This outcome was much encouraged by Buxton, but as David Gutzke has written, it 'was indeed remarkable given the trade's traditional animosity against licensed grocers'. The latter were seen as economic rivals who, while enjoying low overheads and lax supervision, had for years engaged in aggressive commercial practices to undermine the publicans' trade.[59] However, attempts to keep a united Trade front, including the grocers, proved both difficult and divisive. In 1900, agreements between the leaders of the NTDA and the National Federation of Off-Licence Holders' Association to keep a common line demanding both compensation for 'on' licence reduction and preservation of grocers' licences came under intense pressure as groups of publicans made speeches attacking grocers. The 1900 election saw different groups of licensed victuallers producing their own test questions to candidates which ignored the interests of 'off' traders.[60] All these squabbles were symptomatic of a larger dilemma for the Trade. To what extent should they devote resources to the Unionists to fend off the advances of the extreme temperance forces within the Liberal party? Edward Buxton, himself a Liberal, was in no doubt that this was a misguided strategy. At a meeting in September 1900 of the United Parliamentary Council of the NTDA, he warned that 'it is not the part of prudent men to put all their goods onto one ship and to rely exclusively on the support of one political party' since the 'swing of the pendulum' would inevitably put the Liberals in power.[61] Strategic issues here became involved with issues of internal Trade politics. Many council members disputed Buxton's interpretation of the role of the NTDA, claiming that the constituent members retained their own independence of action in these matters; meanwhile, tensions between the Midland brewers and their larger London and Burton counterparts also resurfaced, while tensions and squabbles between licensed victuallers and the brewers remained a complicating factor in attempts to build up Trade unity. In the event, twenty-four English and Welsh Liberal candidates secured Trade neutrality, whereas all but twenty-nine Unionists secured its support.[62]

Buxton's desperate efforts to retain a bridge between the Liberals and the Trade had received the wholehearted support of Herbert Gladstone, the Liberal Chief Whip, but the Royal Commission was to cause the Liberal party, no less than the Trade, major problems. Between 1897 and 1899, the morale of the party was showing signs of improving, with Rosebery and Harcourt both leaving leadership positions. The growing electoral and political power of organised labour seemed to augur well for the party and the Liberals had generally been able to pose as the party of social reform. The temperance issue, however, was fast becoming a thorn in the flesh. On the one hand, temperance reform appealed very strongly to many staunch Liberal supporters in the constituencies. As one of Herbert Gladstone's prominent local supporters reminded him: the 'veto people' were recognised to be among the 'hardest workers in our party'.[63] On the other hand, local veto frightened many of the more influential backers of the party, including retailers like the Gilbey firm, and hardly seemed a popular cause with the English electorate. Herbert Gladstone lectured the new party leader, Campbell-Bannerman: '*We cannot afford* to lose the Gilbeys & all their grocer clients, the Whitbreads Eversheds Buxtons Beaufoys & other men . . . who are more or less connected with the trade'.[64] Gladstone was conscious of this from his own electoral experiences in Leeds in both the 1892 and 1895 elections. At the latter, the popular Conservative millionaire and public benefactor, Col J. T. North, had slashed Gladstone's majority to 96 as drink flowed freely and a host of allied attractions – including the 'Coffee Cooler', a famous boxing champion – were brought in to aid the Unionist cause. By adopting unnecessarily puritanical policies, the Liberals seemed to be alienating many valuable artisan voters.[65]

Accordingly, in the winter of 1897–98 Gladstone, in a series of speeches, criticised the Liberals' association with what was likely to be the ineffective and unpopular policy of local veto. The Liberal leaders of 1893 and 1895, by bringing in their local veto bill without having the power to follow it through, in the process angering the publicans, had been like someone standing harmlessly near a wasp's nest and then deciding to poke a stick into it. The party would be much better advised to reform the licensing authority.[66] In trying to steer the party away from this and other unpopular policy commitments, such as Church disestablishment, Gladstone won support from the right wing or Whig elements of the party and from the Liberal press of the Metropolis, and in so doing was able to build up his own political standing, which had hitherto rested upon his father's reputation.[67] Gladstone had hoped that the Royal Commission would provide a moderate programme of restrictionist reform, embodying useful measures such as restrictions on sales to children, better regulation of public houses and some compensation for reduction in numbers. Such a scheme could unite the Liberals and provide them with ammunition should the Unionists fail to endorse it or deliver it.[68] The divided reports of the Commission upset all these calculations. Peel's minority report was particularly dangerous since it was reasonable enough to attract a wide measure of moderate temperance support, but too extreme to prevent the Trade from taking fright. Generous compensation was essential. 'I fear that without an adequate amount of grease we shall not be able to overcome the friction of the trade at the next or almost any election', he warned Campbell-Bannerman. Efforts to rally a united front of prohibitionists and temperance reformers behind the Peel Report, with the idea of securing local veto at the end of the time limit, were even more alarming since temperance pressure groups would appear to be dictating the licensing policy of the Liberal leadership.[69]

The new Liberal leader, Campbell-Bannerman, showed only a partial awareness of the dangers of the situation by initially referring to the Peel Report as a 'code of reform' which his party might adopt, before watering down his position, on Gladstone's advice.[70] It is clear that political calculation, and even intrigue among the leadership, still played the major part in deciding what should and what should not be Liberal party policy on the temperance question. Just as Harcourt had deliberately adopted an 'extreme' policy in the early 1890s for the sake of electoral and personal advantage, so now Herbert Gladstone and other right wing Liberals strove to avoid making any specific commitment which would weaken their position or harm the electoral fortunes of the party. However, in 1899, with the prospect of a united temperance front behind Lord Peel and Whittaker, it seemed as if the Liberal leaders, whether they liked it or not, would have to endorse some form of comprehensive temperance restriction that included a time limit on licences and a measure of local control. Campbell-Bannerman, who in private was far less favourable to the temperance cause than his public utterances suggested, was certainly pessimistic. His party seemed to be becoming increasingly dependent upon nonconformist radicals for its support. The best they could hope to do was to fight a rearguard action: 'Edward Buxton, Algie West, & Co. . . . wd. like us to give up Local Veto. *We cannot do it*: all we can do is to delay or postpone it in England, under cover of passing it for Scotland & Wales', he calculated at this time.[71] Indeed, the Liberal leader was disconcerted to find himself under attack from two sides simultaneously when he received a letter from 'old Lawson, battle-axe in hand', demanding to know why there had been no mention of local veto for England in his first speech on the subject.[72] Herbert Gladstone, on the other hand, astutely saw a chink of light at the end of the tunnel. An internecine split among the advanced temperance reformers might be the party's salvation:

> I think that the sooner you make it clear that the Veto for England is postponed the better. It will bring the parties of Lawson & Whittaker into conflict and will help us with our brewers & all moderate Liberal reformers. The battleaxe will have first to descend on the heads of the nearest 'traitors' in this case Caine & Whittaker. For the Peel Reporters are the men who threw the Veto overboard.[73]

As A. E. Dingle has observed, 'For almost thirty years Liberal leaders had bemoaned the lack of unanimity within the temperance movement but by the end of the century they were actively encouraging it.'[74]

The tensions which the Royal Commission caused among the Trade and the Liberal party were nothing compared to the disruptive effect it had upon the more 'advanced' sections of the temperance movement. Once again, events were to show how difficult it was for ardent prohibitionist supporters of local veto to compromise or to associate themselves with measures of restrictive temperance reform. The manoeuvres of T. P. Whittaker, one of the temperance Commissioners and Liberal

MP for Spen Valley, were pivotal here. Whittaker, an important figure in the insurance world, was the son of one of the crusading pioneers of the temperance movement and, when appointed to the Commission, had been an orthodox prohibitionist.[75] Once the Commission's reports were published, however, he worked to rally all temperance opinion behind Lord Peel's minority report as the first step towards local option. His strategy was first to secure temperance unity and then to nail the Liberals to such a programme, in return for a temperance compromise on compensation levels and details. Whittaker was optimistic in his ability to persuade his fellow prohibitionists and to isolate Lawson, who he realised would be obdurate.[76] The prohibitionists soon became divided, with some prominent figures such as W. S. Caine, H. J. Wilson, Samuel Pope and Canon Hicks sympathetic to the idea of a compromise around such a general scheme of licensing reform, but others, including Lawson and most of the UKA leadership, obdurate in their opposition.[77] Others, based around the Good Templars, an international prohibitionist group, even founded a National Prohibition Party, and these succeeded in driving W. S. Caine from his candidature for Kilmarnock Burghs in the 1900 election.[78]

After the further massive Unionist triumph at this election, Whittaker renewed his efforts at putting together a broader reform package amid continued controversy within the ranks of the UKA supporters. Initially, the dispute between Whittaker and Lawson had seemed to be one of tactics. However, it soon became clear that questions of tactics raised questions of strategy. In other words, it involved discussion of the *raison d'être* of the prohibitionist agitation and the relevance of the favourite model of direct popular agitation. Lawson's dislike of compromise sprang from his deep mistrust of any political manoeuvring remote from popular agitation. He and other orthodox prohibitionists believed Whittaker's strategy would actually set back reform, as the Trade would be sure to use the Peel proposals as the thin end of the wedge to extract further concessions from the government of the day. They found solace once more for political failure in the knowledge that theirs was a moral as much as a political movement, and in the belief that moral sentiment was best cultivated in the country 'out of doors' rather than in the corrupting corridors of power. By contrast, Whittaker and many of his supporters quickly found themselves moving away from a mere tactical shift towards a strategic reappraisal. They soon found that by working for other reforms besides local prohibition, they were contradicting the prohibitionist premise that *only* through prohibition was there a chance of eliminating the evils of intemperance. This, in turn, led them to question both the prohibitionist conception of political action and the validity of the prohibitionist solution itself. They ultimately found the solutions of prohibition and progressive restriction to be incompatible. The problem was that Peel's minority report did not really provide them with a coherent approach and justification for an alternative policy. This they were to find in a quite different solution in the shape of disinterested management, along the lines of the Gothenburg programme. Here, the work of Joseph Rowntree was to provide them with an alternative approach of greater power.

Rowntree and Sherwell's new approach

The Gothenburg concept of disinterested management, first popularised by Joseph Chamberlain in the 1870s, had continued to attract modest attention from those wishing to engage in small scale experiments.[79] However, Joseph Rowntree was to provide the focus for a more sustained approach. As a Quaker cocoa manufacturer, Rowntree was typical of the class that formed the bedrock of the Victorian temperance movement. His aversion to alcohol was such that he warned his grandchildren that Drink was the 'most dire of all temptations' they would face in their lives.[80] However, in 1892, he 'had come to the conclusion, after a somewhat careful examination of the alleged triumphs of Prohibition especially in New England, that Prohibition was only successful in rural districts or in places where there were facilities within easy reach'. Arthur Sherwell, who had recently come to York to help establish an adult school, became interested and undertook to visit America to research the issue.[81] Rowntree and Sherwell's resulting volume, *The Temperance Problem and Social Reform*, published in 1899, made an immediate impact; it was reviewed in all the major journals and within five years had sold 90,000 copies.[82]

Rowntree and Sherwell's starting point was emphatically restrictionist: 'the present consumption of alcohol in this country is excessive, and ought to be reduced, and that the force of law and of local arrangement should favour sobriety rather than intemperance'.[83] However, licensing reform needed to be enacted as part of a more general programme of reform. In common with Booth and other writers of the 1890s, but unlike the Royal Commission, the authors sought to place drinking in the context of urban industrial poverty and social issues in general. Notwithstanding the great advances in education and the temperance efforts of the past decades in the United Kingdom, they found that the consumption of intoxicants 'is not only excessive, but seriously subversive of the economic and moral progress of the nation'.[84] Unlike the prohibitionists, however, they attributed this, not to the continued sale of alcohol itself but, first, to the dullness and monotony of the lives of the people and the lack of rational recreational facilities and, secondly, to the activities of the Trade, which, they concluded, constituted a 'social and political menace' of the first order. It was their concentration on this second feature which gave their analysis originality. They concluded that the reason why the past efforts of reformers had come to nought was the continued capacity of the Trade, with its 'enormous wealth' and its 'highly efficient organisation', to command the ear of governments and to exert 'a direct and powerful influence upon the electorate'. 'The independence of Parliament and the purity of municipal life are alike imperilled.'[85] It followed that it was necessary to eliminate the motives of private gain from the sale of alcohol.[86]

Sherwell's detailed researches showed the shortcomings of the operation of local veto in North America. In contrast, the experience of Sweden and Norway showed how a system of carefully regulated management in the towns had gone far towards solving the problem of excess drinking. The great achievement of the Gothenburg system had been to take the sale of intoxicants out of interested private hands and to subject it to 'effective restriction and control'. Analysis showed that this restriction 'being locally applied under local representative authority, keeps pace with the Temperance sentiment of the locality'. The number of houses might be speedily reduced; policing tightened up; and barmaids, music, gambling, sales on credit and all the 'adventitious attractions' or 'immoral accessories' of the public house destroyed at a stroke.[87] They concluded that the 'first step in the direction of reform' in Britain would be to give localities the power of granting a monopoly of the entire retail trade either to specially formed disinterested management companies or, under safeguards, to the councils themselves. The profits from the traffic in intoxicants should then be handed over to a central state-controlled authority which would then return the profits to those localities where the scheme was adopted, in ratio to the population and not to the profits earned. These profits would be specially earmarked to provide the constructive side of the reform programme. 'People's Palaces' for rational recreation, arts and exhibitions, educational agencies and popular lecturers, social and recreational clubs, gymnasia, and temperance cafes might all be financed by the profits of the traffic. The public house, shorn of its seductive character, would no longer be able to compete with the brighter and more attractive conditions of the new recreational institutions, and a generation might be reared which would be able to resist the fatal attractions of alcohol and the public house. Such proposals might not solve the entire problem of intemperance, but 'If the proposals fall short of the full aim of the idealist, they in no way conflict with his ideal. They simply lay the foundations upon which he and others may build.'[88]

The most significant feature of temperance politics over the next five years was the way in which Rowntree and Sherwell's ideas formed a catalyst for restrictionist reformers. The shift in Whittaker's position was the most remarkable. His efforts in 1899–1901 had been geared towards marrying the licence reduction proposals of Lord Peel with demands for local veto. However, in the summer of 1903, the first links were forged between the supporters of the Peel Report and the advocates of disinterested management. Lady Helen Somerset and other 'Peelites' came together with Rowntree and Sherwell and drafted a secret manifesto. This was designed to 'form a basis of legislation which may unite the different sections of the Temperance people, and at last give some constructive policy'.[89] It called for compensation money to be raised from the Trade and administered on a national basis by an independent body within a strict time limit. At the end of the time limit there must be 'wide powers of local self-government' including provision for local veto, disinterested control and 'a scheme of constructive reform which should include the provision and maintenance of adequate counter-attractions to the public house'. Local veto found a place in this programme, but it was relegated to a subsidiary position.[90] Whittaker, moreover, was now associating with reformers who were sceptical of local veto, regarding it at best as a harmless irrelevance.[91] A number of prohibitionists were provoked into violent opposition. Rosalind, Countess of Carlisle, who had conducted a personal vendetta against Lady Somerset ever since the days of a bitter split in the British Women's Temperance Association in 1893, objected strongly to space being given for the 'heretical poison' of 'these brilliant but mistaken orators'.[92]

If we take the story beyond the passage of the 1904 Licensing Act, considered in the next chapter, which established a vested interest in English 'on' licences, we find the divisions intensifying and solidifying. Whittaker and his associates were increasingly attracted by the idea of the public resuming the 'full monopoly value' of all licences at the end of the limit; a simple power of local veto would not be enough: full discretionary powers of the widest kind were required, including the power to take the Trade out of private hands.[93] Despite efforts to try to reconcile differences, the chief parties on either side were no longer prepared to place a high premium on unity.[94] The UKA Executive passed a resolution condemning municipalisation of the Drink traffic.[95] Whittaker and his allies, for their part, suppressed the Central Temperance Legislation Board and formed a new organisation, the Temperance Legislation League (TLL), which had Sherwell as its Honorary Secretary.[96] The TLL urged temperance workers to avoid 'the disasters of the past'.[97] 'Unless the private financial interest in the retail sale of drink be eliminated, . . . substantial progress is hopeless'; moreover, the evil of intemperance 'must be fought, not by repressive legislation alone, but by counteracting and constructive effort also'.[98] By 1906, Whittaker was pouring out invective against his former prohibitionist allies in the columns of the public press. Reasonable and practical temperance people, he claimed, had now withdrawn from the active work of the prohibitionist societies, because 'they were sick and weary of the browbeating and denunciation, the misrepresentation and personal abuse which was showered upon those who were making the most promising effort of recent years to lift the legislative phase of the Temperance movement out of the morass of impracticability in which it had so long foundered'. All that was left was 'a stage army' whose organisations lacked power and status and were now comprised of small-minded men, able only to comprehend a policy of destructive wrecking.[99]

The temperance movement entered the twentieth century, therefore, divided into two bitterly warring factions. The prohibitionists upheld the local veto, while the new reformist groupings had come to put their faith in the new principle of disinterested management. Both factions were to battle to impose their views on the Liberal party. Whittaker and his group had managed to attract the interest and backing of many influential Liberals, such as George Cadbury, J. T. Brunner and Robert Spence Watson, as well as many of the traditional moderate temperance reformers who had found their home in the CETS and many who were temperamentally interested in moderate reform.

In retrospect, it is clear that the years after 1895 marked a very significant shift in the temperance and Drink questions. The UKA could no longer exercise a hegemony in the political aspects of the temperance movement.[100] Its financial position and its increasing inability to attract MPs to speak at its public meetings began to give cause for concern.[101] Certainly the prohibitionist forces, especially in Scotland and Wales, remained sufficiently strong (and noisy) to retain some influence among radical Liberal politicians and to prevent the new grouping of reformers, around Whittaker, from establishing an unchallenged supremacy in the movement for reform. Disinterested management *à la* Gothenburg could not simply replace local option schemes as the unchallenged focus of reformers and many socialists, like Snowden, continued to support local veto. The prohibitionists, however, had compounded their difficulties by their inept failure to associate themselves with, and hence gain control over, the moves to introduce restrictionist reforms. Moreover, they still clung to an outmoded model of popular political progress in which party alignment was to be eschewed, notwithstanding the fact that identification with the Liberal party presented their sole chance, now, of achieving their objective. These political failures were compounded by a those at a more ideological level. Between 1895 and 1901, the prohibitionists had lost hegemony over the terms of discourse of the Drink debate. The emphasis had shifted towards such issues as social poverty and national efficiency.[102] Moreover, Rowntree and Sherwell, by pushing forward the concept of public control, had challenged the local veto as a solution to the supposed ills of drinking.[103] Fundamental questions about the nature of the public house and the role of community control were being raised. However, in the meantime, Drink unexpectedly reached the height of political controversy.

5
The High Water Mark of Party Political Controversy, 1902–14

Edwardian Britain saw the Drink question reach heights of acrimony and fierce political dispute, culminating in the controversies of the Liberal government's licensing bill of 1908. This triggered massive demonstrations on either side in Hyde Park, elicited controversial pronouncements from prominent church leaders and contributed to the simmering constitutional crisis of 1909–11. In short, Drink became one of the major conflicts between the parties. This could hardly have been forecast at the turn of the century, when calmer waters had seemed to lie ahead. Then, the pattern had seemed to be set whereby Drink would increasingly be taken out of the cockpit of party politics, with renewed efforts being made by moderate social reformers, church leaders and the like to produce compromise solutions.

The changing social and economic position of the Trade

Changes in the social and economic position of the Trade, particularly regarding the English brewers, were at the root of this change. Beginning in 1887, the large Burton and London breweries were floated on the stock exchange. Following this, the 1890s saw a surge in beer sales and speculative fever about the fortunes of the drink industry, fuelled by a ready availability of cheap money, low raw material prices and buoyant consumer demand as a result of high wages in the economic boom.[1] Competition, particularly in London, was fierce and the large brewers responded by an aggressive policy of purchasing public houses directly and swallowing up smaller breweries, often for the sake of their tied-houses. Whitbread's, for example, doubled its nominal share capital between its flotation in 1889 and 1901, and its leasehold and freehold properties which had been valued at £26,430 in 1886 were set at nearly £2 million by 1907. The Burton brewers followed suit and Allsopp, in particular, pursued a reckless policy of purchase, paying prices many considered 'insane'.[2] The boom decade of the 1890s was followed by a sharp downturn in fortunes after 1900 as 'conditions changed with remarkable rapidity'.[3] *Per capita*, beer consumption fell annually after 1899. Economic recession was partly to blame, but there were also other underlying factors: the rapid shift of working-class expenditure towards consumer durables and the availability of alternatives for leisure expenditure, such as football and cheap railway excursions. Not all sections of the Trade were equally badly hit, as there was a shift towards the consumption of bottled beer at home and more competition from clubs. Many of the largest giants of the industry had been investing heavily in public house property at the very time when the pub was losing its preeminent position as a focus of working-class leisure and culture.[4] The London brewers were particularly badly hit after 1900, with annual reported declines in barrelage of between 2 and 7 per cent.[5]

These changes had two political implications. In the first place, the leading breweries, being overexposed in public house property, were particularly sensitive to attempts at compulsory licence reduction. Secondly, as public companies, large brewers now had to be accountable to a wider public, both for their investment decisions and the conduct of their business. This posed problems once business experienced a downturn after the heady euphoria of the flotation period, but it also presented opportunities. The Trade was no longer a narrow sectional economic interest, but instead could pose as the representative of a major legitimate public interest. Much propaganda could therefore be made of 'widows and orphans', whose welfare depended upon income from brewery dividends and who would suffer if 'confiscatory' schemes were passed. In many ways the temperance lobby and unwelcome government action could provide a lightning conductor that could distract attention away from the mismanagement of some of the large firms, which in the case of Allsopp had been nothing short of catastrophic. The position of the Trade could therefore be moulded much more easily into a more general clash of interest between capital and the collectivist state. Already this had been apparent with the close links between the Trade and the libertarian Liberty and Property Defence League in the 1880s.[6] For temperance reformers, on the other hand, the new potential ability of the Trade to mobilise a vast swathe of shareholders among the ordinary public was an added cause of alarm. For decades the temperance lobby had fulminated against the 'Our Trade, Our Politics' standpoint of the drink interest. However, apart from the role of public houses at elections, this was hardly a matter calculated to arouse great concern among the uncommitted. Both the increasingly national organisation of party politics and the growth in size of Trade components put a different complexion on the matter. Rowntree and Sherwell, in 1899, devoted a whole chapter to the 'social and political menace' posed by the Trade, referring to the effect upon municipal politics, police watch committees and the like.[7] This was one of the factors which led them to advocate state control of liquor. With the controversies of 1904 and 1908, the issue of shareholders' influence became a major concern. The prohibitionist, G. B. Wilson, calculated in 1904 that 167 peers and 129 MPs had interests in brewing and distilling and even such a moderate Liberal as Lord Rosebery spoke in 1908 of the Trade as 'poison[ing] the resources of your political and your municipal life.'[8] Those on the left tended to take at face value the propagandist boasts of Trade organisations: 'It was difficult enough', wrote the Liberal Chief Whip to his leader in 1907, 'when only the big brewer was to be attacked. Now, in place of the big brewer are hundreds, if not thousands, of shareholders; and this with the allied trades revolving around the liquor interest, makes licensing reform peculiarly hard to compass.'[9] The reality was rather less impressive as parsimony, lack of imagination and poor organisation prevented the Trade from realising its full potential in this area in any systematic manner.[10]

The 1902 Licensing Act

Initially, in 1899, the divided reports of the Royal Commission seemed to confirm Salisbury's cynical expectation that it would dampen down the legislative imperative, a view explicitly endorsed by the Home Secretary, Sir Matthew White Ridley, speaking at the Country Brewers' Society annual dinner in 1899.[11] However, Randall Davidson, Bishop of Winchester, who was soon to succeed Temple as Archbishop of Canterbury, took a lead on behalf of social reformers who felt that some small measure of non-contentious reforms common to both reports could be implemented, pending a more radical overhaul of the licensing system. In May 1900, he moved a resolution in the Lords, urging the government to act on such issues as improving policing regulations and tightening the law on sales to children. Although the motion was opposed by the government and lost,[12] Davidson could nonetheless claim something of a moral victory, as Temple and twelve other bishops supported the resolution and there were signs of Conservative discontent at the purely negative approach of the government.[13] Over the next few months, he began to rally opinion in favour of a minimalist, consensus position. The modesty of his proposals meant that he could not arouse much enthusiasm from the temperance groups like the CETS and Lord Peel who, as we saw in Chapter 4, were at this very moment trying to build up a common 'front' for the advanced temperance pressure groups.[14] On the other hand, Davidson's independence from any power base within the temperance movement was a positive advantage.[15] Moreover, the fact that his proposals, by leaving the reform of the licensing authority alone, did not block either local veto or any other reform of the licensing system meant that temperance reformers were not actively hostile.[16]

The Liberal Unionist Francis Fox once again set about rallying support for moderate reform,[17] and a powerful deputation including Algernon West also lobbied the new Home Secretary Ritchie.[18] Notwithstanding his experiences in 1888 and 1890, Ritchie was more 'favourably disposed' than his predecessor, Ridley, had been.[19] Although cautious in public, behind the scenes he urged upon his colleagues a measure of 'useful reform'. 'The demand for legislation does not come merely from those who are opposed to the Government or from extreme men. A large number of our supporters are committed to Temperance reform of some kind, and among them are to be found many of the most influential and moderate men of the party.' Unless some reform was initiated, he felt 'sure a strong outside reaction might easily be aroused'.[20] During the 1901 session, Ritchie first passed a small bill concerning the sale of liquor to children, and then decided to take over and adapt three draft bills of Davidson's and to tackle the problem of 'off' sales from grocers' licences. The end product was the modest but useful Licensing Act of 1902.[21] It changed the laws on drunkenness, improved the machinery of licensing, brought all 'off' licences under the magistrates' control and registered clubs. The only serious opposition came from the 'off' Traders who were isolated.

The significance of this legislation lies in its insignificance. It had taken thirty years to pass a few modest and scarcely controversial reforms which did little more than improve the administration of the existing law. In most other fields of government regulation, such improvements would surely have followed as a matter of course after a combination of pressure from the civil service or public inspectorate, consultation with the relevant industries or trades, and some sort of agitation on the part of the press, eminent public figures or respected reforming institutions. But liquor licensing and temperance reform were a law unto themselves. The question was not, for example, one where there was any simple progression from *laissez faire* to tight governmental control. A pattern of controls and regulations already existed. Difficulties arose because there were fundamental divisions concerning the purpose of control, the nature of the problem, and the means by which a 'solution' could be secured. In 1902, reform was introduced despite, rather than because of, the work of the temperance pressure groups. Ritchie and his colleagues, after their bitter experiences in the past, moved very cautiously. The modest piece of legislation was able to be passed for the following reasons: the neutrality of the temperance forces; the absence of popular excitement on the issue; the lack of opposition from the Trade (other than some 'off' retailers); pressure from moderate Unionist quarters; a degree of cross-party consensus with the Liberals and the sympathetic attitude of the Home Secretary himself. Much of the initiative clearly came from Ritchie himself, as there is no evidence of civil servants at the Home Office playing a proactive role. The legislation itself was simply adapted from Davidson's bills and worked into shape by officials.

The 1904 Licensing Act

Ritchie's legislation was not sufficient to settle the licensing question during the lifetime of Balfour's Ministry. It was, however, not the organised pressure groups on either side of the question, but that sedate body, the English magistrates, who forced the pace. Their position was indeed a complex one. As servants of the Crown, it was their duty to administer the licensing statutes; as representatives of the locality, it was their duty to interpret those statutes in accordance with the needs and requirements of the community; as a quasi-judicial body, they had to assess each case before them strictly according to the rules of law and equity. Their scope for initiative was, in these circumstances, strictly circumscribed. The licensing magistrates did not constitute any bureaucratic force of specialists or form themselves into any institution or organisation which strove to influence government. Their function was essentially passive. The one area where the local benches' decisions could have an impact was in deciding how many new licences should be granted for individual localities. With the rapid expansion of the population into suburban areas, for the first time this offered magistrates a lever: licences would only be granted in new areas if brewers were prepared to surrender several older licences in inner urban districts. The 1890s had seen great attention focused upon the vexed issue of the excess numbers of 'on' licences in urban centres. Such houses were usually insanitary and were portrayed as 'drinking dens' where the hard-pressed publican was perceived as pushing alcohol upon his customers. The decisions in the *Sharp* v. *Wakefield* case of 1889–91 had made it clear that in England, only the 'ante-69' beerhouses enjoyed a statutory right of renewal. Until 1900, however, few benches of licensing magistrates had attempted to reduce or redistribute licences on a large scale, however much they felt convinced that such a move was necessary. Moreover, most justices were naturally reluctant to dispossess individual owners or licensees, and considered the central government had a responsibility to initiate a scheme for licence reduction, along with some form of compensation. In some instances, benches began quietly to reduce licences with the consent of the local brewers, as in Liverpool.[22] However, in 1901, considerable publicity and controversy was aroused by the efforts of the Birmingham justices, led by Arthur Chamberlain (Joseph Chamberlain's Liberal brother), to reduce licences. Over a five-year period, 150 licences had been eliminated as part of a systematic scheme, undertaken in cooperation with local brewers, involving a compensation fund.[23] But, by 1901, this had broken down because of its essentially voluntary character and because it tended to inflate the values of licensed property.[24] Active and well publicised attempts by Chamberlain to extend it aroused the opposition of some local Unionists and of the English Trade as a whole, and ended in failure.[25] Clearly, local initiative was not sufficient.

The government, however, seemed determined to do nothing. Many licensing benches therefore decided that the only way out of their predicament was to act on their own and force the issue. Over the next two years, the situation of the Trade deteriorated rapidly. The effect of non-renewals seemed to be cumulative, and particular attention was focused on the refusal of the Farnham bench to renew 9 out of 45 'on' public houses in their district. This decision had been taken on the recommendation of the county justices themselves and was deliberately designed to arouse opinion throughout the country. 'We were not', wrote one of the justices, 'fighting the question of one or two licenses in Farnham . . . magistrates all over England are making enquiries with a view to following the same course'. Their object was to prove that licensing justices had the power to act administratively as well as judicially.[26] The Farnham justices' decisions were upheld throughout all the process of appeal and, by 1903, other benches sessions followed their example.[27] The position from the Trade's point of view was fraught with serious danger, given the large sums the brewers had sunk in tied-houses and the threat to licensees' livelihood. The loss of a few hundred scarcely profitable houses was neither here nor there, but the precedent might prove disastrous. The Trade could not in these circumstances stand idly by. The law, if need be, had to be changed.

Subsequently, the Liberals made the most of the situation by presenting the 1904 Licensing Act as the direct result of Trade pressure upon the Unionists, the 'capitulation of the State to a powerful and organised interest' and the payment of a long overdue debt by the Conservatives to the Trade.[28] Certainly, the Trade brought all its resources into play in an attempt to push the government into action. Balfour and Ritchie received a deputation representing all sections of the English Trade on 18 March, 1903, protesting at the 'feverish activity' of the justices. Balfour expressed sympathy and roundly condemned the precipitate actions of some magistrates, which, however well intentioned, fell little short of 'unjust confiscation'.[29] When no action was immediately forthcoming, the Trade took steps to support anti-Unionist candidates in the Woolwich and Rye by-elections in March 1903, and had the satisfaction of seeing both seats lost by the government. The view that the 1904 Act was a debt paid to the Trade is supported by the fact that ministers themselves had no desire whatsoever to reopen the licensing issue. Electoral considerations certainly played some part, although ministers were less worried at the Trade's direct electoral impact than its indirect influence on the propertied classes who held brewery shares. There was, Balfour wrote to the King the day before the Trade deputation, an 'intense and widespread' feeling against the justices' actions, 'and as ignorant opinion attributes (most erroneously) what has occurred to the action of the Government, we suffer proportionately in the constituencies'.[30] However, the true picture is more complicated. As David Gutzke has pointed out, the Trade itself was, as ever, not all of a mind on the issue, with some prepared to follow the majority of the Royal Commission in arguing for a levy on the Trade itself whilst others demanded the state compensate them from general taxation.[31] As far as the government was concerned, if ministers had been solely interested in appeasing the Trade, it would have been comparatively easy to have adapted private members' bills which were introduced on behalf of the Trade which offered compensation or a legislative title to licensees. Equally, it would have been even more advantageous to have passed a temporary suspensory act on the eve of the next election. This course was urged strongly by Joseph Chamberlain. He argued forcibly that the 'support of the Publicans is not worth much in itself' and 'becomes important only when they are really excited and alarmed, as they were in 1895'. If, he astutely calculated, 'we do all we are going to do for them, before the General Election, they will have nothing to fear; and they will not work for us out of mere gratitude'; conversely, he believed a temporary act and the promise of full compensation to come would bring out all the Trade support and force the Liberals to declare their own policy.[32]

At first, the Cabinet agreed to proceed along these lines.[33] By December 1903, the new Home Secretary, Akers-Douglas, had sketched out a draft bill giving a five-year right of renewal.[34] A month later, the ministers concerned began to have second thoughts. Balfour and some of his colleagues, along with civil servants at the Home Office, were anxious that the new bill should provide a final settlement of the issue and, if possible, prove 'a distinct contribution to the cause of reasonable temperance'.[35] Balfour was aware of the delicacy of the situation. If the proposed bill failed to give permanent security to licence holders, the Government stood in danger of falling 'between two stools'. It would forfeit the confidence of the Trade without in any way securing the support of temperance sympathisers.[36] Soon the Cabinet as a whole was convinced that it was better to try and settle the question outright before the next election. Akers-Douglas introduced a bill on 20 April, which provided that no English beerhouse or public house licence could be suppressed except on grounds of misconduct without payment to the interested parties of a sum equal to the difference in value in 1904 of the premises with and without the licence.[37] The money for compensation was to come from a levy on all licensed property. The compensation fund was to be administered on a local basis and reduction could only take place to the extent allowed for by the money in the fund or by money borrowed on its security. Licence reduction was in effect to be determined by the justices sitting on the new county compensation authority and the role of the justices in brewster sessions was limited to deciding which individual licences were to be referred to the compensation authority. New licences were to be exempt from the compensation scheme and made to pay a high licence duty.

Ministers were concerned to present the bill as a step forward for temperance, even though they knew they could not secure any support from the temperance movement. The Trade was not given all that it desired. 'The dog was fed with a bit of his own tail', declared Lord Burton.[38] The compensation levy might in the future be used by a hostile government to increase the financial leverage on the Trade. Nevertheless, at last licensees were to have their position recognised in law and, in any event, the Trade could not hope for a better deal from the Liberals. Both the Liberal party and all the temperance pressure groups, including moderates in the CETS, vehemently opposed it on various grounds. The absence of a time limit, it was argued, would block the way for either local veto or disinterested management schemes.[39] Secondly, Parliament by passing the bill would lose the right of gaining for the nation the monopoly value of existing licences. [40] Thirdly, the bill undermined the possibility of local discretion by communities. Finally, the critics challenged the effectiveness of the measure in reducing licences. [41] The Licensing Bill, passed with the aid of the guillotine, brought little political advantage to the Unionist ministers. Opposition from nonconformist Unionists and from the bishops of the Church of England was embarrassing, and there was some unease on the Unionist backbenches.[42] The Liberal leaders gained some tactical advantage in rallying opposition to the Bill, but in the long term the 1904 Act presented them with a difficult problem. Amendment or repeal of the Act would be both technically difficult and politically dangerous.

The 1908 Licensing Bill

The triumph of radical political forces at the election of 1906 filled prohibitionist veterans with enthusiasm and hope. Lawson, who died soon afterwards, was 'confident that the special cause to which he had given his life was now nearing victory'.[43] Outwardly there were signs that this faith would be vindicated. Nonconformity had never before enjoyed such influence within the Liberal party, with over 75 per cent of Liberal and Labour candidates in the election committing themselves to an 'amendment' of the 1904 Act in their election addresses.[44] On 5 April, Campbell-Bannerman and Herbert Gladstone, the Home Secretary, received a deputation of over 100 MPs urging priority for temperance legislation and, five days later, T. Leif Jones (popularly known as 'Tea Leaf'), Lawson's successor as president of the UKA, carried a resolution in the Commons in favour of local option by the magnificent vote of 271 to 44.[45] Such hopes were illusory. The Liberal leaders were scarcely enthusiastic temperance supporters and, furthermore, the emphasis in licensing matters had shifted away from local option or local control towards finance, as Asquith recognised.[46]

Accordingly, by January 1907, the Cabinet had agreed that the 'backbone' of any licensing scheme should be a uniform reduction of licences. Approximately a third of English licences were to be eliminated, according to a sliding scale of licences to population.

Compensation was to continue, but at a reduced rate, and some sort of time limit was to be introduced.[47] The reform which Herbert Gladstone, the Home Secretary, now proposed was rigid and inelastic. Everywhere licences were to be reduced to a statutory limit; compensation was to be organised on a national and not a local basis; the control of the fund was to be vested in the hands of a special licensing commission of three members, sitting in London. This commission, Gladstone admitted, had 'rather a formidable look of centralization', yet it was difficult to see how any substantial reduction measure could avoid such an authoritarian embodiment, especially when obvious exemptions would have to be allowed in business centres or holiday resorts.[48]

The length and nature of the time limit caused the greatest debate within the Cabinet. Should it take the form of a simple limit to the operation of the 1904 Act, thus returning to the *status quo ante*? This was what prohibitionists wanted. Alternatively, should the state acquire the full monopoly value of the licence at the end of the limit? This was strongly advocated by Whittaker and his allies in the TLL, who supported disinterested management. In their view, the Trade should not only have to compensate itself for reduction within the time limit, but should also lay down a sinking fund to meet the total cost of the withdrawal of *all* its licensed property at the end of the limit. Herbert Gladstone fiercely opposed this latter course, which he believed would be to 'court disaster'. The Lords would wreck such a bill on the grounds that it was confiscatory, whereas a mere reduction measure would leave the brewers isolated.[49] The Lord Chancellor, Lord Loreburn, on the other hand, wanted a more radical measure to allow full powers for local veto and local option for reduction to promote 'popular as opposed to bureaucratic government'. Temperance enthusiasts, unless satisfied with the legislation, would, he feared, 'transfer from the Liberal Party to some school of Labour or Socialist thought and they would go over in the conviction that they had been betrayed'.[50] The Cabinet finally settled for a limit of fourteen years, at the end of which the full monopoly value was to be transferred to the state.[51] In this way, there was the full promise of local control and local option for all sorts and conditions of temperance reformers, but this was relegated to a fairly distant future so as not to trouble the essential 'backbone' of licence reduction. In the meantime, temperance reformers would find it hard not to support the closure of one-third of the retail drink outlets in the country.

Opposition to the bill centred less around technicalities of licensing and more upon the general issues of property and confiscation. The opponents of the bill portrayed it as the precursor of socialism: what was done to the brewers today would be done to landlords and colliery owners tomorrow. Balfour hyperbolically described it as 'the greatest injury ever done to public morality.' [52] The Trade used the opportunity of a by-election in Peckham to flex its traditional muscles.[53] However, new methods were also employed. Protests were organised on the part of holders of brewery stock, with widows and poor clergymen being given pride of place, and an association of Brewery Debenture Holders was organised.[54] Randall Davidson, Archbishop of Canterbury, and those of his episcopal colleagues who supported the measure were made the target of a sustained correspondence campaign on the part of disgruntled Tradesmen and brewery shareholders, many of whom threatened to stop supporting Church charities.[55] Otherwise, protest meetings were held all over the country, culminating in a monster Trade gathering in London on Sunday 27 September, when 130 special trains were run to bring Trade employees in 'a jovial mood' to demonstrate in Hyde Park. The Liberal *Westminster Gazette* caustically declared that the demonstrators might have been 'especially chosen to illustrate the ravages of drink on the human frame'.[56]

The bill passed through its stages in the Commons with the help of the guillotine and came before the Lords in November.[57] Some Unionist peers hesitated before throwing out the measure completely. Lansdowne, Conservative leader in the Lords, 'was shrinking from the responsibility' in May and later King George V strongly urged caution upon him.[58] Lord St Aldwyn (Hicks Beach) was another senior peer who believed it best to amend an unpopular bill with the advantage that 'a difficult & dangerous question would be removed from troubling the next Unionist Govt., and the brewers would be saved from the very possible extinction of many of their licences' by punitive taxation in the next budget.[59] Most Unionist peers, on the other hand, believed that the opportunity of simultaneously thwarting the government and striking a blow for the rights of property and the interests of beer drinking labourers too good to miss. The decision to throw out the bill completely was taken before its second reading at a meeting at Lansdowne House which, according to one of those present 'was great fun'.[60]

The licensing question had become caught up in the much broader issues of party controversy at the level of high politics where stakes were high. Both parties were facing a major strategic question of how to respond to the challenge of labour and working-class organisation. For the Unionists, the tariff reform issue, since 1903, had been a cause of profound division. The wholehearted enthusiasts for tariff reform saw it as a proactive policy necessary to meet the unsustainable demands for social reforms which socialists and those on the left were putting forward. The attraction of tariff reform was that it was an issue with a trans-class appeal, and one which could help to cement imperial unity.[61] Others saw tariff reform as a dangerous heresy which undermined the principles of free trade, and which sought to introduce alien programmatic politics into the Tory tradition. Among the Liberals divisions were less clear cut, but the strategic dilemma was how to provide sufficient social reforms to appeal to working-class voters and labour, while simultaneously holding on to middle-class supporters anxious at the prospect of high taxation and excessive state interference.

After their disastrous smash in the 1906 election, the Unionists, notwithstanding their own complex divisions over the tariff issue, had adopted a successful technique of harrying the Liberal government, taking the view that it was 'at bottom, little more than a collection of disruptive log-rolling minority groups, with no natural cohesion and no real identity with the nation'.[62] The temperance enthusiasts were the very epitome of such a minority grouping. The House of Lords was a key element in this strategy and, by 1908, a series of measures, such as the Education Bill, the Plural Voting Bill, and a series of Land Bills had been either defeated or so mangled that they were withdrawn, although the Lords had been careful to allow the passage of some more popular labour and social issues. Rejection of the Licensing bill by the die-hards was seen as a means of deliberately upping the stakes in the battle for democracy. It was essential to defend the power of the Lords against the 'unconstitutional' moves to pass dangerous measures, such as Home Rule, which were pushed upon the government by minorities and which ran counter to the popular democratic wish. As George Wyndham calculated privately to Balfour, 'If the Liberals cannot exist without that, then either there can be no Liberal Party, or no Second Chamber; and if the Liberal Party drive the country into that choice, the country will – I think – prefer a Second Chamber to the Liberal Party'.[63] On the Government side also, the narrow Drink issue was quickly transformed into a higher plane. The bill itself was presented in terms of democratic rights, a means of curbing the power of the liquor monopolists. The conflict, declared Lloyd George, was 'one of those fundamental conflicts between the lowest appetites of the people and their highest instincts'.[64] All this was standard temperance rhetoric of the kind used in the past to justify the local veto; but, after its rejection by the Lords, the bill took its place in the great constitutional struggle for democracy. As Winston Churchill – an unlikely person indeed to find on a Hyde Park temperance platform! – asked, was the Government to rule or was it to be Trade?[65] By opting to throw out the bill the Unionist hardliners had underestimated the capacity of Lloyd George to turn the issue to his advantage. When Lord Riddell breakfasted with him on 24th November, he found the Chancellor 'not at all disturbed by the fate of the Licensing Bill', declaring that a 'thanksgiving service' would take place at the Treasury later that morning as he was looking forward to taxing the Trade.[66] Lloyd George had grasped the interlocking nature of the taxation and social reform questions and, impatient with the Government's lacklustre legislative and reforming record to date, saw the budget not as a mere fiscal device but as a political opportunity. It was a means simultaneously of promoting social reform as a rival to tariff reform, and of breaking the political impasse into which the ministry had become enmeshed.[67] In his budget, he enthusiastically seized upon land taxes and heavier drink licensing duties as the means of simultaneously raising the sums he needed while avoiding taxation, which would hit the middle-class Liberal supporters. The sharply increased manufacturing and retailing licences were also a back door method of reducing the numbers of drink outlets and tackling the problem of monopoly value, a principle of 'high licence' which had been advocated by Rowntree and Sherwell a decade previously.[68]

Despite the high hopes of temperance enthusiasts, the only legislation which the Liberals managed to enact was the Local Veto Bill for Scotland in 1913. The Liberals had long been pledged to this, and 61 of the 72 Scottish MPs returned in 1906 had pledged themselves to supporting this measure.[69] There were some skirmishes between the Lords and the Commons, but the Unionist leaders had now become convinced that local veto in itself would be relatively harmless. There were already large rural areas in Scotland without licences and the population there seemed to suffer no ill effects; if there were other puritanical areas where the majority really wished to put down public houses, there seemed little reason to deny them their pleasure. Spirits could easily be retailed to the few who wished to continue to consume them. All the evidence seemed to suggest that, except in remote Highland areas and possibly in one or two select wards of the larger burghs, the local veto provision would be a dead letter. The Conservative leadership contented themselves with amending the details of the bill. In this somewhat half-hearted manner, local veto finally reached the statute book. The Act was not the result of a great popular crusade but of a deal between the leaders of the two main parties, few of whom cared greatly about the measure one way or the other, or were sanguine as to its likely results. The local option question had in effect been bypassed both by developments within liquor licensing and by new thinking on the temperance question. It was enacted in Scotland not because there was any great hope that it would alleviate intemperance in that country, but because there were areas where the issue was still a living one and because its adherents had an influence among the ranks of the Scottish Liberal party workers out of all proportion to their strength within the community as a whole.

Drink and the nature of politics in Edwardian Britain

What light does the Drink question shed upon the nature of high politics on the eve of the First World War? Before 1899, government licensing bills had been largely the creations of individual ministers, who generally took up the question on their own initiative and pursued it with the minimum of consultation and assistance from their Cabinet colleagues or the Prime Minister of the day. In 1872 and 1893–95, Cabinet committees had been set up but they had exercised little influence or power. Bruce and Harcourt, no less than Goschen, had been able to press ahead with their ill-fated schemes despite the misgivings and doubts of their colleagues, including the Prime Minister. Nor, lower down the political hierarchy, had there been a great deal of coordination or unity on licensing matters within the parties. A large body of Liberal MPs had disliked and even opposed Bruce and Harcourt's plans, and many Unionists had been similarly hostile to the proposals of Ritchie and Goschen. After 1899, however, it is possible to trace some important changes in the pattern of licensing politics at the highest level of British politics. In the first place, licensing now aroused the careful attention of the Cabinet as a whole. In both 1904 and 1908, the details and timings of the licensing bills were carefully considered at Cabinet meetings. Both Balfour and Asquith as Prime Ministers, took an active interest, overshadowing in many respects their Home Secretaries, Akers-Douglas and Herbert Gladstone. In 1904, for example, Balfour's private secretary, J. S. Sandars, conducted highly sensitive and important negotiations with Trade organisations and brewers. In 1908, Asquith remained in close touch with Herbert Gladstone and was responsible for taking many important decisions on such questions as the time limit and compensation. Many other members of the Cabinet showed an equal interest in the issue. In 1908, for example, Lord Loreburn, Lloyd George and John Burns all made known their views, and the Bill was fully discussed in a series of 'pretty lively' Cabinet meetings.[70]

Secondly, both civil servants and representatives of interested pressure groups were beginning to play a more important part behind the scenes. With the possible exception of 1888, civil servants had hitherto taken an extremely passive role in drafting licensing legislation. Bruce in 1871, Kimberley in 1872 and Harcourt in 1893 all appear to have sat down to work out their bills with a single civil servant or parliamentary draftsman, while on occasions sending out for expert legal or fiscal advice. After 1899, civil service initiative was, by later standards, still limited. In 1902, the Home Office officials had no plans of their own and merely set about adapting and drafting Davidson's own bills into a satisfactory and workable form. In both 1904 and 1908, the civil servants played a more important role in determining the details of compensation, licence reduction and the time limit. All these were complicated matters and the detailed memoranda of men like Sir H. W. Primrose, N. J. Highmore, and I. N. Guillemand were invaluable for the Cabinet of the day but, all the same, Herbert Gladstone drafted the outlines of the measure in his own hand. A similar situation prevailed with the interest groups. Before 1899, Selwyn-Ibbetson, Goschen, Harcourt and other licensing reformers to some extent had all had contact with representatives of the various sections of the Trade or the temperance movement, and it was a common practice for ministers to receive formal deputations on the subject. After 1899, however, there were indications that the degree and intensity of lobbying – particularly *informal* lobbying – was gradually increasing. In 1901–02 and in 1908, temperance reformers, such as Davidson, Peel and Whittaker, were able to approach ministers on a more sophisticated basis than had been common in the 1870s or 1880s. In 1906, for example, Whittaker was able to present Gladstone with a long and detailed series of suggestions, which received most careful consideration (and criticism) from civil servants and ministers. Similarly, in 1903–04, Tradesmen were able to exercise considerable influence upon the government simply because the question was so administratively and financially complicated. Alongside this development of informal contact and assistance, there persisted the more traditional methods of 'direct' political persuasion. So long as the drink question aroused great political passions in the country at large, all the ballyhoo of popular demonstration and electoral agitation continued. In some respects, it was all the more marked since the two lobbies on either side, the Trade and the temperance movement, were now more than ever identified with one or other of the two chief parties. Hence, the interest group which was 'in opposition' to the government had to rely primarily on outside, noisy agitation. Even here, however, there were signs that the pattern was being modified. The Trade's sophisticated lobbying of the City and of the Church of England in 1907 and 1908 marks a change from the violent populist agitation of 1871–72. The signs of the new pattern of politics dominant after 1914 are to be found in embryo between 1902 and 1914.

In the long term, liquor licensing was to cease to interest political parties. But there was little sign of this in the decade before 1914. On the contrary, a third feature of these years was the increasing extent to which the parties now appeared to formulate party policy on the licensing question, which was expected to bind together the collective leadership and the rank and file of MPs alike. Serious divisions, of course, persisted within the parties with no less than 14 Unionists voting against the 1904 Bill, and 8 Liberals opposing the 1908 Bill. In both instances, a still larger number swallowed their private scruples and supported the ministry in the lobby. However, this was nothing compared to the cross-voting in the 1880s or to internal party divisions on many other contemporary issues, like tariff reform. In any case, both in 1904 and 1908, the government of the day was determined not to let these internal divisions hinder its policy. On both occasions, the government as a whole was too committed to withdraw gracefully. In 1871 and 1890, licensing had still been seen primarily as the responsibility of a single minister, and, although the licensing episodes of those years reflected badly on the ministry, it was Bruce and Goschen individually who bore the brunt of responsibility. In 1904 and 1908, failure would be the failure of the government and of the party. In 1888 and 1890, Harcourt and Gladstone had been able to harass their Unionist opponents without seeming to do so entirely on party grounds. This, in 1904, was impossible. The more the Liberals confronted the ministry, the more the question could be made into one of confidence in the government. By 1908, party leaders on both sides had come to view the licensing question as an element in the broader political struggle of the time. In due course, the 1908 Bill became a sacrificial victim in the constitutional struggle being waged between Government and Opposition. Here, liquor licensing had become a pawn in an inter-party struggle, just as a decade earlier it had been the plaything of internal Cabinet politics in the struggle between Harcourt and Rosebery.

These factors, although significant, are not in themselves sufficient to explain why liquor licensing in 1904 and 1908 occupied such a dominant position in the struggle between the parties, whereas after 1919 it faded so rapidly from political notice. It was, after all, a period when popular interest in the temperance question was, if anything, on the wane. An explanation must take account of the changing character of the two main parties and the particular terms of reference in which the licensing question was couched. Although the leadership of the Liberal and Conservative parties – the dozen or so political heavyweights whose voice at any time really mattered – had remained substantially similar in background, character and ethos, the rank and file of party activists and backbench MPs had changed in character since 1885, and still more since 1867. On the Liberal side, the representation of non-conformist radicals reached its peak in the 1906 Parliament. On the Unionist side, the representation of property (finance and business) had grown in an equally striking manner. The pattern of politics remained broadly similar, but the terms of reference in which political questions were discussed had changed. The classical Whig and Tory issues and the shades of party or faction inherited from the era of Palmerston had faded, to be replaced by new terms of reference and new distinctions. The protection of property, the threat of socialistic legislation, the rights of the people were now issues which occupied the centre of the debating stage. In 1904 and 1908, licensing bills neatly fitted the broad divisions of ethos between the two parties, just as the polarisation of the Trade and the temperance party to either side of the House tied in with the changing character of the two parties. The licensing issue was posed almost exclusively in terms of property and finance. The question was now interpreted in the light of confiscatory 'socialism' *versus* the rights of property, or of predatory vested interest *versus* the aspirations of the people. In 1908, the licensing question was sucked into the vortex of the constitutional struggle between the Liberal government and the Unionist peers. For Lloyd George, licensing and the subsequent 1909 Budget, in which drink taxes were linked to land value taxes, were means of arousing much needed popular working-class enthusiasm and of cementing a progressive alliance with traditional nonconformist radicalism. The brewers along with the landed class with which they now had such close connections, were an easy target calculated to cement this strategy.[71]

For these reasons, the licensing question in these years came to be posed in party terms, but it would nevertheless be wrong to suppose that ministers had been forced to adopt policies by pressure from within their party or from the interested groups which were allied to them. These pressures played an important part, but they were not, in themselves, sufficiently sustained or coherent to determine the pattern of policy-making. Equally important were administrative pressures in favour of a settlement. The Unionists, in 1904, were faced with the need to settle the process and procedures of licence reduction; the Liberals, in 1908, with the need to adjust the unsatisfactory operation of the 1904 Act. The process of decision-making was highly involved. Pressures from the party, the influence of interest groups, the advice of civil servants, the tactical position in the Commons, the internal balance of the Cabinet: all these contributed to the complex pattern of legislation. A great deal depended upon the terms of reference in which particular issues were couched. In 1904 and 1908, the licensing question was posed in terms which were closely linked with broader party and political divisions. In both 1902 and 1912–13, however, the pattern was very different. In 1902, there was a general agreement to take the issue out of party controversy, indeed even outside temperance controversy. The 1902 Licensing Act (and the 1903 Scottish Act) raised none of the explosive issues of property that divided the parties in 1904 and 1908. Nor did the Act in any way affect the various solutions to the temperance problem championed by the rival temperance groups. All could be sweetness and light, and the measure would pass to the statute book without excitement or controversy.

6
The First World War: Drink and National Efficiency

The outbreak of war in 1914 transformed the whole issue of liquor control. Not only was Drink brought high up the political agenda, but the terms in which the question was debated were recast. Whereas from the 1880s Drink had been seen largely as an aspect of social reform, now it was primarily redefined in terms of national efficiency. It was the effect of consumption of alcohol upon the war effort, industrial production and the availability of scarce raw materials, including food substances, that became the subject of heated discussion and major controversy. In common with other industries, brewing and distilling became subject to much greater degrees of government intervention. The volumes and strengths produced, the raw materials consumed and the prices charged became subject to government control. This was all the more marked since here was an industry which had not been subject to much pro-active interference before, except for taxation and licensing.[1] After 1914, moreover, Drink became the concern of various bureaucratic bodies which often had conflicting interests. In particular, the creation early in the war of the Central Control Board (Liquor Traffic) (CCB) was to bring a wholly new dimension. In contrast to the passive regulation which the conservative Home Office had exercised in prewar days, here was a body which was able to develop a more proactive interest in alcohol policy. It involved many personnel who were new to the question, and who approached the whole issue in terms that were very different from prewar proponents of temperance reform.

National hysteria on Drink

Some attention was paid to the issue of Drink almost immediately after the outbreak of war. The Defence of the Realm Act (DORA) gave the military authorities powers to regulate hours of sale in certain key areas and to control the supply of drink to HM forces, powers which began to be used liberally over the course of the next ten months.[2] The French government had been quick off the mark to impose more general restrictions on sale, and the Home Secretary was asked as early as 10 August, 1914, what powers he or magistrates possessed for reducing facilities for sale. Concern at this time focused upon the threat of riot or public order, especially in connection with the treating of departing troops by enthusiastic civilians, which was giving rise to alarming scenes at railway stations and ports. A government bill which allowed the licensing justices to limit hours of sale was quickly introduced, but only passed after it had been watered down by a watchful House of Commons, so as to require a prior recommendation from the chief officer of police. By the end of the year, almost half the licensing districts in England and Wales had such orders imposed.[3]

March and April 1915 were to see an extraordinary flare up of public hysteria on the subject of Drink. The flames of this were in large part fanned by Lloyd George, but they could only have ignited because there was already a smouldering feeling of discontent. Initially, the normal lines of combat between the Trade and the temperance societies were in evidence. Brewers stressed their patriotic credentials in view of the new beer taxes, while temperance advocates stressed old arguments about the detrimental effects of alcohol consumption upon the national character. By the winter, temperance enthusiasts sensed a new opportunity to call for prohibition, given the stiff actions by the Russian and French governments in prohibiting vodka and absinthe sales respectively. In Scotland, attempts were made to mobilise opinion in favour of the prohibition of spirits, and Bonar Law was warned by supporters of the growing feeling on the subject with crowded meetings and calls for Unionists to consider this policy.[4] On 22 February, 1915, a large meeting, representing important sections of the business, shipbuilding and academic communities, was held in Glasgow and called for prohibition for the duration of the war.[5]

However, new issues soon attached themselves to the Drink question. One was the direct effect upon the military preparation, with drinking by recruits and the problems of refreshment facilities for large encampments of soldiers being highlighted. Lord Kitchener took to warning of the effect of treating and over-indulgence upon his troops – his sister meantime went round addressing temperance meetings – and these warnings were backed by appeals for self-control by both Lord Roberts and Randall Davidson, the Archbishop of Canterbury, although the latter was wary of the Church associating itself with schemes whereby the state would control commodities and materials.[6] Moreover, concern about drinking became linked to a general alarm and unease in conservative quarters and in the churches at the rapidly changing position of many working-class women, who were enjoying separation allowances and unaccustomed freedom and leisure.[7]

It was, however, a speech by Lloyd George at Bangor on 28 February that transformed matters. In it, he dwelt upon the problems of securing the adequate output of munitions and the difficulties industry was having in meeting the demands of war effort. He explicitly linked these problems with Drink. A 'small minority' of workmen were shirking their duty, but this small minority could 'throw a whole works out of gear'. 'What is the reason? Sometimes it is one thing, sometimes it is another, but let us be perfectly candid. It is mostly the lure of the drink.' 'Drink', he went on to declare in words which were subsequently to be quoted *ad nauseam*, 'is doing us more damage in the War than all the German submarines put together.'[8] Historians have suggested different motivations for this outburst. Cameron Hazlehurst has stressed his impatience with Kitchener, with the War Office's inefficiency and with Asquith's sluggish conduct of the war; hence, he was ready to use whatever weapons were to hand to accelerate matters, including a more direct appeal to public opinion.[9] Linked to this was the industrial situation and the necessity, as Lloyd George saw it, for a more active government policy in the management of the war, for which he had argued in a Cabinet paper the previous week.[10] Over the next month, he went on to play a key role in negotiating wide-ranging agreements with the trade unions and in establishing government control over factories. Control over Drink was a part, but a subordinate part, of a broader strategy. Others have stressed also how Lloyd George's own personal predilections and background undoubtedly played a part. Temperance and Drink had always been a cause dear to his heart and to those of his bedrock supporters in North Wales. Dr Turner has suggested that the references to Drink in the Bangor speech were there, at least partly, to soothe his Welsh audience, who were asked to come to hear him on a Sunday.[11] As the former Welsh radical was transmuted into the imperial statesman, so his relations with his former nonconformist power base became strained. An appeal to temperance sentiment was a convenient expedient: one where the nonconformist conscience and the concern for imperial national efficiency, so often at odds, for once pointed in the same direction. Stuart Mews develops this interpretation and presents Lloyd George's interest in the question as motivated by tensions within Welsh nonconformity. In March 1915, the Welsh Liberal nonconformists were furious at a government bill to delay the disestablishment and disendowment of the Church of Wales until after the end of the war and at Lloyd George's justification for this action. Tackling the Drink question 'would not only salve the nonconformist conscience but might also be a means of vindicating the honour of nonconformist Wales' by raising recruits through presenting the war effort as a crusade of the gallant, teetotal young men.[12]

All such considerations of high politics, often involving quite extraneous issues, were important factors. However, there were also bureaucratic forces at work. The Admiralty had for some months wished to extend its powers under DORA from the harbours to the neighbourhood of factories undertaking shipyard work. In early February, Charles Roberts, a strongly pro-temperance junior minister in the government, had already sent Lloyd George a series of long notes on the role of Drink in hampering efficiency in industry.[13] Employers in the shipyards had always been particularly sympathetic to temperance, and it was fairly natural for them to cast a critical eye on drinking, as they faced the difficulties of reaching exacting targets.[14]

Whatever his motives, Lloyd George energetically set about collecting and collating a mass of material about the effects of drinking on production in the shipyards and armaments factories. Dr Turner, in a comprehensive analysis of this episode, has concluded that 'In the later stages a search for information was deliberately confounded with a publicity campaign. Material was collected by prejudiced observers, and failed to face the critical question of whether lost time, which could be documented, was attributable to excessive drinking, which could not. Industrial relations in engineering, shipbuilding, and merchant shipping were historically bad.'[15] Arthur Shadwell, an acute and impartial contemporary observer of the industrial scene, confirms this impression. His first hand investigations showed that 'The whole controversy had been coloured by class feeling.'[16]

During late March and April, Lloyd George mounted a highly successful publicity campaign on the subject.[17] On 17 March, he raised the matter at a conference with trade unionists.[18] Particular prominence was given to the views of a deputation of the Shipbuilding Employers' Federation on 29 March. This included a strong temperance element and called for total prohibition for the duration of the war. Lloyd George agreed that 'nothing but root-and-branch methods will be of the slightest avail in dealing with the evil' and produced yet another eminently quotable refrain in declaring that 'we are fighting Germany,

Austria and Drink; and, as far as I can see, the greatest of these three deadly foes is Drink'.[19] Scarcely surprisingly, feeling in some trade unionist circles was running high against the slurs on the workers. Lloyd George then produced a masterstroke on the same day by seeking an audience with the King in which he explained how a royal example of abstinence would greatly assist coercive measures. A conditional assent in a letter from the King's secretary was then adroitly leaked to the press, so that the King and the royal household became, in effect, bounced into total abstinence for the duration of the war. George V was privately annoyed at the turn of events and years later confessed he was able to continue to drink privately 'under doctor's orders'.[20] However, the public example was followed by sundry other celebrities such as Lord Kitchener and the Archbishop of Canterbury, although notably not by the Cabinet or the House of Commons.[21] Naturally the 'King's Pledge' attracted the maximum of publicity. Nonconformist reaction was to endorse fully the charges against Drink, but even in Conservative circles there was an acceptance that, although the demands for prohibition were wide of the mark, some sort of problem existed. Thus, the *Daily Telegraph* conceded that what in peacetime was 'an economic waste and a social evil' became, in war, 'a black crime against the nation'; while the *Morning Post*, although advocating cautious action, conceded that whatever the government decided was necessary for the safety of the nation must be accepted 'at however great a sacrifice'.[22] In this way, by spring 1915, the Drink question had been reformulated, both in terms of national efficiency and as part of a moral drive to purify the fabric of the nation. The fight against the Hun and against the Demon Drink went hand in hand to assuage the atavistic anti-war proclivities of nonconformity; while the pledge against Drink was seized upon in conservative religious and political circles as a means of cementing national unity on a trans-class basis.

While this publicity was being generated, Lloyd George, behind the scenes, began to investigate a radical solution in terms of the complete state purchase of the whole liquor trade, which preliminary investigations estimated at upwards of £225m. Possibly he had become carried away with the concern about national efficiency, but equally opportunist political considerations may have steered him. One Cabinet colleague reports him as saying on 30 April 'the idea that slackness and drink, which people talk so much about, are the causes of delay, is mostly fudge', rather it was government mismanagement that was the cause of shortages of ships and munitions.[23] Meanwhile, a balanced Cabinet Committee, chaired by Samuel and containing both Trade and temperance sympathisers from all parties, was set up to discuss compensation for the Trade for any restrictions on hours of sale and strengths; and this, in turn, considered the practicality and cost of a scheme for state purchase.[24] Throughout April, a series of complex negotiations took place involving both leading Unionist politicians and the brewers. How was it that such a drastic answer seemed, for a while, to become practical politics? Several factors converged here. The first was that disinterested management, as an alternative solution to the Drink problem, had been gaining ground in temperance circles ever since the publication of Rowntree and Sherwell's volume in 1899. There now existed a significant lobby in temperance circles, stronger at the elite level than the popular, that was anxious to apply these principles to wartime conditions.[25] Secondly, a few leading Unionists, whilst intensely suspicious of Lloyd George, were not unsympathetic to the prospect of some such solution. Bonar Law, for example, 'rather liked' the idea of state purchase from a purely party point of view. 'If it can be carried, which I doubt, it would free us from the Trade incubus and it would really mean the universal adoption of disinterested management in regard to which I have always taken a favourable view.'[26] But the third and most important factor was the changed position of the Trade. Here, it is important to appreciate the dire financial position of many of the larger brewers. In the rush into the property market for tied-houses before 1914, they had paid excessive sums for often dilapidated property. The prospects both of war damage and of further temperance restrictions made a gloomy situation even darker; while for the distillers the prohibition of spirits was by no means out of court. Already, in November 1914, the beer duty had been sharply raised from 7s. 9d. to 23s. per standard barrel of beer.[27] Many Traders began to favour the idea of a complete sell out, provided that compensation was fair. State purchase on favourable terms might actually be preferable to government restrictions and inadequate compensation.

From 25 March 1915 Lloyd George, described by Asquith as being 'red hot' with the plan for drink nationalisation,[28] began negotiating with the brewers and, by the second week of April, Samuel's Cabinet Committee had come up with surprisingly generous terms based upon the prewar stock market valuations.[29] Bonar Law, for the Unionists, offered a somewhat lukewarm neutrality provided the terms for compensation were right.[30] His party was in a somewhat exposed position since the government claimed action against Drink was essential for the war effort. Privately, however, they resented the way the government had 'dragged the King into the controversy' and viewed ministers' manoeuvres with suspicion.[31] Bonar Law was shrewd enough to see that the munitions problem lay at the heart of the matter: 'I think the Government have bungled the whole subject, and the cry about drink is being used partly at least to divert attention from their own shortcomings.'[32] However, he and his colleagues were in something of a cleft stick. The government was now pledged to 'some drastic action' and the Trade would

> come to us as a Party telling us that they are ruined and expect us to oppose it. . . . If we do not oppose what the Government suggest we shall be bitterly attacked by the Trade which will have a great deal of support in our own Party. On the other hand, if we do oppose the proposals of the Government we shall certainly offend a large section of Conservative opinion which has become a little hysterical on this subject.

On balance, Bonar Law felt state purchase and disinterested management to be the best option: not only would it be a genuinely useful reform, but it would cause the Liberals 'enormous difficulty through the opposition of the teetotal fanatics'.[33] This assessment was shrewd, as the Cabinet itself quickly became alarmed at the problems. Asquith was dead against what he called 'the Great Purchase Folly', and many of Lloyd George's colleagues 'seemed terrified at the cost' of the scheme. On 19 April, the Cabinet opted instead for a policy of higher taxation, coupled with widespread powers to take over the whole trade in scheduled areas deemed important for the war effort.[34] This, in turn, came unstuck as the Trade, backed by the Unionists, offered outright opposition to the taxation proposals, and even a series of compromises between the various parties foundered in the House of Commons in the face of fierce opposition from Irish members and backbench Conservatives.[35]

The work of the Central Control Board

The sudden popular interest in Drink, verging on the hysterical, was a classic example of a 'moral panic' in which the media played a role. The climate of opinion had been created in which new initiatives could be taken. This allowed the whole policy agenda to be broadened. Legislation passed on 19 May, 1915 that set up a Central Control Board (CCB) (Liquor Traffic) which was given wide-ranging powers. This new authority could schedule areas that were involved in the production and conveyance of war materials, or where naval or military forces were stationed. In these scheduled areas not only was the CCB given wide powers to regulate the sale of drink, including hours of sale, it might also compulsorily purchase outlets or interests of the Trade.[36] The CCB was to exist only for the duration of the war and the following twelve months. The UKA opposed the idea that any purchase of the Trade in selected areas should be on a permanent basis, although this received the support of Whittaker and other enthusiasts for public control.[37]

A feature of the work of the CCB, evident from the outset, was its independence from the 'vested interests' of the Drink question: the temperance organisations and the Trade. The composition of the CCB reflected the new emphasis on Drink as an industry and a national resource. It contained representatives of employers and labour organisations as well as civil servants from the Home Office and Treasury, and it was only in January 1916 that Henry Carter, a Wesleyan Methodist temperance worker, and W. Waters Butler of the brewers, Mitchells & Butler, joined the Board. The chairman was Lord D'Abernon, a prominent banker and former Liberal MP, who had considerable knowledge of industrial resources.[38] When a local area was considered for scheduling, it was the opinions of the military, local authorities, the licensing magistrates and local employers and trade unionists which were actively sought, although if local religious or temperance societies wished to give evidence they were heard separately.[39] The expectation had been that only relatively small areas would be scheduled for control by the CCB, based on Orders in Council. This was, indeed, the pattern initially. However, the local police and local authorities themselves put pressure on the CCB for extensions for the sake of administrative convenience and, as the war effort consumed more and more areas of industry and public life, so the tendency emerged for whole swathes of country to be scheduled. By the beginning of 1917, only a relatively few rural English and Scottish counties remained unscheduled, with 38 out of 41 million inhabitants living under the control of the CCB.[40]

Although the CCB was created in response to a perceived localised problem concerning military areas and munitions production, its advent coincided with a general recognition that the war was likely to be of long duration, and would have a profound impact upon vast swathes of economic and social life. As Henry Carter, the contemporary historian of the CCB, wrote in 1918: 'Munitions meant much more than shells. Munitions meant clothing and bedding, food and drink, leather and canvas and rubber equipment, chemicals, electrical supplies, all kinds of transport, hospital requirements, building materials, ship-construction, engines of a thousand types, devices for trench warfare, aircraft and artillery.'[41] Alongside this came massive upheavals in family life, relations between the sexes, patterns of work and the distribution of labour. The purchasing power of many industrial workers soared, at the very time when there were limited outlets for leisure or expenditure. Shortages of raw materials and food became pressing, and this affected the drink industry as much as agriculture.[42] Moreover, the intellectual climate moved sharply in favour of the principle of state control over prices, manpower, transport and the regulation of consumption.[43]

Although initially the CCB moved cautiously, towards the end of 1915 it began to develop some far-reaching initiatives. For the first time a bureaucratic body existed which, in contrast to the prewar Home Office, had an explicit role to seek proactive policies towards alcohol control. As Carter later recollected, 'A dual policy was required, in part restrictive, in part constructive.'[44] The restrictive element attracted more immediate attention. The most dramatic move was to reduce the hours of sale for 'on' consumption to five and a half hours in almost all scheduled districts and to introduce the celebrated 'afternoon gap'. The justification here was to ensure that consumption coincided with meal times and to eliminate early morning nips of spirits, afternoon soaking and late-night binge drinking. Clubs were, for the first time, subject to the same hours as public houses. Special hours were applied in some areas: for example, the public houses were kept closed on Saturdays in central Scotland to prevent men visiting them before returning from work on pay day, an interesting early example of the CCB extending its interest into broader social issues.[45] Another measure prohibited 'off' sales of spirits in the evenings and at the weekends. Furthermore, the CCB gradually enforced a policy of dilution of spirits. Various minor restrictions were also imposed, of which the most controversial was the total prohibition of all treating in public houses, designed to meet the problem of servicemen being plied with excessive drinks.

As far as the constructive work of the Board was concerned, the role of the Chairman, D'Abernon, was crucial. He brought a fresh mind to the whole question of alcohol control. Hitherto, in his view, there had never been any proper 'temperance legislation'. 'The whole history of the licensing laws has been one of regulating the trade and meeting the various abuses as they arose.'[46] A proper approach should be based not on dogmatic assertions but on empirical study of the problem. 'In dealing with the various problems connected with the Liquor Traffic a sound administrative policy must be based on a full knowledge of the relevant physiological and other scientific evidence and that, in the numerous cases in which the available scientific information was defective, investigations ought to be promoted with a view to filling the gaps in exact knowledge.'[47] Accordingly, the CCB began to set up a series of committees to research aspects of alcohol consumption, for example, the Women's Advisory Committee which investigated the assertions of increased female drinking and intemperance. Most important in this connection was the Alcohol Committee, formed in November 1916 and chaired by D'Abernon himself, which consisted of eight medical or scientific experts.[48] During 1917 and 1918, this Committee undertook a range of varied research, including experiments on the effects of consuming alcohol on typists' speeds and accuracy and upon manual workers' outputs, on the nutritional value of alcohol, on the effectiveness of prohibition in Russia, and on the nature and value of drunkenness statistics.[49]

From the outset, the CCB took an interest in the relationship between food and drink. One of the purposes behind the restricted hours was to reduce drinking on an empty stomach. D'Abernon believed 'the vital question at the moment for the Central Control Board to consider is whether in the industrial centres an effort can at the present time be made to induce the licensed victualler to become in fact a victualler'. Such a policy would materially reduce working-class drunkenness.[50] Edgar Sanders was sent out on a fact finding mission in September 1915, to tour the (then limited) restricted scheduled areas. He reported that the reception of the restriction orders 'has been unexpectedly gratifying' and that the 'temper of the nation at present is such that the people are waiting to be told what to do, when they will do it cheerfully'. However, on the specific point of the provision of food, he discovered a near universal view among publicans that, except in special houses, the customer would not regard the public house as a place for the provision of food. Nor did the tied-house system or the mechanics of the licensed trade encourage any such initiative.[51] The Second Report of the CCB in May 1916 stressed the desirability of 'vigorous action' to encourage the provision of 'wholesome and sufficient nourishment'.[52] Efforts by the CCB to get the licensing justices to take an interest in the provision of food in licensed premises had disappointing results.[53] However, a more promising area lay in the development of industrial canteens. Right at the outbreak of the war, the Chief Inspector of Factories and Workshops had drawn attention to the difficulties which those workers far from home faced in obtaining midday food. This concern had been amplified by a White Paper of April 1915 on Shipbuilding and Munitions which reported that, in the absence of a mess room or canteen, such workers brought cold food with them which was consumed in a public house where excess alcoholic consumption then incapacitated them for the strain of heavy work. Increased use of night-shift work presented another problem.[54] In July, P. W. Wilson of the People's Palace Association wrote to D'Abernon complaining that 150 of the 200 firms his association had approached with a view to establishing canteens on their premises had either ignored or refused the request; he suggested 'a little tactful pressure by the Board would greatly hasten the extension of this work'.[55] The CCB eagerly took up the question and appointed a Canteens Committee under the chairmanship of the energetic Sir George Newman. The CCB was then given the power to provide such refreshment rooms, either directly or through agents. Initially the Board encouraged voluntary bodies, like the YWCA and the Church Army, to provide canteens,[56] and managed to persuade a reluctant Treasury to provide half the capital cost for canteens for transport or munitions workers. However, as public subscriptions for this work waned, it was obvious by 1916 that the CCB would have to take a more direct role in superintending the process. Employers were given very favourable tax incentives for the provision of the facilities and, in government run factories, the state paid for them, entrusting the CCB with general responsibility for their running. Ultimately, over 900 canteens were provided.[57] By 1917, the CCB had run into bureaucratic squabbles with both Treasury and the Ministry of Munitions, and lost control of their running to the latter, much to the disgust of D'Abernon, who, at the end of the war, described the provision of canteens as 'an integral and essential part of Temperance Reform' that had done much to check insobriety.[58]

The CCB's attitude to women's drinking also reveals how far removed its thinking was from that of traditional temperance opinion. Temperance societies had for long been particularly hot on the question of female drinking or intemperance. The war conditions, when many working-class women were earning good wages and when their male relatives were often absent at the front, focused attention on female drinking and predictably gave rise to outrage on the part of temperance stalwarts. Birmingham was a particular focus of attention. Here, a White Ribbon Bands petition, signed by 37,155 women and girls, alleging widespread female drinking parties and the seduction of girls away from total abstinence, requested that an order be made restricting women under 21 from visiting public houses until the cessation of hostilities. A CCB committee, which included four women and was chaired by George Newman, visited Birmingham on 20–21 July 1915.[59] After taking evidence from justices of the peace, the police, medical persons, welfare workers and supervisors in factories, it concluded that there was no evidence of any recent increase in drunkenness or excessive drinking. The pattern was rather one of a large number of women taking alcohol to a moderate degree. There was a social trend of it becoming acceptable for young women to order drinks without male companions, a trend that was likely to continue. The (male) leadership of the CCB was not so progressive as to view this with equanimity, and alienated Louise Creighton and the Women's Advisory Committee by refusing to publish their conclusions that drinking among women had not increased and that women should be treated just as men.[60] Female drinking continued to be seen as a 'problem' and the CCB was prepared to countenance restrictions on sales to younger women; nevertheless, the answer lay not in negative bans but in a more positive direction, including an 'increase in all forms of wholesome centres of social life and recreation where people may obtain that rest and refreshment of which they stand in need.' A further issue which the investigation highlighted was the unsatisfactory construction of public houses, which made them unsuitable places for women and young persons.[61]

By early 1916, D'Abernon had clearly begun to view the work of the CCB less in terms of the war emergency and more as a solution to the underlying problem of intemperance and the deficiencies of the existing licensing system. Thus, in March 1916, he was in discussion with Samuel, the Home Secretary, about possible schemes for wholesale licence reduction and consequent improvement of the retail trade in areas where the magistrates, police and the Trade might be sympathetic. In June, he received the enthusiastic backing of Neville Chamberlain for trying such an experiment in Birmingham.[62] Meanwhile, the CCB had discovered another method of putting a 'constructive' policy into operation. DORA had given the CCB powers to take over the trade in limited areas, if this was deemed essential for the war effort. Shadwell and Carter, contemporary historians of and apologists for the work of the CCB, have given the impression that the CCB was reluctantly pushed into state control by pressure of events and had no desire to embark on control as an experiment in licensing reform.[63] However, disinterested management by some form of public body had for twenty years ranked as an 'alternative' temperance programme to the local veto and D'Abernon had served as a member of the Surrey Public House Trust Company from its inception.[64] The record shows that almost immediately after the inception of the CCB, D'Abernon's mind was moving in this direction. On 29 May, 1915, Alexander Part of the Home Counties Public House Trust sent the CCB a pamphlet describing his company's work and offering to manage some 70 houses for the Board. Two days later, on D'Abernon's personal instigation, the CCB requested a further twenty copies of the pamphlet and Part was interviewed in June. Negotiations broke down over commercial terms.[65] It is clear, moreover, that when the delegation of the CCB visited Newhaven, the first area to be scheduled for control, they were already toying with the idea of taking over the Trade there. Lord Lytton, Chairman of Part's Trust Company, however, advised in July 1915 that it might be better 'to start the experiment in a district where drunkenness was at present carried to excess, so as to afford a better opportunity of testing the value of our principles of management'. Newhaven, a largely sober town, did not fit this bill. The Secretary of the CCB thanked him for this advice which the Board would certainly bear in mind.[66] Meanwhile, Joseph Rowntree, the veteran champion of disinterested management, sent the CCB a long memorandum giving advice on how a scheme of direct control might work.[67] By August 1915, the Public House Committee of the CCB was examining a report from the Explosives Department of the Ministry of Munitions about the situation at Gretna, which stressed the necessity of controlling the supply of alcohol from the outset. Meanwhile, in the same month, delegates of the CCB had visited the Admiralty establishments at Invergordon and Cromarty, where there was concern about licensing arrangements, and the Admiralty subsequently recommended purchase by the CCB. On 20 September, the Public House Committee recommended outright purchase of the licensed trade in the Cromarty Firth and Gretna areas.[68]

The first six months of 1916 saw these ideas come to fruition. The first small area to be taken over in January 1916 was at an isolated government factory at Enfield Lock, where a deputation of workers had approached the CCB concerning the lack of refreshment facilities and catering, particularly with respect to the night shift. In addition to the inadequate on-site canteen facilities, four neighbouring public houses were taken over and hours of sale, limited to four and a half hours, were redistributed to meet the needs of the various shifts. New canteen facilities were installed and, in due course, two of the public houses 'practically rebuilt'.[69] In April, the problems posed by on-shore influxes of naval ratings in the Cromarty Firth were tackled. Here, thirteen licences, including hotels, were taken over and 'off' sales were restricted to residents.[70] Both these areas were small and had limited implications. The situation on the border near Gretna and Carlisle was altogether more challenging. Here was the venue for experiment which the CCB sought. In Autumn 1915, a decision had been made to develop a very large greenfield site around Gretna for a new munitions factory. From late Autumn to June 1916, the whole area saw a massive influx of construction workers and navvies, many of whom were 'of a migratory class, mostly from Ireland, probably the majority without home associations or other inducements to restraint. They were hard worked, earned high wages, and were likely to feel that they had the excuse, as they had the means, for indulgences in liquor.'[71] Pressure on local housing, shops and licensed premises was enormous and affected the nearby city of Carlisle. The highly-coloured account of the local Wesleyan Minister, Rev. G. Bramwell Evens, gives a flavour of contemporary concern:

> 'The housing problem at once became acute. Small houses were simply stacked with men. . . . At night these men were practically turned out into the street until bed-time. Their landladies did not want them inside the house. . . . It is not to be wondered at that scenes of the most nauseating and degrading character became a common occurrence. Men fought like beasts; fierce fights raged round the doors of the public-houses. The diminished police force was unable to cope with the situation. Almost every alley was littered with prostrate drunken men. The main thoroughfare of Carlisle was Bedlam.'[72]

Edgar Sanders was sent as a representative of the CCB to investigate. He confirmed that conditions were 'appalling' and suggested that direct control by the CCB was 'the only possible way of dealing with this abnormal state of things'.[73]

In subsequent years, apologists for state control were to make much of the reduction in the drunkenness figures brought about by the CCB. However, the presence of 22,000 construction workers would have had only temporary consequences, and their replacement by the 10,000 steadier munitions employees at the factory, many of whom would be women, was always going to lead to improvement. In other words, Carlisle was no Newhaven and provided exactly the fertile ground for the experiment upon which D'Abernon and his colleagues had been pondering. This is not to say that the CCB had any grand design or very clear cut plans; on the contrary, it was faced with making administrative innovations on an unprecedented scale and had to work out many solutions as it went along. Nevertheless, the CCB throughout showed a willingness to extend its control in the area and fight opposition from the Treasury when necessary.[74] By mid-1917, the 'Carlisle scheme', as it became known, covered an area of about 500 square miles either side of the Scottish border with a population of 140,000.[75] From the very beginning, the CCB placed great importance on developing close links with the local community. A local advisory committee was established which contained representatives of elected councils, churches and trades and labour organisations, and of women's bodies. The president was the Earl of Lonsdale and the committee was chaired by F.W. Chance, a prominent JP. The role of this body was less to make policy than to keep the CCB in touch with local opinion. In this it was largely successful, at least as far as elite opinion was concerned.[76] Edgar Sanders was appointed general manager, but the CCB offices in London took a close and sustained interest in the management of the scheme.

Throughout 1916 and 1917, the policy components of the Carlisle scheme were developed. A total of five breweries and 368 licences lay in the area and the first element of the CCB's policy was to establish monopoly control, except over a few high-class hotels. This was essential to suppress 'ill-regulated competition which has been the root cause of so much that is undesirable in our licensing system'.[77] The second element lay in applying the principles of disinterested management. The new 'managers' of the public houses were to have no interest in the sale of intoxicants.[78] The system of direct management, rather than the traditional licence system, was designed to ensure that the instructions of the CCB could be quickly conveyed and enforced. Thirdly, the CCB imposed restrictions on sale that went further than those applied to the normal scheduled areas. Sunday closing was introduced, spirit sales banned on Saturday and 'on' sales prohibited to persons under eighteen.[79] A fourth element was the substantial reduction in licences. Not only did this reduce temptations to drink and unsatisfactory competition, it also offered opportunity for improvements. 'Fewer and better houses' became the watchword of the CCB, although economy was another factor involved.[80] 'The old, evil-smelling, stuffy ramshackle premises with which most towns of any size abound can be closed down, and the trade shepherded into larger, lighter, and more desirable premises.'[81] Small snugs and bars were done away with, in preference for larger more airy rooms which were capable of central superintendence. All outside advertisements were swept away, so the state run houses took on a somewhat antiseptic and rather austere appearance. In addition, one or two major redevelopments took place in selected large taverns, such as the Gretna Tavern, the Citadel Tavern in Carlisle and Gracie's Banking at Annan where restaurant facilities were provided, as well as bowling greens, billiard rooms and even, in the case of the last, a cinema.[82]

D'Abernon proudly considered Gracie's Banking to embody all that was best in the CCB's work. It was 'as different from the ordinary public house as chalk from cheese' and would 'serve as a model of what public houses should be, to the country at large'. In August 1916, he even invited Lloyd George to preside over its opening, on the grounds that it would 'stand as the first real monument and outward symbol of the State's control of public houses, and regarded from this point of view, its inauguration becomes a business of national importance'. Some high profile public event was in his view desirable since, although local public opinion had been won over, 'whilst we have been doing things our detractors have been noisily articulate'.[83] This last remark indicates that, by the latter part of 1916, the Carlisle scheme had already attracted major controversy. Prohibitionists were attacking the temperance credentials of the scheme by attempting to show the existence of concealed drunkenness. Foremost here was the Wesleyan minister, Rev. Stuart Wilson, from Birmingham who in a ferocious pamphlet attempted an exposé of 'state drunkenness' under state management, which in turn sparked a defence from his counterpart in Carlisle, Rev. Bramwell Evens.[84] From another quarter, the brewer, Col Gretton, accused the CCB in Parliament of giving instructions to the police not to make arrests for drunkenness in Carlisle if they could help it.[85] By the winter of 1916–17, the Carlisle scheme, far from being seen as a mere expedient to deal with the temporary problems of munitions workers, was being promoted as a model for the future treatment of the Drink problem. The CCB began to propose state purchase schemes for other areas, such as Chepstow, Bristol, Glasgow and Liverpool.[86] The existing state run schemes began to attract the support of all the veteran exponents of disinterested management, such as Whittaker, Sherwell and the members of the TLL. The secretary of the latter viewed the state management areas as 'experiments of great and permanent value' and the 'right conception of what is needed in the interests of a great social reform'.[87] For D'Abernon and his colleagues at the CCB, however, the Gothenburg system was only a part, albeit a useful element, of the solution: the real lesson of the war was that the quality of state control and direction was key. The work of the CCB showed what could be achieved when positive policies towards alcohol were undertaken by a government department.[88] As the Carlisle General Manager's Report for the last year of the war put it, the opportunity had been taken at Carlisle 'to aim at making the organization of the liquor trade in the area in which the Board were working, a model for the remainder of the community'.[89]

Lloyd George and state purchase

In these circumstances, it was scarcely surprising that supporters of the new approach should have been tempted once again to raise the question of state purchase for the whole liquor trade. Temperance reformers in the North of England and Scotland lobbied the government for action along these lines. Joseph Rowntree, for example, presented memorials signed by clergy, university professors, professional people and leaders of commerce from the leading English industrial cities.[90] However, of more immediate impact upon Cabinet ministers was the threat of food shortages and the need to restrict drastically import of brewers' materials.[91] A further factor was Lloyd George's accession to power as Prime Minister. A week after this took place the CCB, taking advantage of the moment, submitted a memorandum to the Cabinet urging state purchase of the whole trade on the grounds that 'state control has come to be regarded with more and more favour as being the policy which offers the most rapidly effective and the best permanent solution to the problem'.[92] D'Abernon, in a letter to Lloyd George, stressed that further substantial improvements would be impossible under 'the present system of confused Trade competition'; it required 'the State stepping in to clear away the present confusion, and reorganise the whole trade on more economical and scientific lines'.[93] As in 1915, the political difficulties led to caution. Sir George Younger was initially suspicious about Lloyd George's role, but after investigation told Bonar Law he believed that 'No. 10 has no responsibility whatever for the present propaganda. They are endeavouring, if they can, to dampen it down and are inclined to blame some members of the Board of Control for the agitation.' The meddling of the CCB in this question was, he believed, 'asking for trouble with a vengeance' in the House, as it would give the Asquithian section an ideal opportunity for making trouble on the Liberal benches.[94]

At this point, the issue became inextricably caught up with the question of food controls. Already in 1916, as German submarines took their toll of British merchant shipping, the government had placed limitations on the strengths of beers in cooperation with the Brewers' Society.[95] Once again, this allowed opportunity for the prohibition movement to draw new strength. In June 1916, for example, the Strength of Britain Movement was formed, which produced a Memorial subsequently signed by 2,500,000 persons calling for prohibition.[96] However, at the end of the year, there was general alarm about the supplies of grain, and questions had been raised about the use of barley and malt in brewing or distilling and of scarce shipping space for imports for beer raw materials. In response to this alarm, and as part of the new prime minister's energetic pursuit of the war effort, the Ministry of Food was established in December 1916 and Lord Davenport, who was appointed Food Controller, came out with a scheme to reduce beer production to 50 per cent of the 1915 level.[97] For the remainder of its existence, the CCB was to be engaged in bureaucratic tussles with the new Ministry of Food.[98] The CCB protested that such a reduction 'at one stroke would cause hardly less irritation and unrest than a policy of total prohibition'. Reductions needed to be accompanied by a policy of state purchase on grounds of efficiency and also equity, since large profits would be made by brewers from reduced gravities.[99] Although the issue of state purchase was postponed, the CCB continued to undertake preparatory work. It informed the Ministry of Munitions that the Food Controller's restriction, by causing a virtual 'famine' of beer, would be certain 'to produce irritation and resentment amongst the workers in munition areas', and that more comprehensive controls over the industry were necessary to maintain as much barrelage as possible despite the reduction in raw materials.[100] In the meantime, the Cabinet appointed a committee, chaired by Sir George Cave, the Home Secretary, to review the effects of further restrictions on brewing.[101] The Cabinet in due course adopted a less draconian reduction of one-third of the 1915–16 barrelage in agreement with the brewers, along with new taxation proposals suggested by the CCB.

Cave thought it best that his committee should be confined entirely to representatives of the Trade and a few government officials. D'Abernon, in his desire to distance the CCB from unpopular restrictions on beer supply which had 'nothing to do with temperance only with submarines', made the error of agreeing.[102] In the meantime, the committee of the Brewers' Society, alarmed at the prospects of further controls, began serious consideration of the question of state purchase.[103] By 14 March, Cave's committee had come up with its own scheme for control of the Trade. It suggested two bodies: (i) a 'Liquor Committee' of the government composed of five or six members with 'public or official experience' which would be located in the Home Office; (ii) a Trade Management Committee, representative of all sections of the Trade, which would have the job of framing a scheme for the manufacture, distribution and sale of reduced beer. The relationship of the proposed Liquor Committee to the CCB needed 'careful consideration'.[104] This scheme aroused fierce opposition at a very large meeting of the Brewers' Society the following day, which demanded guaranteed payments on the basis of prewar profits, failing that state purchase was preferable.[105] Such terms were unacceptable to the government and Cave's report, when discussed at the Cabinet, suggested either direct control for the duration of the war (along the lines of the railway or coal industry) or state purchase. The former would present grave practical problems, given the fragmentation of the Trade, and the terms of the latter needed to be considered by a Cabinet Committee containing persons not interested in the Trade.[106] On 27 March, the Cabinet heard Cave argue the case for state purchase. There was an urgent need to exercise control so as to eliminate waste and, at present, the liquor trade was being 'killed by inches'. Younger and other experts considered purchase would prove a profitable transaction. However, although opinion was favourable in England and Ireland, 'very strong' opposition might be expected from the temperance movement in Scotland. It was agreed that careful consideration should be given to the political aspects, and the Prime Minister was to consult his Liberal and Labour colleagues on the prospect of passing a bill.[107]

Lloyd George then proceeded to see various temperance deputations, neatly balancing the prohibitionists with the supporters of disinterested management: this was a good way of mounting publicity on the issue.[108] Meanwhile, Lord Milner, who had been charged with drawing up a draft bill on the subject, forcibly presented arguments to the War Cabinet on 4 May in favour of the assumption of state control as soon as possible. At present, he argued, the government was facing 'vehement and growing criticism from the Temperance people for doing nothing' but, in a few months time, 'when the stock of beer runs out, we shall be met with equally violent, or even more violent, attacks from the drinkers'. Control was necessary now, and the purchase need take place only after the war.[109] D'Abernon was by now alarmed at the way matters were shaping. Although he had supported state purchase, this was as a means of bringing about a long-lasting temperance policy. This element seemed lacking in the Milner plan. For one thing, there was a danger of paying far too much for a 'badly damaged' asset. Secondly, at present the Trade was a useful buffer between the CCB and the public; the implications for the CCB becoming responsible for liquor sales without the administrative arrangements of Carlisle were alarming.[110] State purchase was being seen simply in terms of facilitating the provision of weaker beers, and was likely to be discredited in the popular mind because of this. Finally, the new plans said nothing about closing public houses or providing for the 'improvement' in trading conditions. The Cabinet further considered its dilemma between 7 and 9 May. As stocks of malt and barley faced possible exhaustion, 'strong protests' were likely to come from munitions workers and other key areas. On the other hand, the Trade was being ruined and 'such a policy of drift would satisfy no one but those who advocated Prohibition without compensation'. The parliamentary situation remained delicate, with considerable opposition among Liberal backbenchers who normally supported the government.[111] By 31 May, the government had settled on a threefold policy of control, purchase and local option, the emphasis on the last being the means of winning over temperance opposition. In order to achieve the necessary cooperation of the brewers, large concessions were made. Their prewar profits were to be guaranteed until the bill containing the full financial schedule was passed, possibly at the end of the war. Control of the Trade was to be vested in a new body composed of brewers, licensed victuallers and civil servants: the CCB was, Milner believed, regarded by the Trade with 'suspicion and dislike' and was 'not suited to do the actual control'; on the other hand, social reformers would 'be antagonised at the outset if the Board were completely knocked out' so it could not be 'ignored and should be fitted in'.[112]

However, when the Cabinet met on 21 June, it beat a hasty retreat from Milner's scheme, much to his surprise.[113] Instead, Lloyd George adopted an alternative plan, based on a proposals suggested by the leading brewer, Gretton, of Bass, whereby the permitted barrelage could be increased by 20 per cent in return for brewers brewing a weaker beer at a maximum of 1036°.[114] This suggestion chimed in with ideas sent in by the CCB, which argued for increased beer output by providing weaker beer without the necessity for control, as an experimental solution for the next three months.[115] Several factors lay behind this *volte face*. Not only was the War Cabinet preoccupied with more pressing questions, it was also conscious of the political difficulties, with many temperance inclined MPs hostile to state control.[116] Another factor was a shift in attitudes by Gretton, the MP who headed the brewers on Milner's committee, and the brewers. As Dr Turner has suggested in his analysis of the episode, Gretton was probably 'moved by a fear, not of purchase, but of the possibility that the government might take control, impose restrictions which would cripple the Trade, and try to hand the problem back to the brewers at the end of the war'.[117] This interpretation appears more credible if one takes account of the bureaucratic manoeuvrings within Whitehall. Here, the role of the Ministry of Food was crucial. It had engaged in a battle with the CCB over the supply of beer since its creation at the beginning of the year. Now, without authorisation from the Cabinet, the ministry had set up a committee, chaired by Sir Walter Roffey, with a view to overcoming shortages of fuel and manpower by concentrating brewing into a smaller number of breweries, rather than allowing the present situation of most breweries working at less than full capacity to continue. This had the backing of Lord Rhondda, who was studying coal economies. On 11 June, the leaders of the Brewers' Society met Bonar Law, Sir Arthur Stanley, J. R. Clynes of the Food Ministry and Roffey; they made it clear that such a plan for concentration ran directly contrary to understandings made with Lord Milner. Instead, they offered to achieve a twenty-five per cent reduction of fuel by voluntary means.[118] Opinion within the English Trade was now obviously divided on the whole question of control and, as the summer wore on, grass roots elements began to mobilise meetings or agitations of one kind or another against both the idea of state purchase and further control.[119] Throughout the remainder of 1917, the government suffered continued discontent on the issue of supplies of drink. Beer strengths were diluted again, with 1030° becoming standard, and the weaker beer was informally named 'Government Ale'. On the other hand, American pressure for a total ban on brewing was strongly resisted, given the evidence of unrest in industrial areas at existing beer shortages.[120] In these circumstances, weaker beverages were the lesser of two evils. By early 1918, the raw material and food situation was easing and pressure for radical policies faded.

State purchase remained a theoretical possibility, as the government set up three committees to review the financial aspects of state purchase in England, Scotland and Ireland. However, these only published their findings in May 1918, long after the supply shortage had passed. They recommended the purchase of both the manufacture and the supply of alcohol liquor, since most retail outlets were tied to brewers; the total cost based upon average annual profits from 1910 to 1913 was estimated to be some £400 million.[121] Supporters of state purchase persisted in lobbying Lloyd George in favour of action.[122] But Lloyd George had neither the inclination nor the capacity to turn his attention to the question again and, in April 1918, the Cabinet postponed discussion on the reports indefinitely.[123]

During the First World War, Britain became a more sober nation. By the early 1920s, *per capita* spirit consumption had halved from its level just before the war while beer consumption had fallen from 25 gallons to 10. Convictions for drunkenness, although recognised as notoriously unreliable as an indicator of insobriety, also fell markedly from 135,811 to 29,075.[124] D'Abernon and his fellow supporters of the CCB claimed that all this was the direct result of the control policy of the CCB, a view also endorsed by later historians such as Arthur Marwick.[125] However, the pattern of fall in drunkenness in Carlisle was not dramatically different from that of other northern towns, especially if one makes allowances for the peculiar circumstances of the influx of navvies. Nationally the pattern for diminished alcohol consumption had been in place since the 1890s, although the war of 1914–18 does mark a significant acceleration. The higher taxation and the sharply reduced hours of sale must have played a part, as did the 'constructive' work of the CCB. However, it is impossible to separate these factors from the general underlying trend for the growth of alternative leisure pursuits. One lesson, however, was certainly apparent for the Trade. It was possible to actually increase profits while consumption levels decreased. The future lay in rationalisation of assets and the provision of better facilities for a more discerning market. Here, the state control of the CCB was ahead of the notoriously conservative Trade, which was to take on board this lesson in subsequent decades.

Later, the abortive state purchase episodes came to be presented by the advocates of disinterested management as a missed opportunity for radical temperance reform.[126] The divisions between the prewar temperance prohibitionists and the exponents of the Gothenburg system hardened still further, as recriminations set in about who was responsible for the 'lost opportunity' when Lloyd George was in power. Waldorf Astor henceforth championed the concept of state control as the sole means of ridding the polity of the corrupting influence of the Trade, which would otherwise put a block upon all social reform in this area. However, this reading distorts the history of Drink in the war. The major concerns for the Cabinet and the various bureaucracies within government were rather different. The issues that really preoccupied them were such things as food resources, the efficiency of munitions supply, public order, the discontent of the workforce and the effect of temperance measures upon the exchequer. In short, the Drink issue was seen in terms of national efficiency rather than in terms of the effects upon the lives of individuals. Moreover, for the first time the pressure groups and vested interests of the Trade were brought directly into the policy-making sphere. In contrast to the period before 1914, when the Trade was concerned only to minimise government interference and largely to fight either unwelcome legislative proposals or taxation schemes, now the government and the Trade depended upon each other for the detailed administration and working out of policy in the area. This meant that the politics of the Trade, which had many divisions, was also reflected in the politics and discussions within Whitehall.[127] Here again, there were complex factors coming into play. The ministries of Munitions, Food, the Home Office and the CCB all had rather different concerns and ways of looking at the question. There were also the special circumstances pertaining to Scotland and Ireland. Again, state purchase should not be seen crudely as the culmination of the policy of the CCB, in the way in which it was portrayed by its apologist and historian, Henry Carter.[128] Certainly, D'Abernon and the CCB pressed for state purchase in 1916; but, when it became obvious that the purchase scheme being formulated by Milner and the Cabinet would not be a measure of social reform but a mechanism for solving the problems of the drink industry, D'Abernon withdrew his support, although some of his colleagues, such as Carter, remained enthusiasts. For D'Abernon and other key figures in the CCB, such as Sir John Pedder, it was state *regulation* in the interests of the war effort and social amelioration that was important, not the principle of state ownership or, indeed, of disinterested management. Old-style temperance concerns to restrict or eliminate drink *per se* had only a limited place here. Indeed, they were likely to be counterproductive. Thus, excessive restrictions on the sale of beer, whether brought about by the prohibitionists or the Ministry of Food, would sooner or later lead 'to a reaction which will endanger the whole advance in national sobriety which has been attempted during the last three years'. As the war came to its conclusion, the CCB turned increasingly towards the safeguarding of both its own position and the 'steady policy of regulation' and improvement that it had been developing.[129] The CCB had been set up, with somewhat limited aims, to meet an immediate problem caused by the relationship of drinking to the war effort. However, it had quickly developed a bureaucratic interest in the issue of temperance and social reform as a whole. In that sense, it had redefined the temperance issue in terms of a constructive policy of judicious restrictions mixed with modernisation, which D'Abernon and his colleagues saw as going a long way towards providing a solution to the temperance problem. The question was whether such a policy could continue once hostilities ceased.

7
The Postwar Settlement, 1919–21

New directions

In retrospect, it is clear that the Armistice of 1918 marked the beginning of a distinctly new phase in the history of the Drink question. The 'heroic' days of the temperance versus Trade struggle were over. Never again were there to be massive Hyde Park rallies on the subject of licensing reform. Never again would a Prime Minister make a dramatic headline grabbing speech on the question along the lines of those of Lloyd George in 1915. The days were all but over when constituency election campaigns threatened to drown in torrents of beer or prohibitionist hyperbole. This shift reflected broader political and social developments, which had already been in train before 1914 but which were accelerated by the war. Militant nonconformity, if not entirely a spent force, had lost its power and momentum. New thinking in left wing circles analysed the deeper social causes of obvious ills such as drunkenness, and henceforth social reformers concentrated on housing, education and working conditions. The social conditions model of the Drink question became dominant. Moreover, the leisure revolution of the interwar period began to play down the role of the public house in the community, as gardening, organised sports, the cinema and motor bus excursions became the focus of working-class attention. Statistics for both consumption and drunkenness during the 1920s and 1930s bore witness to the sharp diminution in excess drinking. For its part, the Trade began its long delayed process of transformation into a modern manufacturing and retailing business: one which came to realise that increasing gross sales of beverages was not the sole or most efficient means of maximising profit. All these changes which affected the Drink issue directly also went hand in hand with important shifts in the British political system in general. After 1914, the capacity of individual MPs to initiate social reform was greatly diminished. Party programmes and manifestos, although still significant, were ceasing to be the key determinants of policy-making; in many areas the key actors were to be Whitehall departments in association or consultation with interested pressure groups, especially producer groups.

Although these changes were already evident to perceptive contemporaries, the period up to the Royal Commission on Licensing of 1929 was inevitably one where older habits and patterns lingered on before fading away. The Trade took time to adjust to new situations; while the temperance societies, for their part, continued to fight many old battles (not least with each other), and their leaders tended to be ascribed an exaggerated importance as spokespersons on the issue. Popular interest in the issue was not entirely spent, especially in Scotland and Wales. Churchill, for example, was defeated by an independent prohibitionist candidate at an election in Dundee in 1922, and Sunday closing for Monmouthshire aroused popular passions in 1921. Yet the main lines of the Drink question were effectively settled in 1919–21 in such a way as to remove the issue from major controversy for some fifty years. This settlement was basically a conservative adaptation of prewar mechanisms, modified in the light of wartime developments and experience. Although there was no return to the minimal state interference of before 1914, with high taxation and restricted hours being maintained, no proactive alcohol policy was pursued of the kind which the CCB had been developing.

Detailed examination of the politics of 1919–21 should, however, caution us against seeing this somewhat lacklustre approach as being in any sense inevitable. The existence of the CCB had, after all, provided a bureaucratic focus for a policy of progressive temperance restriction. Enough evidence had accumulated to suggest that the state had the potential to develop social policy in this area in ways that had been undreamt of before 1914. Henry Carter's study of the work of the CCB, published in 1918, was in part a propagandist attempt to argue for the continuation of the Board's work after the war. Moreover, many contemporaries, including brewers, temperance reformers and local government leaders, remained unhappy at the authority exercised by the licensing magistrates. The early decades of the twentieth century marked the apogee of local government and it would not, therefore, have been illogical for local authorities to have been given extensive powers over liquor control. In this context, too, the link with housing policy should not be ignored. Temperance concern had always been an important component of the Garden City movement in the early days, and the massive growth of suburbs posed interested questions for liquor licensing in the narrower sense. Another solution would have been the creation of some sort of independent board, rather along the lines proposed for the treatment of the Poor Law or Education. Finally, the advent of the Labour party represented a new potential factor in the complex equation of liquor politics. The attitude of the party on the temperance question had always been ambiguous, but the debates about state purchase and the existence of the Carlisle scheme presented the opportunity for a radical approach along the lines of state control, a policy which would have been doubly attractive had the brewers reverted to their pre-1914 lavish support for the Conservative party.

Controls on production

Three issues required resolution at the end of the war: the extent and nature of controls on the production of beers and spirits, the future of the CCB and the extent to which wartime licensing controls should be relaxed, retained or even extended. All three issues were somewhat intertwined. The strict wartime controls on the quantity of liquors had stemmed from the shortage of raw materials and had never been a prime concern of the CCB, although it had been more enthusiastic about the parallel restrictions on strengths. The process of dismantling this network of control took place in stages and was completed by June 1921, with the most important restrictions on beer being eliminated by mid-1919.[1] It is not necessary to give a detailed account here, but the process illustrates the interdepartmental tensions within Whitehall at this period. Soon after the end of the war, there was evidence of discontent among workers at the maintenance of what were widely seen to be vexatious restrictions. Early in May 1919, for example, the Cabinet considered a letter from Ben Tillett complaining of the inability of his constituents to obtain liquor on Easter Monday, and warning that the consequent 'serious discontent' was fast 'becoming a scandal and interferes with the disciplinary work of the Union'.[2] The Ministry of Food experienced 'exceptional pressure' from many quarters for liberalisation of controls. It, in turn, urged the abandonment of controls in view of agitation and reported disturbances in the country, trusting upon 'natural circumstances to prevent abuse'. Both Roberts, the Food Controller, and Austen Chamberlain, the Chancellor of the Exchequer, felt themselves in a difficult position since no ministerial colleague was responsible for the CCB and liquor regulation in general.[3] The brewers, particularly those of high quality, high gravity beers, were involved in complex negotiations with these ministers and were putting pressure on them. Sydney Nevile, who led a deputation on the subject, was, according to his own account, able to persuade the Chancellor that the poor quality of beer brewed was jeopardising the revenue as well as destabilising the Trade.[4] On the other hand, D'Abernon took a different view. He believed that it was the quantity not the quality of beer that was the real cause for popular discontent. He and H. A. L. Fisher, President of the Board of Education, who chaired the Cabinet Committee on Liquor Restriction policy, were wary of taking the brewers' assurances at face value and of simply adding to their profits.[5] Fisher went so far as to assert that control over the gravity of beer was 'one of the most important measures for effective temperance which the Government can take'.[6] D'Abernon, moreover, was particularly concerned to safeguard to the last some control over strengths of beers brewed and their prices in the interests of temperance. He circulated a paper in February 1920 which claimed that an 'appalling rate' of increase in drunkenness was a result of previous relaxations and failure to accompany increases in strength with higher taxation. Stung by this, Chamberlain got the Customs and Excise to work on D'Abernon's statistics and somewhat gleefully refuted them.[7] When the Board of Trade and the Treasury were finally able to prevail upon the Cabinet to abolish all control over prices and strengths of beer in July 1921, the Treasury noted, with scarcely concealed distaste, that the sole reason they had lasted so long after the end of the war had been 'the desire to keep alive a form of control which has been regarded in some quarters as effective for the prevention of drunkenness'.[8]

The future of the CCB and of liquor control

These battles over the control of output illustrate how, in the new political order, bureaucratic politics were coming to play an important part in Drink policy. They also reveal the relative isolation and weakness of the CCB. This was all the more marked given the general popular sentiment against wartime regulation and control. D'Abernon and the CCB leaders sought the transfer of its power to 'a new authority, suitable to peace conditions'.[9] The objective here was to provide a means to continue the temperance policy which D'Abernon and his colleagues had come so enthusiastically to endorse. In March 1919, D'Abernon set out his ideas in notes for Fisher. Specifically, he recommended broken and shorter opening hours, 'non deleterious' strengths, 'adequate' price levels along with the provision of non-alcoholic refreshment. Equally important, however, was the necessity for an 'efficient system of central control and initiative'. The old pre-1914 system had failed because the licensing justices 'were not strong enough to resist trade pressure, and they had no enlightened and scientific policy'. He suggested this body be attached to the newly created Ministry of Health as soon as possible 'to avoid the dangers which must result from a gradually weakening authority'.[10] The choice of the Health Ministry was significant, since it would be far more proactive in liquor and temperance policy than the Home Office.

The weakness of D'Abernon's position lay in this inability to mobilise any coherent pro-reform lobby in the face of strong postwar moves for general derestriction. Not only did the mainstream militant temperance societies remain wedded to local veto, hoping for great things from the 1913 Scottish Local Option Act, due to come into force in 1921, but the supporters of state purchase mobilised for one last ditch effort. Spring 1919 saw a certain amount of jockeying for position. Fisher's Cabinet Committee comprised G. H. Roberts, (the Food Controller), R. Munro, (Scottish Secretary), Lord Milner, J. H. Thomas (representing labour), D'Abernon and Astor, with Pedder and Sykes serving as official Home Office and CCB advisers.[11] Milner quickly circulated a lengthy and powerful memorandum pointing out that the Cabinet already possessed a 'deliberately adopted' policy of state purchase and local option, formulated in May 1917, which 'still holds the field'. At present there was a danger with piecemeal relaxation of slipping into 'the old state of things' with 'a return of all the old evils'. He concluded that

> 'Before we engage once more in the old interminable and never really effective efforts to prevent the abuse of liquor by imposing restrictions upon the various private parties who are interested in its sale, I think we ought to make up our minds whether the only radical remedy for such abuse – the elimination of private interest in the sale of drink – which we certainly contemplated and almost adopted two years ago, is to be finally abandoned, and if so, why?'[12]

On the Committee, Milner could count on the support of Astor and Thomas; on the other hand, Munro warned that Scottish temperance opinion would not accept state purchase.[13]

By the end of May, the Committee presented the Cabinet with its report. It unanimously rejected any return to prewar conditions. 'Moderate opinion' all over the country wished to maintain the 'essential principles' of the wartime regulations which had brought about such a 'large improvement in sobriety, public order and public well-being'. If this opinion were flouted, the Government would be likely to face criticism 'on all sides'. Even within the Trade, 'large and important' sections did not wish to return to the old state of affairs. The Committee outlined a policy of continued restrictions along the lines which D'Abernon had advocated. However, when it came to considering the broader constitutional framework the Committee was less helpful. It outlined three possible options: (i) the transfer of all licensing and liquor powers to newly established licensing commissions, subject to parliamentary control, for the constituent countries of the UK; (ii) as (i) but to include the opportunity of large regional areas to opt for either prohibition or state purchase on triennial polls; (iii) state purchase for England and Wales along the lines of the 1917 policy. Policy (i), while likely to be opposed by the Trade, would be acceptable to the 'temperance party' and most moderate opinion; policy (ii) had the advantage of being 'more constructive' and opening the way to future reform while avoiding the political unpopularity of state purchase; on the other hand, it was potentially complex and, like many compromises, ran the risk of maximising opposition. The Committee felt unable to make any clear recommendation, especially in such a politically sensitive area where the choice 'turns partly upon the broadest considerations of general policy and finance, and partly upon an estimate of the present state of public opinion.'[14]

Such an indecisive approach was hardly likely to stimulate action, and the next few months saw a dangerous slippage in the situation from the point of view of the CCB. Fisher's committee had strongly recommended that parliamentary publicity should be given to instructions for some kind of interim regulation before the Whitsun recess, but no action had been taken. The political dangers of Drink were such as to put off all but the most stalwart. Certainly, there was the feeling that 'moderate opinion' would be disenchanted if an opportunity was not taken to capitalise on the wartime advances. But such moderate opinion was always somewhat nebulous, hard to gauge and of uncertain electoral weight. Organised political nonconformity was sharper in its intensity and more predictable in its direction. Here, the Prime Minister did not go short of advice, often in terms of anger mixed with sorrow. The *Methodist Times*, for example, while lamenting the 'strained relations' between the Free Churchmen and Lloyd George, was yet prepared to give him the benefit of the doubt on most matters, but Drink was a touchstone of principle: 'Let him bow himself in the house of Sir George Younger, and in that act he will sever himself from the confidence of Free Churchmen all over the country.'[15] The problem was, first, that Lloyd George needed the political support of Younger and the Unionists and secondly, that there was no indication whatsoever that the nonconformist orientated temperance forces could agree upon a common platform. Hence his lukewarm interest. He informed Seebohm Rowntree in August that he knew nothing of the present position of the Drink state purchase proposals and was conscious of 'the difficulty of such a measure on account of the opposition it would meet from the Independent Liberals and some teetotallers.'[16]

Throughout 1919, the CCB had to fight a rearguard action in which it was repeatedly forced to lower its sights. In April, its officials even appeared optimistic that the unpopular, 'no treating' regulations could be retained.[17] During the summer the Board, as we have seen, had had to give way on the issue of limiting strengths of beverages, as well as relaxing a range of other controls. By late summer, it seemed that even the continued restrictions on hours of sale might be in jeopardy.[18] In early July, D'Abernon arranged for both Henry Carter and Sydney Nevile, his fellow Board members who represented 'moderate' opinion on both sides, to pen letters, expressing their apprehension at the abolition of all controls, and he duly forwarded these letters to Lloyd George and Fisher.[19] Later in the month, officials in the CCB drafted a somewhat desperate memorandum for D'Abernon to circulate to the Cabinet. The cumulative effect of successive relaxations of wartime controls was such that 'a point has now been reached at which the Board can do little if anything to meet demands pressed by this or that section of the public for further relaxations, without undermining the whole fabric. It is very difficult, however, for the Board without express Government support, to withstand the pressure which is being brought to bear on them at the present time.' The benefit to the nation of the knowledge gained and advances made in wartime would be lost if further relaxations took place before a final legislative settlement was made. It was 'therefore of imperative importance that a definite mission or mandate should be conferred upon the Board for the period which must elapse before the establishment by Parliament of a new authority'.[20] Notwithstanding efforts of Pedder to use the Whitehall network to arouse the interest of senior ministers, no action was taken along the lines indicated, despite the fact that Bonar Law had announced on 2 July that the government intended to create a new Licensing Commission, under ministerial control, to replace the CCB.[21]

The 1921 licensing compromise

In the meantime, initiatives were being taken by a select group of brewers. Even before the end of the war, in late 1917, Sir Richard Garton, an industrialist with interest in supplying fermentable sugars to brewers, along with Edward Giffard of Barclay Perkins, had consulted with the heads of some of the major brewing firms about a possible postwar initiative. This group had urged a 'constructive' approach to the problems of the Trade, and now 'agreed that, with the end of the war, an active and clear cut policy of construction would be needed in all industries, especially our own'. They asked Sydney Nevile, who shared their views and who was a member of the CCB with good Whitehall contacts, to help them. Over a series of dinners and weekends spent in the pleasant surroundings of Giffard's yacht or his Surrey home (where his neighbour, Lord Justice Parker, was able to drop in to offer sympathetic advice), they drafted the outlines of a new licensing policy.[22] During the course of 1919, their proposals were reported to the Brewers' Society and hence to the NTDA which set up a committee to draft a bill. This was finally introduced by Col Gretton MP, of Bass's, into the Commons in March 1920.[23]

The motives of the brewers are succinctly recalled by Nevile, who was clearly in his element in mobilising support:

> . . . we found ourselves in a dilemma. There was intense public resentment against the continuance of restrictions long after the war had ended, aggravated by the knowledge that the temperance enthusiasts had tried to use the war to further the cause of prohibition; there was a conviction that it was the influence of social reformers that led to this prolonging of controls. We thought it possible that this resentment might lead to public and political agitation to enforce a complete return to pre-war conditions which we ourselves did not desire.[24]

Nevile and his associates had long taken the view that insobriety was not only undesirable in the public interest, but was also actually inimical to the commercial interests of the Trade itself. The future lay in improved public houses with greater leisure amenities. Apart from the renewed danger of future government regulation or even a state takeover (perhaps at the hands of a future Labour government), the greatest stumbling block to the implementation of such a policy lay in the restricted and unsympathetic attitude of the licensing benches. After 1900, the licensing benches had acted somewhat erratically: in some areas refusing applications by brewers to enlarge or improve premises, even as part of deals in which numbers of old, run down inner-city houses were traded in. Accordingly, Gretton's Bill proposed a drastic limitation on the autonomy of licensing benches through the establishment of judicial tribunals which were to operate on uniform principles over large areas, with further recourse to a single appeal authority presided over by a High Court Judge. The bill became unofficially known as the 'The Brewers' Litany Bill', following the quip by J. S. Eagles of the CCB that it could be summarised as pleading 'from the Injustices of the War, and the Justices of the Peace, O Parliament deliver us!'.[25] In the more measured terms of an official minute, the Home Office conceded that the bill was technically an 'excellent piece of work', but dismissed it as a reforming measure: the 'main effect and . . . main motive of the changes is to ease the places where the Trade finds the system pinches'.[26] The bill, as introduced, appeared perhaps deceptively bland: what it in fact did was to turn licensing from an administrative to a judicial responsibility of the justices, and effectively to recognise a security in licensed property thus protecting the vast sums tied up in public houses.

This point was not lost upon temperance leaders nor indeed by many licensing magistrates themselves, who, Nevile noted, 'were united in attaching great importance to their duties which they most jealously guarded'. This factor and 'other repercussions' led Nevile and the brewers 'to think again, to trust to argument, gradual persuasion and steady propaganda to ensure a more reasonable attitude towards improvement in licensing administration'.[27] The understandable passivity of the government was bound to come to an end at some time since there was a statutory requirement for the CCB to be wound up on the signing of a peace treaty. In November 1920, the government, following the advice of Fisher's Cabinet Committee, somewhat abruptly announced the transfer of the Board's powers to the Home Office as a temporary measure, without consulting either the CCB or the Trade. This caused some considerable protest, not only from ardent temperance enthusiasts but also Conservatives who viewed with some dismay the prospect of a government department running a commercial liquor business in Carlisle. The Attorney General reported to the Prime Minister that 'there is real and widespread antipathy to departmental control as such' and urged further delay and caution.[28] Sydney Nevile was also 'furious, for I was convinced that what the country needed was an Act which would establish stable conditions, and this pernicious proposal would leave the industry as a political pawn', in the process destroying his hopes of a 'constructive' policy.[29] Nevile himself, although holding an official position in the CCB, wrote a critical letter in *The Times* in which he protested at the failure of the government to deploy the knowledge and resources of the CCB after the war in the pursuit of a constructive social policy.[30] The government bill was withdrawn on 14 December and uncertainty prevailed as Gretton prepared to introduce a second, but more moderate, brewers' bill in early 1921. Sykes, the Secretary to the CCB, failed to get an interview with the Prime Minister and Bonar Law, found himself 'in a very difficult position', admitted he 'felt in the dark as to the mind of the Government and the Prime Minister'.[31] At this point, the broader political pressures became irresistible as 166 MPs signed a resolution calling for the final winding up of the CCB and a largely attended meeting of Unionist MPs on 15 March demanded the ending of all remaining wartime restrictions.[32] Accordingly, on 22 March, the Cabinet decided to reconvene Fisher's committee, which now lacked D'Abernon, Milner or Astor, but included Munro, Sir George Younger, Baldwin, Lords Lytton and Peel, T. A. Lewis and the Attorney General.[33]

The committee had before it a sort of valedictory plea from D'Abernon, now serving as ambassador in Berlin, in favour of a state sponsored scheme, funded by the taxation levied on the Trade, for the purposes of creating modern and well constructed public houses along the best managed lines.[34] However, in its deliberations on 5 and 18 April, the committee plumped for caution. It concluded that any proposal to create a new central commission or board which might be best able to 'make a general and scientific survey of the liquor problem' would provoke such opposition in Parliament as to delay the bill; hence, it was prudent to leave administration to the magistrates. It seemed best, moreover, to take off the Whips on the reading of Gretton's Bill. On 20 April, the committee was hastily summoned an hour before the full Cabinet met and decided to recommend that further relaxations on hours of opening be announced during the forthcoming debate as a means of further placating restive backbench MPs. Most of the discussion at the full Cabinet which followed centred around the tactics of how to deal with Gretton and the wide measure of support he was receiving on the Unionist side. But the general aim of government policy was agreed to include the promotion of the 'improved' public house, the granting of some sort of appeal from magistrates' decisions, autonomous treatment for Wales and – vaguely – the creation of 'some more central authority, free from political pressure, for surveying and co-ordinating the liquor policy of the country as a whole'.[35]

Lloyd George had no wish to add Drink to the rapidly mounting political problems of his coalition. He wanted to settle the question with the minimum of risk. On 22 April, the morning of the scheduled second reading of Gretton's bill, he hastily summoned a meeting of the members of the Cabinet Committee and those members of the CCB who could be found, for a general discussion. He suggested a deal whereby the brewers agreed not to press Gretton's bill further in return for an 'agreed' government sponsored measure; this the brewers, despite some recriminations from the licensed victuallers, accepted.[36] The device Lloyd George hit upon was one which had been used periodically during the war of a 'round table conference' of interested MPs from either side of the question who would be charged with hammering out a legislative formula. In this case, the conference was given the remit to consider 'how best to adapt in times of peace the experience obtained during the period of war' in connection with the licensing laws.[37]

This conference succeeded better than Lloyd George could have hoped. Even the Brewers' Society itself had not initially been optimistic. However, several parties had an interest in a negotiated settlement. The brewers in return for a measure of security were quite prepared to compromise on hours of sale and other matters. Many on the temperance side were keen to safeguard the restricted hours and tighter regulations while they could.[38] It was those like Astor, who still dreamed unrealistically of state purchase, who were most suspicious of the brewers' motives.[39] Between April and June, the arrangements and details for the conference were worked out between Gretton and the Congregationalist minister, T.T. Broad, Coalition Liberal MP for Clay Cross and a temperance supporter. Broad found Gretton to be 'in a reasonable mood' throughout the negotiations and the government to be 'grateful' for the progress being made and 'extremely anxious to get this thing out of the way'.[40] The round table conference sat in June under the chairmanship of the Attorney General; it consisted of eighteen MPs: four each from the temperance and Trade sides, two representing clubs, four neutrals, and two each from the government and the Labour opposition. The groundwork laid by Gretton and Broad was built upon and a deal on hours rapidly reached.[41] A draft government bill was ready by 16 July and endorsed by the Cabinet despite some objections to the prospect of the Home Office conducting state trading at Carlisle.[42] The bill passed smoothly through Parliament with unusual rapidity and was quickly followed by a comparable Scottish Act.[43]

For the future, the most significant feature of the 1921 Act was the restriction on hours. The weekday hours of opening were fixed at nine in

London (between 11.00 a.m. and 11.00 p.m.) and eight in the rest of the country (between 11.00 a.m. and 10.00 p.m.); Sunday hours were more restrictive. Magistrates were given powers of discretion regarding the hours within these limits which soon gave rise to some anomalies, for example, with pubs on the North side of Oxford Street closing an hour later than those on the South side! A compulsory afternoon break of two hours was imposed and this was to remain in the eyes of many foreign visitors and tourists as a fine example of British eccentricity until the 1970s in Scotland and 1990 in England. Temperance advocates made clear that in no sense did they regard the 1921 Act as a satisfactory settlement of the question: it was merely a wise and expedient measure which preserved the useful wartime advances at a time when they were subject to criticism; the way ahead lay for some more radical reform along the lines of local control.[44] They could, however, point to some successes. The restricted hours eliminated the worst excesses of early morning indulgence, all day soaking and late night binges which had been present before 1914; and it must be remembered that some rural parts of the country, which had escaped the DORA regulations, now came under restricted hours for the first time. The brewers had had to concede on Sunday closing in Monmouth and on various other matters such as the abolition of the 'bona fide traveller'; the Carlisle scheme was preserved (although prohibitionists detested it) and taxation on alcohol remained far higher in real terms than in pre war days. On the other hand, if the longer view is taken, it is hard to escape the conclusion that the larger brewers were the long term gainers. They had achieved some measure of security for their property by a clause which limited the unfettered discretion of the justices;[45] and, above all, they had avoided the creation of some kind of an independent Licensing Commission which would have provided a focus for a future more pro-active temperance policy. A settlement of some sort had been enacted and, so long as the Conservatives remained in the ascendant, there seemed little to fear for the future, particularly as the popular enthusiasm for temperance seemed on the wane. The passage of prohibition legislation in the United States may have appeared disturbing at first, but it soon became apparent that the evident shortcomings of that policy could be used to advantage.

Drink and the new political order

The details of the politics of liquor in 1918–21 are interesting, not because the 1921 Licensing Act was in itself a particularly important milestone, but because they illuminate the workings of the political system in connection with the Drink question. Several general conclusions may be drawn. In the first place, the political parties tended to avoid any specific policy programme on the issue. This reflects the peculiarly opaque nature of the party system at this time. The confusions in Liberal party politics and the very ambiguous position of Lloyd George meant that the natural focus for a 'temperance policy' was removed from the scene, in striking contrast to 1904–08. Temperance sentiment among Independent Liberals and some Coalitionists was a factor to be taken into account, but this acted normally in a negative manner, as when ideas for state purchase or extensive state control were ruled out of court in Scotland on account of the prohibitionist sympathies of many Scottish Liberals. The position of the Labour party had never been very clear on the issue and, as we shall see in Chapter 8, it became even more muddied after the war, with a threefold division between prohibitionists, nationalisers and libertarians. Unionist sentiment was, as ever, largely pro-Trade and it was susceptible to the popular demands for the removal of controls. It was the threatened revolt of Conservative backbenchers over Gretton's 1921 Bill that was a key factor in stimulating Lloyd George into action. However, the party was never unanimous on the issue. Some considered the party to have been over generous to the brewers in 1904, and more were concerned not to dismantle all wartime controls entirely. H. A. L. Fisher, in 1920, warned Lloyd George that the alienation of moderate temperance opinion could be a threat to the Coalition: he was being 'deluged with manifestos and memorials from the Temperance Party' and he instanced the decision of the Bishop of Croydon and the moderate Temperance Council of the Christian Churches to oppose the Coalition candidate in the Louth by-election.[46] Moreover, in the persons of the Astors, the Conservative party had acquired two vociferous temperance champions, deeply hostile to the Trade, who acted as a focus for temperance opinion in the party: their papers contain a significant amount of correspondence on the subject with clergymen, public school masters, magistrates and local party workers of Conservative persuasion. Perhaps the greatest indication of the inability of the party to make an impact was the retention of the Carlisle scheme, which aroused considerable hostility among free marketers in the party and some unease among Conservative Cabinet ministers themselves.

By contrast, the focus of policy-making had shifted markedly to Whitehall departments. A second feature which emerges from the 1919–21 politics of Drink is the clash of departmental policy lines and the capacity of individual civil servants to pursue strategies. Whereas the CCB continued to wish to steer the consumer away from stronger ales in the interests of temperance, the Food Controller's department and later the Food Department of the Board of Trade wished to see liberalisation of supply after the end of the war. Thus, in June 1921, Frank Coller of the Board of Trade assured Arthur Towle, the Manager of the Midland Hotel Services Department and a former civil service colleague, that for over two years he had 'been trying to get rid of the Orders affecting the prices and gravity of beer. I have not succeeded yet although I have contrived to get some slight modification.'[47] Under D'Abernon's chairmanship, the CCB had been no mere administrative body, implementing DORA regulations in the interests of wartime efficiency. It had built up a 'Drink policy' which it sought to promote in the interests of national efficiency for peace as well as war. Licensed reduction, improved and salubrious premises, the provision of canteens, refreshments and amusements, shorter hours along with a range of temperance restrictions had been part of this, but D'Abernon had wanted to see the creation of a strong, new Licensing Commission which would take the lead in forcing the brewers to plan a new pattern of retailing and which would also conduct scientific analysis into all aspects of the alcohol question. Similarly, officials in his department, like Sir John Pedder, had over the years developed a kind of proprietary interest in the Carlisle scheme and were prepared to defend it from attacks from any quarter, including guerrilla skirmishes from the Treasury, ever eager to pare down expenditure.[48] D'Abernon's general policy was supported by the newly formed Ministry of Health which expressed concern about the effects of drunkenness upon health, especially that of women.[49] But other Whitehall departments had different perspectives. The Board of Trade wanted liberalisation of trade; the Customs and Excise was worried about the revenue; and the Treasury was concerned to cut back expenditure.

A third point which clearly emerges from the politics of Drink between 1919 to 1921 is the adeptness of the leaders of the Trade. The small group of larger brewers around Giffard, Garton and Gretton had a clear strategy and were able to exploit their connections. Once state purchase fell off the political agenda in 1918, and once the popular mood was in favour of derestriction, they could swim with the tide. But equally important were their connections with Whitehall. Sydney Nevile put his finger on this as a key factor:

> The helpful attitude of the industry, too, during the war had resulted in personal friendships and mutual respect between some of us in

> the Trade and the Government. Perhaps never before had brewers and the executive heads of Government departments worked so closely together – the gulf of suspicion and mistrust between the Trade and the Government and its various departments had been largely bridged.[50]

Certainly the contrast with the battles of 1904 and 1908 and the very negative attitude of the Trade then is striking. The connections forged at this period between civil servants and the Trade persisted into the interwar years. Sir Edgar Sanders, a former Chairman of the Magistrates' Association who was appointed Manager at Carlisle, went on to become Director of the Brewers' Society in the 1930s; while Sir John Pedder, the leading Home Office expert on licensing, on his retirement in 1932 went on to serve on the Board of Watneys for seventeen years.[51] Such connections are all the more significant when it is remembered that these officials had been promoting a modestly restrictionist outlook. As in other areas of industrial and commercial life, the First World War had proved that government had need of producers and manufacturing pressure groups when it sought to regulate. Hence, the development of what Middlemas has termed a degree of 'corporate bias'. In this connection, it is interesting that in the round table licensing conference of 1921 the formula adopted by the government of equal numbers of Trade, temperance and 'neutral' MPs was drawn from the model of the two sides of industry. The problem on the temperance side was that although they had individuals, such as Henry Carter, who were influential, as societies and organisations they had lacked the expertise or power to deliver resources which, for example, trade unionists enjoyed in matters of labour politics.

This deficiency might have been compensated for had the temperance societies been able to mount a coherent political campaign. But they were handicapped by the endemic divisions within their midst. There were three main groupings. First, there was D'Abernon and the body of opinion centred around the CCB, which was anxious to develop a constructive state liquor policy in the interest of national efficiency. D'Abernon could count on the active support of Henry Carter, now a leading influence on social questions in the Methodist Church; he also enjoyed a certain amount of sympathy and support from temperance activists for the maintenance of wartime controls. But this fell far short of support for the constructive and 'scientific' analysis for which D'Abernon yearned. The Society for the Study of Inebriety, which he himself had joined, was another source of support. This body argued for the development of the wartime controls. However, the Society was neither organisationally nor attitudinally equipped to embark on a lobbying campaign.[52] Secondly, there were the old devotees of the Gothenburg system, like the Rowntrees, who now rallied enthusiastically in support of the disinterested management of the Carlisle scheme. These were joined by the supporters of state purchase, in particular Milner and Astor. Astor's disappointment in 1917 had encouraged him to develop an attitude towards the Trade every bit as hostile as the prohibitionists. 'When we talk of temperance extremists don't let us forget that every brewer is an extremist', he lectured Broad during the 1921 negotiations.[53] Such ferocity ill fitted either the views or the approach of D'Abernon. The issue of state ownership and control of the Trade therefore muddied the waters of the restrictionist position. Finally, there were the prohibitionists, who concentrated upon the winning of local veto and upon Sunday closing. They regarded the improvers in Carlisle as 'doing the Devil's work' and, as Wilfrid Lawson a generation before, had scant interest in any scheme of licensing 'reform'. Developments in the United States blinded them to the erosion of their power base in the UK. All these divisions were to emerge in debates about Carlisle and the improved public house in the next decade to which we now turn.

8
Decades of Improvement: The Interwar Years

The 1921 settlement dashed the hopes of all those wanting some radical departure in government policy towards Drink. Moreover, the interwar decades saw a sharp waning in the influence of the temperance societies at the local level, except in parts of Scotland. Ernest Selley, a supporter of public ownership of the Trade, who conducted an exhaustive study of drinking habits in the 1920s, was regretfully informed by temperance activists and others that their organisations 'are today but a shadow of their former selves', and this impression is borne out by statistics for membership.[1] Nevertheless, the very extent of the changed climate provided some opportunities for campaigners. Church leaders, social workers and the medical profession continued to show an active interest in alcohol and its connection to more general social or health issues. The very decline of the temperance issue allowed new opportunities to redefine the Drink question in broader social terms, relating it to the behaviour of young people, the provision of leisure facilities, or advertising. The fact that alcohol was less intimately connected with working-class lifestyles also removed one barrier to policy initiatives. The emergence of the Labour party as a party of government also provided an opening for the development of a more proactive social policy towards Drink.

Continuation of the old attitudes

In the 1920s, few of these opportunities were taken by the temperance leaders, who continued to be torn apart over the issue of local veto versus public control, until a rather belated and panicky reaction to the Brewers' advertising offensive in the 1930s brought about new thinking and a measure of cooperation. The continued divisions within the temperance movement are revealed by the unhappy experiences of Waldorf Astor who, like others before him, was to receive scant reward for a decade of effort and financial support, and retired from the field in disillusion. Astor was an unlikely temperance enthusiast, but his service on the wartime CCB had strengthened his bitter hostility to the role of the Trade in public life.[2] At the CCB, he had not proved to be the easiest of colleagues. Sydney Nevile took little trouble to hide his dislike in his autobiography written forty years later, while D'Abernon privately described Astor as 'a sentimental, priggish millionaire, dog-stupid with an exaggerated sense of his own importance.'[3] On the other hand, as a wealthy Conservative and newspaper magnate, he and his formidable wife, Nancy, possessed a vast and influential range of social contacts. As his favoured policy of state purchase no longer was practical politics, in 1921 Astor set about trying to rally the two wings of the temperance movement as well as outside opinion in favour of a united attempt to allow local communities to rid themselves of the Trade. He attracted the support of Bishop Burge of Oxford, who enthusiastically welcomed the opportunity 'of lifting the whole problem on to the level of a combined effort on the part of *all* men of goodwill to use the experience which these last years have brought us, and to deal with the matter as a part of reconstruction and social reform'.[4] The resulting 'Oxford Bill' allowed localities a threefold choice of no change, no licence, or disinterested management by means of polls every four years.[5] Where the bill differed from nineteenth-century schemes was the large size of the areas proposed and the creation of a framework of administration which comprised a Liquor Management Board appointed by the Home Secretary, a Central Advisory Committee, made up of representative interests, and local advisory committees. This echoed the administrative pattern of the old CCB. The bill was introduced for several years in the House of Lords and in 1924 attracted the support of 50 peers, including the whole episcopal bench. The bill is interesting in so far as it reveals first, a continued concern among non-party elites with the temperance question, secondly, the old attachments to the idea of local control and finally, the continued endemic divisions among the temperance lobby. A round table conference was held in January 1922, designed to allow temperance societies to present a united front at the forthcoming election, but a larger delegate conference broke down in acrimony as prohibitionists refused to agree to cease hostile criticism of disinterested management. In turn, the supporters of state purchase, like Arthur Sherwell, rounded on the prohibitionists and refused to cease active campaigning for their own solution of public control, linked to disinterested management.[6] Although the 'Oxford Bill' continued to be introduced in Parliament on an annual basis, it had no real head of steam; even so, as late as 1928 Astor had hoped that the Liberal party might adopt it as policy.[7] By this time, Astor had concentrated on funding a 'Drink Enquiry' (although even here its results disappointed him). By 1933, Astor had joined the eminent company of politicians who had, since 1870, been disillusioned with the temperance movement, complaining to Philip Snowden that despite the fact he had sponsored regular weekly articles in *The Observer* for many years, 'the temperance movement never backed us up. They did not even support us by buying the paper.'[8]

Such divisions among temperance pressure groups were nothing new but, before 1914, they could at least be compensated for by influence within the Liberal party. After 1921, this was not the case, and the failure of the temperance lobby to mobilise effectively at the very time when much elitist opinion was more favourably disposed was a debilitating weakness. Part of the explanation for such truculence lay in the fact that the United States offered prohibitionists the prospect of a dream come true, and they naturally exulted in such a development in what was becoming the most economically advanced country in the world. British prohibitionists had their own more modest expectations in the form of local option in Scotland under the Temperance (Scotland) Act of 1913, which came into effect in 1920 after the seven-year time limit. The rather puny results were cruelly to illustrate the weaknesses both of the temperance movement and the whole concept of the local veto. The Act provided for polls to be held in whole burghs and in rural parishes with a choice of no licence, licence limitation and no change.[9] Although a broad based campaign for limitation as well as no licence might have maximised support, the pro-local veto Scottish societies resolutely ignored this and set up a National Citizens' Council in order to coordinate a prohibition campaign. A chain of no licence committees was set up and, by the close of 1920, 5,706 meetings had been organised, at a cost of £21,419, often with the active help of church ministers.[10] For its part the Trade, mobilised a counter-campaign. The Scottish whisky distillers engaged professional staff and mobilised their retailers. In the autumn of 1920, the entire staff of whisky companies were sent out to campaign.[11] In the event, out of the total of 1,215 Scottish areas, a mere 37 areas opted for limitation and 36 for local veto.[12] The areas going dry were either remote rural ones, strongly influenced by puritanical religion, or wealthy residential, professional suburbs of Glasgow, Rutherglen and Greenock. In neither category could there be said to be a major problem of intemperance.[13] An exception was the small but expanding town of Kirkintilloch, a young community fast becoming a satellite of Glasgow. Here, figures of arrests for drunkenness had been high and an active temperance movement existed. In 1920, the local establishment – the local council, the Catholic leader of the local miners' association and the Labour M. P., Tom Johnston – came out strongly for prohibition. The victorious temperance forces subsequently claimed a great victory for the local veto here, declaring that drunkenness had diminished, conditions in homes improved and savings bank deposits greatly increased. One public house was converted into a cinema and others ended up as a bookshop, a dairy and an ice cream parlour. But the temperance success was short lived, prohibition being overturned by the subsequent poll in 1926.[14] The new uses to which the old premises were put indicates that it was the cultural changes that were significant. The social changes which the twentieth century was bringing to this youthful community were accelerated and assisted by the vote, rather than caused by it. Elsewhere, local prohibition carried some of the disadvantages which opponents of local veto had always predicted. In Stornaway and Wick, large numbers of drinking clubs grew up and elsewhere boundaries were a problem, for example the Isle of Arran, which was split down the middle into wet and dry parishes.[15] By 1968, the number of dry areas had shrunk to 20 and limitation areas to 17.[16]

The Labour party and the Drink question

The stunted performance of local veto, even on the fertile ground of Scotland, illustrates very clearly the fading appeal of the traditional prohibitionist cause in contrast to the United States. The advocates of the rival policy state control were to fare little better. We have already seen how, before 1914, the Labour party held no very coherent view on the Drink question. Advocates of public control, such as the Webbs, faced opposition equally from orthodox prohibitionists and from libertarian socialists. These divisions were exacerbated after 1918.[17] At the end of the war, a determined attempt was made to get the Labour party to endorse nationalisation of the Trade. Seebohm Rowntree took an initiative in this and arranged a meeting at the House of Commons on 5 June, 1918. As well as MacDonald and J. H. Thomas, the group included Arthur Sherwell and, amazingly, Waldorf Astor. The presence of a Conservative MP, a millionaire and a newspaper magnate to boot, at a caucus hoping to influence the Labour party in favour of nationalisation of an industry shows how the Drink question could break all the normal rules.[18] MacDonald and Thomas believed that the Labour party was sympathetic to nationalisation but was in no way ready to press for it. They agreed to take steps to 'deepen the interest' in the subject by inspiring articles in trade union and socialist publications. The following summer, the campaign was put on a more formal footing with the employment of Arthur Greenwood and J. J. Mallon (later warden of Toynbee Hall) as officials in a Labour Campaign for the Public Ownership and Control of the Liquor Trade. Rowntree was to bankroll the operation.[19] Mallon, Greenwood and Thomas energetically attempted to mobilise support, for example by convening a 300-strong delegation of trade unionists to examine Carlisle.[20] By 1920, the new body had enlisted supporters among many local parties and, early that year, got the party's advisory committee on the temperance question to recommend that the party 'actively pursue a policy of state purchase.'[21] Labour supporters of state purchase rehearsed all the normal arguments in favour of taking the private profit out of drink sales, but also laced them with a vitriolic attack upon the capitalist nature of the brewers and other Trade organisations.[22]

However, it soon became clear that rank-and-file Labour activists, trade unionists and MPs were split three ways on the issue. On the one hand, the proponents of state purchase came under considerable pressure from many of their membership in favour of relaxing controls. Liberals, such as T. P. Whittaker and Theodore Carr, MP for Carlisle, despaired of Labour's timidity in the face of such working-class demands.[23] The links with working men's clubs was also a factor here: many of these had significant interests in brewing and many working-class licensed victuallers were Labour sympathisers. In addition to this, many trade unions in heavy industry, for example iron and steel, maintained beer drinking to be a necessary refreshment for workers and strongly fought to oppose unnecessary restrictions. Other socialists took a libertarian view on principle and considered much of the attack on working-class drinking as a slur upon the workers.[24] Indeed, such was the strength of pro-Trade sympathy in the parliamentary party that a motion to support Gretton's Licensing Bill in 1921 was only narrowly defeated at a private meeting.[25] There is some evidence of murkier connections. Mallon, when standing at Watford, claimed to have been approached by someone purporting to speak for the local licensed victuallers' association who offered 'votes and money if I promised to do what the Trade required', and he knew of other cases where Labour candidates were offered up to £300 towards election expenses, if they stood against pro-temperance Liberals.[26]

On the other side, a good number of trade unionists and party workers, especially in Scotland and Wales, were inclined towards prohibition or orthodox restrictions and were fiercely opposed to the idea of the state condoning the traffic.[27] This body of opinion, surprisingly, now found a leader in Snowden, who proceeded to recant his earlier interest in state control. Writing in 1921, he pointed to three factors which had led him to change his mind. First, was the 'remarkable advance' of prohibition among the English speaking peoples, which strongly suggested that the road to prohibition should not be blocked. Secondly, he had been impressed by the beneficial effects of restrictive measures in the war. Thirdly, the financial condition of the country militated against state control; moreover, in this connection, the creation of a vast 'vested interest' would substitute a 'public cupidity' for a 'private interest'.[28] Matters came to a head at the Scarborough Party Conference in June 1920, when Snowden used procedural devices to outmanoeuvre the pro-nationalisation lobby. The Scottish miners used their weight in the Miners' Federation to pass a resolution in favour of comprehensive local option (including disinterested management) as opposed to all-out public ownership. Greenwood described this to J. S. Sanders, the General Manager at Carlisle (who was in regular sympathetic correspondence with him and Mallon), as 'a serious setback to our work'.[29] Some debate continued within the party and a special sub-committee of the party Executive, chaired by Sidney Webb, was set up in 1922 to work out a definitive policy. But given the threefold split, this wisely avoided specific policy commitments, concluding there was 'no single panacea', and produced a form of words which more or less anyone could subscribe to.[30] Although Labour remained more sympathetic to temperance-inspired legislation than the Conservatives, the party took no significant initiative until Herbert Morrison pressed for the state control of licensing in the New Towns after the Second World War.

The Carlisle scheme

Once the 1921 Act settled the narrower aspects of the licensing question, the Conservative governments of the interwar years had no incentive to take further initiatives. However, the continued existence of the Carlisle scheme, and the smaller Scottish state trading areas, kept open a debate on the role of the state and the whole *raison d'être* of licensing. Carlisle was important in several respects. In the first place, it kept alive controversy; secondly, it generated a degree of paternalistic pride on the part of Home Office officials; and thirdly, it provided an alternative model of government policy towards Drink.

As far as controversy was concerned, the officials managing Carlisle and their supporters had the strange experience of being bombarded with criticism from two opposing sides at once: the prohibitionists and the Trade. Indeed critical accounts of visits to Carlisle by prohibitionist Good Templars and the like were regularly quoted with approval in the unlikely columns of the Trade press. Prohibitionists set out to discredit the experiment and thus destroy the case for disinterested control. Two sorts of evidence were used. One was lurid first-hand accounts by observers of drunkenness in the streets, the failure of the police to enforce the law, overcrowding and serving of drunken customers and (especially) the incidence of female drinking and 'improper' conduct.[31] Another, and perhaps more telling, source was the official statistics for drunkenness, crime and the like. These tended to show that, notwithstanding sharp improvements in the war, Carlisle in the 1920s fared no better than comparable small industrial towns in Lancashire. For their part, although outright nationalisation was fading as a threat, the large brewers feared, with some justice, an extension of the Carlisle 'experiment' into other areas, with consequent reduction in licensed houses and buying out of brewing interests. Such opposition was eagerly taken up by many Conservatives, anxious to attack the whole idea of state trading. Throughout the 1920s, Col Holbrook MP, whom Home Office officials minuted as having a 'bee in his bonnet' about Carlisle, tabled a series of awkward questions and motions on the subject.[32] At the local level, it seems Trade representatives were not above acting as *agents provocateurs*. In July 1925, for example, a group of gentlemen posing as tourists (who were identified as belonging to the Trade Defence Association) went on a sort of tour of the state run areas of Scotland. At Dingwall, after 'snooping around' the accommodation, they attempted to obtain drink from the bars to take away (against the regulations). Arriving at Invergordon at 2.45 p.m., they peremptorily requested a late lunch. A Miss Ferguson supplied this only to be met with the request at 3.15 p.m. for a bottle of whisky, out of hours. On her refusal, 'they kicked up a fearful fuss'. The local state manager then telegraphed ahead to forewarn his colleagues up the railway line and furnish a description of the party.[33] As for Carlisle itself, judging by the numerous enquiries and delegations sent to examine the operation of the system, drinkers there must have become quite inured to the appearance of thinly-described clergymen and the like in the bars, who would periodically quiz them on the merits or otherwise of state control. Once the novelty had worn off, the city seems to have accepted the new order without difficulty. Initially there had been bitter complaints about the quality of 'state beer', but this is partly explained by the fact that the advent of state control coincided exactly with the sharp reduction in gravities all over the country.[34] Later civic leaders tended to support the scheme, as did Theodore Carr, the city's MP.[35] However, by the late 1920s, some observers could complain that the real problem in Carlisle was apathy. Few civic leaders or church ministers bothered themselves with the scheme and seemed surprised to learn that they were the subject of interest by investigators.

A particularly interesting aspect of the Carlisle scheme is the extent to which it became a sort of protégé of some of the Home Office officials. These took positive steps to defend it and to present it in the best possible light, even when they were serving sceptical Conservative ministers facing political criticism on the issue. The continued existence of Carlisle after the war owed as much to expediency as deliberate intent. The Geddes Report on Public Expenditure in 1920 gave a cool assessment of its financial benefit and was critical of the idea of the state trading. It judged that the only reason for its continuance could be as a social experiment, but the Home Office officials considered that what they termed this 'somewhat ill-informed and half-hearted' condemnation would let them off the hook, especially as no one wanted to complicate other Geddes-inspired legislation with the liquor question.[36] As we have seen, the 1921 Licensing Act was rather a rushed job, very much the result of a lowest common denominator. It was easiest to simply transfer the responsibility for Carlisle and the Scottish areas from the CCB to the Home Office with the minimum of upheaval.[37] There was some recognition at the political level that success had been achieved at Carlisle during the war, but Conservative ministers were cool towards the idea of a government department undertaking a purely commercial enterprise. In 1923, in the face of an onslaught from Col Holbrook and other Tory backbenchers, serious consideration was given to the idea of divesting themselves of responsibility. The government was reported to be 'opposed alike to the extension of the experiment to other areas, and to the disposal of the Carlisle Undertaking to private enterprise . . . they were not anxious to take the initiative in altering the existing state of things, but . . . their commitments as a Government prevented them from giving active support to State trading in any form.' Ideally they would have liked to transfer the undertaking to some trust or independent, non-profit-making concern.[38] However, a Cabinet paper counselled caution: not only were the financial returns on

Carlisle now highly favourable and the time to dispose of capital assets unfavourable but, for technical reasons, the transfer of licences to the private sector would need legislation in an already overcrowded session. Such considerations of political expediency probably weighed more with ministers than the positive arguments, which stressed the support of 'responsible opinion' in favour of the scheme and the opportunity it allowed the state to get 'a useful inside knowledge' of licensing law and administration.[39]

Ministers, including Home Secretaries, at this period had no interest in liquor issues and were only too content to fight shy of the question;[40] but among some Home Office civil servants we can trace a positive endorsement, if not paternal benevolence, towards Carlisle. Thus, they were angry at the Geddes Report and the efforts of the Treasury to restrict expenditure on Carlisle in 1920–22; they carefully arranged visits of various dignitaries to the City; and they took a hand in helping to prepare evidence from Carlisle for the 1929–31 Royal Commission so as to present the scheme in the best possible light. 'Some Govt.', wrote Sir John Pedder, in briefing Arthur Henderson for a Parliamentary Question in 1924, 'before long must tackle this question; and it is to be hoped that the answer will be found in obtaining powers for the extension of public ownership whether to the country at large or area by area. Both methods have their difficulties but they ought not in either case to be insurmountable.'[41] Officials found Henderson's Conservative successor, the somewhat prickly Joynson-Hicks – universally known as 'Jix' – far less pliant on the subject, even though he was a teetotaller and, in his youth, had been a regular platform speaker for the CETS.[42] In 1928, Hinshelwood drafted a Cabinet paper setting out the Government's response to Balfour of Burleigh and Astor's 'Oxford Bill' which, while pointing to flaws in the Bill, counselled caution. A 'very large and influential section of the community' believed improvements to be necessary and it was important for the government not to appear to offer mere obstruction; moreover, as Carlisle already existed, 'the Government will I think have to be careful to avoid creating the impression that they are hostile to their own work in the existing schemes'. Sir John Pedder, in an approving gloss on his junior's work, noted that if 'the general view of the S of S and Cabinet is to say Yes to this Memo. I think the spokesman of the Govt. could make an effective and useful (politically as well as socially) speech.' Jix's reaction was apoplectic when the memo was put up to him. 'This memo does not represent my views', he scrawled in his red ink, 'I am opposed to Local Option and to State Management. I have only tolerated the reviled [?]

socialism of Carlisle because I found it in operation but the Party to which I belong hates it.'[43] In the revised version, which went to Cabinet, the Home Secretary, while conceding it was necessary to keep Carlisle in place, urged that the Government spokesman in the Lords should categorically renounce any further extension of public ownership of the drink trade.[44]

That ministerial views could at times be so much at odds with the ideas of officials is undoubtedly due, in part, to the dominant position and influence of Sir John Pedder, Assistant Secretary at the Home Office at this period. Pedder, described by Sydney Nevile as 'a typical civil servant of the highest class' who hid his human qualities under a somewhat bureaucratic manner, had spent all his career on liquor licensing. In 1896, as a clerk, he was already composing memoranda for the Home Office on the main points of the licensing law and, by 1915, such was his expertise that he was the obvious choice to be the senior official on the Central Control Board, where he acted as deputy to D'Abernon; on the Board's abolition he went on to chair the advisory council on the State Management areas.[45] On his retirement in 1932, it was noted that he had a 'knowledge of the whole subject of liquor control which is probably unique and it will not be easy to supply the deficiency.'[46] Pedder's wartime work made him an enthusiast for state control and 'improvement'. In 1922, amazingly, he even flirted with the idea of speaking at a Cambridge Union debate in favour of state purchase, only being dissuaded by 'trepidation among the powers that be at the risk of political controversy'.[47]

The Carlisle scheme, which was really on quite a modest scale, attracted attention and interest for two reasons. The first was because it offered an example of state management of a normally commercial enterprise at a time when state involvement in a range of industries, such as electricity, railways and the new radio broadcasting, was subject to political controversy. The second reason lay in its apparent ability to offer an alternative model as a 'solution' to the Drink issue. Here, the concept of disinterested management seemed to hold the key. The concept, first advocated by Chamberlain in the 1870s and popularised by Rowntree and Sherwell in 1899, had become the magnet for temperance enthusiasts who had turned their back on prohibition and the local veto. Before 1914, there had been various experiments at implementing the idea, for example by two commercial organisations, the People's Refreshment House Association, formed by the Bishop of Chester, and Public House Trust Companies headed by Sir Edward Grey of Fallodon. However, these had been small scale operations, only totalling some 500 houses altogether scattered over the country in predominantly rural communities.[48] Carlisle was different. Here, the whole trade was taken over, except for four high class hotels, in a 500 square mile area; Licensing matters were removed from the control of the magistrates and a board of management, superintended from London and advised by a local advisory body, administered the regulations and decided policy. Managers were given a commission of 75 per cent on the sale of food and 25 per cent on non-intoxicants, and were otherwise simply given a wage. In most cases initially, former licensees were taken on by the State Board. Sometimes there appears to have been an interesting culture shock in store for them. Henry Carter, for example, relates how once the General Manager, who happened to be visiting a bar, intervened to stop one such bar manager

> from again serving a customer who had already consumed a fair quantity of liquor. The manager – who was the former licensee – protested that the man 'could carry more liquor without getting into trouble with the police'. The General Manager explained that from the point of view of the Board this idea was totally wrong. At the end of a long argument the ex-licensee exclaimed, 'Of course, I can easily work that way if the Board want it, if you tell me that I'm not to be dismissed for letting down the trade.'[49]

In order to superintend such a high-minded approach to drinking, the Board appointed its own inspectors to supplement the police force. However, the operation of the Carlisle scheme was to cast doubt on the extent to which disinterested management really was a sufficiently robust concept on which to base a policy solution.[50]

The 'improved' public house and disinterested management

Disinterested management was, however, only part of the approach. Linked to it was a deliberate policy of transforming the public house itself. The general state of public houses in 1920 was far from satisfactory. Most were cramped, overcrowded and unhygienic. Both Selley and Vernon, who analysed the Drink issue in the 1920s, concluded that most public houses were simply drink shops.[51] Lord D'Abernon, who considered the reconstruction of licensed premises to be a key element in social reform, believed that a measure of state intervention would be the stimulus to encourage the brewers to take the initiative in improving their premises; moreover, under unregulated competition there was a tendency for bad houses to drive out good.[52] Carlisle provided the opportunity to experiment in this field. Carlisle premises, in common with those in most smaller Northern towns, were certainly substandard. Nearly half the existing public houses were closed, while the rest were radically 'improved'. Improvement tended to take the form of ripping out partitions, improving sanitation and providing 'air, light and publicity'. Good quality furnishings were provided in keeping with the latest, rather austere, fashions of the time. There seems, indeed, to have been some initial complaint about the removal of 'snug' bars, but the general consensus was that, after a decade, the Carlisle drinkers were satisfied with their regime.[53]

There was, however, a real ambiguity about the purpose and the nature of the 'improved' facilities to be provided in the state run enterprises. This dichotomy went back to the early days of the concept of disinterested management. The Scandinavian approach had been to regard the new system as a means of catering for a human frailty in a way that minimised risk, rather in the way that present day supporters of legalised brothels argue their case. Austerity was the order of the day in such bars, with 'perpendicular' drinking at the bar encouraged. The provision of counter-attractions had long been seen as an element of the new policy, but this could be interpreted in different ways. In the late nineteenth century, some English Gothenburg reformers, such as Jayne, the Bishop of Chester, inclined to a different view that the reformed public house should be wholesome and attractive. On the other hand, Rowntree and Sherwell, the chief protagonists of disinterested management, made no secret of their distaste for 'the theory of recreative attractions' in their volume describing British 'Gothenburg' experiments.[54] In Carlisle, all advertisements for the sale of intoxicants were removed and the sale of food was encouraged in most houses, with a select few being developed along popular restaurant lines. During wartime, the emphasis in the scheme had certainly been upon the elimination of drunkenness and the promotion of temperance; however, in peacetime a subtle shift took place. By 1925, for example, a new policy was introduced for providing comfortable women's bars, in place of the previous practice of encouraging women to drink in side passages or in spartan standing bars.[55] By 1927, Eagles privately conceded to Nevile that 'our first improvements were necessarily tentative, and were in some ways misguided; I think we studied economy to excess.' Eagles certainly saw Carlisle not as a mere commercial enterprise but as 'a sort of missionary centre', but the gospel which was preached was, by this date, not one of temperance *per se* but of 'the improved public house'.

> If the work here is well done, the idea of public house improvement will spread to other places, partly through people who have seen it in operation here, and partly through the sort of cachet of respectability and publicity which any idea gets when the Government takes it up. Licensing Magistrates will increasingly tend to drop their antediluvian notions about increased facilities for drinking; brewers who have been starving their houses . . . will see what we are doing and will wake up to their own shortcomings.[56]

Sydney Nevile, who had served on the wartime CCB, enthusiastically endorsed all these sentiments. He served for long years as an unpaid technical adviser to the state run brewery largely because of his passion for promoting the idea of the improved public house.[57]

Nevile had campaigned for a 'constructive' Trade policy even before 1914, when he had been 'an object of suspicion; accused now of hypocrisy, now of insincerity, now of being a crank.'[58] After 1920, when employed by Whitbread, he took every opportunity to promote his ideas. 'We believed that a general improvement in tone and conduct would promote sobriety, and diminish the hostility of many social reformers.'[59] Whitbread and other brewers in the South East wanted to take advantage of the new swathes of suburbia to provide a completely different class of house. Large palatial premises were the fashion of the day: 'We were already thinking in terms of houses with a large room to seat say three hundred people for concerts, and perhaps half the number for meals, with other resources on a similar scale.' Although experience showed that more moderate-sized premises were usually more satisfactory, 'at that time spectacular houses appeared to be one method of attracting attention to the new movement'.[60] Whitbread set up a special Improved Public House Company in order to manage the catering and other demands posed by the new brand of houses. Even if the new houses were not on a gigantic scale, the transformation was often striking. H. L. Grimston of Barclay's recounted how, when one of his firm's improved houses was reopened, a woman came into the bar, took one look and cried 'Gor lummy, the House of Lords' before bolting. Grimston went after her and soothed her down with a free drink![61]

Apart from such temporary consumer reaction, the brewers' conception of the new model pub met with opposition from temperance enthusiasts, some social reformers, but also from many benches of magistrates. Structural alterations which increased facilities for drinking required the approval of local justices. Here, there were important regional variations. Some benches pursued an obstructive policy; the majority insisted on the surrender of numbers of redundant licences for the granting of a new one or a consent to a major refurbishment.[62] In Middlesex, however, magistrates were more sympathetic and even went so far as to urge on licensing benches throughout England the desirability of a uniform practice which would include the encouragement of the provision of large rooms and the elimination of small standing room only bars.[63] Feeling in some quarters ran high. Thus, during the 1920s, the whole tenor of debate had shifted towards the nature of the public house in a rapidly changing society where mobility and leisure patterns were in a state of flux.

Joynson-Hicks, who served as Home Secretary throughout Baldwin's 1924–29 Government, had not the slightest interest in opening up the licensing question. Inquiries on the subject, he warned, were 'always troublesome', compounded in his case by his teetotalism and ex-temperance background and the false expectations which this raised on the part of reformers.[64] However, elite opinion, even in his own party, remained anxious. His hands were somewhat forced by Lord Salisbury and Conservative peers who in 1924, when in opposition, had pledged the Conservatives to support the then Labour government's idea of an inquiry into disinterested management.[65] Accordingly in 1925 Salisbury, 'uneasy at an attitude of blank negation on Licensing Reform', persuaded the Cabinet to set up such an inquiry, maintaining that developments along these lines represented the best prospect of 'advance' on the question whilst acting fairly towards the Trade.[66]

The difficulties of the resulting departmental committee under the chairmanship of Lord Southborough revealed all too starkly the weakness of the claim of disinterested management to provide an alternative model of the Drink question. Its report in 1927 cast doubt on whether the two forms of liquor retailing – conventional retailing and disinterested control – were really as distinct as was commonly supposed. Many brewery owned houses were staffed by salaried managers, while it was open to question whether so-called disinterested management could be wholly disinterested, since managers here had an indirect interest in the 'success' of their houses in commercial terms, if only because of their prospects of promotion to management of a larger house. Despite a somewhat lukewarm endorsement of the achievements at Carlisle, the committee concluded that here was a useful experiment and recommended, without being specific, further trials of state management: 'Experimental work of this kind is, in our view, of great value . . . in our opinion the most important aspect of the State schemes, in their postwar development, is that they provide an unfettered opportunity for making and testing such experiments.'[67]

The somewhat vague report, dismissed by the Home Secretary as unhelpful, concealed a tortured proceedings about which the Chairman freely vented his feelings in private letters to the Home Secretary. Not only half his membership, including the 'most important', had deserted him for more pressing work, the remainder had quickly 'ceased to take an interest in the Terms of Reference', which had been couched rather narrowly, so as to exclude a general review of liquor licensing let alone any broader investigation into alcohol. Moreover, the whole issue of Drink and improved houses seemed 'as broad and deep as that of Catholic and Protestant, Free Trader and Protectionist, the Home Ruler and the Ulsterman, or the Red and White Rose. The divergences of opinion among witnesses and judges alike is inborn – it is in the blood.' Even the three KCs on the Committee had been inclined to base their conclusions on preconceptions rather than the evidence before them. The fundamental difficulty, however, was the fatal ambiguity about what was meant by the 'improved' pub. Was it to be a sanitised public house, where customers could drink a good quality product in decent but plain surroundings free from the pushing attentions of the landlord, or was it to be something in the forefront of leisure developments? In this connection Southborough cited 'Gracie's Banking', which was one of the Carlisle scheme's most ambitious developments at Annan across the Scottish border. Here were to be found a billiard saloon, a cheap restaurant, a cinema in an adjacent building, bowling and putting greens and an area for playing quoits. 'We saw women there playing bowls; young people can frequent it; it is not a place so I am informed, which would commend itself if the licensing justices were the authority. On the other hand it is very attractive and I can well imagine there would be an uproar if it and several other places somewhat of the same kind were suppressed.' Here was indeed an 'improvement' on the squalid beerhouses which such developments replaced, yet he could not help wondering if it was 'not a grave mistake to establish such places as . . . licensed premises of the character of a restaurant in which games are played? Do not such houses attract a class of person who would not go to a public-house? Youths and young women for instance? If people want to play games why should they go where intoxicating liquor is sold?'[68] Such questions went to the heart of the debate about the 'improved' public house. The fact was that the state run, 'disinterested' Carlisle scheme and the practices of the brewers were rapidly converging in the same direction, as Sydney Nevile had always hoped they would. The future was to lie in commercial exploitation of the pub as a leisure facility with as much profit coming from non-alcoholic ancillaries such as soft drinks, food and games as from the liquor itself. The pattern was already set, even though it was only as late as the 1960s that it became universal all over the country.

The Royal Commission, 1929–31

After the Southborough inquiry, Joynson-Hicks came under pressures from various quarters to take some action. Temperance reformers wanted various restrictions (especially on clubs and laws regarding the presence of children); high-minded supporters of disinterested management sought more experiments as recommended by Southborough; conversely many Tradesmen and some Unionist associations redoubled their hostility to state trading and demanded further relaxations of wartime restrictions; the licensed victuallers, for their part, had their own grievances on tied-houses and against the existence of clubs and the laws regarding 'off' licences.[69] Even some benches of magistrates demanded action of some sort against anomalies and abuses of the law.[70] Joynson-Hicks took the obvious line of least resistance and in 1929 recommended the appointment of a Royal Commission. The first Labour government had been on the point of making such a move in 1924, and there was a general feeling that it was over a generation since the last such major investigation on the subject.[71] But, for the government, the main concern was to shelve an awkward question, in this case conveniently until well after the next general election.[72] A separate and parallel commission was established for Scotland.

The Royal Commission, like its predecessor, displayed all the defects of its breed. It did not help matters that its Chairman, Lord Amulree (formerly Sir William McKenzie) was, within a year, appointed Air Minister in the second Labour government. Apart from raising a nice constitutional point as to the propriety of his continuing – just the sort of issue on which Home Office civil servants excelled in writing lengthy memoranda – this had the effect of limiting the initiatives which could come from the body. That no one was judged capable of substituting for him revealed the uninspired composition of the Commission which 'was mainly composed of persons who have publicly given expression to specific points of view on the licensing question.'[73] The result of such partisan composition was the usual plethora of minority reports or notes of dissent, provoked largely by the virtues or otherwise of state trading in Carlisle; only 16 out of 19 members signed the majority report. The brief of the Commission was not only to examine the licensing laws, but to examine 'the social and economic aspects of the question'. Evidence was taken on medical, economic and social aspects; but, by its nature, the question and answer format was not suited to producing original research.

The Commission was encouraged by the decline in drunkenness and intemperance since the 1890s. Social factors were held to be important here, but war inspired restrictions, especially regarding opening hours, were also given their due. Against this, the Commissioners felt that the possibilities of further state action to reduce undesirable excess drinking 'have not yet been exhausted'.[74] The majority report ruled out radical departures such as local option or state purchase (the latter on financial grounds); it was, however, generally favourable to disinterested management at Carlisle, where the public monopoly control was seen as a matter of key importance, and suggested in rather cautious and vague terms that further trials in public ownership might be made.[75] The Commissioners believed the question of improved public houses to be a matter of the 'greatest importance': the best type of improved pubs were 'a direct discouragement to insobriety'. Licensing justices and the Trade should be encouraged to pursue a policy of improvement and the report suggested various technical changes in licensing procedures to facilitate this.[76] In addition, the report recommended the establishment of a National Licensing Commission, 'an indispensable part of a satisfactory system of licensing administration.' This would allow a more active policy of licence reduction and improvement; at present the Home Office was hampered by a lack of direct administrative responsibility. The proposed new Commission should 'be divorced as far as possible from Parliament and Government'. It would play a role in stimulating schemes of licence reduction; the delimitation of licensing policy for new 'development areas'; the facilitation of extension of public ownership in appropriate areas and the collection of data on licensing matters.[77] A year of economic and political crises, 1931 was scarcely the most propitious of times for a Royal Commission to report, and its rather unexciting suggestions attracted little interest outside specialist circles. In a broader sense, too, the Commission came at the wrong time. Many of the issues to which it devoted attention, like local option, disinterested management and licence reduction, were really by now *passé*. By contrast, other concerns upon which the Commission touched, such as the medical effects of alcohol, drinking and motoring, the impact of advertising and the role of alcohol in the leisured society, were to attract attention a generation later.

New issues: medical aspects; Drink and advertising

It is appropriate to conclude this survey of the interwar decades by touching upon some of these new concerns. Ever since the 1890s, medical opinion had come round to a more critical view of the physiological merits of alcohol, even if the more lurid claims of prohibitionists were not accepted. There had been division between the teetotal, temperance doctors and those concerned to see alcoholism as a medical problem of addiction, who clustered around the Society for the Study of Inebriety. Now a further school had arisen, initially based around the Scientific Advisory Committee to the CCB. The focus here was a concern with the economic rather than the medical effects of alcohol. D'Abernon had been keen to sponsor research on the effects of alcoholic intake upon such activities as typewriting, memory tests and muscular activity such as weight-lifting.[78] After the war, work continued along these lines in the Medical Research Council and by H. M. Vernon and others.[79] Lord Astor also commissioned such work as part of his 'Drink Enquiry', which had separate panels of experts investigating such aspects as poverty, national efficiency, public expenditure, medical and physiological effects.[80] The position of these 'moderationalists' was that small quantities of alcohol had no effect upon the individual's capacity to function normally, but that significant intakes had an adverse effect. This group stressed its 'scientific' credentials and largely succeeded in establishing their paradigm as the ascendant one. However, as Joanne Woiak has pointed out, the results were far from conclusive and the research 'was clearly designed to provide a scientific rationale for particular drink control measures, and furthermore was sponsored by the very people who put forward these measures.'[81] However, after the winding up of the CCB little or no research work was directly sponsored by government departments into the area of alcohol and national efficiency. It was quite beyond the scope or the inclination of the Home Office. Nor does the Ministry of Health seem to have been concerned at the medical aspects: the only ministry file in the Public Record Office in this period which the author has unearthed relates to the question of hygiene in glasses and other apparatus used in public houses![82]

The issue of advertising, by contrast, exploded shortly after the Royal Commission reported. Temperance opinion had always disliked the way a 'pernicious' substance was allowed to be freely advertised and the Royal Commission shared some of this unease, estimating the annual total spent as being at least £2 million. In arguments that foreshadowed the later debates about smoking, the Commission felt that this advertising was not limited to mere brand substitution but had the effect of swelling total demand, in particular appealing to the 'rising generation'. It expressed 'some alarm' at this, but was at a loss to suggest any countermeasures.[83] It was the rash decision of the brewers to experiment with collective advertising which really sparked off controversy. Impressed by the 'Guinness is good for you' adverts and by a successful advertising campaign by the Spanish government to arrest falling sales of sherry, leading brewers suggested a similar campaign to combat falling beer sales. The Brewers' Society appointed Nevile to chair a small committee to carry the matter further. Here, he received the enthusiastic backing of the newly appointed director of the Society, Sir Edgar Sanders, who had previously been General Manager at Carlisle. Sir Edgar had become an enthusiast for advertising when employed by Lord Leverhulme, and now went around addressing various county associations of brewers to rally support for a scheme.[84] But it was a copy of his rather ill-judged remarks, intended only for circulation among brewers, which caused something of a storm when, to his dismay, it was obtained and then gleefully disseminated by the temperance lobby.[85] Sir Edgar called for 'a great national effort to arrest the falling consumption' of beer. 'We want', he declared, 'new customers. We want to get the beer-drinking habit instilled into thousands, almost millions, of young men who do not at present know the taste of beer.' He further raised the spectre of the corruption of the press when he stated: '. . . if we begin advertising in the Press we shall see that the continuation of our advertising is contingent upon the fact that we get editorial support as well in the same paper. In that way it is wonderful how you can educate public opinion generally without making it too obvious that there is a publicity campaign behind it all.'[86]

Sir Edgar's remarks had the immediate effect of uniting the temperance forces which had hitherto been in a state of disarray over the issue of state management. Henry Carter's Methodist Church Temperance and Social Welfare Department joined the UKA in supporting a programme of legislation.[87] An 'emergency council' was formed with the Archbishop of York, Philip Snowden and Astor as joint presidents, and another 70 vice presidents comprising eminent people from all walks of life. Because of the furore, the brewers seriously considered abandoning the plan but proceeded cautiously.[88] The result was widespread advertising hoardings with the theme of 'Beer is Best' (sometimes impishly defaced with the words 'Let Alone' by temperance artists). In 1935 Lord Arnold, who had been Paymaster General in the previous Labour government, introduced a bill into the Lords to ban such advertisements, arguing that it was the duty of the state to restrict and control such highly undesirable advertising, just as it was its right and duty to restrict the sale of alcohol. This was rejected by the government on the grounds of freedom, but the brewers were sufficiently disturbed to think it 'vital' that the bill be rejected by a large majority of their lordships.[89] The Ministry of Health interviewed Saunders on the subject but felt no inclination to take action.[90] This incident offers a foretaste of some of the issues of the post–1945 period: the corporate and commercial power of the drinks industry, the manipulation of the mass market, the concern for health and the role of government as a regulator.

The interwar decades had indeed seen a substantial change in the nature of the Drink question. They had begun with a lively debate about national efficiency and the prospect that prohibition might make advances in the international arena. State purchase had support in some quarters, and disinterested management had seemed to offer an alternative model of temperance restriction. But, after 1920, it gradually became clear that the decline in *per capita* consumption and of intemperance achieved in the war was no mere blip but part of a national trend. No longer could the 'Drink Problem' be described, in the much quoted words of the Royal Commission of the 1890s, as a 'gigantic evil'. The licensing laws gradually secured general acceptance and the strength of the temperance movement ebbed away, although it retained a significant amount of support among Labour MPs. The prohibitionists were obviously greatly discouraged by the failure and repeal of prohibition in the United States. Local option ceased to appeal and gradually the idea of disinterested management also lost its integrity and its force, to become subsumed in the general issue of the 'improved' public house. The Carlisle scheme had presented a most interesting experiment in social administration, but the distinctive point of the operation became lost to sight, as the administration there lost its original *raison d'être*. When, in 1937, the Conservative MP for the City, Brigadier-General Spiers, moved an adjournment debate on the subject, the focus of his attack was simply the 'socialist' nature of the 'coercive' regime there, the temperance issues scarcely surfaced.[91] In this new climate, there was opportunity for temperance forces to act in a more harmonious manner, as shown by their front against the advertising of beer and their subsequent adoption of a united programme of restrictionist reform. The decades of 'improvement' had changed not only the social context of the Drink question, but also the nature of the Trade and the political context in which the issues were debated. New aspects, such as health, advertising, drink/driving, regulation of monopoly and town planning, were emerging.

9
Policy Fragmentation 1945–70: Three Case Studies

Drink had a low political salience in mid-twentieth-century Britain. The temperance movement was now both weak in terms of popular support and remote from political influence.[1] Nor was the drink industry yet organised into a powerful, leisure pressure group lobbying for shifts in policy. In contrast to 1914–18, despite some lobbying in nonconformist circles[2], no political attention was paid to alcohol in the Second World War, except for such technical matters as compensation for bombed public houses. *Per capita* consumption levels had declined sharply since 1900 and were low by international standards. The World Health Organisation (WHO) put Britain bottom of the league in terms of severe alcoholism.[3] Nor did Drink offer much anxiety on account of public order or in relation to other social ills. In short, there was a widespread consensus in government and among the political and social elite that Drink was no longer a 'problem'. Nevertheless, the 1945–1970 period is interesting insofar as new alcohol related questions came on the political agenda, albeit not as major issues. Drink also offers us an insight into the changing nature of the policy process in postwar Britain. Until the 1930s, debate had largely centred on a single issue: the 'temperance question', which was generally seen as a social problem in its own right, although one having ramifications into other areas. Contemporaries' perceptions and approaches to it varied enormously, but stemmed from the six Victorian models which we analysed in Chapter 2. The First World War saw some redefinition along lines of national efficiency with new interests and parties becoming involved; nevertheless the issue was still largely seen as a *distinct* problem, and the focus for handling it lay in a combination of licensing controls and taxation policy. After 1945, there was a fragmentation of alcohol policy. Aspects of Drink became hitched up with other concerns and the issue was defined in various ways. In place of the earlier patterns of interplay between political parties and well organised pressure groups, with politicians, social reformers, bishops or other notables sometimes mediating between them, we can see the development of discrete policy centres with various fluid networks interacting with them. In place of the pivotal role played by the Home Office and for a while the CCB, we find different departments occupying these centres. Thus, the Home Office is interested in public order aspects and the narrow question of licensing; Town and Country Planning in drinking as a leisure activity; Transport in drink and driving; Health in alcoholism and drinking as a public health issue; Trade and Industry in the economic aspects of drinking; and the Exchequer in the fiscal and financial aspects of alcohol consumption. In the latter part of the twentieth century, a variety of policy discourses ebb and flow and coexist with each other. Such discourses reflect the dominant concerns and ideological viewpoints of the professional and voluntary groups which make up the various policy communities as well as the prevailing fashions and dominant concerns of broader policy areas, like the health service, road safety or retailing. In this chapter, rather than attempting a comprehensive history of the state and alcohol, we will examine three case studies of policy-making in the twenty-five years after 1945: liquor licensing and the New Towns; policy towards alcoholism; and drink/driving.

The New Towns and state control, 1945–52

Planning had become the watchword of the day by 1945. The bold creation of New Towns was both the expression and symbol of the new, rational social order which politicians and administrators aimed to achieve. The story of the New Towns has been frequently studied, but the legislation, passed by the Attlee government in 1949, to place all alcohol outlets in them under state control, has been ignored.[4] Yet, in its original conception, the plans would have placed whole swathes of the Home Counties under a Carlisle-style management, since intermediate areas between nearby New Towns were to be included. The legislation and its subsequent repeal by the Conservatives, before it became effective, caused tensions within Whitehall and controversy outside.

The garden city movement had been linked to liquor licensing from the very beginning. The Victorian, paternalist pioneers of model communities, like Saltaire and Bourneville, had banned alcohol from them. However, Ebenezer Howard in the 1920s had envisaged the new garden cities as adopting a variety of expedients, including conducting the liquor trade themselves.[5] Lord Reith's 1946 New Towns Committee, which laid out the principles for the new bodies, broke new ground by seeing public houses as providing vital leisure and refreshment facilities and a means of cementing the new communities.[6] However, the New Towns Act of 1946 was silent on the subject.[7] The Whitehall body responsible for the New Towns was the Ministry of Town and Country Planning (MTCP), established in 1942. This department was already administering a scheme, based on recommendations of the wartime Morris Committee, whereby licensing planning bodies were set up in areas that had suffered extensive bomb damage, and this involved extensive cooperation with the brewers.[8] Here, committees negotiated with interested parties for the removal of old licences into new overspill areas, often across the existing licensing areas. In March 1946, however, civil servants at the MTCP quickly realised that such a scheme could not easily work in the proposed New Towns where the population would be drawn from a variety of areas. Any general reform of the licensing process in accordance with modern planning thinking, although desirable, would be bound to be controversial and it was best to work out some transitional mechanisms, such as the creation of a 'central clearing house'.[9] However, they soon faced a difficulty on account of sharp divisions in the Trade between the central Brewers' Society, dominated by the large companies anxious to 'give the public the service they require' in the new communities, and the Essex and Hertfordshire Brewers' Association, representing the local brewers, who resented this outside intrusion and wanted to supply new houses themselves.[10]

For those at the MTCP, the matter was essentially a technical one and they saw it in the light of planning policy. However, the sudden involvement of the Home Office sharply raised the stakes. Its interest in the question actually had a long gestation. At the height of the war, Herbert Morrison, when Home Secretary, had enthusiastically asked his permanent secretary, Sir Alexander Maxwell, to prepare a case for Cabinet to extend the state controlled Carlisle scheme all over the country as part of a reconstruction policy. After researching the question Maxwell, although seeing 'big social and economic advantages', reluctantly concluded that he could find little ammunition to justify such a scheme, but that the issue was clearly one for general planning and postwar development.[11] However, the Home Office was already responsible for the Carlisle state management area and, in 1944–45, considered extending its area and the scope of the scheme in the interests of assisting economic development in Cumberland, for example providing better hotel accommodation. Chuter Ede, Morrison's successor as Home Secretary in the Attlee Government, was wary of the likely political furore, but suggested consulting Morrison's Lord President's Committee before authorising inquiries which he hoped would be 'on somewhat wider lines than that proposed.'[12] The ground was, therefore, exceptionally fertile when J. J. Mallon, the Warden of Toynbee Hall, wrote to Sir Alexander Maxwell in August 1946, arguing the case for state control of licensing in the New Towns. Mallon had promoted the campaign in the Labour party for public control of the Drink trade in the 1920s. He now pointed to the unfortunate lack of any concerted policy before the war in new suburban estates, and argued that the New Towns provided an ideal opportunity for disinterested management to allow 'houses to be run in such a way as to afford really good social facilities without a vested interest in pushing the sale of liquor. The public houses should form part of the necessary social facilities and not be regarded as multiple shops for the sale of liquor.'[13] Mallon then energetically mobilised a lobby, attracting the support of Henry Carter, Seebhom Rowntree, Lord Harmsworth, Earl Lytton and R. L. Reiss, the Vice-Chairman of the Town and Country Planning Association.[14] In October 1946, a powerful deputation, including several MPs, argued their case before Lewis Silkin (the Minister at MTCP), J. Westwood (the Scottish Secretary), and Sir Frank Newsom (a senior Home Office official). The public house, they argued, had failed to adapt and offered 'nothing to the youth of today'; here was a means whereby the pub could become the centre of recreation.[15] The ministers present – as well as Chuter Ede and Maxwell who were unable to attend – were strongly impressed by these arguments. Maxwell privately regretted that 'we did not think of this question at the time when the New Towns Bill was being prepared; it will now, I fear, be difficult to get the necessary legislation.'[16]

Mallon's lobby was supported by a rather disparate, but potentially powerful, coalition. There were socialists who saw this as a logical area for nationalisation, rather like the road haulage industry which the Labour government was now preparing to take over, all the more appealing because of the brewers' long support for the Conservative party. Others, like the Rev. Henry Carter and Seebhom Rowntree, approaching from the temperance angle, had no interest in this, but saw the idea as the culmination of the old principle of disinterested management.[17] Yet others, such as Reiss, were attracted by the town planning aspects. However, although their minister, Lewis Silkin, seemed impressed, civil servants at the MTCP quickly became uneasy, and then exasperated, at the turn of events. They wanted to use the existing planning and New Town machinery to tackle the problem.[18] They complained that the 'the Home Office and the Scottish Office were rather anxious to load the dice in favour of State ownership and to sweep aside the provisions of the Licensing Planning Act'. Conditions in Carlisle were hardly typical and the rather antiseptic public houses there could not fulfil the role envisaged by Lord Reith's Committee. Moreover, the large brewers, with whom the ministry was cooperating well, were pressing to become involved.[19] Finally, the policy would be reckless since the New Town Act obliged the new development corporations to safeguard the right of those already resident in the designated areas to carry on their businesses 'as far as practicable'.[20] There then followed a highly technical – and at times tetchy – series of exchanges between the MTCP and the Home Office about the nature of the licensing processes as they affected the New Towns.[21]

In the early summer of 1947, with matters bogged down in technicalities, the young Evelyn Sharp – later to find fame as the redoubtable 'Dame' in the Crossman Diaries – began to handle the issue for the MTCP. She saw at once that the policy of state management could bring wider dangers for her department. The brewers would object very strongly and the MTCP might be charged with some breach of faith, particularly by the existing liquor interests in the designated areas. Furthermore, it would have a knock on effect on the costs of extinguishing redundant licences in London. Even more seriously, there might be adverse repercussions for the popularity of the whole New Towns enterprise.[22] The Brewers' Society did indeed get wind of the state management idea, and mounted an intensive lobby of its own.[23] A high level delegation met both Chuter Ede and Lewis Silkin and their officials in October 1947. Sydney Nevile, who was their principal speaker, stressed that they had 'for many years been doing all they could to improve public houses' despite prejudices against them; state management would be a 'great discouragement to brewers in their plans for public house improvement in general'.[24] At a subsequent meeting, the brewers sensed the divisions between the two ministries, with the MTCP being more favourable to them.[25] The brewers stressed that they had long experience in providing attractive environments, a wide range of choice of product and landlords who, in contrast to state managers, could foster friendship and confidence with the public.[26]

Matters became even more uncomfortable for civil servants at the MTCP when the chairmen of the New Town development corporations began to take umbrage. They were not all of a piece on the matter, some favouring state management, some private enterprise, while others a third solution of control by the development corporations themselves. However, members of the Harlow corporation were reported to be disturbed at the likely repercussions of such controversy upon the whole project.[27] Lord Reith at Hemel Hempsted doubted whether state management was remotely suitable, urging someone in the MTCP to get in touch with 'the Carlisle panjandrum' to assess the prospects: if the Home Office wanted the state to control drink outlets, then it was better if the development corporation did so 'since the Corporation is, after, all a form of the State'.[28] Evelyn Sharp seized on this 'third option', informing the Home Office in November 1947 that it was 'pretty certain' her minister would favour individual control by the corporations, a suggestion that Newsom of the Home Office found 'rather disconcerting', as such a course had been explicitly ruled out in an earlier draft paper endorsed by all three ministers for the Lord President's Council.[29] The MTCP, stumped on this, thought it best not to reply to this letter, but recommended – in classic Whitehallese – the line that 'having regard to the strong views expressed by several of the corporation chairman, the minister is not now satisfied that we can dismiss this alternative without further consideration.'[30]

This rearguard action bought time but was ultimately to no avail as the MTCP, a new and junior ministry, was outgunned by the Home and Scottish Offices and also faced the enthusiasm of Herbert Morrison. In April 1948, the Lord President's Committee duly approved the Home Office plan, which was in turn endorsed by the Cabinet in July, the Home Office meanwhile stressing how the Carlisle model involved a degree of decentralised management.[31] Nevertheless, the announcement of legislation led to great unhappiness among some of the corporation chairs. Lord Reith, for example, declared bitterly that the news had come as a 'great shock' to him, and Sir Thomas Bennett and Mr Heal complained that the corporations were being 'set at naught' by the Home Office, a department 'with which Corporations had no control and over whom they had no influence'.[32] Morrison was warned that Reith was 'violently' opposed to the policy, and the permanent secretary of the MTCP warned that he was having 'a great struggle' to dissuade the chairmen and others in the corporations from openly opposing the proposed bill. They were particularly sensitive at being gagged by collective 'ministerial responsibility' since they were not members of the government and some even were independent members of the House of Lords.[33] They also feared lest the New Towns might come to be regarded as general experimental areas and consequently 'a lure for cranks of all sorts'. Consequently, the permanent secretary impressed on Silkin the need to soothe the 'injured feelings' in 'our corporations'.[34] Members of the influential Town and Country Planning Association, with which the MTCP had a close relationship, were also upset that Reiss's presence on Mallon's original deputation had been taken as an endorsement of their views.[35] Disputes between the MTCP and the Home Office on technicalities continued with mounting acrimony throughout the winter.[36]

By the end of 1948, the issue had reached the public arena and a great deal of lobbying from interested parties took place. Seebohm Rowntree reported that the Home Secretary was very concerned to get support from influential people from all parties in support of the measure, especially from the town and country planning movement, and he, Astor, Mallon, and his secretary G. R. Lavers did their best to stir this up.[37] The Trade press carried highly critical accounts and a gamekeeper turned poacher, J. S. Eagle, formerly General Manager of Carlisle but now employed by Whitbread, wrote articles in several national newspapers, much to the indignation of Home Office officials.[38] Eric Tetley, the Chairman of the Brewers' Society, wrote to Herbert Morrison expressing the 'surprise and dismay' of the Society at the proposed legislation which had been undertaken without any warning or consultation with the industry. The industry had built up a track record of providing improved public houses and had been looking forward to planning to provide for the New Towns.[39] The Trade managed to patch up its own differences in the face of a common enemy and the Brewers' Society set up an Action Committee. This met weekly to mobilise a public opinion offensive while encouraging and coordinating grass roots activity.[40] There was much hostile coverage in the popular press, with talk of pubs being renamed the 'Attlee Arms' or the 'Morrison Shelter'.[41]

The issue seemed to have potential for turning into a party political controversy over Drink, a scaled down 1908 episode. Morrison certainly seemed keen to up the stakes. In his own hand, he drafted a furious riposte to Col Tetley complaining about the 'hysterical propaganda' in the *Morning Advertiser* and reminisced about how the Trade 'gone into politics against the Liberal Government' of his youth, warning that if it entered the party political arena again 'it would be inviting serious consideration as to its future'. Civil servants at the Home Office expurgated all of this from the official reply, but this did not stop the Lord President from using nearly identical language in the peroration of his second reading speech in the Commons.[42] Other supporters of state management excitedly entertained visions of the Labour government putting the nationalisation of the drink trade in their manifesto for the 1950 election, even fantasising that it might replace steel nationalisation as a priority.[43] However, this assessment was quite exaggerated as few Labour MPs saw alcohol as a major issue, and many had been cool about the New Towns Licensing Act (with 2 voting against and no less than 87 abstaining). Moreover, sections of the temperance movement, like the UKA, remained deeply opposed to the concept of public control. Nevertheless, the large brewers were certainly alarmed, fearing the measure would be 'the thin end of the wedge of nationalisation of the industry'.[44] However, they took the view that a cautious approach was best. Both at a private meeting with Lord Woolton and at a friendly meeting with the Home Affairs Committee of the Conservative party, it was agreed that there should be no organised opposition from the shareholders, and instead the focus should be on grass roots meetings emanating from the retailers.[45] Later, the Trade should avoid any partisan identification at the forthcoming general election.[46] The large brewers were actually far more worried about the moves against the tied-house system, which attracted support among Labour MPs, when Geoffrey Bing began tabling a series of private members bills on the subject. This was dangerous, since it threatened to drive a wedge between the brewers and sections of the retail trade.[47] The danger of the New Towns legislation was less its direct effect than its potential to undermine relations with the governing party. The softly-softly approach, moreover, soon bore dividends in the shape of concessions from the Home Office. The most important here were the withdrawal of the idea of state control for all 'adjacent and intermediate' areas, and an agreement to give local advisory committees discretionary power to allow existing licences in the New Towns to continue in private hands.[48] After their return to office in October 1951, Conservative ministers rapidly decided to repeal the New Towns provisions of the 1949 Licensing Act before they had become operational, and this was achieved the following year with no political or public excitement.[49]

Several interesting features emerge from the New Towns episode. Firstly, state management was now debated largely in terms of planning rather than disinterested management or temperance. The discourse and terms of debate had shifted. However, the question was one where technical issues blended in some way with broader political agendas of socialism or temperance. Secondly, the policy process was heavily influenced by the bureaucratic interests involved. Both the MTCP and the Home Office had their own interests and perceptions of the problem.[50] Both, moreover, represented important client groups, the town and country planning movement and the Carlisle scheme respectively, for which they acted as patrons. Ministers had a broader interest and officials at the MTCP were handicapped by Silkin's sympathy for state management; but even he was an enthusiastic defender of his department's interest on the more technical aspects.[51] Thirdly, the policy process now revealed the involvement of broader para-government bodies such as the New Town corporations whose support was necessary for the successful implementation of a policy, but who did not fit easily into the workings of classic ministerial responsibility. Fourthly, the gestation period of the policy reveals how the issue came onto the agenda as a result of technicalities and this, as much as ministerial direction or clear vision, was the driving force behind many of the early moves. Finally, the issue shows how dramatically the framework of policy debate can alter. Viewed from an age influenced by New Right faith in the market, the idea that the state, in whatever guise, was best placed to provide leisure facilities appears extraordinary.

Policy towards alcoholism, 1945–75

If the New Towns initiative saw new policy objectives grafted on to old solutions, policy towards alcoholism was more of a *tabula rasa*. As we saw in Chapter 4, the issue of 'habitual inebriates' had attracted attention in Victorian times. A medical lobby had grown up, centred around the Society for the Study of Addiction, that maintained that alcohol abuse was the result of a medical addiction. The moves to establish institutional asylums for 'inebriates', based on the rather weak Habitual Drunkards legislation, was stillborn, and there was little coherent policy pressure from this direction partly on account of differences between biomedical and psychotherapeutic approaches.[52] By 1945, medical treatment for people with alcohol problems was virtually nonexistent in the National Health Service (NHS), and what hospital treatment there was came under the aegis of mental health wards of hospitals, themselves Cinderellas of the NHS.[53] Neither the British Medical Association (BMA) nor the Medical Research Council (MRC) was interested in the issue in the early 1950s. For its part, the Ministry of Health (MoH) had no proactive stance on the issue of drinking, considering alcohol consumption to be neither a problem nor a health related issue. When Home Office officials in 1957 wrote to ask if the MoH could help reduce drunkenness among young people, there being an upsurge of offences, they were rebuffed with the comment that this was 'a social rather than a health problem' and so outside the Ministry's competence.[54]

However, a combination of factors was bringing about change. One was the emergence in the United States of a strong paradigm that saw alcoholism in terms of a treatable disease, rather than resulting from individual moral failings or social conditions. Such a viewpoint was particularly pressed by psychiatrists, who in turn dominated a WHO committee in 1951, which portrayed alcoholism as a serious social problem that governments, the health services and voluntary bodies ought to tackle. Throughout the early 1950s, the WHO provided a focus for international pressure on the subject, as well as a definition of an alcoholic. E. M. Jellinek, a consultant to the WHO, developed and publicised the disease concept of alcoholism and came to influence sections of psychiatric and medical opinion in Britain.[55] Jellinek's view was that alcoholism was both a misunderstood and underestimated problem. His estimate was that there might be some 400,000 people in Britain suffering from various forms of the 'disease', most of whom were a far cry from the vagrants or mentally ill persons on the street who tended to be identified with the condition. Professional opinion in Britain was not entirely united on the issue, but the addiction disease model became more generally intellectually acceptable. It also had the advantage of bolstering the claims of expertise of those psychiatrists and other professionals who worked in this area. There were, however, some significant differences in approach. One centre was Warlingham Park Hospital in Surrey where Max Glatt, a psychiatrist, after trial and error, had established a dedicated in-patient treatment unit for alcoholics that combined drug treatment with group therapy sessions. Results here were relatively favourable. By 1955, Glatt was advocating in *The Lancet* and other medical fora the establishment of a network of regional special treatment centres.[56] Civil servants at the MoH were well aware of the Warlingham Park approach. Another centre of experimentation was the Maudsley hospital, London, under the Dean of Psychiatry, D. L. Davies, which spread influence throughout a wider network. Here, the emphasis was more on drug treatment but also on the wider socio-psychological contexts of alcoholics. Alcoholism here was seen as being related to other psychological problems.[57] Alcoholics Anonymous (AA), voluntary associations of alcoholics seeking mutual self-help, another influence from the United States, began to flourish in Britain during this time and enjoyed close links with the Warlingham Hospital, where their group therapy approach was actively encouraged.[58] An AA deputation met civil servants at the MoH in 1954 to urge the case for more hospital beds specially dedicated for alcoholics, as was the case in the United States. Although all these bodies had many important differences of approach, they were united in a common belief that alcoholism was a medical disease which deserved more attention from the authorities and for which 'science' could provide an ultimate answer. Their terms of discourse helped define the nature of the problem.[59]

During the 1950s, however, officials at the MoH remained cautious. For one thing, there did not seem to be any evidence of a massive or pressing unmet demand for services of the NHS on this issue: feedback from GPs showed they diagnosed few patients as alcoholics, and there was little evidence of alcoholics not being able to be admitted to hospitals. Secondly, they were aware of the differences in approaches among the medical and psychiatric professions. AA were firmly told, in 1953, that medical treatment was the responsibility of the doctor in charge and that the minister did not feel he should himself sponsor applications of any particular treatment or therapy.[60] Dr Mackay, who after 1954 was senior medical officer at the Board of Control, the regulatory body over the mental health field, was sympathetic to the medical approach, but he maintained the MoH's position of seeing alcoholism as a symptom rather than a disease and hence an element of broader mental health problems. A variety of different treatments and approaches were therefore appropriate.[61] Finally, there was great uncertainty about the prevalence of the problem. Jellinek's high estimates were contradicted by far lower estimates based on a survey of GPs by Dr Parr in 1957.[62] A civil servant in 1956, faced with constructing a reply to a correspondent regarding statistics of alcohol related disease or accidents, minuted that 'I very much doubt whether we have any report or statistics on the incidence of disease relating from alcohol (there is no mention of the subject in the 1954 report of the CMO)'; the correspondent was therefore referred to the National Temperance Society as the most likely source of information![63]

Towards the end of the 1950s, there was a significant shift. The MoH was faced with handling an increasingly critical correspondence with GPs, clergy, MPs and others complaining about the inadequacy of information on the subject or the lack of suitable treatment facilities.[64] In 1957, the Chief Medical Officer's Report mentioned alcoholism at some length, conceding that the condition had a public health dimension.[65] Alcoholism itself, however, was of low public salience and it was only a surge in drunkenness convictions at this period that impelled any initiative. The BMA and the Magistrates' Association had set up a joint committee to consider matters of common interest relative to the medical aspects of legal offences and, in 1958, this body turned to the problem of the rehabilitation of vagrants, and hence to the more general issue of alcoholic addiction. The Committee was impressed by the experimental approach of the treatment unit at Warlingham Park and co-opted Glatt on to it. This seemed to offer the prospect of a 'cure' rather than a mere temporary detoxification provided by an 'ordinary' mental hospital. Accordingly, it recommended the establishment of regional specialist in-patient alcohol treatment centres on a regional basis, linked to psychiatric medicine.[66]

These recommendations surfaced in the public domain in 1961, but the MoH was already becoming anxious. 'Alcoholism', minuted one official in September 1960, 'seems to be a matter about which we are gradually coming under increasing pressure and I have the feeling it would be wise to give it some special attention.'[67] Interdepartmental meetings with the Home Office and the Prisons Service followed and it was agreed to ask the Standing Committee on the Mental Health Advisory Committee for advice on the best treatment and to encourage research through the MRC or a social survey to discover the incidence of alcoholism.[68] Such a move had dangers for 'it is almost inevitable whatever the terms of reference we devise, that we shall get recommendation for something to be done'; it was 'the sort of inquiry that is likely to strike the headlines and will be almost certainly represented as indicating an alarming increase in alcoholism'.[69] However, these developments coincided with a change of personnel among the medical advisers of the ministry, with Dr (Brigadier) Phillipson taking over responsibility for all addiction issues. Phillipson was attracted to the idea of alcohol units and quickly got to know all the leading actors in the alcohol field.[70] The move to favour specialist treatment units also coincided with more general developments in the NHS. One was the desire of Enoch Powell, the minister after 1960, to bring about more planned, evenly distributed care. Another was a shift of emphasis towards building new better designed hospitals rather than providing more beds. This went along with a greater emphasis on more specialist units in general; in fact, medical advances and changing practice meant that there was spare ward space which was suited to the development of alcohol or drug addiction units.[71] All these different factors came together to produce a policy shift within the MoH. Group therapy was now seen as 'an essential part of the treatment, and was much preferable to the present practice of a large number of hospitals treating very small numbers of patients'. Officials recognised that 'this would involve a change in stated policy'.[72] The culmination of the new policy came in the recommendation to Regional Health Authorities of the creation of specialist in-patient units for the treatment of alcoholism and alcoholic psychosis,[73] although the references to the effectiveness and desirability of group therapy were much toned down after representations from those professionals sceptical of its effectiveness.[74]

The policy shift was, in reality, far less dramatic than it may have appeared and certainly did not represent any conversion by the lay civil servants in the MoH. A variety of factors had pointed to the need for action along *some* novel lines, and the Warlingham Park model, pioneered and advocated by Glatt and his associates, ideally fitted the bill. It was a 'way of being seen to take action', whereas advocacy of the Maudsley approach of treating alcoholism alongside other mental disorders meant more of the same.[75] The 'policy solution' had two further advantages. Firstly, Dr Davies and the Maudsley school, while sceptical of the value of in-patient specialist units, saw the initiative as a way of raising the profile of alcoholism, directing resources towards it and initiating change.[76] Hence, damaging public disputation could be avoided. Secondly, under the organisation of the NHS, the Regional Health Authorities and not the ministry officials were responsible for the implementation of the policy. In practice, the implementation was patchy and allowed a great deal of flexibility. Only thirteen treatment units were operational by 1968.[77] Moreover, Betsy Thom's research has shown that 'from the start, the units differed in their approach to treatment and in the range of services offered – a reflection, in part, of differences between Regions in perceptions of local need, of available resources, and of past history of service provision'.[78] An extreme example was All Saints Hospital, Birmingham, where the newly appointed Medical Director in February 1964 found that the 'regional unit' for alcohol treatment, which the ministry had been assured was in existence, consisted only of a cocktail cabinet which had been purchased by a predecessor to provide authentic atmosphere for aversion therapy. This cabinet had been locked away in a 'small side ward in a remote part of the hospital' pending the planning of the unit which had never materialised![79] Such elasticity in the policy allowed for considerable diversity of practice among the policy implementers and specialists.[80]

By the 1960s, officials at the MoH had come to accept that alcoholism was a medical condition, that it should be treated under the NHS and that the ministry had the responsibility of disseminating information and guiding policy on the matter, subject to the advice of professionals. However, it would be wrong to portray them as wholehearted converts to the disease and treatment model of alcoholism. For one thing, they remained uncertain about the size of the problem and conscious of the weakness of the research base upon which policy was grounded. There was, for example, an absence of data about the age and social class of those currently treated.[81] Even in 1965, it was conceded that 'little is known in the Department' about research in the field and any national survey would be 'difficult and expensive'.[82] Secondly, they were extremely averse to proactive promotion of any treatment facilities. Alcoholism was referred to as a 'submerged problem'; there was a danger of being 'overwhelmed' by artificially generated demand; money and personnel might be diverted 'away from other fields which might be regarded as more urgent'.[83] Officials were reluctant to take initiatives in an area of uncertainty: 'Although we should like to do what we can to prevent alcoholism it is not a subject on which issue of general publicity is likely to help much at all.'[84] A third and more fundamental issue was a degree of scepticism about the definition of alcoholism itself. Jellinek's attempts to refine the concept by classifying different types of the 'disease' seemed to suggest that the whole concept was merging into the more general and familiar one of intemperance, or what soon became termed 'problem drinking'. Officials were reluctant to go down this route, and one of the arguments against suggestions for health education on the subject was that 'we must obviously be careful to avoid seeming to campaign against drinking as such'.[85]

This somewhat ambivalent approach is also to be found in the MoH's response to the parallel establishment of the National Council on Alcoholism (NCA) in 1962. This had its roots in the voluntary sector, with the initiative coming from the Rowntree trust (W. B. Morrell being a particular advocate), doctors, various churchmen and some connected with the temperance movement.[86] The idea of this initiative, which was again modelled on practice in the United States, was to provide information about alcoholism and also advice, ideally through local centres. The national Marriage Guidance Council provided some sort of model for the new body.[87] However, the original objectives also included the more ambitious goals of conducting research on alcoholism, and generally 'gradually to create a "climate" of opinion in which this serious illness can be discussed, admitted and accepted without shame or self-reproach'. The body saw itself as providing leadership 'to plan a long range approach' to the problems and in convincing '"decision makers" in Government and Industry that money and manpower can be saved, and much unhappiness avoided, by a new, objective approach to alcoholism'.[88] However, the focus of the NCA was rather distant from the political pressures placed upon the ministry. In all its pamphlets and publicity, the NCA stressed the way alcoholism affected the ability of 'normal' people to function properly in their everyday lives. Examples it offered included such vignettes of middle-class life as the father with a drink problem having to ask an uncle to stand in to give his daughter away on her wedding day.[89] By contrast, most of the high profile attention to alcoholism centred on the problem of down and outs, or what was termed 'Skid Row' alcoholics. A series of awkward parliamentary questions from MPs in the early 1960s focused on this and, after 1964, the Chancellor of the Duchy of Lancaster, Douglas Houghton, energetically pressed the ministry on the issue of homeless single people. He argued for an interdepartmental initiative involving the Home Office and the Ministry of Housing as well as the Simon Community.[90] Again, this impinged on divisions among the experts in the area, with tensions between another voluntary body, the Camberwell Council on Alcoholism, which was partly pioneered by Dr Griffith Edwards of the Maudsley Hospital and which undertook a social, community approach with emphasis on public health and hostels.[91] Another problem lay in the difficulty of the MoH finding funding for a voluntary body, as it had no statutory authority powers so to do and faced hostility from the Treasury in extending grants to such bodies.[92] The NCA was finding it difficult to raise public funds as alcoholism lacked the pulling power of other disabilities.[93] Moreover, officials were frustrated at the failure of the NCA to fulfil its stated aim of undertaking research into the issue and were extremely sceptical of the NCA's emphasis on health education.[94] Interdepartmental problems were another problem. A working party on policy towards habitual drunken offenders between 1967 and 1971 was undermined by the reluctance of either the Home Office or the MoH to take responsibility for the policy.[95]

By 1970, we can detect the beginnings of another significant policy shift in the ministry. Previously officials had been extremely reluctant to move beyond a narrow definition of alcoholism as a 'disease', which had become the dominant thinking in the 1950s. Thus, in 1960, in the internal debate about the possibility of setting up a joint sub-committee of the Medical Advisory Committee and the Standing Mental Health Advisory Committee, it was stressed that any inquiry should be firmly limited 'to treatment as opposed to prevention' which would otherwise open 'too wide a vista'.[96] The following revealing comment also illustrates the MoH's reluctance to support health education on the subject.

> In the past couple of years I have seen several suggestions that there ought to be a health education campaign on alcoholism, but at no stage has anyone suggested the form it should take or given any

> evidence that any particular form of health education is likely to be effective. We have also discussed the difficulty of drawing a line between a campaign against alcoholism and against drinking.[97]

Lack of expertise in the field, the absence of a research base, a scepticism about the claims of medical experts and a reluctance to be drawn into old style temperance debates are all evident here. However, by 1966, when this was written, there were dissenting voices as other civil servants felt that there was a case for further action.[98] Partly, this reflected departmental divisions within the ministry. However, other factors were coming into play. One was the sevenfold increase in hospital admissions for alcoholism from 1954 to 1964, along with an increase in convictions for drunkenness in the 1960s and consequent political pressure, with parliamentary questions and debates on the subject.[99] More importantly, there was a shift in the dominant thinking among the medical and psychiatric professionals away from the concept of distinct in-patient treatment units towards more community-based care. This shift, which has been extensively studied by Dr Thom, tied in with more general health fashions in the 1970s. It was linked with criticisms of the unitary disease theory of alcoholism and the tendency to define the issue in looser terms of 'problem drinking' or 'alcohol dependence'. In turn the interest of a wider – and more prestigious – range of medical opinion became attracted to alcohol issues, especially as the view took root by the late 1960s that there was a correlation between overall levels of drinking in the nation and levels of mortality from alcohol related diseases.[100] This intellectual shift in the medical and psychiatric community was accompanied by further organisational changes, notably the transfer of responsibility for habitual drunken offenders from the Home Office and the creation, in 1967, of a new voluntary body, the Medical Council on Alcoholism, which acted as a pressure group within the medical profession.[101] The new intellectual emphasis tied in with the Department of Health and Social Security's developing interest in health education, particularly as regards smoking and diet.[102] The post–1970 focus on the drinking habits of the nation as a whole greatly extended the target groups and the number of organisations and interests involved in the making of policy. The emphasis became less on issues of 'treatment' and more on influencing alcohol consumption within the population as a whole and the management of alcohol problems. This wider emphasis, however, brought the Department into conflict with other departments after 1970.

Drink and driving

Policy towards alcoholism was debated in a narrow professional and governmental arena and caused scarcely a ripple in the public realm. By contrast, the initiatives on drinking and driving could hardly have enjoyed a higher media and political profile. The popular as well as the quality press carried frequent – and often lurid – stories on the issue from the mid–1950s, and Barbara Castle introduced the breathalyser in 1966 in the full glare of TV cameras. Drink/driving legislation was discussed at Cabinet level and was regarded as having a potential electoral impact. Moreover, the move towards restriction in this sphere contrasted with the general liberalisation on alcohol issues at this time.

Such public exposure was all the more remarkable, given the lack of interest in the issue immediately after the war. Driving after drinking alcohol in large quantities had long been recognised as an undesirable practice, but was regarded in much the same light as individuals using industrial machinery or undertaking building work. Since 1925, it had been an offence to be 'drunk while in charge' of any mechanical vehicle, but drivers were only prosecuted on the grounds that that they had been 'incapable' of controlling their vehicles, in other words in an extreme state of intoxication. Juries, as opposed to magistrates, moreover, were notoriously inclined to give the accused the benefit of any doubt. The growing popularity of the motor car and the development of large suburban public houses on arterial roads had drawn attention to new issues of road safety, not least the danger to pedestrian drinkers as they left public houses. In 1945, the advisory Road Safety Committee of the Home Office and Ministry of Transport (MoT) considered the earlier Alness Report, which had first suggested voluntary blood tests as an aid for prosecution. This idea was summarily rejected, but a series of apparently moderate suggestions by Sir Alker Tripp of New Scotland Yard, which included notices warning against drinking and driving at public houses, the siting of licences away from main roads, and the harmonisation of evening closing hours, was no less vehemently opposed by the Home Office, which raised a series of negative technical objections.[103] The MoT had more of an interest in road safety *per se* but, in 1953, had refused to support campaigners in Birmingham who had wanted to put up anti-drink/driving posters on the grounds that they criticised even the moderate use of alcohol.[104] Furthermore, the MoT had strong reservations to the idea of making it an offence to drive with a specified level of alcohol in the bloodstream on the grounds that 'it is probable that public opinion is not yet ready for a revolutionary change of this kind', and that the somewhat arbitrary working of such a law 'would probably contravene British ideas of fair play'.[105]

Yet when these words were penned in the Ministry in 1955, the beginnings of a sea change in attitudes were evident. Several factors worked together here. Firstly, there was the model of the Scandinavian countries where laws were passed making it an offence to drive with only modest levels of alcohol in the bloodstream. The law there was firmly enforced with roadside checks and blood tests at police stations. Soon a culture developed of not drinking and driving. Other European countries and American states began to adopt similar provisions, albeit less draconian. This provided reformers with a clear cut policy target. Secondly, there emerged a lobby in Britain in favour of change. Foremost here were the Pedestrians'Association (PA), the Royal Society for the Prevention of Accidents (RoSPA) and the BMA, who were supported by temperance and church groups. The PA was more of an 'outsider' group and had poor relations with RoSPA, which it saw as too pro-motorist and too closely linked to the MoT.[106] Graham Page, a Conservative MP who was Chairman of the PA, began to introduce bills for tightening up the law, including a legal limit and roadside tests, and he collected a cross-bench group of influential MPs who harried Macmillan's government with awkward parliamentary questions. By 1960 the BMA, for its part, demanded that police be given the power to stop cars and require their drivers to undertake chemical tests.[107] This lobbying tied in, thirdly, with growing media interest in the subject. The findings of a government financed investigation by Professor Drew of Bristol University, based on simulations of driving conditions, received widespread and somewhat sensational coverage in the popular press and the government was, wrongly, accused of trying to suppress its results.[108] The Christmas casualty toll in 1959 was particularly alarming – deaths showed a 78 per cent increase over 1958 – and papers began to talk in terms of 'slaughter on the road' and the 'scourge of the drunken driver'. Some police chiefs began to call openly for a move towards a Scandinavian approach.[109]

Finally, between 1955 and 1960, scientific and technical research began to change officials' attitude within the MoT. Research work in various countries showed that even low levels of alcohol had an appreciable effect, and that the judgement of drivers and their reaction times generally began to be significantly impaired above 50 mg of alcohol per 100 ml (roughly a couple of pints of beer). These findings were endorsed by Professor Drew's experiments, which had resulted from a research programme jointly sponsored after 1953 by the Medical Research

Council (MRC) and the Transport Road Research Laboratory and which were known in the MoT by early 1956.[110] The problem was that at the level when performance deteriorated, the driver would show no visible signs of inebriation and could certainly not be classed as 'incapable'. These physiological studies were reinforced by analysis of accident figures. Sample investigations by the Road Research Laboratory suggested that 17 per cent of road accidents showed evidence of someone involved having been drinking (although this included pedestrians) and that after 10.00 p.m. the figure rose to a staggering 62 per cent. This contrasted with the official figure of 0.57 per cent of accidents caused by 'drunkenness'.[111] In other words, the number of convictions for drunken driving marked the tip of the iceberg of the problem.

A head of steam was building up for a change of policy. Nonetheless, there were also important braking forces. One was the technical uncertainly of measuring blood/alcohol levels. Breath testing equipment was in its infancy, untried and expensive; blood testing involved a doctor and was thought not to be universally acceptable; urine testing was discovered by a BMA committee in 1960 to be the least reliable. Another was the uncertain state of public opinion. Although officials were aware of a Gallup poll of 1955 which indicated a 75 per cent approval for roadside tests, they were equally aware that the motoring organisations, with which the MoT enjoyed very close relations, were opposed to changes in the law on the grounds that it would be an infringement of liberty. Denis O'Neill, the head of the Road Safety Division of the MoT, in 1956 wanted 'a lot of convincing that we have yet reached the point in this country where we ought to try to work the [Swedish] system'.[112] Another stumbling block was the conviction that different persons would be affected differently by the same quantity consumed. Any blood/alcohol level fixed would therefore risk being unfair to individuals.[113] Furthermore, responsibility for any policy would have to be shared with the Home Office, for it radically affected the role of the police and the magistrates. All sorts of difficulties needed to be addressed. When would the police be justified in stopping motorists? What was to be done with those refusing to give a sample? If drink limits were imposed, how would this relate to the existing law on drunkenness? What would the effect be on police/public relations?

Up till late 1959, the line taken by the MoT in the face of parliamentary pressure from Graham Page was to stonewall. O'Neill felt that ministers would have one day to take 'an exceptionally difficult decision' whether to replace the existing policy of leaving judgement on intoxication to the courts with one of absolute scientific blood/alcohol tests.

But he found the Drew report 'extremely disappointing' as it had made no attempt to relate the results to the normal drinking patterns of the subjects or different temperaments, nor had it analysed the effect of alcohol on performance in actual driving conditions. It was of little practical help to the ministry.[114] This was not the view taken by the Chief Medical Officer of the MRC who urged the necessity for further research and policy development.[115] The Lord President of the Council, Lord Hailsham, who was responsible for the MRC, was shaken by a hostile line of questioning in the House of Lords on the government's inaction in June 1959 and seven months later wrote to the MoT in a 'personal capacity', reflecting on his own experiences of drunk driving cases as a QC, and urging the creation of a new offence of drunk driving based on compulsory, scientific tests, 'a question to which I have given much thought'.[116] However, by this date the MoT was headed by a new, dynamic minister, Ernest Marples, who was convinced of the seriousness of the problem and particularly keen to take action. He thought 'there would be strong support in Parliament for drastic action to be taken against the drunken driver' and that 'public opinion, as far as I judge it, is ready for stern action by the Government'.[117] He sent a small working party of officials to visit the Scandinavian countries to investigate the systems there.[118]

The new enthusiasm of the MoT for Scandinavian-style legal limits, however, quickly ran into the cautious approach of both the Home Office and the legal departments. Officials there pointed out the opposition of many police forces and were particularly anxious that a simple legal limit might have little relationship to the actual capacity of individuals. They were also deeply worried about both the scientific and legal technicalities. 'It looks as if the Home Office does not want omelette on the menu because they cannot bear the thought of breaking eggs' was the despairing comment from the Road Safety Division of the MoT.[119] The matter could not be resolved at official level and, in March 1960, it went to the Home Affairs Committee of the Cabinet. Lengthy and convoluted discussions followed at ministerial level, not helped by erratic changes of position by Lord Hailsham and Charles Hill, the Chancellor of the Duchy of Lancaster, and by the unexpected presentation halfway through of a report by a BMA committee which cast doubt on the accuracy of urine tests, which had hitherto been the politically preferred option.[120] In the end, the cautious approach of the Home Office, the Attorney General and the Scottish Office prevailed over Marples's bolder vision. The Road Traffic Bill of 1961 contained clauses which would make it an offence to drive when control of the vehicle was 'impaired' by alcohol (as opposed to the driver being 'incapable') and which allowed a chemical test taken in a police station to be used as evidence in a court. A level of alcohol of 150mg per 100ml was to be taken as a proof of impairment. This was a very high level (roughly equivalent to two-thirds of a bottle of whisky) but courts would be expected to convict at lower levels if the evidence of the police was that 'impairment' had taken place. However, the police were not given powers to stop motorists at their discretion and the chemical tests would only take place if drivers had been involved in an accident. The Bill also gave ministers powers to introduce breath testing machines at a future date if they wished. The Bill was finally passed in the following session, 1962.[121]

The 1962 Act was a cautious piece of legislation which represented the lowest common denominator of consensus.[122] Sir Richard Nugent, the parliamentary spokesman for the motoring organisations, declared that he was a 'reluctant convert' to a closer definition of drunk driving and thought the government had followed the right approach to blood tests; however, he warned against moving further to spot checks or 'drink traps'.[123] But many parliamentarians criticised the legislation as weak and likely to be ineffective, among them Lord Denning, Lord Silkin, Lord Lucas, and the Bishop of Chester; while, in the Commons, the Opposition spokesman argued the case for a statutory blood/alcohol limit.[124] Ironically, all these reservations had been fully shared by Marples himself, who had warned his colleagues that 'to introduce a Road Safety Bill with these present proposals will almost certainly evoke strong criticism in the press and in Parliament, as a result of which we shall be under severe pressure to accept more far reaching provisions'.[125]

Marples was proved to be correct. RoSPA changed its policy in favour of the introduction of legal limits as a result of pressure from its grass roots.[126] This was a body with which the MoT enjoyed an extremely close relationship as part of its policy community. The Ministry's officials in the Road Safety Division managed to tone down the reporting of this shift, but privately felt 'that there was something to be said for a softening up of public opinion'.[127] The official line to 'wait and see' how the 1962 Act worked could not survive the change of government in October 1964, since the new Labour minister, Tom Fraser, had supported a legal limit in Opposition and had rather rashly hinted at legislation before Christmas 1965 in an ITV interview.[128] However, momentum had already been generated within Whitehall before the general election, with a working party of civil servants from the Home Office, the MoT and representatives of the Police established in January 1964 to look at the practicality of breath testing. This working party, set up as result of furore following what an editorial in the *Daily Telegraph* called 'the ghastly carnage' on the roads over Christmas 1963, worked on the assumption that a legal limit was to be introduced, following evidence of a shift in public opinion, and that testing in police stations (although not at the roadside) would henceforth be compulsory.[129] Meanwhile, the MoT launched an expensive advertising campaign in Christmas 1964 to educate the public on the dangers of combining moderate drinking with driving, and ministers persuaded Page to withdraw his latest private member's bill in return for a promise of government legislation.[130]

By 1965, the terms of debate marked an advance from 1960/62. There was now a more general acceptance of the idea that driving beyond a blood/alcohol limit should be an offence in its own right and that 80 mg per 100ml was the appropriate level.[131] The motoring organisations themselves were prepared to accept this but would resist any lower level. The main bone of contention was now the issue of the police using 'random' roadside breath tests to screen out drivers who, if showing positive, would be subjected to a blood test at a police station. This the motoring organisations hotly resisted as an 'unjustified intrusion into the life of the individual'.[132] On this point, there followed a strange reversal within Whitehall. The Home Office, which in 1960 had been a braking force, took the view that as ministers wanted a tough bill, then there should be tough enforcement: random roadside tests would be more practicable and less invidious for the police than the alternative of exercising discretionary powers. Otherwise, the police would be criticised for lying in wait outside public houses, golf clubs and the like.[133] The police representatives on the joint working party, which was split on the issue, actually took quite a contrary view.[134] These reservations were shared by both Sir Thomas Padmore, permanent secretary of the MoT, and Tom Fraser who feared that any political fallout would land on their heads, and so urged a more cautious approach.[135] In the end, the Home Office line triumphed. Several different considerations were at work here. Legal experts at the Home Office felt – rightly, as events turned out – that it would be difficult to frame effective legislation that required the police to have reasonable suspicion before administering tests. Their inclination was reinforced by the hawkish views of the teetotal George Thomas, Under-secretary at the Home Office, who repeatedly stressed how horrified the country was at the death toll.[136] This view found support lower down in the road safety divisions of the MoT itself, where officials, unlike their seniors, were not concerned with wider political calculations.[137] Finally,

Fraser was desperate to act quickly before Christmas to shore up his fading political reputation, as he had failed to secure Treasury funding for another drink/drive publicity campaign and so could be persuaded to make concessions.[138]

The breathalyser will forever be associated with Barbara Castle, who replaced the much criticised Tom Fraser as Minister of Transport.[139] It has been seen as one of the ways in which she challenged the power of the motoring lobby. In reality, Castle inherited both the policy and approach from her department. Like Fraser, she argued firmly, but initially unsuccessfully, in Whitehall against random testing on grounds of political expediency.[140] The fact that the motoring organisations were opposed and both police and trade unionists divided, weighed heavily with the higher echelons of the MoT, as against the inclinations of their own road safety divisions.[141] But it was the willingness of the Conservative Opposition to capitalise on the issue that forced the Cabinet into a U-turn and to abandon random testing when the Road Safety Bill was reintroduced after the 1966 election.[142] This aspect, Castle admitted, had aroused more than just disagreement but even 'in some quarters almost hysterical and irrational opposition'.[143] She insisted, however, on tightening up the penalties, introducing an automatic disqualification for 12 months for drivers who exceeded the limit.[144] Even if Castle's contribution to the policy was by no means original, she was able to provide an unprecedented public relations boost to the new law on account of her unique, high profile media presence. Her long-suffering husband, Ted, had to limit himself to simple tonic water, a drink he disliked, at parties and pubs as the press 'tracked us everywhere'.[145] However, far from 'coming a cropper' over the law as she feared, she felt herself to be 'sailing through': it 'has been astonishingly well-received and the press and TV have done a magnificent job of putting it across'. The next Christmas casualties were 'dramatically down'.[146]

In reality, the debate over random testing was somewhat overstated, since the Act gave the police wide powers for breathalysing motorists for any minor, moving road offence, such as driving with faulty brake lights.[147] However, the Act proved rather difficult to enforce as, for a period, the courts allowed motorists to exploit a good many loopholes, as the Home Office had foreseen. In one notorious case, a motorist was actually acquitted on the grounds that the policeman was not wearing his hat and therefore not strictly 'in uniform'.[148] Moreover, the deterrent effect of the Act began to wear off and accident figures involving drink and driving began to rise again. The issue continued to be of such high profile that Harold Wilson's political press secretary, Gerald Kaufman, even warned him in 1968 – at the nadir of the government's popular standing – that a perceived failure in this, hitherto seen as one of their positive achievements, could rebound badly on its whole credibility. Kaufman's idea for more proactive police enforcement, however, floundered on the obduracy of James Callaghan, the new Home Secretary.[149]

After 1970, pressure continued from the BMA and the road safety lobby for a tightening up in the law. A feature of the post-1970 period, moreover, was the very large expenditure on anti-drunken driving publicity: by 1987 this ran at £2.5m, which was five times the amount the Health Education Authority was able to spend on alcohol education in general.[150] The Drink trade also showed itself keen to publicise the dangers. Partly as a result, the climate of opinion had shifted further, with even the motoring organisations supporting 'discretionary' tests. The departmental Blennerhasset Committee of 1975 supported tightening up of the law, but both technical problems and the parlous political state of the Labour government delayed implementation. Norman Fowler's Transport Act of 1981 certainly tightened the law, although discretionary testing was rejected.[151] The 1980s saw new groups, such as the Campaign against Drink Driving and Alcohol Concern, campaigning on the issue and working with the Department of Transport. However, no new issues of principle were at stake and the focus has been on modifying an existing approach and administrative framework. By the late 1990s, controversy in the road safety area had shifted to the question of speed as a factor in road deaths.

The story of policy towards drink/driving between 1955 and 1970 is one of policy innovation. A variety of different factors came into play to bring about change. There was the backcloth of mounting, clear scientific evidence that here was a problem, reinforced by the example of foreign countries that pointed the way towards policy solutions. In contrast to alcoholism, where the experts' definition of the problem was unclear and always shifting, here it was the technical ways of implementing policy that presented the main point of difficulty. Public opinion and media pressure for action was another important background force; but politicians and officials right up till the 1970s were extremely cautious in how they interpreted this and were perhaps unduly wary of a political backlash. Obviously public opinion itself was something that could be manipulated, for example by the publication of a White paper in 1965, and by Barbara Castle's media blitz in 1967. It is interesting to note that neither of the traditional two combatants on Drink issues played a major role. The temperance groups and churches certainly supported those pressing for restrictions, but their position, that this was part of a more general alcohol problem, made little impact. On the other hand, the Trade took a fairly passive role, since it judged that it was neither a popular nor a crucial issue on which to fight, and also because sections of the Drink industry, like the 'off' Trade, had much to gain. Indeed, as early as 1951 the National Trade Defence Association, both genuinely concerned at the issue and also conscious that 'this was perhaps the only heavy stick the Temperance Party have left to beat us with', had circulated licensees about the dangers of drunken driving and had offered cooperation with RoSPA on the issue.[152] Later, it donated money.[153] In 1967, the breathalyser caused divisions between the licensed victuallers and the brewers; the latter tried hard to prevent the publicans from launching a campaign to get the public to write in protest to MPs. Although the policy was one that fundamentally involved Drink, it tended to be redefined in terms of a road safety issue. Here, the tendency was for greater regulation and control, for example MOT tests and safety inspections, in contrast to alcohol consumption where liberalisation was becoming the dominant mood. Pressure for and against innovation came from a whole mixture of professional and interest groups of one kind or another: the motoring organisations, chief constables and other police bodies, the Law Society, the BMA, safety bodies like RoSPA and the PA and a number of technical advisory bodies within Whitehall. All of these had well-established access to civil servants and formed parts of complex policy communities, especially since Scotland was also involved. Civil servants at the MoT found influential bodies from within their policy community ranged on different sides. Within the Whitehall departments, a peculiarly rich combination of policy streams interacted over the fifteen year period. First, there were the rival departmental bureaucratic interests of the two principal departments, the Home Office and the MoT, as well as minor players like the law officers and the police. Then came the technical advice. This followed a pattern and time span of its own and was not always welcome, insofar as it might be inconclusive (for example, the working party on breath testing in 1964–65), inconvenient (for example, the BMA's doubts about urine testing in 1960) or unhelpful and unduly academic (for example, Drew's findings in 1956–58). Thirdly, there was the somewhat erratic factor of strong ministerial interest (for example, Marples, Hailsham, Fraser, George Thomas) or lack of interest (for example, Watkinson before 1959 or Callaghan in 1968). Finally, the macro political scene impinged at various points, such as the imminence of an election, the size of the ministry's majority and the interest of Cabinet ministers, and even the Prime Minister, in electoral advantage. The result was a peculiarly rich policy soup.

10

Epilogue: A Brief Sketch of the Period after 1970

The story of government and alcohol over the last thirty years can offer interesting insights into the policy process in the modern British state. It should provide future historians, with access to official records, a rich seam of material to quarry. The period was one of enormous changes in the backcloth to the policy process. The drinks industry itself underwent profound transformations, with the distinction between wine or spirits and brewing largely disappearing as the large brewers diversified into, first, the wine business and, later, leisure areas, such as hotels and catering. Furthermore, the drinks sector, in common with many other consumer areas, was internationalised as the largest firms became multinationals. The retail market saw equally dramatic changes. Consumer taste shifted away from beer towards wines and the more exotic spirits. The role of advertisers in steering this market by means of the manipulation of images became particularly important. Alcoholic beverages became an important area of sales in supermarkets. Drinkers demanded higher standards in public houses, with a marked increase in demand for better food, non-alcoholic drinks and more sophisticated amenities. The 'on' sales area also diversified with niche markets developing for traditional 'real ale', and the period saw the impact of an articulate, consumer pressure group, the Campaign for Real Ale (CAMRA), which was sharply critical of the big players in the drinks industry. Broader cultural and intellectual changes were also significant. Britain became a more secular and culturally diverse society during this period. There was a marked shift towards libertarianism in many areas, along with resistance to the idea of both the nanny state and social engineering. Attitudes towards the consumption of both legal alcoholic drinks and illegal soft drugs consequently became more relaxed, although this was punctuated by periodic moral panics. By contrast, attitudes towards tobacco consumption became markedly more censorious. In ideological terms, we find a shift after 1980 towards free market and economic liberal ideas, along with scepticism about the capacity of centralised government agencies to provide effective services. The health policy area witnessed especially complex developments, both in terms of organisation and ideology, one of these being more emphasis on preventative medicine. Finally, the structural framework of the policy process was altered as the European Community extended its competence, particularly in areas of trading and taxation. In the face of such complex developments, it is hardly surprising to find the policy fragmentation, which we noticed from 1945 to 1970, becoming more marked. By the 1980s, it was estimated that no fewer than 15 government departments or agencies had an interest in policy towards alcohol sales, each with its own bureaucratic viewpoint or interest.

A strong feature of the period after 1970 was the redefinition of the Drink issue as chiefly a health problem by those opposed to alcoholic consumption. The old UKA was supplanted in terms of public profile by the United Kingdom Temperance Alliance Ltd, a charity, which emphasised educational work and which broadened its interest into other addictive areas.[1] The emphasis was on policies based on scientific research which were politically practicable. The leaders of this 'new temperance movement' had close associations with the National Council on Alcoholism, and themselves established an educational Institute for Alcohol Studies in 1983.[2] The new generation of temperance workers showed an interest in areas such as community work and primary care for those suffering from alcohol abuse. Hence, they downplayed teetotalism and became part of a much broader alcohol control or 'misuse' lobby which attracted considerable support from influential quarters in the medical and academic world, and which established international links, particularly in America. From 1970, the Department of Health (DHSS, for most of the period) acted as a centre of a policy community with an interest in promoting control policies. This marked a shift from the pre–1970 Ministry of Health where, as we saw in the last chapter, officials had been reluctant to go down this road. Several factors were at work here.[3] Firstly, the DHSS had already shifted away from accepting the disease model of alcoholism, requiring in-house treatment, and had come to stress the importance of community care as part of a more general treatment of 'problem drinking': itself a far more elastic concept than 'alcoholism'. This was accompanied by the transfer of responsibility for habitual drunkard offenders from the Home Office to the DHSS. Secondly, the DHSS by the late 1970s accepted a policy of aiming to reduce the overall level of alcohol consumption. Particularly influential here was a 1979 report by the Royal College of Psychiatrists. Essentially, this accepted the consumption model based on the works of the French statistician, Sully Ledermann, which maintained that the higher the level of overall consumption in society, the higher the corresponding harm from alcohol abuse.[4] This was reinforced, thirdly, by statistical evidence that showed a significant rise in both consumption figures and alcohol related diseases from the 1950s to the 1980s. This consumption model, fourthly, chimed in well with the general interest shown by health policy-makers from the early 1980s in preventative medicine, an area previously neglected. Thus, the promotion of 'sensible' drinking could be seen as a laudable policy objective, along with encouragement to reduce intakes of fat and sugar, to take aerobic exercise and to stop smoking. Finally, all this shift was facilitated by a series of health ministers from both main parties – Sir Keith Joseph (whose uncle was chair of the National Council on Alcoholism), David Owen, David Ennals and Sir George Young – who were interested in alcohol issues and sympathetic to control policies.[5]

By the 1970s, a lobby in favour of more coherent alcohol control policies was exerting significant influence for the first time since 1918. The more robust attitudes towards smoking (involving educational expenditure, sharply increased taxation and controls on advertising and smoking at work) provided a model here. The DHSS supplied a focus for an advocacy coalition. However, the lobby faced formidable problems. Most notably the mechanisms for pursuing the policy lay quite outside the ambit of the DHSS and its allies. Taxation was the preserve of Customs and Excise, liquor sales outlets came under the Home Office, and advertising was under the auspices of independent regulatory bodies. Moreover, the suggested policy mechanisms themselves were by no means watertight. There was evidence that increased taxation led to smuggling or – as the EC's single market developed – legal importation. Demand for beer, in particular, was fairly inelastic.[6] Restrictions on sales were a far more difficult proposition than in the time of the First World War, given the popularity of supermarket sales. Critics could also produce evidence that restricted hours for 'on' sales actually encouraged 'binge drinking' and alcohol problems. The weakness of the alcohol control lobby was graphically illustrated by the fate of the report on alcohol by the Central Policy Review Staff (CPRS). The CPRS chose alcohol policy as one of its subjects for investigation precisely because it fell across so many existing departmental lines. Its draft report in March 1979 came down firmly in favour of control policies and also the creation of an advisory council on alcohol policies which should coordinate and monitor policies. This caused great internal controversy within Whitehall, with stout resistance coming from those departments keen to promote tourism and employment. This sensitive report was never published in Britain but was leaked and eventually published independently in Sweden.[7] The DHSS's policy document, *Drinking Sensibly*, which came out in 1981, emerged as a result of a long series of interdepartmental clashes and revisions. It was an equivocal document which, though endorsing a health education programme against alcohol abuse and urging responsible advertising, backed away from using taxation as a tool to discourage consumption.[8]

The alcohol control lobby faced numerous difficulties. The Drinks industry was well organised and powerful with no less than five alcohol companies ranking among the largest fifty companies in Britain in the mid–1980s. Its strong representation in Parliament, particularly among the Conservative party, was ultimately less important than its influence in Whitehall. It gave employment to some 450,000 persons and provided wealth and prosperity. Hence, ministries such as Food and Agriculture, Employment, Trade and Industry, and the Treasury had an interest in opposing restrictive measures. The tourist industry was another powerful ally. Added to which, public opinion poll evidence showed that the new temperance emphasis on alcohol control was deeply unpopular, except in the important area of drink/driving. Finally, the alcohol control lobby itself was far from homogeneous. Important groups like the BMA gave only a sporadic interest, preferring to husband their resources by concentrating on tobacco and, on occasions, drink/driving rather than overall consumption issues. The variety of conceptual approaches also undermined unity of action. In 1971–72, for example, several medical bodies and individuals, adhering to the disease model of alcoholism, declined to give evidence to the Erroll Committee on liquor licensing on the grounds that they were concerned with alcoholism not the sale of alcohol.[9] Furthermore, in the early 1980s, in the aftermath of the CPRS debacle, the DHSS was embarrassed by acrimonious divisions between the existing four voluntary Alcohol bodies, and three of them were subsequently replaced by a single government funded charitable body, Alcohol Concern.[10] There is evidence also for considerable internal divisions between policy factions within the DHSS in the early 1980s. The department was also finding it difficult to keep control of policy, where so much of the implementation was in the hands of voluntary or decentralised agencies outside its immediate command.[11] Nevertheless, Alcohol Concern provided a focus throughout the 1990s in raising critical questions about the patterns and levels of consumption. It is no accident, given the contentious nature of the alcohol policy area, that alcohol education has been one area that has flourished. As Rob Baggot has put it, this has been 'an island of consensus', with the large alcohol companies themselves anxious to promote 'sensible' or moderate drinking, which is portrayed as being in their interest.[12] In 1989, the drinks industry itself set up the Portman Group, which called itself 'an initiative against alcohol abuse' and which proved effective in low key lobbying in Whitehall. An area where the education campaign has made an impact has been the popularisation of the concepts of 'safe limits' based on 'units' of alcohol consumption, introduced by the Health Education Council in 1987, which soon acquired public recognition. The low levels at which these were set appear to have been reached somewhat arbitrarily;[13] but it is an indication of how far they had become enshrined as articles of faith that the government's sensible attempts to refine them by stressing daily rather than weekly limits in 1995 met with a storm of protest from alcohol control enthusiasts.[14] Another area of change has been the discouragement by employers of lunchtime drinking on the grounds that 'driving a desk' under the influence was asking for trouble. However, restrictions on advertising have been through voluntary codes.[15]

Almost all scholarly writing on alcohol in Britain after 1970 has been by authors broadly sympathetic to alcohol control.[16] It has therefore tended to concentrate on explanations for the lack of success of such policy. Although important, there is a danger lest this perspective provides a single dimensional picture of the policy process which both underplays the cross-cutting tensions in the period and exaggerates the cohesion of the lobbyists on either side. A good example of such complexity is provided by the ill-fated attempts by Lord Young, when Secretary of State for Trade and Industry, to open up the beer trade to free market competition in 1989. Mrs Thatcher's governments had shown scant regard for vested interests, even among groups formerly supportive of the Conservatives, and had shown a zeal for using free market mechanisms to open up trades or professions to market forces. Lord Young attempted to force through a report of the Monopolies and Mergers Commission which proposed a drastic curbing of the tied-house system. This led, initially, to divisions between the large and the smaller brewers. There then followed a largely successful rearguard action by the Brewers' Society, first to ensure the unity of the brewing companies, and then to lobby Conservative MPs and Whitehall ministries. The original proposals were watered down and, even then, the larger brewers were able to steer the implementation of the proposals to their own advantage. CAMRA and other consumer groups were dismayed and discomforted.[17]

This whole episode also revealed deep tensions between the brewers and their tenants. This was also a factor in the long saga of the liberalisation of the British licensing laws after 1970. Maudling, the Home Secretary in the Heath government of 1970, regarded the licensing laws as archaic, and pressure was coming from both the Monopolies Commission and the tourist industry for liberalisation. Departmental committees were set up to consider the question, the Erroll Committee for England and Wales, and the Clayson Committee for Scotland. Both reports recommended extension of permitted hours of sale including the abolition of the 'afternoon gap' introduced in the First World War, along with various other reforms, such as allowing children under 14 to sit in licensed premises subject to certain conditions. Their reports had contrasting fates. The Clayson report received a broader range of support because it justified its findings on medical grounds – liberalisation was seen as a means of reducing 'binge drinking' before closing time – and because the Scottish licensed victuallers wanted relaxation of their existing, very restricted opening hours. This left the alcohol control lobby, who saw longer hours as an encouragement to consumption, isolated. By contrast, in England and Wales strong opposition emerged both from the publicans, who did not want to face increased competition or to work longer hours, and from the medical lobby. As a result, after the Scottish Licensing Act of 1976, the law in Scotland went from being more restrictive to more liberal than that in England and Wales.[18] The government remained officially neutral on the issue for a while. However, opinion in the Home Office had come round to the view that more liberal licensing hours were beneficial in curbing binge drinking and the evidence from Scotland, though fiercely fought over, suggested that the liberalisation there had been successful in this respect, as well as widely popular. Following pressure from backbenchers along with a campaign for flexible opening by the group 'FLAG', which was able to unite the licensees, the brewing, leisure and tourist industries, the government in 1987 finally allowed more flexible opening in England and Wales by abolishing the afternoon gap.[19] Evening closing at 11.00 pm, however, was retained, although the Labour government in 2001 produced a White paper recommending its abolition, following support from the police.[20]

In contrast to the period before 1945, licensing laws were no longer seen as a key factor in the issue of alcohol policy. This reflects both the free availability of alcohol from supermarkets and other outlets, and the vastly more civilised ambience of public houses: by the early 1990s catering accounted for an average 25 per cent of pub turnover.[21] In 2002, responsibility for licensing was transferred from the Home Office to the Department of Culture Media and Sport in a move that went largely unremarked. Proposals are under discussion at the time of writing in 2003 to switch licensing decisions from magistrates to local councils, perhaps allowing more flexibility in policy, ironically something which had been advocated by temperance restrictionists in the 1880s. The liberalisation of the liquor licensing laws in Britain over the past thirty years reflects the general growth of libertarian attitudes, in contrast to the United States, where more censorious attitudes towards drinking have once again become more fashionable. However, this increasingly relaxed attitude has been punctuated by periodic minor 'moral panics', fanned by a sensationalist media. These have been related to the more general problem of loutish behaviour and youthful hedonism in late-twentieth century Britain. One such episode was the link between alcohol and football hooliganism in the 1970s, which led to restrictions on the serving of alcohol on trains and in football grounds. Another was the attention given to late night disorders among young revellers at closing time in 1988, with the term 'lager louts' being coined.[22] Another was a concern about under-age drinking in 1997, fanned by the extraordinary decision of the drinks manufacturers to market fruit flavoured alcohol drinks, popularly termed 'alcopops'. None of these moral panics has had the force or appeal of the armaments scare of 1915; moreover, others not related to alcohol have been equally or more potent, for example those about AIDS, teenage pregnancies, drug taking at late night raves, and paedophilia. However, they have been enough to ensure that Drink remains an issue of controversy beyond the concerns of the alcohol and health lobby. The excessive binge drinking by young people, including those under 18, has continued to cause widespread concern.[23] Not only are the health implications striking, but there is also a visible impact on public behaviour. In fact, the relationship of Drink and law and order has attracted much more popular attention and concern than Drink as a health problem. This is particularly linked with the issue of drinking among youths, so that many 'nightclub' areas of British cities on a Friday and Saturday begin to remind one of the descriptions of pre-CCB Carlisle in the First World War. It is perhaps surprising that the alcohol control lobby, in contrast to its interest in health aspects, has not directed more attention to this problem, including the obviously very lax enforcement of the laws against under age drinking and the failure of magistrates to respond to residents' concerns. However, at the time of writing, February 2003, there are indications that both the Home Office and the Prime Minister's Strategy Unit are considering a strategy to tackle Britain's alcohol-fuelled yob culture. The target here will be so-called 'hazardous drinkers', who are not alcoholics, but who may periodically indulge in heavy bouts of drinking which lead to antisocial, or even criminal, behaviour.[24]

Policy towards alcohol in Britain at the start of the twenty-first century remains complex in character, far more so than a hundred years ago, when it could be identified more narrowly in terms of liquor licensing.[25] Even in the area of taxation alone, for example, the Treasury has to take into account the conflicting interests of raising revenue, meeting macro-economic targets, satisfying the health lobby and ensuring the well-being of the drinks industry, and taking account of the pressures from the EC for a single market. A feature of the policy area, common with others, has been the growth of complex policy communities or policy networks and the dependence of government at the centre upon professionals for contributions in both the formulation and the implementation of policy. Although the alcohol manufacturers retain close links with the Conservative party, party polarisation on Drink is largely a thing of the past, with New Labour's policies indistinguishable from those of their opponents.[26] More significant for the policy process are the vested interests and competing outlooks of the numerous Whitehall departments, along with quasi-governmental agencies, that have an interest in alcohol. The policy perspectives of these departments have changed over time, being shaped both by political or governmental imperatives and by changes in the intellectual framework or the policy discourse. Writers interested in the 'new temperance' agenda of alcohol control often bemoan the lack of an overall and coherent policy towards alcohol of the sort advocated by the CPRS. They tend to explain this in terms of the strong vested interests of the drinks industry. However, such policy dissipation, it might be argued, is the norm rather than the exception in contemporary Britain. It has been of feature of policy towards drugs, inner city decay, equal opportunities, climate change, training in the workforce, rural deprivation, sustainable development, the environment and social exclusion. It is not for nothing that Tony Blair has called for 'Joined-up Government' with efforts being made in the Cabinet Office to coordinate policy. But this is the Holy Grail of political aspiration. Efforts to achieve such cohesion are invariably politically costly and often disruptive, or even counterproductive. At all events Drink, compared to the areas just cited, is now far down the list of both government and popular concern, and is unlikely to be the recipient of any such special treatment.

11
Drink, the Political Process and Policy-Making in Britain

The previous chapters have told a detailed story of the politics of Drink in Britain over a long period. In this final chapter, we will first examine what the history reveals about the changing nature of the British political system, then draw some brief comparisons both internationally and with similar policy areas, and finally relate it to some theories of the policy-making process.

Drink and the British political system

The high politics of the Drink issue indicates that the political system in Victorian Britain was both complex and flexible. Drink does not easily fit into some of the dominant interpretations. Most historical writing on the politics of this period revolves around three themes or debates. One, following Ostrogorski's analysis, concerns the rise of organised mass parties and the question whether this led to a fundamental shift in the nature of constituency, parliamentary and governmental politics. Another, is the question as to whether an era of community politics in the mid-century was replaced by one of class politics, and whether the Liberal party was capable of responding appropriately to this shift. A third theme, following Dicey and also the Fabians, is the growth of government and whether an age of *laissez faire* was being replaced, or at any rate modified, by the rise of collectivist or interventionist government.

Certainly, in the period before 1880, the Drink question very much reflects a concern that social policy matters should not be subsumed into the cockpit of party battle.[1] Attitudes towards the question reflect the older Whig and Tory views that the political elite should be insulated from popular or democratic pressures. Selwin-Ibbetson's 'dread' of the Drink issue becoming subject to popular agitation in 1869 reflects awareness of the way in which liquor could have a destabilising and degrading effect upon elections, and also of the capacity of 'teetotal fanaticism' and other popular zealotry to subvert the measured deliberations of Westminster politicians. Hence, the reluctance of many MPs to countenance the transfer of licensing to elected boards or to municipal control. Parliament was the accepted forum for the resolution of licensing matters, but during this period most parliamentarians were well insulated from the world of intemperance and public drinking, and moved cautiously on the question being for the most part sceptical of the efficacy of legislative measures. They were wary of taking far-reaching initiatives in an area that so intimately affected the lives of the working classes and felt a special responsibility to take cognisance of the wishes and desires of those who were not directly represented in the political system. The widely differing models of the Drink question and the conflicting recipes for reform did nothing to penetrate the fog that surrounded the question. However, where there seemed an overwhelming desire for action on the part of the unenfranchised – for example, Sunday closing in Ireland and Wales – they were prepared to pass legislation in the face of opposition from the Trade. Major initiatives, like Wellington's Beer Act of 1830, Gladstone's grocer licences of 1860 and Bruce's licensing bills in 1871 and 1872, required government initiative and became linked with extraneous political calculations. However, many legislative initiatives or committees of inquiry came as a result of individual experts or enthusiasts: Buckingham in the 1830s, Villiers in the 1850s, Selwin-Ibbetson and Lawson in the 1860s, and Dalrymple, Chamberlain and Cowen in the 1870s. This followed the pattern of many other areas of social policy such as the Factory Acts, merchant shipping legislation and the repeal of the Contagious Disease Acts.

Does the Drink story uphold the widely held view that the 1870s mark a watershed in British politics concerning the rise of party? Certainly, after 1870, many radical politicians were seduced by a model of progress being secured through the party machine. These were the years of the caucuses of the National Liberal Federation and the rise of the party machine, regarded so balefully by Ostrogorski and many other contemporary observers, such as Dicey.[2] The new electorate required large scale organisation on the part of political parties and factions, and these organisations, at first local caucuses but later national party machines, had taken upon themselves the responsibility for formulating 'policy' which was then to be pushed upon the leaders of the political parties. In the eyes of the leaders of the caucus – the young

Chamberlain, Schnadhorst, and Spence Watson – this development was eminently 'democratic'. The objective of the National Liberal Federation, for example, was seen as ensuring 'the direct participation of all its members in the direction of its policy and in the selection of those particular measures of reform to which priority shall be given'.[3] Here, apparently, was a mechanism to allow the people a voice in the creation of social and political policy; and democracy through popular political parties was seen as supplementing or even supplanting the direct agitation.[4] Some radicals, sympathetic to temperance reform, slotted the Drink issue into this perspective. G. O. Trevelyan, Cowan and, above all, Joseph Chamberlain, all took up licensing reform in the 1870s precisely as part of a broader radical agenda to promote local self-government or municipal improvement, and as a means of driving the Liberal party towards the agenda of nonconformist radicalism. They were clearly interested in fitting the issue into an ideological schema of democratic party politics in which the Liberal party was the force that would sweep away unresponsive and privileged aristocratic government. As the influence of nonconformist radicals grew in the constituencies, so the tendency developed for the Trade and the temperance movement to align themselves locally with the rapidly evolving party machines, a process helped by the move of the more right wing Liberals away from Gladstonianism to Unionism in 1886. By the compensation battles of 1888 and 1890, Drink had become an issue which was seen to affect the fortunes of the government as a whole. In the 1890s, local option was an element of the Newcastle Programme of 1892 and some senior Liberal politicians, such as John Morley, Lloyd George and Harcourt, saw party political advantage in the issue; the latter, indeed, notwithstanding his abhorrence in the 1870s to 'grandmotherly legislation', did all that he could to use the issue to embarrass the Unionists. By 1904 and 1908, licensing had become a major element in party manifestos, and the fate of the legislation of those years became linked to issues of the highest importance, for instance reform of the House of Lords.

Nevertheless, equally, the Drink question cautions us against hastily seeing the 1870s as some kind of a dramatic turning point marked by the rise of the mass party. For one thing, there remained a place for the 'freelance' reformer right up to the First World War, as the experiences of Randolph Churchill, Frederick Temple, Randall Davidson and Bishop Jayne were to show. More fundamentally, Jon Lawrence, although primarily concerned with the low politics of constituency and popular politics, has challenged the near-universal view among historians that the late-nineteenth century witnessed the triumph of party organisation in British politics. He points, among other things, to tensions within local parties (on precisely issues like temperance), the incompleteness of political elites' control over popular politics, and the existence of organised 'sabaltern' groups within parties, such as the Irish, radicals and nonconformists.[5] Our high politics perspective shows a similar complexity. Various factors acted as a counterweight to party polarisation. One such was the endemic internal divisions and jealousies among both the Traders and the temperance societies. The 'off' trade retained close links with the Liberals, and the large brewers themselves became alarmed at their exposure when they were identified with one party, particularly after 1890, when they were vulnerable to a collapse in property prices for licensed houses.[6] The more moderate temperance reformers in the CETS retained strong links with the Unionist parties. Moreover, many Conservative politicians, like Randolph Churchill in 1890, Balfour in 1895 and Astor after 1916, were uncomfortable at being branded as belonging to the 'beer and bible' party. Bonar Law in the First World War even referred to the 'Trade incubus' which weighed upon his party. The reforming efforts of Ritchie in 1888 and 1902, and Goschen in 1890, did not stem from a specifically Conservative 'policy' towards licensing. In 1888, Ritchie adapted his proposals from the plans of Liberal predecessors; the 1902 Act stemmed from non-partisan efforts of Randall Davidson; and the licence reduction scheme in 1890 was very much the personal brainchild of the Chancellor. The Conservative compensation schemes of 1888 and 1890 initially attracted the support of both Liberal leaders and moderate MPs; it was only when they aroused agitation outside that Harcourt and Gladstone began to consider what political capital could be extracted from the issue. Furthermore, it was only when disquiet was reflected within the parliamentary context – in threatening to drive a wedge between the fragile parliamentary coalition of Conservatives and Liberal Unionists – that the issue really aroused the political interest of Liberal MPs. The Conservatives MPs were less concerned about the rights and wrongs of compensation – a truly tedious issue – and more about the obstruction of the Liberals which extended the sessions into July, so interfering with the racing season, and which threatened the credibility of the Unionist alliance. Here, the Drink question only became political, in the sense of party political, because it indirectly affected more obviously party political matters, namely the Unionist alliance on Ireland.

The resistance to party polarisation was compounded by the ideology of the prohibitionists themselves. Although Sir Wilfrid Lawson, in

1889, privately likened the Liberal party to a 'big salmon' which 'we the prohibitionists, have hooked . . . and are now "playing" with the object of landing him as soon as possible',[7] he singularly failed to exploit the opportunity of such links, refusing, for example, to give any proactive assistance to Harcourt in 1893 and 1895. Throughout the last quarter of the century, the UKA experienced exquisite tension between its vision of itself as a trans-class, trans-sectarian and trans-political, populist movement and the realities of cooperating with the political party that claimed the allegiance of the vast majority of its supporters. This was evident both among the UKA's local branches and at the parliamentary level, as the experiences of W. S. Caine, torn between his temperance militancy and his support for the union with Ireland, showed.[8] The mythology of the Anti-Corn Law League's 'victory' in 1846 cast a long shadow. The temperance militants were mesmerised by the apparent way in which the League had triumphed through popular agitation alone. As a result, the movement 'out of doors' was seen as all-important, the process of parliamentary legislation secondary and unimportant. Prohibition, like the cause of free trade, had 'sprung out of the soil'.[9] Cobden and the other leaders of the Anti-Corn Law League had never enjoyed a majority in parliament but had nonetheless forced a government to concede their cause.[10] There would be three stages in any agitation: 'first popular, then parliamentary, and lastly governmental – the last two rapidly following upon the development of the first'.[11] This seductive model, which saw all elite politicians as generally timid, corrupt or stupid encumbrances to the path of enlightened and altruistic popular radicalism, had widespread appeal during the mid-Victorian period. Leaders of all popular 'agitations' revered the triumphs of the anti-slavery and the Anti-Corn Law movements.[12] Liberal politicians themselves were not averse to playing on it, as in the case of Gladstone with the Bulgarian atrocities agitation in the late-1870s. However, most leaders of popular agitations during this period showed at least some capacity to compromise with party leaders or legislators, for example the Reform League, the Liberation Society and the campaign against the Contagious Diseases Acts. The prohibitionists, however, proved peculiarly reluctant to compromise their strategy right up till 1914 and, in the process, alienated a host of politicians who might have been prepared to help them, including such heavyweights as Bruce, Chamberlain, Ritchie and Harcourt. Several factors came into play here. First, the strategy did seem to have some success in a *negative* way insofar as popular pressure, refracted through Parliament, caused governments of both parties to abandon 'unsatisfactory' licensing reform schemes in 1871, 1888, and 1890 which would block local veto. Secondly, the self-righteous purity of the populist, agitational model blended with the absolutism of the prohibitionist ideology. Licensing reform (other than the local veto) meant condoning the hated traffic: 'The Alliance', declared Lawson, 'went for the overthrow of the trade and for no such Utopian scheme as would tinker with it.'[13] Secondly, the ideological gulf between restrictionist and prohibitionist reformers after 1870 time and again destroyed the prospect of a united front and led to mutual recriminations. Finally, in a strange reversal of the normal tendency, the parliamentary leadership in the shape of the veteran, Sir Wilfrid Lawson, proved particularly unresponsive to the idea of compromise. The force of popular opinion was what mattered, once he had that behind him, 'there will be no difficulty in marching on to victory'.[14] As late as 1900 when, under pressure from sections of the UKA executive to rally around the Peel Report, he resisted the politics of compromise. 'It is', he lamented, 'an age of "new diplomacy" and I suppose I am an old fogey, too conservative to trot along in the new and seductive paths which some of our friends seem to have discovered.'[15] It was, he complained, 'the "wise men" who are the plague of my life – the men who want to go round instead of to go straight', 'the sooner the better in my opinion that we revert to our old agitational position, and leave legislation to the legislators'.[16]

All sorts of factors, therefore, prevented contemporaries from viewing Drink and licensing reform through party political spectacles. Similarly, it does not exactly fit into an interpretation which sees a shift from community to class-based politics in the last quarter of the nineteenth century. As David Dixon has stressed in his study of gambling, the blind alleys and lost causes of history tend to be screened out of historical interpretations if they do not conveniently fit conventional political divisions; yet they may reveal important truths.[17] As early as the 1830–60 period, both free licensing supporters and the prohibitionists showed elements of class politics, combined with what were both economic and moralistic issues. Much was made of the mobilisation of the labouring people against a remote, unelected and unresponsive aristocratic class who were portrayed either as maintaining monopoly or as foisting unwelcome dens of vice upon the labouring classes. But equally, the issue could be seen in individualistic and religious terms, or as part of communities' search for autonomy and democratic government. We find similar complexities in the period after 1870. On the one hand, groups like the Liberty and Property Defence League attempted, with some success, to fit the moves for reduction of licences or for local veto into an outlook that fiercely challenged the advance of 'confiscatory socialism'.[18] Opposition to the 1908 Licensing Bill was mobilised from among the many shareholders in breweries. On the other hand, the interest in public control over the Trade which became so marked in the late 1890s came partially from advocates of public ownership *per se*, but more so from those motivated by the need to control the political and social 'menace' of the Trade. Later these included the Astors, prominent Conservatives. The labour movement from the very start was deeply divided on Drink issues.[19] In the early twentieth century, the Labour party itself suffered a threefold division on the issue: some activists advocating prohibition, some public control and others hostile to state intervention at all.

In his influential study of the British political tradition over the past two hundred years, W. H. Greenleaf has portrayed political development in terms of dialectic between the growing pressures of collectivism and the opposing libertarian tendency. He shows that all three main political creeds reflected this tension, with collectivist and liberal elements to be found within each.[20] Temperance and liquor issues reflect this complexity. Drink did not fit comfortably into liberal, conservative or socialist perspectives. However, neither do the Victorian models of the Drink question, which we considered in the first chapter, readily fit into an individualist/collectivist framework. Prohibition, a supremely interventionist doctrine, was argued in terms of an extension of local liberty. Moreover, as Geoffrey Searle has argued, the early Victorian period, far from witnessing the ideological triumph of free trade, sees a complex array of doubts expressed about capitalism and the market from a variety of sources, and not just those favouring collectivist regulation. For their part, the prohibitionists argued for restrictions and intervention on liberal grounds, as the demand for drink was seen as artificially created by those who traded in it.[21] Moreover, prohibitionists, eager for one form of draconian regulation, were fiercely opposed to restrictionist reformers, who advocated far-reaching state restriction though control by elected boards or, even more unacceptable, direct public management of the liquor traffic. Advocates of the Gothenburg system agreed on the need for collectivist control of Drink, but were deeply divided as to whether this was best achieved by a public body, a local council or an independent charitable trust. It is only after 1914, with the advent of the CCB, that we find a more clearly articulated demand for state intervention in the interests of national efficiency. Although the Fabians in the 1890s were interested in the Drink question at this time, it is significant that the Society found the issue an uncongenial one. The issue of municipal control was clouded by the hostility of disinterested management enthusiasts to the idea of the local community profiting from the traffic. There was little scope for the permeation of Fabian ideas at the elite level.

Elite politics brings us to interpretations of politics that have stressed the autonomy of high politics. Maurice Cowling and other exponents of the concept of 'high politics' have reacted against Whig or progressive liberal interpretations which tend to see reform in terms of concession to political and social pressures from below. They argue that the climate of parliamentary opinion 'was *affected* by extra-parliamentary forces, but not created by them', and the connections 'between the closed world in which decisions were taken and the external pressures it reflected' were 'so devious and diverse' that no necessary connection can be drawn between them.[22] Faction and personal ambition or frustrated ambition are critically important in the fluid world of Cabinet and parliamentary high politics, and the actions of politicians must be explained 'by relating them to the actions of other politicians'.[23] The world of high politics was a closed one in the sense that the political prima donnas of the time 'were bound to see more significance in the definite structure of relationships at Westminster, than in their contacts with the world outside'. For this reason, it is misleading to talk in terms of a dialogue between leaders and governed and 'explanations of Westminster should centre not on its being at the top of a coherently organised pyramid of power whose bottom layer was the people, but on its character as a highly specialised community, like the City or Whitehall, whose primary interest was inevitably its own very institutional life'.[24] The extension of the franchise and the increasing need to manipulate rather than to influence the electorate brought no change to this esoteric character of high politics. Political leaders 'had as little intention as their predecessors of encouraging the electorate to enter into the high places of power. What they wanted the electorate to want was not participation but vicarious satisfaction at the leadership of the politicians who operated the system or claimed the right to operate it in the future.'[25] The importance of parties lies not, as historians tend to suppose, in their continuity, but in their fragility and in the continued possibility of their disruption.

Politicians certainly recognised the necessity of a gulf between private belief and public rhetoric on the Drink issues, along with the need for elasticity in policy pronouncements. Thus, Gladstone's ostensible support for temperance legislation after 1870 was at odds with his personal opinions. Chamberlain and Harcourt, in 1895, could indulge in a tongue-in-cheek exchange of private correspondence, pointing out how each had reversed his position between the 1870s and the 1890s on local option.[26] Lloyd George in 1915, whilst fanning the hysteria on wartime drinking, could admit in private that it was mostly 'fudge'. Certainly, a remarkable feature of the period before 1914 was the opportunities open to the political prima donnas of the day to take initiatives on social policy questions with a free hand, untrammelled by the constraints of the civil service, pressure groups, political parties or Cabinet colleagues. Some leading politicians took up the licensing question, not through personal choice, but as a matter of duty, like the workhorse Ritchie in 1888, 1890 and 1902. But it was more common for leaders voluntarily to seize hold of the question. Chamberlain in 1876, Churchill and Goschen in 1890, and Harcourt in 1893–95 are all examples of this. None of them had pressing departmental reasons to take up licensing, and none – with the possible exception of Chamberlain – had any great knowledge of Drink issues, although they were willing to undertake research on the topic.[27] Their motives were varied. At one level, these statesmen had every desire to do something to alleviate the terrible evil of intemperance, and to settle an awkward and tiresome administrative problem. But, at another level, they were equally determined to reap the maximum electoral or personal advantage from the issue. Thus, in the context of high politics, Chamberlain's espousal of municipal control over liquor in 1876 owed something to his confidence in municipal self-government, but more to his tactical need to acquire the support of nonconformist Liberal activists in his challenge to the Liberal leadership. Randolph Churchill's sudden conversion to temperance reform after his fall from office owed something to a study of urban conditions, but more to his desire to pose as a radical Tory democrat and to his desire to embarrass his rivals on the Tory front bench. Goschen's decision to pose as a temperance reformer in 1890 owed something to his shock at the millions wasted on beer and spirits, but more to his need to solve an awkward fiscal dilemma and to scotch the threat from Randolph Churchill. Chamberlain's cooling enthusiasm for local veto and growing desire to see equitable compensation owed something to a 'maturer' consideration of licensing, but more to his shift from Gladstonian Liberalism to Unionism.[28] Harcourt's local veto bills of 1892–95 owed something to electoral considerations, but more to his desire to find a weapon with which to outsmart his arch rival, Rosebery, in the bitterly divided Liberal cabinets of 1892–95. Lloyd George's exaggerated rhetoric in 1915 owed something to his concern at the problems in the munitions and shipbuilding, but equally served to appease his Welsh nonconformist supporters and to consolidate his position in the Cabinet. The state purchase schemes of 1915 and 1917 similarly need to be understood, both in the context of the supplies for the war effort and the complex high politics of the War Cabinet. After 1921, Drink issues rarely received such attention from the top elite but, in the 1960s, both Marples's and Castle's strong commitment to the breathalyser had the additional advantage of raising their personal profile in their respective Cabinets. Explanations in terms of high politics see authority not as a means of achieving policy, but policy as a means of achieving authority. On their own, they can be unduly desiccated insofar as they stress context too much and content too little, and simplify the interaction between low politics and high politics. However, they add a dimension to our understanding of the policy process. The channels by which reformist legislation got onto the agenda were manifold. Direct popular agitation fostered by outside groups, pressures from political parties, lobbying by groups or factions within parties and individual initiative by statesmen all could play a part.

In the nineteenth century, given the passivity of the Home Office, there was no bureaucratic focus that could act as a stimulus for self-generating government growth. There is no real scope for MacDonagh's model of government growth to be applied in our case history, given the absence of an inspectorate and the lack of any clear policy trajectory towards intervention.[29] It is interesting to speculate whether things might have evolved differently had Bruce's original 1871 plan of setting up a public house inspectorate gone ahead. Nevertheless, the conservative nature and culture of the Home Office, with its essentially passive outlook on the liquor question, was in a negative way able to define the culture and terms of reference. Its dominant ethos was to preserve the existing regulatory system as opposed to experimenting with restriction or prohibition: paradoxically its position on gambling was the reverse, where it fiercely defended a prohibition on off-course betting against those who argued for regulation.[30] The degree for policy initiative across Whitehall varied, with officials in the Board of Trade being more proactive on account of their different career backgrounds.[31] However, it is interesting that during this period much of the initiative comes from localities, with initiatives stemming from the Liverpool free licensing experiments of the 1860s, from Chamberlain's experiences and preoccupations in Birmingham in the early 1870s, from the licensing reduction scheme of Arthur Chamberlain in Birmingham in the 1890s, and from the Farnham magistrates' bench after *Sharp* v. *Wakefield*. After this case, the magistrates had acquired a lever with which to exert pressure on the government, which became marked after 1900. Had control over liquor licensing been entrusted to local bodies, as many restrictionists advocated, then a different pattern may have emerged. As far as licensing legislation was concerned, however, ministers seem to have been very much on their own. Thus, in 1872, Kimberley, the Colonial Secretary, had to draft in his own officials to clear up the debacle of Bruce's licensing proposals; and, in 1893, we find Harcourt and his son sitting up half the night trying to draft a workable local option bill. By 1908, there was more sign of a civil service input and advice on legislative schemes, but even then the Home Secretary, Herbert Gladstone, wrote pages of draft proposals for the licensing bill in his own hand.[32] He and the Lord Chancellor, Loreburn, were to have a decisive clash in the Cabinet on the nature of the Bill, reflecting their own intense interest in and mastery of the technical details of the scheme.

After 1914, there is a sharp shift in the focus of policy-making. The new CCB provided a bureaucratic force with an active interest in pursuing a policy shift towards restriction. This was a body that, from very early on, was not simply reacting to events, but was actively seeking to promote a policy initiative viz. the direct management by the state of the liquor trade in selective localities. Under the enthusiastic leadership of Lord D'Abernon, the CCB pursued a policy of research into the effects of consumption in a variety of contexts in the new light of national efficiency. It was able to redefine the problem and link the Drink issue with quite new areas, such as the provision of canteens in factories. The First World War, however, saw the dramatic widening of the policy arena away from issues such as taxation and licensing to encompass issues such as national efficiency and food production. Here, we find clashes of departmental interest with the CCB engaged, first, with a clash with the Ministry of Food and then in a rearguard, and ultimately unsuccessful, battle to preserve its existence in the face of opposition from the Treasury and parliamentary opinion. However, the issue of state purchase in both 1915 and 1917 had far greater political repercussions where the stakes were high. Here, it was figures such as Lloyd George, Bonar Law and Lord Milner who played a crucial role, and the question was removed from a purely Whitehall arena. Once the CCB was abolished in 1919, its proactive restrictive policies fell by the wayside, although the modicums of limitations such as the restricted opening hours and high taxation remained, and the Home Office continued to exert a sort of proprietorial protection over the Carlisle scheme.[33] Our case studies after 1945 reveal that bureaucratic inputs into the policy process were of major importance, although stimulus for change often comes from outside groups or political forces. The New Towns story shows a fierce struggle between the MTCP and the Home Office to control policy in the area of Drink as a leisure pursuit. Similarly, in the case of drink/driving, the Home Office and the MoT struggled to ensure that their respective priorities and perspectives were to the fore. Civil servants had plenty of scope to define the terms in which alcoholism or drunk driving was discussed. The episode of the CPRS report reveals a particularly sharp clash of Whitehall departments with the MoH ultimately being outgunned and defeated by a coalition of other departments. The issue of alcohol control after 1945 had fragmented, so that a whole range of Whitehall interests were involved. It all illustrates very well the way in which British government during this period was characterised by interdepartmental turf wars and clashes, with the Cabinet system providing resolution of conflict.

As well as the rise of bureaucratic influence, the first two decades of the twentieth century also witnessed a greater impact upon policy-making by the vested interests involved. Keith Middlemas, writing primarily about industrial relations, has gone so far as to claim that, shortly after, the British political system shifted from one of a parliamentary democracy to one of 'corporate bias' in which two parallel political systems coexisted.[34] In the nineteenth century, the Trade exerted influence primarily through demonstration and deputations to ministers. Bruce, in 1871, failed to consult the brewers about his scheme. By the 1890s, the larger brewers were attempting to influence ministers in a more direct away, but the process was haphazard, for example the links between J. Danvers Power and his relative W. H. Smith. Their focus remained on electoral politics but they faced the problems of endemic divisions within the Trade, with smaller country brewers and licensed victuallers often at odds with the large brewery companies. Notwithstanding the temperance reformers' lurid pictures of the political 'menace' of the Trade, their bargaining position was weak at the turn of the century as they found themselves exposed financially and linked uncomfortably with one political party. The First World War saw ministers, officials and representatives of the Trade cooperating on policy issues far more closely, for example on the use of raw materials and taxation. The round table licensing conference of 1921, which shaped licensing policy for the next fifty years, was the very epitome of corporate style bargaining. In the interwar years, a number of influential intermediaries between the government and the brewers played an important role in lubricating relations between

Whitehall and the Trade. A pattern emerged of key governmental figures such as Sir John Pedder, Sir Edgar Sanders and J. S. Eagle moving from government to serve on Trade bodies. Nothing illustrates the shift in political strategy more than the contrast between the brewers' activities in opposition to the 1908 Bill with that offered to the 1948 New Town legislation of the Attlee Labour government. In the former case, there were massive public demonstrations and electoral activity. In the latter, the brewers, although in contact with Lord Woolton of the Conservative party and masterminding a newspaper campaign critical of the government's plans, were most careful to avoid any overt electoral involvement. By the 1960s, over the question of the breathalyser, the brewers had become even more discrete. They distanced themselves from the campaign of some of the licensed victuallers against the new proposals, and took a low profile on the issue. By the time of the CPRS report in 1982, the political discussions that mattered seems to have been entirely shielded from public view. The Brewers' Society lobbied hard in Whitehall for the suppression and modification of the CPRS report so that the government paper, *Drinking Sensibly* was acceptable: 'the Society has been working with the Civil Servants and Ministers of the relevant Departments to try to ensure that when the paper was published it would be a moderate, balanced document. It is very gratifying that our efforts have been so successful.'[35]

Richardson and Jordan have spoken of Britain in the postwar world becoming a 'post-parliamentary democracy', where policy communities of interest groups around Whitehall departments, rather than parties or Parliament, are the chief actors in the policy process.[36] The case studies of policy on alcoholism and drink/driving provide plenty of evidence for the importance of policy networks as a key focus in the post-1945 period. The MoT in the 1950s and 1960s had conflicting pressures as the road safety lobby and the motoring organisations came into conflict. In the case of alcoholism, the terms of discussion of the problem were determined by the expert groups who happened to be in ascendancy at any particular time, with officials exercising a moderating influence. On the other hand, the post-1945 case studies also show that Parliament still played an important role. On drink/driving, it was the Pedestrians' Association and the Conservative M. P., Graham Page, that did much to get the issue on the agenda, perhaps more so than the Royal Society for the Prevention of Accidents, which was more of an establishment or Whitehall orientated body. Again, in the case of policy on alcoholism in the 1960s, it was pressure from MPs, GPs and members of the public, as well as the professional medical world, that helped highlight the need for initiative. In a more negative manner, it was coolness among Labour MPs that dampened down the potential of licensing in New Towns to become yoked to the general issue of nationalisation versus private enterprise in the 1950s. Another feature during this period is that the interest (or, on occasions, the lack of interest) of individual ministers, irrespective of party and sometimes bureaucratic position, plays a key role in determining the policy agenda. Without Morrison's fierce enthusiasm on the issue, it is hard to imagine the New Towns liquor legislation going as far as it did. Lord Hailsham, Marples and George Thomas all promoted the case for drink/driving legislation. Barbara Castle, while cautious on the issue, was able to steer the implementation of the policy in a high profile manner. On the health policy side, Sir Keith Joseph, David Owen and Sir George Young all played a helpful role in orientating the DoH to take an interest in the health aspects of alcohol consumption. The media also played a role in getting the issue on the agenda.

Some comparisons: contrasting policy agendas

Detailed comparative analysis of policy towards Drink lies beyond the scope of this book. However, our study indicates that the area of alcohol policy in Britain has been rather more complex and contested than in other industrial countries over the period. In France, the question has been seen predominantly in terms of health. The importance of wine in both that nation's diet and commerce, and the pattern of slow and steady rather than binge drinking, along with the absence of any marked evangelical Christian movement, meant that the organised temperance movement was weak. The policy concentrated around the issue of discouraging excessive soaking and reducing excess, overall consumption; hence, the policy arena tended to be colonised by medical experts. By contrast, a robust temperance movement emerged in Germany, but was not, as in Britain, part of a larger mosaic of progressive liberal causes. Total abstinence was not a key feature and the movement was elitist and worked from the top downward.[37] In Scandinavian countries, on the other hand, there was a robust temperance movement with strong grass roots support. The policy adopted here was a combination of local option and municipal control, a combination which avoided the interminable jealousies between prohibitionists and restrictionists in Britain. In Sweden, the importation and distribution of alcoholic drink came to be largely controlled by a state monopoly and later, in the twentieth century, a rigorous alcohol control policy was pursued, aimed at reducing consumption. Policy patterns here chimed in with the egalitarian and strong communitarian political culture, and with a tradition of strong paternalistic, even authoritarian, regulation from the state. In the United States, as is well known, there was a strongly contested battle between the drink interests and prohibitionists, with little margin for intermediary regulatory or restrictionist approaches. The Manichaean outlook, which saw the world in terms of a clash between good and evil, favoured first, the religious model, regarding the problem as one of the moral failings of individuals, and later, the prohibitionist outlook, which saw the drinker as a helpless victim of an evil force. Here, prohibitionists dominated the political agenda until the 1930s. Later, after the collapse of prohibition, the alcohol question came to be dominated by the disease model of alcoholism, which adopted an individual perspective – again in absolutist terms – and which was colonised and determined by medical experts.[38]

Even this brief sketch prompts one significant reflection: the dominant agenda or discourse of a policy area can vary enormously. Constitutional, social and political factors all help determine the terms of reference of a policy 'problem'. As David Fahey has pointed out, a variety of factors acted as a brake on the progress of prohibition in Britain as opposed to the United States: the constitutional structure, which allowed less room for local initiative and experiment; the relative weakness of evangelical Protestants and organised women's movements, the higher social standing of brewers, the widespread affection for the 'local pub', the one-sided temperance links with the Liberal party and the failure of the prohibitionists (especially at the turn of the century) to dominate the terms of discourse of the debate.[39]

Other comparable issues in Britain point to the elasticity of both the policy agenda and the terms of debate. The rise of a movement against alcohol in mid-Victorian Britain was accompanied by popular agitations against smoking, gambling, the state regulation of prostitution and the use or trade in opiates. Anti-smoking movements could make no headway in Victorian Britain on account of the strongly individualist approaches to the subject. The sole exception was juvenile smoking, where the issue came to be seen in terms of stunting an immature individual's development, and so could be linked to Edwardian issues of national efficiency and racial degeneration. After 1950, the issue becomes transformed as the evidence mounted of the undeniable damaging health effects of consumption. Arguments against smoking changed from a moralistic to a health orientation. Even here, initially, the dominant paradigm was based on helping the individual smoker, and only in the last quarter of the twentieth century shifted to a more collective one of public health.[40] In comparison with Drink, however, the parameters and shifts on the question, as well as the politics, seem a good deal more clear cut. Gambling was another area where moralist and religious debate mingled with economic arguments. As far as working class gambling was concerned, the dominant policy before 1930 was far more influenced by issues of social control than in the case of Drink. A policy of prohibition on off-course racing betting was pursued and defended by the Home Office, the very department which paradoxically had fended off demands for prohibition of alcohol. As with temperance reform, the moralistic anti-gambling pressure groups faded in strength after 1914. Interestingly there was 'spill-over' from the Drink policy area as advocates of state regulation in gambling pointed to the supposed success of the CCB. Later, in the 1960s, the 'compulsive gambler', who suffered from excessive behaviour, was discovered, again following the example of the disease model of alcoholism.[41] Prostitution, like Drink, has been throughout a hotly contested policy area. Early in the nineteenth century, some reformers challenged the accepted tolerant view of it by portraying it as an 'intolerable evil' which threatened the social order. Later, this view was opposed by those regarding it as primarily a social evil best contained by police and medical regulation. Feminist and socialist perspectives added new and cross-cutting complexities and, to this day, there is no consensus on the causes or significance of the phenomenon.[42] Very dramatic shifts have occurred in the policy arena of drugs. The early nineteenth century saw general social use of opium, which was perceived as possessing useful medicinal properties. By the late Victorian period, however, the medical and pharmacist professions had effectively gained control of its use, which was henceforth defined in terms of addiction. The contrast with alcohol at this period is striking. This laid the seeds for the later development of drugs policy which is best seen in terms of 'creative tension' between concepts of treatment and of control, with a contested area between civil servants, the medical profession and the police. Explanations for the shift in the late-nineteenth century have to take into account not only the development of public health, but also social factors such as the growing professionalisation of medicine, and the growing articulation and influence of the new professions.[43]

Drink and the policy process

All the above examples show the importance of the intellectual frames of reference of the policy process. As Virginia Berridge has stressed, 'what most needs analysis is not the dimensions of a problem but the definition of it. It is the establishment of attitudes and perceptions, of shifts in focus and ways of looking at things which should concern us.'[44] The story of the politics of Drink certainly reveals that a simple rational actor view of the policy process, which sees policy-makers facing a problem – albeit complex – and then working out solutions, is in itself inadequate, as it leaves so much out of the frame.[45] Certainly it is true that contemporaries in the period from 1850 to 1920 tended to speak in these terms, talking of the 'temperance problem' and agonising or fiercely clashing with each other over the 'solutions'. It was also a period, in contrast to that after 1945, when policy had a simple focus, parliamentary legislation, which leant itself to classification in terms of stages of the political process. This classification seemed fitted to a liberal model of the political process in which demands for change were seen as 'coming up' to the political elite, whether through direct popular pressure, political parties or the influences of pressure groups of one kind or another. However, as our analysis earlier in this chapter has shown, the erratic way in which, at the level of high politics, the political prima donnas of the period took up the question, either for personal or party advantage or as a means of 'fixing' another policy – Wellington and agricultural unrest in 1830, Gladstone and the commercial treaty with France in 1860, Ritchie and local government in 1888, Goschen and his budget in 1890, Lloyd George and the munitions issue – undermines any rational policy-making perspective. Politics is about more than problems and policy.

A more fundamental problem with rational actor accounts of the policy process is that they play down the ideological spectacles with which a policy problem is viewed or approached. In the middle of the nineteenth century, we find different models of the Drink question vying for supremacy based on *a priori* assumptions and value judgements that were radically different: free licensing, moral suasion, prohibition and regulation. But beyond that, the particular contested ground over which policy centred, what we may term the tactics as opposed to the strategy of the question, varied strikingly. At the risk of some simplification, the following is a summary of how the contested ground varied:

1830–70	The market: trading practices
1860–95	Local control over licensing
1880–1914	Licence reduction schemes; merits of the Gothenburg scheme
1914–20	Hours of sale and CCB controls
1920–40	Improved public house; merits of state management

Thus, the debate on the Drink question at any time during this period, although involving fundamental and important issues and perceptions, nevertheless often appears, from the perspective of a later generation, to be fought out in exceedingly narrow terms of reference. The policy debate is therefore heavily circumscribed and bounded, to an extent greater than that allowed by Simon in his conception of 'bounded rationality'.[46]

The narrow terms of reference of the debate at any time is further illustrated by the content of the two Royal Commissions on liquor licensing, and various other inquiries between 1830 and 1970. Such inquiries, according to a rational actor perspective, should be expected to be critical in unearthing data and clarifying policy options. Their terms of reference tended to be tightly drawn concerning aspects of liquor licensing, which hardly encouraged them to undertake research. Moreover, their very composition – packed with interested parties – ensured either a divided (1899) or an anodyne (1931) report. Home secretaries and leading ministers cynically viewed these bodies as lightning conductors which allowed them to shelve actions. The appointment of the Erroll Committee of 1971 was instrumental in another sense. It was clearly a device by Maudling to 'soften up' the ground for liberalisation, hence the strong presence of consumer and business personnel among its members. By contrast, the various parliamentary inquiries of the early nineteenth century into the 1830 Beer Act and free trade issues had more influence on legislators.

A feature throughout the history of Drink is the high degree of uncertainty against which legislators and policy-makers operated and the limitations of research into the question. Despite the superfluity of prose written about Drink before 1914, those making policy remained in many respects astonishingly ignorant about what they were legislating on at that time. The world of the public house, to say nothing of the working man's club, was alien to most legislators or policy-makers and it was one equally foreign, because generally despised, to temperance workers. As two commentators wrote in 1901: 'To most of us the public-house is as little known as China . . . How few of our cocksure reformers have troubled even to enter it!'[47] The result was that a number of nostrums – that publicans 'pushed' drink on their customers or that intemperance was linked to the excess number of outlets – went largely unresearched. Rowntree and Sherwell's book was influential on account of its rare research into the problems of one policy solution, local veto, in New England. It is true that temperance activists, like their counterparts in anti-gambling and other similar movements, were assiduous in reinforcing moral and religious arguments with facts and figures from both the social sciences and the medical world.[48] Elite policy-makers were bombarded with data about the social costs of intemperance.[49] The problem was that the causation links between alcohol and crime or other social evils, on which some of the data centred, depended upon subjective interpretations. Even basic statistics could be elastic and contested. Joseph Chamberlain warned a Select Committee of the House of Lords in the 1870s that he could make the statistics of convictions for drunkenness in Birmingham ten times as bad by tightening up policing: 'just one turn of the screw would bring in ten times the number'.[50] *Per capita* consumption figures were a far tighter source of data. But rather than themselves guiding policy, their interpretation depended upon the intellectual paradigm being adopted. Thus, later, when the disease model of alcoholism was to the fore in the early 1950s, *per capita* consumption was irrelevant; but once the Ledermann hypothesis had gained support by the 1970s, consumption figures became an important indicator of 'problem drinking' for the DHSS. In short, scientific research was itself a tool in the struggle for dominance over the policy area. The marked lack of consensus among Victorian medical opinion of the merits of alcohol and the causes of 'habitual drunkenness' prevented any emergence of policy control by the medical profession, as so strikingly happened with opiates at the end of the nineteenth century. In the early twentieth century, there was a threefold battle between temperance doctors, the Society for the Study of Inebriety (advocating the disease model of alcoholism) and the new moderationists in the Medical Research Council and the CCB. All 'manipulated medical-scientific knowledge and employed the rhetoric of objectivity in their efforts to gain a position of cultural and scientific authority on the alcohol question.'[51] The rational actor model of policy sees empirical research as determining policy, but in our history research facts tended to follow policy prescriptions rather than determine them. Moreover, once the institutional basis for mobilising research was removed, it could wither on the vine, as happened after the demise of the CCB, despite the efforts of outsiders like Astor. Indeed, by the 1950s, Whitehall departments seemed both bereft of a research base and lacking in a research culture. No attempt was made to research the likely needs of leisure in the New Towns, and the Carlisle 'experiment' had merely drifted along with the Home Office, having no thought of systematically analysing its operation. Likewise, we find the civil servants at the MoH in the 1950s quite bereft of information about the extent of alcoholism in Britain. The departments involved in drink/driving policy appear to have been very much in the dark about the popularity of legislation; and the politicians then seem quite as uncertain and nervous about its political fallout as their predecessors in the 1890s were concerning the relative electoral muscle of the temperance and Trade groupings. Indeed, the Brewers' Society was better informed about public opinion than the government as a result of commissioning two professional public opinion surveys on the subject.[52]

Decision-making in uncertainty, the confusion of policy means and ends, the erratic nature of policy-making and the interplay of complex interests and organisations are all factors which underpin the model of disjointed incrementalism presented by Charles Lindblom. This is generally seen as the polar opposite to rational actor approaches to the policy process. Policy-makers are seen as 'muddling through'. Small incremental steps are the natural outcome in a democracy, as a plethora of decision-makers impact on the process. These include actors at relatively low levels in the political or administrative hierarchy. Incremental shifting, rather than heroic change, is seen as the normal state of politics in a democracy. Policy is a continuum, and the implementation of policy will itself often substantially shape the policy process. Moreover, decision-makers in the real world often pay as much attention to the means as to the ends of policy.[53] At first blush, the story of Drink seems to offer some good examples of this perspective. We may point to the incremental development of the Carlisle scheme in the interwar years, and the way it was shaped by local administrators and protected by the Home Office, without any strategic direction. The New Towns story shows a complex picture of how technical needs, as much as political direction, brought the issue to the fore. The intricacies of drink/driving policy in the Macmillan government reveal an intriguing melange of factors in the Cabinet committee with the erratic contributions of ministers such as Lord Hailsham, unexpected and unwelcome scientific research findings, interdepartmental interests and technical legal factors all intruding. The perspective might also be applied to the fiasco of Bruce's 1871 legislative efforts and the Unionists' licensing problems of 1890. However, the history of Drink in Britain also starkly reveals the inadequacies of the model, which is always most at home in explaining settled conditions. It ignores the driving force of general political ideologies. One thinks of the free licensing and prohibitionists in the mid-nineteenth century, the way the issue became bound up with the debate on 'socialist confiscation' after 1900, or the passion of Herbert Morrison for public control. It plays down the way in which the force of events can lead to radical policy shifts, for example the First World War, and it underestimates the capacity both of politicians, like Lloyd George, and administrators, like D'Abernon, to impose a vision on the process to use legislation or new institutions to steer the process. Nor does the model serve to explain the even more involved policy processes of the post-1945 world. The drink/driving case study, for all the complex forces involved, could also be read in terms of the rational actor model and conventional liberal views of democracy. After all, there was a full debate in the public arena and in Parliament, as well as Whitehall, and a range of policy options were fully clarified and discussed, despite the intrusion of technical factors.

Powerful insight into the policy process has been provided by writers who stress the importance of institutions in the policy process. Particularly influential has been the bureaucratic politics model of Graham Allison. Here, policy is seen to emerge less as a result of the intentions of politicians, but more from the interactions of bureaucracies within a government. The standard operating procedures of different organisations and the clash of rival departments are key factors. 'Where you stand on an issue depends upon where you sit.'[54] The history of Drink shows many examples which support this perspective on the policy process. The Admiralty, a department previously as far removed from the Drink question as possible, forced it on the agenda in the early months of the First World War to further its own interests in extending control over the shipyards. The CCB for its part, once set up, established its own policy ethos and battled fiercely with the Ministry of Food. The case studies of the New Towns and drink/driving show plenty of examples of interdepartmental clashes with politicians and civil servants fighting their departments' causes. We also find important differences within the hierarchies of an individual department, with, for example, the road safety division of the MoT anxious to tighten up the law, while the top civil servants are concerned about the political repercussions for their minister. However, like disjointed incrementalism, the focus on the politics of organisations leaves out of the picture broader political and ideological forces. It is not good at explaining why in some case 'normal' bureaucratic politics operates, whereas at other times political priorities or sudden shifts in definition of a problem can transform the policy arena.[55] It also downplays what Jenkins and Gray have termed the extrinsic influences – as opposed to the intrinsic bureaucratic interests – upon ministers and civil servants which 'arise from the divergent backgrounds and developments of individuals and groups'.[56] In the drink/driving example, we may point to the staunch teetotalism of George Thomas, Marples's forceful character, and Lord Hailsham's experience as a QC with drunken driving cases. In the earlier period, it is not possible to build up a picture of bureaucratic politics in a policy area that was then singularly lacking in bureaucratic involvement, whatever the case in other areas such as education or railway regulation. Similar considerations apply to theories of policy networks, which are most appropriately used when issues of implementation are at stake which in turn determine the nature of the policy, for example over the use of the breathalyser or the operation of regional units on the treatment of alcoholism. Policy networks appear to be more significant in the post-1945 period than earlier.

In the past twenty years, policy theorists have been particularly interested in broadening the approach to policy analysis by seeking to link economic, political and social forces to the power of ideas and belief systems. The 'new institutionalist' school has provided one such perspective. Its exponents seek to show how institutions themselves shape ideas and determine the capacity of groups to influence policy and respond to societal and other pressures. They help to set the norms of behaviour and the political agenda. Institutions can be a force for change, as well as stability, as institutional apparatus may provide a powerful focus for shifting dominant policy consensus.[57] Such an approach seems to provide some useful insight regarding the Drink story. Parliament in the nineteenth century was the focus for alcohol policy, and was imbued with an outlook that favoured regulation and modest restriction, through the licensing laws, rather than more proactive policies or outlooks that might have been pursued by local municipal bodies. The traditional model of regulation was also reinforced by the passive outlook of both the Home Office and the local magistracy, both of which approached the question through legalistic terms of reference. These institutional arrangements made it difficult for those advocating free licensing, prohibition or temperance restriction to make headway. Hence their interest in devices like the local veto or locally elected boards of control. The contrast with the First World War is striking. Here, the CCB provided more than a mere bureaucratic focus for policy. D'Abernon and his colleagues developed almost a missionary zeal for the twin policies of restriction and the improved public house brought about by state management. They were equally dismissive of both the old regulation and the nostrums of the temperance movement. They were convinced that they could 'solve' the Drink problem by their new restrictive policies, which were underpinned by 'scientific' research. With the demise of the CCB came the end of such a proactive alcohol policy. Moving on to the post-1945 period, the pattern of policy-making is shaped in many respects by the strong departmental focus of Whitehall and the mechanisms of Cabinet coordination. Such structures encouraged the fragmentation of policy in the alcohol area and its redefinition in such terms as town planning, road safety, health, and consumer rights. 'New institutionalist' approaches have been particularly popular in the field of comparative government. Certainly, as noted earlier, one of the factors explaining the divergent paths taken on the issue by Britain and the United States is the contrasting constitutional framework of centralised parliamentary system as opposed to devolved federalism. However, a 'new institutionalist' approach leaves a good deal out of the frame. It downplays the significance of cultural and economic forces and the opportunity they allow for the mobilisation of pressure groups. It also ignores the important perspective of high politics where political heavyweights, such as Harcourt, Lloyd George or Herbert Morrison, could use the issue to further their own personal or ideological interests. Competing ideas, moreover, sometimes provide powerful free-floating forces even when not entombed in institutional structures.

Majone's view that 'We miss a great deal if we try to understand policy-making solely in terms of power, influence, and bargaining, to the exclusion of debate and argument' has unearthed a rich seam of debate.[58] The concept of 'social learning' developed by Heclo has also been particularly influential. Heclo, in his comparative study of the development of social policy in Britain and Sweden, saw bureaucratic 'middlemen' playing a key role in the development of policy. These were mediators in a competing market for social policy ideas. Both social and conventional political pressures were important factors, but the bureaucrats, operating in a situation of collective puzzlement, were continually adopting fresh techniques or adapting foreign experiences to meet the pressures placed upon them and to overcome the failures of the past.[59] Building on both approaches, Paul Sabatier has developed a comprehensive model of policy change that attempts to combine the insights of bureaucratic politics with a proper recognition of ideological and broader political forces. Put simply, he portrays the policy arena in terms of contests at any time between competing 'advocacy coalitions', broad based collections of individuals who span the worlds of political parties, pressure groups, journalism and academe. Ideas are the 'glue' which hold such coalitions together. Within the fluid world of policy subsystems, advocacy coalitions battle for supremacy. At any time, there is liable to be a dominant advocacy coalition whose values and belief system penetrate and, in some respects, shape the policy-making institutions; this coalition is able to set the intellectual framework within which individual policy decisions are made. 'Policy oriented learning' is the process by which rival advocacy coalitions strive for advantage. As the world changes and policy outputs require adjustment, so the rival coalitions are continually seeking to outlearn each other in order to make sense of the world around them. The policy process will be affected by exogenous factors: both relatively stable ones, like the cultural climate or the constitutional framework, and unexpected ones such as the impact of a war, a change of government, particular scandals or events or the sudden intrusion of another policy subsystem. Sabatier maintains that belief systems of the various advocacy coalitions are organised in hierarchical, tripartite layers. 'Deep core' beliefs underpin each coalition. Higher up come policy beliefs containing fundamental value priorities relating to the policy area, including perceptions of causation and strategies for realising core values within the subsystem. Finally, there are narrower beliefs regarding specific regulations or evaluations of applied policy. Whereas deep core beliefs will be held tenaciously, those in the last category are likely to be sacrificed or modifed in the light of the process of policy-learning. Sabatier presents various hypotheses which can be researched empirically in order to test the applicability of the model. He suggests, for example, that where deep policy beliefs are in dispute in a policy arena, the line up of allies and opponents will tend to be rather stable over a decade or so. Furthermore, the core policy attributes of a governmental programme will be likely to remain largely intact, so long as the dominant advocacy coalition remains in power. 'Significant perturbations' external to the policy subsystem will be needed to allow a complete shift in the relative influence of advocacy coalitions.[60] Peter Hall has adopted a broadly similar approach by stressing the importance of policy paradigms underpinning the policy process. Policy-learning takes place at different levels: the overarching goals that guide policy in a particular field; techniques or policy instruments used to attain those goals; and finally the precise settings of those instruments. Whereas normal incrementalism characterises change at the latter two, more fundamental change at the first and deepest level will require more obviously political or strategic policy-learning, which may lead to the emergence of a new policy paradigm. The particular pattern of the paradigm shift will be determined, not simply by the force of arguments, but by political events and the institutional structures and 'ancillary resources' of the competing factions. Sets of ideas, just as much as institutions or political developments or bureaucratic manipulation, shape the policy-making process: indeed, the two should be seen as interacting and reinforcing each other.[61]

Our story of Drink suggests that there is some mileage in these approaches.[62] The Victorian period saw a clash of coalitions of interests which were underpinned by robust policy paradigms. The concept of an advocacy coalition is a useful one, as the various rival camps included politicians, pressure groups, journalists, church leaders and other elite opinion leaders. The free licensing paradigm for a while contested with some success the traditional belief in regulation, but was undermined by empirical evidence unearthed by parliamentary inquiries (policy-learning), which discredited its policies. There then followed a period when two rival advocacy coalitions, traditionalist regulators and prohibitionists, competed fiercely. Because these coalitions shared fundamentally different assumptions, it was a dialogue of the deaf with engagement only on the third level of policy technicalities. As Sabatier predicts, the line up of coalitions was stable over a long period. After 1880, changes in more general social thinking encouraged the support of restrictionist reformers. Both the prohibitionists' borrowing of local veto from America and restrictionists' advocacy of the Gothenburg system may be portrayed as policy-learning. The First World War provided a major exogenous shock to the system, which allowed the new restrictionist policy paradigm to triumph, at least temporarily. Some civil servants, such as Sir John Pedder, the Home Office's leading technical expert on licensing matters for a long period, may be seen as 'policy brokers' struggling to adapt existing procedures in the light of new thinking and new political pressures. On a less grand scale, the approaches of Sabatier and Hall do provide some useful perspectives on the alcoholism and drunk/driving case studies after 1945, with the civil servants as sceptical 'policy brokers' caught between competing advocacy coalitions.

Nevertheless, our history also suggests some serious problems with the approaches. A difficulty with Hall's approach is the vagueness which he gives to the concept of policy-learning, which seems to be applied to goals, techniques and settings. The learning process may vary in nature in different arenas of the policy process. Sabatier's concept of advocacy coalitions underpinned by rival deep core policy beliefs also may be seen to be problematic. The restrictionists, in the 1870–1900 period, developed a distinctive approach. But it is doubtful if this constituted a policy paradigm. Many came to the question from quite different assumptions and with different core beliefs. Thus, we find T. P. Whittaker, a disillusioned prohibitionist, moderate reformers in the CETS, social reformers or medical people all grouped together. Moreover, when restrictionist ideas were dominant after 1914, they were championed by D'Abernon who despised the temperance movement's approaches and emphasised his different 'scientific' approach. Similarly confusing are the odd alliances that sometimes occur. Thus, in the 1920s, the Trade and free market business interests are found fighting alongside prohibitionists to discredit the Carlisle experiment. All these had very different core beliefs. Likewise, Carlisle is defended by temperance enthusiasts such as the Astors and Rev. Henry Carter, by the progressive brewer, Nevile, and by Sir John Pedder and bureaucrats at the Home Office. Another problem is that the actors in the policy process may have a variety of fundamental beliefs. The prohibitionists, before 1914, were driven by their belief in the iniquity of alcohol, but they were almost equally moved by their faith in the agitational model of political progress. Similarly, we find Joseph Chamberlain's belief in municipal enterprise and D'Abernon's faith in scientific research as powerful driving forces. Rowntree's perception of the Trade as a corrupting and subversive influence on politics reflected a core faith in the rational, liberal, democratic process. In short, should we see the core beliefs as those pertaining to the Drink question or should we analyse other fundamental ideological beliefs? A moral suasionist position on alcohol is upheld by Lord Salisbury, a conservative thinker, by John Stuart Mill and even by some socialists. Cardinal Manning's Catholic faith, Lawson's radical liberalism, Ulster Protestants' Orange outlook and socialists' desire to attack capitalist brewers can all be found nestling in the prohibitionists' camp. All this rather undermines Sabatier's contention that it is 'basic ontological and normative beliefs' which comprise the belief systems that underpin policy positions. A further difficulty lies in the way in which the technical policy devices themselves became imbued with passionate commitment on the part of the protagonists. Thus, local veto became the lodestone for the prohibitionists and the Gothenburg system, and later Carlisle, for restrictionist reformers. Often, technical solutions rather than deep core beliefs seem to have shaped the balance of parties. Equally striking is the way in which the same technical solution could take on new meanings and be used for different ends at different times. Disinterested management is a case in point. Originally conceived as a temperance device, it later came to be justified as a means of providing an improved leisure facility, and by the 1940s as an element of social democratic planning.

The concepts of advocacy coalitions, different layers of the policy process and the interaction of ideas and institutional forces provide useful insights. However, the approaches by Sabatier and Hall may be more applicable to rather limited or technical areas of policy or particular episodes of change than large policy canvasses, like Drink, education or health. Their tendency to approach the question in dichotomous terms is not very helpful in an area where there were more than two competing policy nostrums. As Peter John has also noted, the models tend to assume stability in the policy process, and see the key catalyst for change as coming from external 'shocks'. This underestimates both the latitude of individual politicians and the creative conservatism of bureaucrats to steer the policy direction and to manipulate agendas.[63]

A feature of our analysis throughout has been the way in which the Drink question has been made to serve a variety of political and administrative agendas and been couched in a variety of different discourses. In this connection, John Kingdon has produced a model of the political process that stresses the extent to which it is in eternal flux with policy outcomes stemming from a variety of shifting pressures.[64] He sees three 'streams' – problems, policies and politics – which are largely independent, with each having its own dynamics and rules. Problems are public matters that require attention. But what is crucial is the way in which they are defined and categorised. Politicians, bureaucrats, journalists and pressure group activists and so on are policy entrepreneurs who attempt to fit solutions to problems, and who may have their own agenda. Finally, political events, such as swings in the public mood or election results, influence how the problems are defined and how they are prioritised. The separate streams come together at certain critical times, and then 'Solutions become joined to problems, and both of them are joined to favorable political forces.'[65] Kingdon suggests that from time to time a policy 'window' opens when the three streams converge and when an opportunity arises for taking an initiative. Windows close as regularly as they open, and a successful outcome depends upon seizing the right moment. Both ideas and political events make an impact upon what is a 'policy primeval soup', but equally there is spillover from one policy area to another, and policy-makers learn from each other. The situation is always one of flux in which the streams of problems, policy and politics are continually interacting.

Baumgartner and Jones have similarly seen agendas as important facets in their concept of 'punctuated equilibrium'.[66] They point to how settled policy consensus may be suddenly overthrown. Policy monoplies abound in different areas where the dominant actors or institutions are able to control the policy agenda. However, if an outside group can redefine a problem area, then the way may be opened for a dramatic shift. 'Issue definition, then, is the driving force in both stability and instability, primarily because issue definition has the potential for mobilizing the previously disinterested.'[67] New agendas and the accompanying new ideas that go with them can introduce new groups into the policy area, with the result that change can come about very quickly. Similarly, the venue where a policy is discussed and contested is also important. By shifting a policy location from one venue to another, the policy entrepreneur in government will have a greater chance of bringing about change and of linking new solutions to old policy problems. Ideas, interests, political events and institutions are all important in determining the outcomes of the policy process.

Both these approaches, which stress the importance of agendas and the definitions of problems, along with the complicated interactions of policy problems with solutions, have a lot of resonance in relation to our case story. Restrictionist reformers in the nineteenth century were able to widen the scope of the Drink issue by associating it with local government reform; on the other hand, they were unable to change the venue of decision-making from central to local government, which handicapped their advances. In the period after 1895, temperance reform attracted a good deal more support from social elites because of the way some reformers were able to present it as part of a problem of social poverty and national efficiency. The 1830 Beer Act could be seen as an excellent example of a briefly open window, when the problems of distress in rural areas and of excess spirit drinking, the policy prescriptions of free traders and the political concerns of Wellington's ministry all pointed to a radical solution. Similarly, the Licensing Act of 1904 resulted from a combination of factors: administrative pressures from the magistrates, the electoral impact of the Trade and the political calculations of Cabinet ministers. The First World War can offer similar examples of problems, bureaucratic policies and political pressures all coming together to provide an open window for facilitating initiatives such as the setting up of the CCB and, later, the abortive attempts at state purchase. We have already seen how technical solutions themselves were adopted to solve other problems. Take the case of disinterested management. Chamberlain used it to promote municipal aggrandisement, Rowntree and Sherwell as a means of purifying political life, D'Abernon as a means of promoting national efficiency and workers' productivity, and Pedder as a device to improve leisure facilities. In the case of the New Towns episode, technicalities put the issue on the agenda but these quickly blended with broader political priorities. With alcoholism policy in the 1960s, it was political pressures that demanded attention and here we see civil servants seizing upon the technical solution of in-patient treatment units largely because some initiative had to be taken, and this seemed the only credible policy available. After 1970, the shift of the MoH towards a more proactive alcohol policy reflected a redefinition both of the ministry's general outlook on preventative medicine, and a shift in the attitudes of the medical profession towards alcohol with the disease model in abeyance. Drink/driving shows yet another example of the importance of definitions and agendas. Those arguing for legislation on the issue had to change the terms of reference away from the liberty of the individual towards road safety. By contrast, the wider anti-alcohol lobby was unable to present it in terms of an alcohol question with repercussions for other areas of control; and the brewers, happy with the definition in terms of road safety, were astute enough to avoid much controversy on the issue.

Any model is a simplification into which the complexity of the real world of policy-making rarely fits. The approaches in terms of agendas and discourses we have considered do have some weaknesses. Reflecting their American origin, they fail to distinguish sufficiently between the roles of politicians, bureaucrats and professional advisers, crucially important in a country with a strong party tradition like Britain. Apart from their quite different roles, strong cultural traditions underpin each. Kingdon seems to lump them in the policy stream with little differentiation. Distinctions between low and high politics are not really addressed, and the personal manipulations and autonomous position of senior politicians, so stressed by Maurice Cowling, are not addressed. A further weakness is the way in which the issue of power is somewhat glossed over, particularly Lukes's second and third dimensions.[68] The passive power of powerful economic interest groups to shape the political process or keep items off the agenda is not really addressed. The perceived power of the Trade did much to constrain politicians before 1914, and its behind-the-scenes influence shaped the position of some Whitehall departments at the time of the CPRS report in the 1980s. Similarly, other capitalist pressures played a role in shaping the opinion in 1919–21 in favour of the scrapping of wartime controls. Nor is attention paid to the capacity of a political class to shape and structure the state in the way that the Conservatives did in the 1980s. Nevertheless, our study does reveal how, even in a country as politically finely structured and stable as Britain, there is ample opportunity for social policy questions to be transformed by a change in the discourse or definition of the policy question (or in Baumgartner and Jones's terminology, 'agenda'). When such a change of discourse is accompanied by a major bureaucratic shift ('venue'), the changes can be dramatic indeed, as the case of Drink and the First World War illustrate. However, both 'agenda' and 'venue' are themselves likely to continue to be heavily contested and affected by the normal operations and interactions of both bureaucratic and political high politics, as participants, with their own personal motives and agendas, continually strive to manipulate the events or opportunities around them. Here, the forces of institutional conservatism tend to have the cards stacked in their favour. Sometimes, moreover, significant policy change can come about as a result of a more gradually shifting consensus, without there being any dramatic institutional shifts. At all events, the story of the politics of Drink in Britain since 1830 teaches us that the intellectual framework is just as significant as its institutional counterpart when it comes to shaping the policy process.

Notes

1 Introduction

1 *Report of Royal Commission on Liquor Licensing Laws*, Majority Report, p. 2, *PP.*, 1899, (C.9379), XXXV; Noel Buxton and Walter Hoare, 'Temperance Reform', in ed. C. F. G. Masterman, *The Heart of the Empire*, (1st publ. 1901), ed. Bentley B. Gilbert (Brighton: Harvester Press, 1973) pp. 165–210.
2 Brian Harrison, *Drink and the Victorians: The Temperance Question in England 1815–1872* (London: Faber & Faber, 1971; 2nd edn, Keele: Keele University Press, 1994); T. R. Gourvish and R. G. Wilson, *The British Brewing Industry, 1830–1980* (Cambridge University Press, 1994).
3 A. E. Dingle, *The Campaign for Prohibition in Victorian England: The United Kingdom Alliance 1872–1895* (London: Croom Helm, 1980); D. A. Hamer, *The Politics of Electoral Pressure: A Study in the History of Victorian Reform Agitations* (Hassocks: Harvester, 1977); Lilian L. Shiman, *Crusade against Drink in Victorian England* (London: Macmillan, 1988); David Gutzke, *Protecting the Pub* (Woodbridge: Boydell, 1989); David M. Fahey, 'Temperance and the Liberal Party – Lord Peel's Report, 1899', *Journal of British Studies*, 10, (1971) pp. 132–59; David M. Fahey, 'The Politics of Drink: Pressure Groups and the British Liberal Party, 1883–1908', *Social Science*, 54, no.2 (1979), pp. 76–85; David M. Fahey, 'Drink and the Meaning of Reform in Late Victorian and Edwardian England', *Cithara*, 13, no.2 (1974), pp. 46–56 ; David M. Fahey, 'Brewers, Publicans, and Working-Class Drinkers: Pressure Group Politics in Late Victorian and Edwardian England', *Histoire Sociale-Social History*, 13, no. 25 (1980), pp. 86–103.
4 Betsy Thom, *Dealing with Drink: Alcohol and Social Policy: from Treatment to Prevention* (London: Free Association Books, 1999), pp. 23–5.
5 Rob Baggott, *Alcohol, Politics and Social Policy* (Aldershot: Gower, 1990).
6 Matthew Hilton, *Smoking in British Popular Culture 1800–2000: Perfect Pleasures* (Manchester University Press, 2000).
7 Virginia Berridge, *Opium and the People: Opiate Use and Drug Control Policy in Nineteenth and Early Twentieth Century England* (London: Free Association, 1999).
8 *Independent*, 22 and 24 August, 1988.
9 *Ibid.*, 27 October, 1990.
10 Peter John, *Analysing Public Policy* (London: Pinter, 1998) gives a useful analysis.

2 The Drink Problem in Early Victorian Britain, 1830–70

1 11 Hen.VII, c.2; C. M. Iles, 'Early Stages of Public House Regulation', *Economic Journal*, 12 (1903), pp. 251–62.
2 Andrew Barr, *Drink: a Social History* (London: Pimilico, 1998) p. 9.

3 James S. Roberts, *Drink, Temperance and the Working Class in Nineteenth-Century Germany* (London: Allen & Unwin, 1984) p. 2.
4 F. Engels, *The Condition of the Working Class in England*, W. O. Henderson and W. H. Chaloner (eds) (Oxford: Blackwell, 1958) pp. 116, 141–3.
5 G. B. Wilson, *Alcohol and the Nation: a Contribution to the Study of the Liquor Problem in the United Kingdom from 1800 to 1935* (London: Nicholas & Watson, 1940) p. 335.
6 Brian Harrison, *Drink and the Victorians: The Temperance Question in England 1815–1872* (London: Faber & Faber, 1971) pp. 40–1.
7 Martin J. Wiener, *Reconstructing the Criminal: Culture, Law, and Policy in England, 1830–1914* (Cambridge University Press, 1990) p. 11.
8 Harrison, *Drink*, pp. 37–63.
9 *Ibid.*, p. 319.
10 Roberts, *Drink, Temperance in Germany*, pp. 2–3.
11 Cobden to Joseph Livesey, 10 October, 1849, quoted Henry Carter, *The English Temperance Movement: a Study in Objectives* (London: Epworth, 1933) p. 12.
12 Province of Canterbury, *Report by the Committee on Intemperance for the Lower House of Convocation* (London: Longman, 1869) p. 3; *Reports from the Select Committee of the House of Lords . . . into the prevalence of the habits of intemperance . . . PP*, 1878–9, (113), x.
13 *Parliamentary Debates*, 3rd series, 205, col. 1063, (3 April, 1871).
14 *Ibid.*, 251, col. 475, (5 March, 1880). Cf: 'after the ladies had left the dinner-table he . . . confessed himself somewhat indulgent to that occasional excess in social drink which is wholly due to social feeling and temptation. He cited the opinion of some great employer of labour not unfavourable to the character of occasional drunkards.' F. E. Hamer (ed.), *Personal Papers of Lord Rendel* (London: Benn, 1931) p. 54. Cf. Roy Jenkins, *Gladstone* (London: Macmillan, 1996, Papermac edn) p. 417.
15 J. S. Mill, *On Liberty*, ed. R. B. McCallum (Oxford: Blackwell, 1946) p. 73.
16 *Ibid.*, p. 52.
17 Sir William Harcourt, quoted Harrison, *Drink*, p. 210. Twenty years later Harcourt became a leading supporter of local veto.
18 Harrison, *Drink*, pp. 107–46.
19 *Temperance Record*, 4 March, 1871, p. 49. See also Joseph Livesey, *Free and Friendly Remarks upon the Permissive Bill, Temperance Legislation and the Alliance* (Preston 1862); Joseph Livesey, *True Temperance Teaching: showing the errors of the Alliance and the Permissive Bill* (London: Tweedie, 1873); Joseph Livesey, *True Policy Vindicated: a friendly Correspondence between Joseph Livesy and Mr T. H. Barker . . .* (Manchester: UKA [1870]).
20 *Preston Temperance Advocate* quoted Carter, *Temperance Movement*, p. 60. See also Livesey's evidence to the Commons Select Committtee on Intoxication among the Labouring Classes, *PP*, 1834, (559), VIII, qq. 1025–1163.
21 Oliver MacDonagh, *Early Victorian Government 1830–1870* (London: Weidenfeld & Nicolson, 1977).
22 Bright to Hannah Sturge, 24 September, 1873, Hannah Sturge Papers, Friends House Library, MS Box 10 (3) 7, cited Harrison, *Drink*, p. 449. For similar sentiments, see *Parliamentary Debates*, 3rd series, 175, cols. 1402–3, (8 June, 1864).

23 H. J. Leech (ed.), *The Public Letters of the Right Hon John Bright, MP* (London: Sampson Low, 1885) p. 172.
24 Charles Dickens, *Sketches by Boz*, ch. 22 (Illustrated Library edn, London, Chapman & Hall: 1874) pp. 215–16.
25 Harrison, *Drink*, pp. 387–405; Brian Harrison, 'Two Roads to Social Reform, Francis Place and the "Drunken Committee" of 1834', *Historical Journal*, 11, (1968), pp. 272–300.
26 9 Geo. IV, c.61.
27 Wilson, *Alcohol*, p. 98.
28 29 Geo.II, c.12; 9 Geo IV, c.58.
29 Wilson, *Alcohol*, p. 416.
30 *Parliamentary Debates*, 3rd series, 219, col. 563 (20 May, 1874).
31 *First Report from the Select Committee appointed to inquire into the state of the Police of the Metropolis, . . . , PP*, 1817, (233), VII, report p. 21. For examples of alleged malpractices, see *Reports from the Select Committee appointed to examine into the system under which public houses, hotels, beer shops, . . . are sanctioned and regulated . . . , PP*, 1852–3, (855), XCXXVII, evidence qs. 984, 1729, 4079, 7415.
32 T. R. Gourvish and R. G. Wilson, *The British Brewing Industry, 1830–1980* (Cambridge University Press, 1994) p. 5.
33 Evidence of N. Palmer, Recorder of Great Yarmouth, himself a holder of 'very extreme views on these kind of lines', *Reports from the Select Committee appointed to examine into the system under which public houses, hotels, beer shops, . . . are sanctioned and regulated . . . , PP*, 1852–3, (855), XCXXVII, qs. 1673–6, 1729–31.
34 Sidney and Beatrice Webb, *The History of Liquor Licensing in England, principally from 1700 to 1830* (London, Longman: 1903) p. 114.
35 For typical expressions of this view, see letters from 'a thirsty soul', *The Times*, 14 May, 1857, p. 10; 8 June, 1857, p. 12; 15 June, 1857, p. 7; 7 May, 1860, p. 12. See also Harrison, *Drink*, p. 65. The view that the big London brewers unloaded an inferior product on their tied houses underlay the questioning of the 1830 Select Committee which inquired into the sale of beer in England, *Report from the Select Committee appointed to inquire into the Laws and Regulations which restrict the Sale of Beer by retail, PP*, 1830, (253), X.
36 Ker Seymer, *Parliamentary Debates*, 3rd series, 145, col. 1496, (10 June, 1857).
37 Substances like coculus indicus and copperas were believed to have such effects. For adulteration, see Gourvish and Wilson, *Brewing Industry*, pp. 6–7.
38 In Scotland a separate prohibitionist society, the Scottish Permissive Bill Association, was established in 1858, although personal and regional jealousies as much as policy divisions were important, P. T. Winskill, *The Temperance Movement and its Workers: a Record of Social, Moral, Religious and Political Progress*, 4 vols (London: Blackie, 1890–92), vol. 3, pp. 38–9, 89–96.
39 James Kneale, 'The Place of Drink: Temperance and the Public, 1856–1914', *Social and Cultural Geography*, 2, no.1, (2001), p. 47.
40 Dawson Burns, *What the Alliance is and what it is not* (Manchester UKA: [c.1854]) p. 5.
41 UKA, *Annual Report*, 1857, p. 5.
42 Harrison, *Drink*, pp. 210–12.
43 *Ibid.*, pp. 230–4.

44 *Alliance News*, 21 January, 1871, p. 44.
45 An example being Wilson Patten's Sunday Closing Act of 1854 which the UKA presented as being 'based upon a fallacy'. Its repeal 'is an absolute gain. It demonstrates once again the impossibility of successful compromise with the traffic, and it renders even more evident the truth that restriction and regulation must never be confused with total prohibition.' UKA, *Annual Report*, 1855, p. 13.
46 *Report from the Select Committee appointed to inquire into the extent, causes, and consequences of the prevailing vice of Intoxication among the Labouring Classes of the United Kingdom . . .* , *PP*, 1834, (559), VIII; Harrison, 'Place and "Drunken Committee"', *loc. cit.* The Committee's report is printed in Wilson, *Alcohol*, pp. 148–52.
47 *Parliamentary Debates*, 3rd series, 175, col. 826 (30 May, 1864).
48 Wilson, *Alcohol*, p. 197; Harrison, *Drink*, p. 346.
49 *Parliamentary Debates*, 3rd series, 215, col. 676 (7 April, 1873).
50 16 and 17 Vict., c.67; Winskill, *Temperance Movement*, vol. 3, p. 37.
51 Brian Harrison, 'The Sunday Closing Riots of 1855', *Historical Journal*, 8 (1966), pp. 23–65.
52 Gourvish and Wilson, *Brewing Industry*, p. 3.
53 Accounts on which this paragraph draws are to be found in Gourvish and Wilson, *Brewing Industry*, pp. 6–15, and Harrison, *Drink*, pp. 74–86.
54 *Report from the Select Committee appointed to inquire into the state and management of Beershops*, *PP*, 1833, (416), XV. See also box of correspondence from magistrates to the Home Office, House of Lords Record Office, P.O./12/1–3.
55 Gourvish and Wilson, *Brewing Industry*, p. 17.
56 *Parliamentary Debates*, 3rd series, 4, col. 506, (30 June, 1831).
57 *Report from the Lord's Select Committee appointed to consider the question of the Acts for the Sale of Beer . . .* , *PP*, 1850, (398), XVIII; *Reports from the Select Committee appointed to examine into the system under which public houses, hotels, beer shops, . . . are sanctioned and regulated . . .*, *PP*, 1854, (367), XIV.
58 *Ibid.*
59 23 and 24 Vict., c.27. For details, see Harrison, *Drink*, pp. 248–50.
60 *Parliamentary Debates*, 3rd series, 157, col. 1307 (26 March, 1860).
61 Gladstone to Baines, 24 February, 1860, Gladstone Papers, Add. MSS, 44530, f. 160, quoted Harrison, *Drink*, p. 248.
62 *Parliamentary Debates*, 3rd series, 156, col. 1841 (27 February, 1860).
63 For a full account, see evidence of J. J. Greig and S. Rathbone, *Reports from the Select Committee of the House of Lords . . . into the prevalence of the habits of intemperance . . . PP*, 1877, (171), XI, qs. 1–398. Efforts were made to introduce special licensing legislation for Liverpool along these lines in 1862 and 1865 which met Gladstone's approval, Gladstone, PRO HO 45/7268/1–6; minute, 30 January, 1863, Gladstone Papers, Add. MSS, 44399, fols.184–5.
64 Harrison, *Drink*, p. 349.
65 UKA, *Annual Report*, 1857, p. 18.
66 'How to Stop Drunkenness', *North British Review*, 22 (February, 1855) pp. 455–84. Local veto was only one of a series of suggestions put forward and Buxton later described the idea as hasty, crude and impractical, *Parliamentary Debates*, 3rd series, 175, col. 1418, (8 June, 1864).
67 Harrison, *Drink*, pp. 252–4.

68 See typical speeches by Lawson, *Parliamentary Debates*, 3rd series, 175, cols. 1390–8 (8 June, 1864); *ibid.*, 196, cols. 637–48 (12 May, 1869); *ibid.*, 203, cols. 169–79 (13 July, 1870).
69 Harrison, *Drink*, pp. 198–9; John Prest, *Liberty and Locality: Parliament, Permissive Legislation, and Ratepayers' Democracies in the Mid-Nineteenth Century* (Oxford University Press, 1990).
70 National Temperance League, *The Temperance Congress of 1862*, (London: W. Tweedie, 1862); *Proceedings of the International Temperance and Prohibition Convention* (London, 1862).
71 Norman R. Longmate, *The Waterdrinkers: a History of Temperance* (London: Hamilton, 1968), pp. 144–57; Harrison, *Drink*, pp. 212–14.
72 *Alliance News*, 16 August, 1862, p. 261.
73 *Ibid.*, 8 August, 1968, p. 253; Akroyd to H. Bruce, 19 January, 1869, PRO HO 45/8263/2.
74 National Union for the Suppression of Intemperance, *Annual Report*, 1872; J. A. Bremner, Chairman, National Association for the Promotion of Social Science, *Transactions*, 1871, p. 4; *The Times*, 14 October 1871, p. 4.
75 32 and 33 Vict., c. 27. The Act applied for one year only and was renewed annually until its provisions were consolidated in the Licensing Act of 1872. The 'ante-69 beerhouses' were to retain their position.
76 *Parliamentary Debates*, 3rd series, 212, col. 974 (11 July, 1872).
77 *Ibid.*, 210, cols 1415, 1413 (17 April, 1872).

3 Drink becomes a Party Political Issue, 1870–95

1 Dilys Hill, *Democratic Theory and Local Government* (London: Allen & Unwin, 1974) pp. 46–75; B. Keith Lucas, *The English Local Government Franchise: a Short History* (Oxford: Blackwell, 1952) pp. 82–115.
2 Chamberlain's speech of 26 November, 1886, C. W. Boyd (ed.), *Mr. Chamberlain's Speeches*, 2 vols (London: Constable, 1914) p. 114; John Morley, *Liberalism and Social Reforms* (London: The Eighty Club, 1889) p. 17.
3 Gladstone to J. G. Dodson, 10 January, 1882, Gladstone Papers, Add. MSS, 44252, f. 142, quoted Keith-Lucas, *English Local Government Franchise*, p. 108.
4 R. M. Gutchen, 'Local Improvements and Centralisation in Nineteenth Century England', *Historical Journal*, 4, 1 (1961), pp. 85–96.
5 *Parliamentary Debates*, 3rd series, 175, cols. 1402–7 (8 June, 1864).
6 Robert Thorne, 'The Movement for Public House Reform 1892–1914', p. 232, in Derek J. Oddy and Derek S. Millar (eds), *Diet and Health in Modern Britain* (Beckenham: Croom Helm, 1985) pp. 231–54.
7 Lilian L. Shiman, 'The Church of England Temperance Society in the Nineteenth Century', *Historical Magazine of the Protestant Episcopal Church*, 41 (1972), pp. 179–95; Lilian L.Shiman, *Crusade Against Drink in Victorian England* (London: Macmillan, 1988).
8 Anstruther, *Parliamentary Debates*, 3rd series, 210, cols. 1420–1 (17 April, 1872). For exposition of the Association's policy, see *The Times*, 18 February, 1869, p. 5, 8 June, 1869, p. 12, 9 June, 1869, p. 5, 18 February, 1870, p. 9.
9 *Ibid.*, 22 November, 1871, p. 8.

10 *Parliamentary Debates*, 3rd series, 196, cols. 673–5 (12 May, 1869); *ibid.*, 203, col. 187, (13 July, 1870).
11 Gladstone to Bruce, 1 April, 1871, Gladstone Papers, Add. MSS, 444539, ff. 187–8.
12 *Brewers' Guardian*, 20 November, 1871, pp. 343–4; H. A. Bruce, *Letters of the Rt. Hon. Henry Austin Bruce GCB, Lord Aberdare of Duffryn*, 2 vols (Oxford: priv. printed, 1902), vol. 1, pp. 318–19.
13 Sir Algernon West, *Recollections 1832–1886*, 2 vols (London: Smith, Elder, 1899), vol. 1, p. 351. Also Ethel Drus (ed.), '"A Journal of Events during the Gladstone Ministry, 1868–74" by John, First Earl of Kimberley', *Camden Miscellany*, vol. 21 (London: Camden Society, 1958) p. 30.
14 Brian Harrison, *Drink and the Victorians: The Temperance Question in England 1815–1872* (London: Faber & Faber, 1971) p. 263; Lord Brabourne, Political Journal 1874–78, Kent County Record Office, U951/F27/5, ff. 10–12. For contemporary criticism of Bruce's performance at the Home Office, see H. Fawcett, 'The present Position of the Government', *Fortnightly Review*, New Series 10 (November 1871), pp. 544–58.
15 Harrison, *Drink*, pp. 263–5.
16 *Ibid.*, pp. 265–6.
17 *Parliamentary Debates*, 3rd series, 206, col. 949 (17 May, 1871), quoted Henry Carter, *The English Temperance Movement: a Study in Objectives* (London: Epworth, 1933) p. 164. See also Harrison, *Drink*, p. 269.
18 Drus, 'Journal of Events', *loc. cit.*, pp. 29–30.
19 Paul Smith, *Disraelian Conservatism and Social Reform* (London: Routledge & Kegan Paul, 1967) pp. 167–70.
20 Harrison, *Drink*, p. 276.
21 Quoted R. C. K. Ensor, *England 1870–1914* (Oxford University Press, 1936) p. 21.
22 Smith, *Disraelian Conservatism*, pp. 189–90; H. J. Hanham, *Elections and Party Management: Politics in the Time of Gladstone and Disraeli* (London: Longman, Green, 1959) pp. 222–5; E. J. Feuchtwanger, *Democracy and Empire* (London: Edward Arnold, 1985) p. 78; Harrison, *Drink*, pp. 279–84.
23 *Parliamentary Debates*, 3rd series, 218, col. 1244 (27 April, 1874).
24 Smith, *Disraelian Conservatism*, pp. 208–13.
25 For example, he wrote at length on this aspect to Disraeli in December 1972, quoted *ibid.*, p. 170.
26 Drus, 'Journal of events', *loc. cit.*, p. 22.
27 Roy M. MacLeod, 'The Edge of Hope: Social Policy and Chronic Alcoholism 1870–1900', *Journal of the History of Medicine and Allied Sciences*, 22 (1967), pp. 218–22, upon which this account draws.
28 Quoted *ibid.*, pp. 221,225.
29 42 and 43 Vict., c.19.
30 D. A. Hamer, *The Politics of Electoral Pressure: a Study in the History of Victorian Reform Agitations* (Hassocks, Harvester: 1977) pp. 184–99.
31 David W. Gutzke, *Protecting the Pub: Brewers and Publicans Against Temperance* (Woodbridge: Boydell Press, 1989) p. 9.
32 Harrison, *Drink*, p. 267.
33 G. O. Trevelyan, *Five Speeches on the Liquor Traffic* (London: Partridge, 1872) pp. 21–2.

34 Speech to the Tynemouth Liberal Association, December 1879, E. R. Jones, *The Life and Speeches of Joseph Cowen, MP* (London: Sampson, Low, Marston, Searle & Rivington [1886]) p. 146.
35 Speech in support of the Blue Ribbon Army, Newcastle, 19 January, 1884, Cowen Papers, B.302.
36 *Parliamentary Debates*, 3rd series, 229, cols. 866–7 (17 May, 1876).
37 James B. Brown, 'The Temperance Career of Joseph Chamberlain, 1870–1877: a Study in Political Frustration', *Albion*, 4, (1972), pp. 33–4.
38 E. E. Gulley, *Joseph Chamberlain and English Social Politics* (New York: Columbia University Press, 1926).
39 Brown, 'Temperance Career', *loc. cit.*, pp. 31–3.
40 D. A. Hamer, *Liberal Politics in the Age of Gladstone and Rosebery: a Study in Leadership and Policy* (London: Oxford University Press) p. 51.
41 J. Chamberlain, *Licensing Reform and Local Option*, (Birmingham, [1876]) p. 12. Cf. Evidence to Select Committee of House of Lords on Intemperance, *PP*, 1877, (171), XI, q. 2571.
42 S. Wieselgren, *The Gothenburg System: its Origins, Objects and Effects*, (Gothenburg, 1886); E. R. L. Gould, *The Gothenburg system of Liquor Traffic* (Washington: US Department of Commerce and Labour, 1895).
43 Chamberlain to J. Collings, 10 April, 1876, J. Chamberlain Papers, JC/5/16/51; J. Chamberlain, 'The Right Method with Publicans', *Fortnightly Review*, New Series 19 (May 1876), pp. 631–51; Brown, 'Temperance Career', *loc. cit.*, pp. 34–5.
44 Chamberlain, *Licensing Reform*, p. 21.
45 In the House of Commons, 51 Liberals and one Conservative supported his plan while 19 Liberals and 84 Conservatives opposed it. Chamberlain faced similar disappointment in presenting his idea before a select committee of the House of Lords, Brown, 'Temperance Career', *loc. cit.*, pp. 38–40.
46 Chamberlain at general meeting of the Birmingham Liberal Association, 22 November 1877, *Alliance News*, 1 December, 1877, p. 771. Lawson opposed the idea of municipal control.
47 *The Times*, 18 July, 1892, p. 7; 7 April, 1893, p. 11; 7 July, 1894, p. 13.
48 41 and 42 Vict., c.72; 44 and 45 Vict., c.61. Both acts permitted sales to *bona fide* travellers.
49 *Reports from the Select Committee on Sale of Intoxicants on Sunday (Ireland) Bill . . .*, *PP*, 1877 (198), XVI.
50 In October 1866, a body called the Central Association for Stopping the Sale of Intoxicating Liquor on Sundays had been founded as an offshoot from the British Temperance League. This body enjoyed close links with the UKA but attracted considerable sabbatarian support, including in 1880 the two Anglican archbishops. Harrison, *Drink*, pp. 257–8.
51 For Example, T. E. Ellis, *Speeches and Addresses*, A. J. Ellis (ed.), (Wrexham: Hughes, 1912) p. 183. For detailed analysis, see W. R. Lambert, 'The Welsh Sunday Closing Act', *Welsh History Review*, 6, no. 2, (1872), pp. 161–87.
52 Lawson to Bright, 15 September, 1878, Bright Papers, Add. MSS, 43389, ff. 289–94. UKA, Minute Books, 11 September, 1878; 9 October, 1878.
53 Lawson to Bright, 1 November, 1878, Bright Papers, Add. MSS, 43389, ff. 299–303.
54 *Parliamentary Debates*, 3rd series, 278, cols. 1280–1379 (27 April, 1883).

55 Harcourt to Gladstone, 26 April, 1883, Gladstone Papers, Add. MSS, 44198, ff. 48–9.
56 Gladstone to Harcourt, 19 January, 1885, *ibid.*, f. 164.
57 P. T. Winskill, *The Temperance Movement and its Workers: a Record of Social, Moral, Religious and Political Progress*, 4 vols (London: Blackie, 1890–92) vol. 4, pp. 145–6; *Alliance News*, 1 December, 1887, p. 817. The initiative characteristically collapsed after further internal disputes among the breakaways. This was the culmination of a lengthy period of disputes about whether local direct veto parties should be formed in constituencies, Hamer, *Politics of Electoral Pressure*, pp. 243–55.
58 *The Times*, 22 October, 1879, p. 10.
59 Caine to A. Balfour, 28 July, 1878, UKA Minute Books, 8 March, 1882.
60 National Temperance League, *Temperance Congress, Liverpool June 1884*, (Liverpool: N. T. L., 1885); *Alliance News*, 5 July, 1884, pp. 421–2.
61 Hamer, *Politics of Electoral Pressure*, pp. 256–67.
62 Quoted William Saunders, *The New Parliament, 1880* (London: Cassell, 1880) p. 43.
63 There were, however, several instances of vigorous Trade support for Conservatives at the local level where the Liberal was a strong temperance supporter. An example is the Southwark by-election of 1880, Sir Edward Clarke, *The Story of My Life* (London: Murray, 1918) pp. 154–60.
64 Smith to Cairns, 13 March, 1884, Cairns Papers, PRO 30/51/5.
65 Hamer, *Politics of Electoral Politics*, p. 256.
66 'Rough Notes' by Arthur Sherwell on an MS of H. Carter re Orgins of Gothenburg, Methodist Church Archives, Division of Social Responsibility, MA.243.
67 *Parliamentary Debates*, 3rd series, 323, cols. 1665–6 (19 March, 1888). He did, however, hint that the Government would not consider the licensing clauses as vital to the bill.
68 G. B. Wilson, *Alcohol and the Nation: a Contribution to the Study of the Liquor Problem in the United Kingdom from 1800 to 1935* (London: Nicholas & Watson, 1940) p. 380.
69 The justices at Kendall had refused to renew a remote licence at Kentmore on the grounds that it was no longer required. The Northern brewers unwisely challenged this unsuccessfully in Court of Queen's Bench in May 1888. It then became a test case and was finally decided against the Trade in the House of Lords in 1891.
70 *Parliamentary Debates*, 3rd series, 323, cols. 1667–70 (19 March, 1888). A. E. Dingle, *The Campaign for Prohibition in Victorian England: The United Kingdom Alliance 1872–1895* (London: Croom Helm) pp. 108–9.
71 *Parliamentary Debates*, 3rd series, 324, col. 1407 (16 April, 1888); *Alliance News*, 7 April, 1888, pp. 277–8; UKA, *Annual Report*, 1887–88, p. 6.
72 Winskill, *Temperance Movement*, vol. 4, p. 220; PRO MH/19/72–73; Dingle, *Campaign for Prohibition*, p. 113.
73 See long series of meetings CETS, Legislative Sub-committee, minutes, 7 March to 12 May, 1888, Lambeth Palace Library.
74 Dingle, *Campaign for Prohibition*, p. 110.
75 Harcourt to Gladstone, 7 June, 1888, Gladstone Papers, Add. MSS, 44201.
76 Harcourt to Morley, 10 June, 1888, Harcourt Papers /17.

77 *Parliamentary Debates*, 3rd series, 324, cols. 1364–8, (16 April, 1888); 'Memorandum of Events, 1880–92', J. Chamberlain Papers, JC/8/1/1, section XI, p. 5.
78 Dingle, *Campaign for Prohibition*, p. 119.
79 John Newton, *W. S. Caine, M. P. A Biography* (London: Nisbet, 1907) p. 195.
80 *The Times*, 24 May, 1888, p. 7; *Pall Mall Gazette*, 25 May, 1888, p. 7; *Saturday Review*, 26 May, 1888, pp. 612–13; *Spectator*, 26 May, 1888, pp. 709–10. Purely local issues were also important, Dingle, *Campaign for Prohibition*, p. 117.
81 Dingle, *Campaign for Prohibition*, p. 120; *Pall Mall Gazette*, 9 June, 1888, p. 7; *St James's Gazette*, 9 June, 1888, p. 9. See also letters from Conservatives, *The Times*, 7 June 1888, pp. 5, 9; 9 June, 1888, p. 13.
82 Memo, CETS Legislative Sub-Committee, 13 June, 1888, ff. 60–3. This lengthy account of sensitive negotiations was later ordered to be crossed through in the minute book as it contained 'reports of conversations, which ought not properly to be included in the minutes'. *Ibid.*, 19 June, 1888, f. 65.
83 For his Dartford speech of October 1886, *The Times*, 4 October, 1886, p. 10. For his analysis of the Drink problem at Walsall, *The Times*, 30 July, 1889, p. 10.
84 *Parliamentary Debates*, 3rd series, 343, cols. 1698–1723, (29 April, 1890). Churchill spent a fair amount of time on the issue corresponding with Trade representatives, Sir Wilfrid Lawson, and fellow politicians like Harcourt. See Lord Randolph Churchill Papers, 1/25/3345 *et seq.*
85 *Parliamentary Debates*, 3rd series, 343, col. 697 (17 April, 1890).
86 Goschen to Salisbury, 10 April, 1890, Goschen to W. H. Smith, 9 April, 1890, Salisbury Papers.
87 Gutzke, *Protecting the Pub*, pp. 102–5.
88 Memo by J. D. Power for W. H. Smith, n.d., Hambleden Papers, PS/15/26.
89 The extra duty on beer had been levied as a temporary measure in 1889.
90 *Parliamentary Debates*, 3rd series, 343, cols. 732–6 (17 April, 1890). Ritchie worked out the accompanying legislation, PRO CAB 37/27 nos.24, 27.
91 Nancy E. Johnson (ed.), *The Diary of Gathorne Hardy later Lord Cranbrooke, 1866–1892* (Oxford University Press, 1981) p. 111.
92 Dingle, *Campaign for Prohibition*, p. 125.
93 *The Times*, 8 May, 1890, p. 7.
94 *The Times*, 9 June, 1890, p. 10; *Alliance News*, 13 June, 1890, pp. 380–3.
95 Chamberlain, 'Occasional Diary, 1890–96', 17, 18 June, 1890, J. Chamberlain Papers, JC/8/1/5.
96 Dingle, *Campaign for Prohibition*, pp. 126–9; Hamer, *Electoral Pressure*, pp. 256–67; Newton, *Caine*, pp. 211–22.
97 Harcourt to Lewis Harcourt, 14 May, 1890, Harcourt Papers /651, quoted Dingle, *Campaign for Prohibition*, p. 125.
98 Sir Richard Temple, *Life in Parliament: being Experiences of a Member in the House of Commons from 1886 to 1892 Inclusive* (London: Murray, 1893) p. 272.
99 Johnson, *Diary of Gathorne Hardy*, p. 772.

100 Curzon to Churchill, 12 June, 1890, Lord Randolph Churchill Papers, 1/26/3581.
101 Hamilton Diary, 13 June, 1890, Sir Edward Hamilton Papers, Add. MSS, 48653, f. 35.
102 Harcourt to Lewis Harcourt, 21 June, 1890, Harcourt Papers /651; Dingle, *Campaign for Prohibition*, p. 127.
103 Dingle, *Campaign for Prohibition*, pp. 132–6.
104 W. S. Caine, 'The Attitude of the Advanced Temperance Party', *Contemporary Review*, 63, (January 1893), pp. 54–5. See also *Alliance News*, 5 August, 1892, p. 505.
105 Trevelyan to Caine, 25 August and 25 October 1892, quoted Newton, *Caine*, p. 260.
106 Speech at the Eighty Club, 19 November, 1889, Morley, *Liberalism and Social Reforms*, p. 18.
107 Dingle, *Campaign for Prohibition*, pp. 137–8.
108 Dingle, *Campaign for Prohibition*, pp. 141–4. Relations between the two were strained since Lawson had refused to support Caine in his re-election attempt at Barrow in 1890, preferring to support the orthodox Liberal.
109 *Sunday Closing Reporter*, March 1893, p. 10.
110 UKA, *Annual Report*, 1892–93, p. 6. See also *Alliance News*, 3 March, 1893, pp. 138–9 and 10 March, 1893, p. 156.
111 Lawson to Harcourt, 8 March, 1893, Harcourt Papers /145.
112 Dingle, *Campaign for Prohibition*, p. 148.
113 Harcourt to Lawson, 19 March, 1894, Harcourt Papers /147, quoted Dingle, *Campaign for Prohibition*, p. 156.
114 *Ibid.*, p. 138.
115 S. L. Gwynn and G. M. Tuckwell, *The Life of the Rt. Hon. Sir Charles W. Dilke, Bart., M.P.*, 2 vols (London: Murray, 1917), vol. 2, p. 566.
116 Arnold Morley to Gladstone (reporting Harcourt's views), 1 January, 1891 (misdated '1890'), Gladstone Papers, Add. MSS, 44254, ff. 67–8.
117 Harcourt to Morley, 15 July, 1892, Harcourt Papers /24 quoted Dingle, *Campaign for Prohibition*, pp. 141, 169.
118 Gynn and Tuckwell, *Life of Dilke*, vol. 2, p. 566.
119 Hamilton Diary, 23 April, 1895, Hamilton Papers, Add. MSS, 48666, f. 106. An impression confirmed by Rosebery, the Prime Minister, *ibid.*, 30 April, 1895, f. 115. According to Sherwell, 'Bryce in discussing the matter with me very frankly a few years afterwards, condemned their folly in introducing the local bills very strongly – especially the 1895 Bill after the lesson of 1893. It was done solely to placate Harcourt. "We" (ie the Cabinet) he told me, "were all against it, but you know what the position was. Harcourt was sore over his disappointment (ie the premiership), we decided against judgement to give him his his way on this. We were wrong; it was a bad blunder against the interests of the Liberal Party, but it was done to placate him" ', 'Rough Notes' by Arthur Sherwell on an MS of H. Carter re Orgins of Gothenburg, Methodist Church Archives, Division of Social Responsibility, MA.243.
120 Peter Stansky, *Ambitions and Strategies: the Struggle for the Leadership of the Liberal Party in the 1890s* (Oxford University Press, 1964).
121 *The Times*, 15 November, 1894, p. 6.

122 G. R. Askwith, *Lord James of Hereford* (London: Benn, 1930).
123 Dudley W. R. Bahlman (ed.), *The Diary of Sir Edward Hamilton* (Hull University Press, 1993), entry 30 April, 1895, p. 297; Dingle, *Campaign for Prohibition*, pp. 166–8.
124 Lewis Harcourt Journal, Lewis Harcourt Papers, quoted Dingle, *Campaign for Prohibition*, p. 161.

4 New Departures and Old Orthodoxies, 1895–1902

1 D. W. Bebbington, *The Nonconformist Conscience. Chapel and Politics, 1870–1914* (London: Allen & Unwin, 1982) p. 46.
2 *Temperance Chronicle*, vol. 30, p. 122.
3 Gerald Wayne Olsen, '"Physician heal thyself": drink, temperance and the medical question in the Victorian and Edwardian Church of England, 1830–1914', *Addiction*, 89, (1994), pp. 1167–76.
4 Robert Thorne, 'The Movement for Public House Reform 1892–1914', in Derek J. Oddy and Derek S. Millar (eds), *Diet and Health in Modern Britain* (Beckenham: Croom Helm, 1985) pp. 246–7.
5 Martin J. Wiener, *Reconstructing the Criminal: Culture, Law, and Policy in England, 1830–1914* (Cambridge University Press, 1990) p. 12.
6 G. R. Searle, *The Quest for National Efficiency: a Study in British Politics and Political Thought, 1899–1914* (London: Ashfield Press, 2nd edn, 1990).
7 David E. Wright and Cathy Chorniawry, 'Women and Drink in Edwardian Britain', *Historical Papers/Communications Historiques* (1985), pp. 128–9.
8 *Report of the Inter-Departmental Committee on Physical Deterioration, PP*, 1904, (Cd.2175), XXXII; David W. Gutzke, *Protecting the Pub: Brewers and Publicans Against Temperance* (Woodbridge: Boydell Press, 1989) pp. 243–4; David W. Gutzke, '"The Cry of Children": The Edwardian Medical Campaign against Maternal Drinking', *British Journal of Addiction*, 79 (1984), pp. 71–84.
9 Joanne Woiak, '"A Medical Cromwell to Depose King Alcohol": Medical Scientists, Temperance Reformers, and the Alcohol Problem in Britain', *Histoire Sociale/Social History*, 27 (1994), p. 340.
10 *Ibid.*, pp. 346–7.
11 *Ibid.*, pp, 356–7.
12 Amy A. Pratt, 'Approaches to Alcoholism in Mid-Victorian England', *Clio Medica*, 9, no.2 (1974), pp. 93–101.
13 Peter McCandless, '"Curses of Civilization": Insanity and Drunkenness in Victorian Britain', *British Journal of Addiction*, 79 (1984), pp. 49–58.
14 Virginia Berridge, 'The Society for the Study of Addiction 1884–1988', *British Journal of Addiction*, 85 (special issue) (1990), pp. 991–9.
15 Woiak, 'Medical Cromwell', *loc. cit.*, pp. 358–60.
16 Roy M. MacLeod, 'The Edge of Hope: Social Policy and Chronic Alcoholism 1870–1900', *Journal of the History of Medicine and Allied Sciences*, 22, no.3 (1967), p. 244.
17 A House of Lords Select Committee on intemperance in 1878 had already highlighted this lack of consensus. *Reports from the Select Committee of the House of Lords . . . into the prevalence of the habits of intemperance, . . . PP*, 1878–79 (113), X, pp. 569–71; Woiak, 'Medical Cromwell', *loc. cit.*, p. 357.

18 There had always been those who, as a result of their own personal experience of the slums, had questioned the view that drinking caused men to become poor. In the 1880s, many sensational and widely publicised accounts of working-class life had stressed how the public house and drinking were often the only refuges from a miserable and debilitating existence. [A. Mearns *et al.*] *The Bitter Cry of Outcast London*, (originally published 1883), A. S. Wohl (ed.), (Leicester University Press,1970); G. Sims, *How the Poor Live* and *Horrible London* (London: Chatto & Windus, 1889), (essays originally published 1883); Rev. D. Rice Jones, *In the Slums. Pages from the Notebook of a London Diocesan Missionary* (London: Nisbet, 1884).

19 For discussion on this point, see H. M. Lynd, *England in the Eighteen-Eighties* (London: Oxford University Press, 1945) p. 85. For the temperance question and poverty see J. B. Brown, 'The Pig or the Stye: Drink and Poverty in late Victorian England', *International Review of Social History*, 18, (1973), pp. 380–95.

20 T. S. and M. B. Simey, *Charles Booth: Social Scientist* (London: Oxford University Press, 1960) p. 180. Cf. J. A. Hobson: 'we must learn to discriminate the two questions: "Drink as a cause of Poverty", and "Drink as determining who shall be poor"', *Commonwealth*, June 1896, p. 209, quoted Brian Harrison, *Drink and the Victorians: The Temperance Question in England 1815–1872* (London: Faber & Faber, 1971) p. 399.

21 Asa Briggs, *Social Thought and Social Action. A study of the Work of Seebohm Rowntree, 1871–1954* (London: Longman, 1961) p. 30 *et seq*; see also the reflection of these views in A. Sherwell, *Life in West London: a Study and a Contrast*, 2nd edn (London: Methuen, 1897); D. B. Foster, *Leeds Slumdom* (Leeds: priv. printed, 1897); Lady H. Bell, *At the Works. A Study of a Manufacturing Town* (London: Edward Arnold, 1911).

22 John Burns, *Labour and Drink* (London, 1904).

23 J. B. Brown, 'The Pig or the Stye', *loc. cit.*, pp. 389–94; James Kneale, 'The Place of Drink: Temperance and the Public, 1856–1914', *Social and Cultural Geography*, 2, no.1 (2001), pp. 53–4.

24 Philip Snowden, *Socialism and the Drink Question* (London: Independent Labour Party, 1908) pp. 93, 101, 167–9.

25 'Municipal Drink Traffic', *Fabian Tract* no.86 (1899), (6th edn) p. 18.

26 E. R. Pease, *The Case for Municipal Drink Trade* (London: P. S. King, 1904) p. 13.

27 George Whitely to Campbell-Bannerman, 1 March, 1907, Campbell-Bannerman Papers, Add. MSS, 41231, f. 233; cf. Harcourt's description of liquor licensing as 'a very nasty piece of navigation & any channel is full of sunken wrecks of all description', Harcourt to Churchill, 26 January, 1890, R. Churchill Papers, 1/25/3384.

28 George W. E. Russell, *Sir Wilfrid Lawson: a Memoir*, (London: Smith Elder, 1909) p. 229. See also: UKA, *Annual Report*, 1894–95, p. 6; J. Whyte 'The Prohibitionists in Politics', in Guy Hayler (ed.), *The Prohibition Movement: Papers and Proceedings of the National Convention for the Prohibition of the Liquor Traffic* (Newcastle: North of England Temperance League, 1897) pp. 275–9.

29 Jon Lawrence, *Speaking for the People: Party, Language and Popular Politics in England, 1867–1914* (Cambridge University Press, 1998) pp. 213–4.

30 *Westminster Gazette*, 13 August, 1895, pp. 1–2; David M. Fahey, 'The Politics of Drink: Pressure Groups and the British Liberal Party, 1883–1908', *Social Science*, 54, no.2 (1979), pp. 78–9. The defeated member for Coventry claimed that the election had turned almost exclusively on local veto: the 'Temperance Party, who boasted beforehand that they would fight like cats, did not fight at all . . .' The sooner the party threw the measure overboard the better, *The Times*, 29 July, 1895, p. 10.
31 Sir U. Kay-Shuttleworth to Spencer, 23 July, 1895; Peter Stansky, *Ambitions and Strategies: The Struggle for the Leadership of the Liberal Party in the 1890s* (Oxford University Press, 1964) p. 179.
32 Arnold Morley to Gladstone, 19 July, 1895, Gladstone Papers, Add. MSS, 44254, f. 272, quoted Gutzke, *Protecting the Pub*, p. 123.
33 *Licensed Victuallers, Official Annual*, 1896, quoted Joseph Rowntree and Arthur Sherwell, *The Temperance Problem and Social Reform* (7th enlarged edn, 1899), (London: Hodder & Stoughton, 1899) pp. 100–1.
34 *The Times*, 22 July, 1895, p. 8.
35 *Temperance Chronicle*, 28 February, 1891, pp. 98, 103; *Alliance News*, 6 March, 1891, p. 166; 11 December, 1891, pp. 810–11; W.O, Hanlon to Asquith, 25 November, 1891, PRO HO 45/9862/B13433.
36 A. F. Hills, 'Proposed Temperance Legislation', *The National Temperance Congress*, 1895 (Chester: NTL, 1895), pp. 185–99; Hills, Minutes of Evidence Royal Commission on Licensing, *PP*, 1899 (C.9075), XXXIV, qs.72,106–97; UKA, Minute Books, 3 February, 1894.
37 James E. G. De Montmorency, *Francis William Fox* (London: Oxford University Press, 1923) pp. 27–9; Westlake, Minutes of Evidence Royal Commission on Licensing, *PP*, 1899, (C.9075), XXXIV, qs.67,107, 67,170; Harcourt to Caine, 28 November, 1892, Harcourt Papers /144.
38 J. Mann, Minutes of Evidence Royal Commission on Liquor Licensing, *PP*, 1899, (C.9075), XXXIV, qs. 70,642–6; D. Lewis, *Temperance Reformers and the Threefold Option* (Glasgow, 1897); J. Hunter, *The Threefold Option Criticised* (Glasgow, [1897]).
39 David M. Fahey, 'Drink and the Meaning of Reform in late Victorian and Edwardian England', *Cithara*, 13, no.2 (1974), p. 51.
40 Bebbington, *Nonconformist Conscience*, p. 46.
41 *The Times*, 8 February, 1896, p. 12. Prohibitionists regretted the CETS's failure, but were not slow to draw the moral that 'moderate' proposals and methods were futile, UKA, *Annual Report*, 1895–96, pp. 31–4.
42 De Montmorency, *Fox*, pp. 27–32.
43 Buxton to Harcourt, 7 December, 1892, Harcourt Papers /144.
44 For Example, Riley Smith, *Brewers' Guardian*, 25 February, 1896, p. 47.
45 *Parliamentary Debates*, 4th series, 39, cols. 245–55 (27 March, 1896).
46 Bonsor to Salisbury, 2 August, 1895, Salisbury Papers. For public statement, see meetings of National Trade Defence Fund, Westminster Palace Hotel, 29 October, 1895, *Morning Advertiser*, 30 October, 1895, p. 4.
47 Bonsor to Salisbury, 30 January, 1896, Salisbury Papers. Fox had preferred the idea of a Select Committee of the Commons, believing that such a body would be closer to those who might subsequently legislate. However, the Trade 'for many reasons' preferred a Commission. In this way, they would

be likely to secure a more direct representation of their interests. Fox *et al.* to Balfour, 10 September, 1895, PRO T 1891A/14399.

48 De Montmorency, *Fox*, pp. 31–3.

49 Caine seemed fully aware of this cynicism when he wrote in 1897: 'I do not see how we can report before 1899. We shall fulfil the main object with which we were appointed, viz: that of postponing to the next parliament all practical legislation on the Drink question,' W. Rathbone to E. L. Fanshawe, 8 June, 1897, quoting letter of Caine, Rathbone Papers, IX.5.4.

50 The temperance members were: W. Allen, MP, Sir Charles Cameron, W. S. Caine MP, Rev. H. H. Dickinson, Sir W. Houldsworth, MP, J. H. Roberts, MP, Bishop F. Temple and T. P. Whittaker, MP. The Tradesmen were H. Ginling, H. H. Riley-Smith, Sir F. Seager Hunt, MP (replaced by E. N. Buxton, MP in 1898), S. Hyslop, C. Walker, A. Money Wigram, S. Young MP, Sir G. Younger. The neutrals were: Peel, West, Lord de Vesci, the Earl of Jersey (replaced by Lord Windsor in 1897), A. M. Gordon, W. Graham, A. Johnston and J. L. Wharton, MP.

51 UKA, *Annual Report*, 1895–96, pp. 8–9. Lawson described it as a *'Commission pour rire'*, Russell, *Lawson*, p. 234; on the other hand Whittaker, already showing signs of his later flexibility, 'hoped to do great things by a searching cross-examn. of the pro-Drink witnesses', S. N. Wiliams to A. McDougall, 28 April, 1896, UKA Minute Books, 29 April, 1896.

52 For Example, *Morning Advertiser*, 1 April, 1896, p. 4.

53 *Brewing Trade Review*, 1 December, 1898, pp. 421–2.

54 Sir H. Cosmo Bonsor to Salisbury's Secretary (marked 'strictly private'), 6 November, 1898, Salisbury Papers.

55 The somewhat unedifying details of the power struggle between West and Peel were exposed to the public view early the following year: Sir Algernon West, 'The Two Reports of the Licensing Commission', *Nineteenth Century*, 47 (February 1900), pp. 260–74; T. P. Whittaker, 'The Temperance Reply to Sir Algernon West', *ibid.*, (March 1900), pp. 510–25. See PRO HO 45/10151/20998/39 for manoeuvring on the relative status of the reports.

56 *Final Report, Royal Commission on the Liquor Licensing Laws, PP*, 1899, (C.9379), XXV.

57 Frank Bealey, J. Blondel and W. P. McCann, *Constituency Politics: a Study of Newcastle-under-Lyme* (London: Faber & Faber, 1965) pp. 64–5.

58 Gutzke, *Protecting the Pub*, pp. 133–4.

59 *Ibid.*, pp. 135–6.

60 *Ibid.*, pp. 137–41.

61 UPC Meeting 25 September, 1900, verbatim shorthand notes LVNDL Minute Book 25 September, 1900, quoted *ibid.*, pp. 142–3.

62 For a full account on which this draws, see *ibid.*, pp. 141–52.

63 Joseph Henry to H. Gladstone, 9 December, 1897, Herbert Gladstone Papers, Add. MSS, 46036, f. 66.

64 Herbert Gladstone to Campbell-Bannerman, 12 December, 1899, Campbell-Bannerman Papers, Add. MSS, 41215, ff. 169–70. In April 1899, Walter Gilbey indignantly demanded that the Liberal Chief Whip, Herbert Gladstone, intercede with temperance elements to get a compromise on 'off' licences and, when that failed, his partner, Charles Gold, MP,

announced that 'he had ceased to support the Liberal Party', Gilbey to H. Gladstone, 19 April, 1899, Viscount Gladstone Papers, Add. MSS, 46057, ff. 154–7; A.Woodehouse to H. Gladstone, 16 December, 1899, *ibid.*, ff. 232–4, quoted Gutzke, *Protecting the Pub*, pp. 131–32.

65 George Ratcliffe, *Sixty Years of it: being the Story of my Life and Public Career* (London: A. Brown, 1935) p. 95.

66 *Manchester Guardian*, 24 November, 1897, p. 7; *Leeds Mercury*, 8 January, 1898, p. 7. See also Sir Charles Mallet, *Herbert Gladstone: a Memoir* (London: Hutchinson, 1932) p. 161.

67 H. Gladstone to Campbell-Bannerman, 12 April, 1899 and Memorandum by Gladstone, 14 June, 1899, Campbell-Bannerman Papers, Add. MSS, 41215, ff. 66–70, 70–2. *Westminster Gazette*, 29 November, 1897, p. 1; 1 December, 1897, p. 1; 7 January, 1898, pp. 1–2; *Speaker*, 15 January, 1898, pp. 67–8.

68 'I assume', his brother wrote to him in February 1899, 'we are all agreed that it is most important to get a unanimous report so as to give the Government no excuse for not dealing with the question . . . What is important is [that] the question should be settled by the present Government.' Henry Gladstone to Herbert Gladstone, 16 February, 1899, Viscount Gladstone Papers, Add. MSS, 46045, ff. 193–4.

69 Herbert Gladstone to Campbell-Bannerman, 19 November, 1899, Campbell-Bannerman Papers, Add. MSS, 41215, ff. 144–50.

70 For a full account, see David M. Fahey, 'Temperance and the Liberal Party – Lord Peel's Report, 1899', *Journal of British Studies*, 10 (1971), pp. 132–59.

71 Campbell-Bannerman to Spencer, 12 December, 1899, Spencer Papers, 1899 A-R, quoted, D. A. Hamer, *Liberal Politics in the Age of Gladstone and Rosebery: A Study in Leadership and Policy* (Oxford University Press, 1972) p. 21, n.1.

72 Lawson to Campbell-Bannerman, 7 December, 1899; cf. also J. Kempster to Campbell-Bannerman, 20 December, 1899; Lawson to Campbell-Bannerman, 20 December, 1899; Campbell-Bannerman Papers, Add. MSS, 41235, ff. 130–3, 148–9, 152–6; Campbell-Bannerman to Herbert Gladstone, 11 December 1899, Viscount Gladstone Papers, Add. MSS, 45987, f. 56.

73 H. Gladstone to Campbell-Bannerman, 12 December, 1899, Campbell-Bannerman Papers, Add. MSS, 41215, ff. 171–2, quoted Fahey, 'Peel Report', p. 147; Dingle, *Campaign*, pp. 175–6.

74 *Ibid.*, p. 176.

75 For his father, see Thomas Whittaker, *Life's Battles in Temperance Armour*, (London: Hodder & Stoughton, 1884). For his early contributions, see for example, *Alliance News*, 25 October, 1879, p. 676; 28 October, 1892, p. 709; *Dublin Review*, (July 1879), pp. 1–32.

76 H. Gladstone, Political Diary, April 1899–1900, Viscount Gladstone Papers, Add. MSS, 46483, ff. 30, 34, 38, 40; Whittaker to H. Gladstone, 5 November, 1899, *ibid.*, 46057, ff. 206–11; Fahey, 'Peel Report', *loc.cit.*, pp. 140–1.

77 *The Times*, 22 November, 1899, p. 11; 7 December, 1899, p. 6; Fahey, 'Peel Report', *loc.cit.*, pp. 144, 149–51.

78 For a full account of these divisions, see *ibid.*, pp. 155–7. For the complex situation at Lincoln, see Charles Roberts to J. Whyte, 9 October, 1900, UKA, Minute Books, 10 October, 1900.

79 David W. Gutzke, 'Gentrifying the British Public House, 1896–1914', *International Labor and Working Class History* (1994), no.45, pp. 29–43.
80 'Temperance Reminiscences written down by Joseph Rowntree for his Grandchildren, 1914', Joseph Rowntree Papers, JR93/V/3.
81 *Ibid.* Rowntree's reflections in 1892 were published as Joseph Rowntree, *A Neglected Aspect of the Temperance Question*, (York, 1892).
82 Anne Vernon, *A Quaker Businessman* (London: Allen & Unwin, 1958) p. 134; H. V. Emy, *Liberals, Radicals and Social Politics*, (Cambridge University Press, 1973) p. 130.
83 Rowntree and Sherwell, *Temperance Problem and Social Reform*, p. xiv.
84 *Ibid.*, p. 598.
85 *Ibid.*, pp. 88–114.
86 *Ibid.*, p. 540.
87 *Ibid.*, pp. 434–508.
88 *Ibid.*, p. 604.
89 Lady Somerset to Bishop Randall Davidson, 27 August, 1903, Davidson Papers, 1903/S9.
90 The manifesto was leaked to the *Birmingham Daily Mail*, 19 October, 1903, p. 2, reprinted *The Times*, 20 October, 1903, p. 8.
91 For example, scornful comments Lady Somerset to Davidson, 9 September, 1903, Davidson Papers, 1903/S9.
92 Lady Carlisle to Whyte, 25 November, 1903, UKA Minute Books, 2 December, 1903. For divisions within the BWTA, see K. Fitzpatrick, *Lady Helen Somerset* (London: Cape, 1923) pp. 165–8; Lady Carlisle to Whyte, 28 November, 1903, UKA Minute Books, 2 December, 1903.
93 Peel, Whittaker, *The Times*, 21 November, 1905, p. 4; T. P. Whittaker, 'A Temperance Policy for the Liberal Party', *Liberal Magazine*, 3, no.142, pp. 350–7.
94 H. J. Wilson, to UKA Executive, 15 August, 1904, UKA Minute Books, 17 August, 1904. Also A. F. Hills, *ibid.*, 15 December, 1905.
95 *Ibid.*, 28 September, 1904; cf. also UKA, *Annual Report*, 1904–05, pp. 17–18; Lawson, *The Times*, 18 October, 1905, p. 4.
96 Lord Peel chaired the inaugural meeting and became President. Other prominent supporters of the new body were: Sir W. H. Houldsworth, Lady Somerset, T. W. Russell, Frederic Harrison, Lord Courtney, J. T. Brunner, R. Spence Watson, George Cadbury, Prof. Marcus Dods, Rev. C. Aked, Rev. C. Silvester Horne, A. Guthrie.
97 *The Times*, 13 December, 1907, p. 17. See also Arthur Sherwell, *Licensing Reform. Address . . . at the National Liberal Club on 2 December, 1907* (London: Political Committee of National Liberal Club, 1907).
98 Whittaker interviewed in *Tribune*, 30 August, 1906, repr. *Temperance Reform, a Policy of Inclusion* (TLL pamphlets, 1906), no.6, p. 5. See also TLL, *The Place and Scope of Local Veto in Temperance Reform*, Pamphlet, B. Series, no.2, [c.1911], *passim*; T. P. Whittaker, 'Practical Temperance Reform', *Twentieth Century Quarterly*, no.2, (August 1906), pp. 48–51.
99 Whittaker, *Tribune*, 4 September, 1906, repr. TLL, *Temperance Reform Who has Changed Front?*, Pamphlet series, p. 16; also Whittaker, 'Practical Temperance Reform', *loc. cit.*, p. 52. Cf. John Hilton, *Tribune*, 31 August, 1906.

100 Dingle, *Campaign for Prohibition*, p. 176.
101 Memorandum on the Present Financial Position, UKA, Minute Books, 27 March, 1901; UKA *Annual Report*, 1900–1, p. 7; *ibid.*, 1902–03, p. 11. Dingle, *Campaign for Prohibition*, pp. 200–1.
102 David E. Wright and Cathy Chorniawry, 'Women and Drink in Edwardian Britain', in *Historical Papers/Communications Historiques*, 1985, pp. 123–5.
103 David M. Fahey, 'The Politics of Drink in Britain: Anglo-American Perspectives', *Proceedings of the Ohio Academy of History* (Ohio, 2000) p. 3 (also available on website of Alcohol and Temperance History Group, *www.athg.org*

5 The High Water Mark of Party Political Controversy, 1902–14

1 T. R. Gourvish and R. G. Wilson, *The British Brewing Industry, 1830–1980* (Cambridge University Press, 1994) pp. 267–83.
2 *Ibid.*, pp. 271, 276.
3 *Ibid.*, p. 284.
4 *Ibid.*, p. 285; David W. Gutzke, *Protecting the Pub: Brewers and Publicans Against Temperance* (Woodbridge: Boydell Press, 1989) p. 164.
5 Gourvish and Wilson, *British Brewing Industry*, p. 296.
6 Edmund Bristol, 'The Liberty and Property Defence League and Individualism', *Historical Journal*, 18 (1975), pp. 761–89; N. Soldon, '*Laissez-Faire* as Dogma: The Liberty and Property Defence League, 1882–1914', in Kenneth D. Brown (ed.), *Essays in Anti-Labour History: Responses to the Rise of Labour in Britain* (London: Macmillan, 1974) pp. 208–33.
7 Joseph Rowntree and Arthur Sherwell, *The Temperance Problem and Social Reform* (London: Hodder & Stoughton, 7th edn, 1899) ch. 2.
8 G. B. Wilson, *Alcohol and the Nation: a Contribution to the Study of the Liquor problem in the United Kingdom from 1880 to 1935* (London: Nicholson & Watson, 1940) p. 185.
9 George Whitely to Campbell-Bannerman, 1 March, 1907, Campbell-Bannerman Papers, Add. MSS, 41231, ff. 232–3, quoted Gutzke, *Protecting the Pub*, p. 229.
10 *Ibid.*, pp. 223–9.
11 *The Times*, 9 November, 1899, p. 7; *Brewers' Journal*, 15 November, 1899.
12 *Parliamentary Debates*, 4th series, vol. 82, cols. 1004–28 (8 May, 1900); G. K. A. Bell, *Randall Davidson, Archbishop of Canterbury*, 2 vols (London: Oxford University Press, 1935), vol. 1, pp. 323–4; Ridley to Salisbury, 2 May, 1900, Salisbury Papers; *Parliamentary Debates*, 4th series, vol. 82, cols. 1023–8, (8 May, 1900).
13 Bell, *Davidson*, vol. 1, p. 325; E. N. Buxton to Davidson, 9 May, 1900; Davidson Papers, Temperance and Licensing Box; John M. Lee to Davidson, 12 May, 1900; Fox to Davidson, 24 May, 1900, *ibid.*, 1900/T2.
14 CETS, *Annual Report*, 1899, p. 17. See also E. S. Howard, *Why the Church of England Temperance Society supports Lord Peel's Report* (London: CETS, [c.1901]). Howard and other officials of the Society were among the keenest supporters of Whittaker's efforts: E. S. Howard to F. Eardly-Wilmot, n.d.,

Eardley-Wilmot to Davidson, 10 July, 1900, Davidson Papers, 1900/ T2; Eardley-Wilmot to Davidson, 14 May, 1900, *ibid.*, Temperance and Licensing box. The rank and file were less extreme, and the Society also agreed to support proposals embodying the 'common ground' between the two reports of the Commission; E. S. Howard, *Practical Suggestions for the Improvement of the Existing Licensing Laws and their Administration, based upon the Points of Agreement in the Royal Commission Reports* (London: CETS, [c.1900]); E. S. Howard, *What is Practical in the Way of Temperance Legislation?* (London: CETS, [1902]).

15 Davidson to G. E. Hitchcock, 16 June, 1902, Davidson Papers, 1902/F2; Davidson to Lady H. Somerset, 2 September, 1903, Davidson Papers, 1903/S9.

16 Peel to Davidson, 15 March, 1900, Davidson Papers, Temperance and Licensing box; Peel, *The Times*, 30 October, 1901, p. 8; John Newton, *W. S. Caine, M.P.: A Biography* (London: Nisbet, 1907) pp. 294–8; T. W. Russell, *Parliamentary Debates*, 4th series, vol. 89, cols. 595–607 (20 February, 1901); *ibid.*, 101, cols. 1441–4 (30 January, 1902).

17 James E. G. De Montmorency, *Francis William Fox* (London: Oxford University Press, 1923) p. 35.

18 *The Times*, 17 January, 1901, p. 10.

19 Sir John Kennaway to Davidson, 31 December, 1900, Davidson Papers, Temperance and Licensing Box.

20 Memorandum on Temperance Legislation by Ritchie, 30 January, 1901, PRO CAB 37/56/no.13. Also Memorandum by Ritchie, 15 November, 1901, PRO CAB 37/59/no.117.

21 2 Edw. VII, c.28. A year later a broadly similar measure was passed for Scotland, 3 Edw. VII, c.25.

22 Samuel Smith, *My Life-Work* (London: Hodder & Stoughton, 1902) p. 293.

23 Arthur Chamberlain, *Licensing in the City of Birmingham* (Birmingham: Cornish Bros. [1902]) pp. 9–12.

24 *The Times*, 30 August, 1901, p. 9.

25 Arthur Chamberlain came to view the trade with some bitterness and took a prominent part in the subsequent agitation against proposals for compensation, much to his brother's embarrassment. James L. Garvin and Julian Amery, *The Life of Joseph Chamberlain*, 6 vols (London: Macmillan, 1932–69) vol. 5, pp. 172–3; *The Times*, 29 July, 1903, p. 10, 23 September, 1903, p. 4, 11 March, 1904, p. 8, 15 April, 1904, p. 5.

26 A. W. Chapman to Davidson, 6 October, 1902, 4 November, 1902, Davidson Papers, 1902/F2.

27 Gutzke, *Protecting the Pub*, p. 154.

28 Campbell-Bannerman, *Parliamentary Debates*, 4th series, 134, col. 924, (10 May, 1904); Asquith, *ibid.*, 139, col. 98, (29 July, 1904). John Burns confided similar sentiments to his diary, so it was not just rhetorical hyberole, John Burns Diary, 20 April, 1904, Burns Papers, Add. MSS, 46322, f. 17.

29 *The Times*, 19 March, 1903, p. 10.

30 Balfour to King Edward VII, 17 March, 1903, PRO CAB 41/28/6.

31 Gutzke, *Protecting the Pub*, pp. 155–6.

32 Note of conversation between Chamberlain and Charles Vince, Birmingham political agent, quoted Garvin and Amery, *Chamberlain*, vol. 5, p. 173.

33 Balfour to King Edward VII, 16 June 1903, PRO CAB 41/28/11.
34 Memoranda on Licensing by Akers-Douglas, 3 December, 1903, 1 February, 1904, PRO CAB 37/59/117 and 37/68/17.
35 J. S. Sandars to Balfour, 14 and 20 January, 1904, Balfour Papers, Add. MSS, 49762, ff. 20, 46.
36 Balfour to Sandars, 17 January, 1904, *ibid.*, fols. 35–7.
37 *Parliamentary Debates*, 4th series, 133, cols. 696–758, (20 April, 1904).
38 *Brewers' Guardian*, 10 April, 1905, p. 61. For analysis, see Gutzke, *Protecting the Pub*, pp. 155–6.
39 *Alliance News*, 19 May, 1904, p. 341; *Temperance Record*, 1 June, 1904, pp. 55, 255–6; *Chronicle*, 6 May, 1904, pp. 226–7.
40 Joseph Rowntree and Arthur Sherwell, *Public Interests or Trade Aggrandisement?* (London: P. S. King, 1904) p. 9. Articles by Rowntree and Sherwell, *Daily News*, 6, 13, 16, and 23 May, 1904.
41 On this last point, the critics were proved correct. Although Akers-Douglas predicted an annual rate of 2000 suppressed licences a year, in fact over the next thirty years a mere 18,611 were eliminated, partly this was the result a legal judgement in 1906 which ruled that the market value of a licence had to be taken into account. Akers-Douglas, *Parliamentary Debates*, 4th series, 134, col. 994 (10 May, 1904); Wilson, *Alcohol and the Nation*, pp. 111–2; Gutzke, *Protecting the Pub*, pp. 156–7.
42 Lloyd George to William George, 23 June, 1904, quoted William George, *My Brother and I* (London: Eyre & Spottiswoode, 1958) p. 171.
43 George W. E. Russell, *Sir Wilfrid Lawson: a Memoir* (London: Smith Elder, 1909) p. 261.
44 Liberal election addresses at Library of the National Liberal Club.
45 *The Times*, 6 April, 1906, p. 4; *Parliamentary Debates*, 4th series, 155, cols. 1233–68, (10 April, 1906).
46 Asquith to Herbert Gladstone, 24 September, 1906, Viscount Gladstone Papers, Add. MSS, 45989, f. 148.
47 Notes by H. Gladstone, *ibid.*, 46092, ff. 1–2; Memoranda and Reports on the Licensing Bill, 7 January, 1907, Viscount Gladstone Printed Papers, B.P. 2/4 (3).
48 Memo for the Cabinet on the Licensing Bill, 9 December, 1907, *ibid.*
49 Memo for Cabinet by Gladstone, 23 November, 1907, *ibid.*
50 Memo for the Committee of the Cabinet on Licensing by Lord Loreburn, 15 January, 1908, PRO CAB 37/91/3. For similar views, Loreburn to Campbell-Bannerman, 10 March, 1906, Campbell-Bannerman Papers, Add. MSS, 41222, ff. 164–5.
51 Lord Ripon to King Edward VII, 17 January, 1908, Campbell-Bannerman to King Edward VII, 12 February, 1908, PRO CAB 41/31/37, 42.
52 Viscount G. Cave, *The Licensing Bill, 1908. The Case Against the Bill* (London: National Union of Conservative and Constitutional Associations, 1908); F. E. Smith and E. E. Williams, *An Essay on the Philosophy of the Licensing Bill* (London: P. S. King, 1908); F. E. Smith and E. E. Williams, *The 'Facts' and 'Arguments' of Sir Thomas Whittaker, M. P., An Examination* (London: P. S. King, 1908); Walter Long, *Parliamentary Debates*, 4th series, 187, cols. 1282–4, (9 April, 1908); Peter Rowland, *The Last Liberal Governments: The Promised Land 1905–1910* (London: Barrie & Rockliff, Cresset Press, 1968) p. 161.

53 Philip Snowden, *An Autobiography*, 2 vols (London: Nicholson & Watson, 1934), vol. 1, p. 187. Cf. also C. Masterman, *The Condition of England*, J. T. Boulton (ed.), (London: Methuen, 1960) pp. 99–102.
54 For Example, *Morning Advertiser*, 19 March, 1908, p. 5, 26 March, 1908, p. 5, 30 March, 1908, p. 5; *Brewers' Gazette*, 26 March, 1908, pp. 222–3, 23 April, 1908, p. 299; *The Times*, 19 March, 1908, p. 11.
55 A whole box of such letters survives in the Davidson Papers, Temperance and Licensing, 1907–08 Box.
56 Quoted Rowland, *Last Liberal Governments*, p. 161. See also *The Times*, 28 September, 1908, p. 7. Estimates of numbers ranged from a quarter to three-quarters of a million.
57 Gutzke, *Protecting the Pub*, pp. 170–1.
58 J. S. Sandars to Balfour, 8 May, 1908, Balfour Papers, Add. MSS, 49765, f. 164; Thomas Newton, *Lord Lansdowne: a Biography* (London: Macmillan, 1929), p. 368; Rowland, *Last Liberal Governments*, p. 161.
59 St Aldwyn to Balfour, n.d. but August 1908, Balfour Papers, Add MSS, 49695, ff. 167–70.
60 Lord Willoughby de Broke, *The Passing Years* (London: Constable, 1924) p. 247.
61 E. H. H. Green, *The Crisis of Conservatism: the Politics, Economics and Ideology of the British Conservative Party, 1880–1914* (London: Routledge, 1995).
62 Bruce K. Murray, *The People's Budget 1909/10: Lloyd George and Liberal Politics* (Oxford University Press, 1980) p. 56.
63 J. W. MacKail and G. Wyndham, *Life and Letters of George Wyndham*, 2 vols (London: Hutchinson, [1925]) vol. 2, p. 643.
64 *The Times*, 27 March, 1908, p. 13.
65 *Ibid.*, 27 July, 1908, p. 17.
66 Lord Riddell, *More Pages from my Diary 1908–1914* (London: Country Life, 1934) p. 10.
67 Murray, *People's Budget*, pp. 67–8, 109.
68 *Ibid.*, p. 108; Joseph Rowntree and Arthur Sherwell, *The Taxation of the Liquor Traffic*, 2nd edn (London: Macmillan, 1908); Gutzke, *Protecting the Pub*, pp. 175–6.
69 J. W. Gulland, *Scotland Sober and Free* (Glasgow, 1909) pp. 6–7.
70 J. A. Spender, *The Life of the Right Hon. Sir Henry Campbell-Bannerman*, 2 vols (London: Hodder & Stoughton, 1923), vol. 2, p. 377.
71 Murray, *People's Budget*, p. 4.

6 The First World War: Drink and National Efficiency

1 T. R. Gourvish and R. G. Wilson, *The British Brewing Industry, 1830–1980* (Cambridge University Press, 1994) pp. 317–8.
2 Henry Carter, *The Control of the Drink Trade: a Contribution to National Efficiency, 1915–1917* (London: Longman, Green, 1918) pp. 18–27.
3 *Ibid.*, pp. 27–33.
4 *Ibid.*, p. 46; G. A. Frank Knight to Bonar Law, 16 December, 1914, Bonar Law Papers, HLRO, BL/35/5/42; J. P. Maclay to Bonar Law, 12 January, 1915, *ibid.*, 36/1/17; National United Temperance Conference deputation, 24 February, 1915, *ibid.*, 36/4/67.

5 Stuart Mews, 'Urban Problems and Rural Solutions: Drink and Disestablishment in the First World War', in Derek Baker (ed.), *The Church in Town and Countryside. Studies in Church History*, vol. 16 (Oxford: Blackwell, 1979) pp. 57–8.
6 Carter, *Control*, pp. 24, 40, 51.
7 Mews, 'Drink and Disestablishment', *loc.cit.*, pp. 452–5.
8 *The Times*, 1 March, 1915.
9 Cameron Hazlehurst, *Politicians at War July 1914 to May 1915: A Prologue to the Triumph of Lloyd George* (London: Cape, 1971) pp. 196–200, 210–2; also A. J. P. Taylor, *English History 1914–1945* (Oxford University Press, 1965) pp. 28–9.
10 Committee of Imperial Defence Paper G.7, 22 February, 1915, PRO CAB 37/124/40 quoted John Turner, 'State Purchase of the Liquor Trade in the First World War', *The Historical Journal*, 23, (1980), p. 595.
11 *Ibid.*, pp. 594–5.
12 Mews, 'Drink and Disestablishment', *loc. cit.*, pp. 464–5. He goes on to point out that Lloyd George also attempted to represent the postponement of Welsh disestablishment as a bargaining counter which could be used to extract temperance reform from an unwilling Conservative party, *ibid.*, pp. 470–1.
13 Charles Roberts to Lloyd George, 9 February, 1915, Lloyd George Papers, HLRO, LG/C/4/1/17.
14 Gerry R. Rubin, *War, Law and Labour: The Munitions Acts, State Regulation, and the Unions, 1915–1921* (Oxford University Press, 1987) p. 181.
15 Turner, 'State Purchase', *loc. cit.*, p. 599.
16 Arthur Shadwell, *Drink in 1914–1922: a Lesson in Control* (London: Longman, 1923) pp. 22–3. The official report later found no significant evidence for increased drinking on the Clyde since the outbreak of war, *Report and Statistics of Bad Time Keeping in Shipbuilding, Munitions and Transport Areas, PP*, 1914–16, (220), LV, pp. 3, 24.
17 Diary of Sir J. Herbert Lewis, 30 March, 1915 and 23 October, 1915, MS 231, National Library of Wales, quoted Mews, 'Drink and Disestablishment', *loc. cit.*, p. 467.
18 *The Times*, 18 March, 1915; Carter, *Control*, p. 49.
19 PRO CAB 37/126; *The Times*, 30 March 1915; Shadwell, *Drink*, p. 14; Carter, *Control*, p. 50.
20 A full account is given in Mews, 'Drink and Disestablishment', *loc. cit.*, pp. 467–9, 476.
21 Correspondence Lloyd George and Lord Stamfordham, secretary to King George v, 29–30 March 1915, Lloyd George Papers, HLRO, LG/C/5/11–14.
22 *Daily Telegraph*, 1 April, 1915; *Morning Post*, 31 March, 1915.
23 *Lord Riddell's War Diary 1914–1918* (London: Nicholson & Watson, 1933), entry 10 April, 1915, p. 74.
24 Turner, 'State Purchase', *loc. cit.*, pp. 599–600.
25 The various elements of this included Whittaker and the TLL; Rowntree and Sherwell; Earl Grey sponsoring Alexander Part's scheme for the extension of Trust management. See Alexander F. Part, 'Licensing Reform a New Policy', *Nineteenth Century*, 77 (January 1915), pp. 60–71; Grey to Bonar Law, 14

December, 1914, urging Part's ideas as the foundation of a Unionist policy, Bonar Law Papers, HLRO, BL/35/4/37.

26 Bonar Law to Austen Chamberlain, 2 April, 1915, quoted Turner, 'State Purchase', *loc. cit.*, p. 600.

27 Gourvish and Wilson, *Brewing Industry*, p. 318.

28 The Earl of Oxford and Asquith, *Memories and Reflections*, 2 vols (London: Cassell, 1928) vol. 2, p. 68.

29 *Report of the advisory committee on proposals for the state purchase of the licensed liquor trade, PP*, 1916 (Cd.8283), XII, p. 529; Turner, 'State Purchase', *loc.cit.* pp. 602–6 gives a detailed account upon which this draws.

30 Bonar Law to Lloyd George, 7 April, 1915, Bonar Law Papers, HLRO, BL/37/5/15.

31 Lansdowne to Bonar Law, 1 and 5 April, 1915, *ibid.*, 37/1/1, 9; Austen Chamberlain to Bonar Law, 4 April, 1915, *ibid.*, 37/1/7; Carson to Bonar Law, 5 April, 1915, *ibid.*, 37/1/11; Lord Midleton to Bonar Law, 6 April, 1915, *ibid.*, 37/1/14.

32 Bonar Law to Lord Midleton, 8 April, 1915, *ibid.*, 37/5/16.

33 Bonar Law to J. P. Croal, 17 April, 1915, *ibid.*, 37/5/19.

34 Asquith, *Memories*, pp. 73–4; Younger to Bonar Law, 21 April, 1915, Bonar Law Papers, HLRO, BL/37/1/57, quoted Turner, 'State Purchase', *loc. cit.*, p. 603.

35 A detailed account is given in *ibid.*, pp. 604–6.

36 Carter, *Control*, pp. 62–3; Shadwell, *Drink*, pp. 25–8.

37 *Parliamentary Debates*, (HC), 71, cols. 1369–1436 (10 May, 1915).

38 He had served in 1912 as Chairman of a Royal Commission investigating the industrial resources of the Dominions.

39 *Second Report of the Central Control Board (Liquor Traffic), PP*, 1916, (Cd.8243), XII, pp. 5–6. For 'a very carefully drawn up' statement on CCB policy on this point, see Addison to Samuel, 7 December, 1915, PRO HO 185/263.

40 Carter, *Control*, pp. 127–34.

41 *Ibid.*, p. 79.

42 *Ibid.*, pp. 77–119.

43 E. M. H. Lloyd, *Experiments in State Control: At the War Office and at the Ministry of Food* (Oxford University Press, 1924) pp. 259–65; Frank H. Coller, *A State Trading Adventure* (London: Oxford University Press, 1925) pp. 9–21.

44 Carter, *Control*, p. 118.

45 Shadwell, *Drink*, pp. 36–9.

46 Notes by D'Abernon on the History of Licensing, n.d. but probably September 1915, PRO HO 45/353.

47 D'Abernon, Minutes of Advisory Alcohol Committee of CCB, November 1916, PRO HO 185/228. See also his remark that hostility to temperance reform would diminish 'if the Temperance position is confined to the limits of demonstrable facts and is protected by scientific proof', notes for speech to CETS, Annual Meeting, 15 May, 1917, PRO HO 185/242.

48 Michael E. Rose, 'The Success of Social Reform? The Central Control Board (Liquor Traffic) 1915–21', in M. R. D. Foot (ed.), *War and Society: Historical Essays in Honour and Memory of J. R. Western, 1928–1921* (London: P. Elek, 1973) pp. 71–84 provides a useful analysis of some of the 'constructive' research of the CCB.

49 The papers and minutes of the Committee are to be found in PRO HO 185/228.

50 Notes by D'Abernon, PRO HO 45/353.
51 Edgar Sanders to D'Abernon, 6 September, 1915, 6 October, 1915, PRO HO 185/353.
52 CCB., *Second Report, loc. cit.*
53 Shadwell, *Drink*, pp. 47–9.
54 Carter, *Control*, pp. 183–4.
55 P. W. Wilson to D'Abernon, 22 July, 1915, PRO HO 185/228, quoted Rose, 'Success', *loc. cit.*, p. 76.
56 Meeting to consider provision of refreshment houses, PRO HO 185/242.
57 *Third Report of the Central Control Board (LT), PP*, 1917–18 (Cd.8558), xv, pp. 9–12; Carter, *Drink*, pp. 185–91; Shadwell, *Drink*, pp. 51–4; Rose, 'Success', p. 76.
58 D'Abernon to R. S. Meiklejohn of the Treasury, 14 December, 1918; Meiklejohn replied that, with the end of the war, expenditure on canteens was not a proper charge on Munitions. If the Government saw fit to promote temperance reform by subsidising the meals of the working classes, then it should apply to the War Cabinet and the Treasury. However, the Treasury was 'besieged with requests' for social amelioration and it seemed difficult to justify subsidising a class who 'notoriously at present are receiving very high wages'. Meiklejohn to D'Abernon, 23 December, 1918, PRO HO 185/263. Unsuccessful efforts indeed were made by the CCB as late as March 1919 for the transfer back to their control of canteen administration on the grounds that it was 'an integral part of their system of liquor control'. CCB Minutes, 18 March, 1919, PRO HO 185/229; Rose, 'Success', *loc. cit.*, p. 77.
59 The women included representatives of the Welfare Department of the Ministry of Munitions and a factory inspector from the Home Office.
60 Correspondence Louise Creighton and D'Abernon, February–April 1916, PRO HO 185/258.
61 CCB Women's Advisory Committee Papers, PRO HO/185/238. Thomas Nixon Carver, *Government Control of the Liquor Traffic in Great Britain and the United States* (New York: Oxford University Press, 1919) pp. 129–35
62 Memo re conversation with Sir H. Samuel, 14 March, 1916, Neville Chamberlain to D'Abernon, 26 June, 1916, PRO HO 185/263.
63 Carter, *Control*, p. 200; Shadwell, *Drink*, pp. 56–7.
64 David W. Gutzke, 'Gentrifying the British Public House, 1896–1914', *International Labor and Working-Class History*, 45 (1994), p. 39.
65 Correspondence between D'Abernon and Alexander Part, 31 May–12 August, 1915, PRO HO 185/343.
66 Earl Lytton to D'Abernon, 20 July, 1915, Sykes to Lytton, 4 August, 1915, PRO HO 185/343.
67 Memo by Joseph Rowntree, n.d. but 1915, Astor Papers 1053/2.
68 CCB, Public House Committee, Minutes, 3 August, 20 September, 1915, PRO HO 185/213.
69 Carter, *Control*, pp. 172–4; Shadwell, *Drink*, pp. 57,59–60; G. R. Rubin, *Private Property, Government Requisition and the Constitution, 1914–1927* (London: Hambledon, 1994) p. 95.
70 Carter, *Control*, pp. 174–6; Shadwell, *Drink*, pp. 59–60.
71 Carter, *Control*, p. 198.

72 G. Bramwell Evens, *The Truth about Direct Control in Carlisle* (London: P. S. King, [1917]), p. 4.
73 Precis of evidence to Royal Commission on Licensing, 1929–31, Brewers' Society Papers, MSS 420/304.
74 Correspondence between Treasury and CCB, 17 April and 11 July, 1916, PRO T 112; Public House Committee, 3 August and 20 September, 1915, PRO HO 185/213; Rose, 'Success', *loc. cit.*, p. 78.
75 Carter, *Control*, pp. 200–4; Shadwell, *Drink*, pp. 60–3. The CCB was to be embarrassed by a long-running legal dispute about the methods and terms of compensation for some of the undertakings it took over, see Rubin, *Private Property*, pp. 93–112.
76 Documents on Constitution of Carlisle Local Committee, May 1916, PRO HO 185/8; Carlisle, Local Committee Minutes, PRO HO 285/9; Rose, 'Success', *loc. cit.*, p. 80. The General Manager's annual reports regularly made much of the degree of local support for the scheme, for example, *General Manager's Report to the Central Control Board for the Year ending 31 December 1919*, *PP*, 1920 (Cmd.666), xx, p. 20.
77 CCB, *Carlisle and District Control Area. General Manager's Report to the Board, 1918–19*, *PP*, 1919 (Cd.137), xxiv, p. 11.
78 Report of Col David Davies regarding administration of public houses and canteens in Annan District, 5 July, 1916, PRO HO 185/227.
79 Sunday closing was largely introduced so as to bring the English areas round Gretna into line with Scottish practice.
80 Shadwell, *Drink*, pp. 67–8.
81 CCB, *Carlisle General Manager's Report*, 1918–19, *loc. cit.*, p. 12.
82 Carter, *Control*, pp. 209–14; Shadwell, *Drink*, pp. 70–7; Derek H. Aldcroft, 'Control of the Liquor Trade in Great Britain', in W. H. Chaloner and Barrie M. Ratcliffe (eds.), *Trade and Transport: Essays in Economic History in honour of T. S. Willan* (Manchester University Press, 1977) pp. 247–8.
83 D'Abernon to Lloyd George, 19 August, 1916, PRO HO 185/263.
84 Rev. Wilson Stuart, *The Carlisle and Annan Experiment under the Central Control Board (Liquor Traffic)* (Birmingham: Templar Printing Works, [1917]); Evens, *Truth about Direct Control*; Rose, 'Success', *loc. cit.*, p. 80.
85 *Parliamentary Debates*, (HC), 93, col. 985, (8 May, 1917); for correspondence between D'Abernon and Gretton on the subject, 9–25 May, 1917 see PRO HO 185/263.
86 CCB, Public House Committee Minutes, PRO HO 185/213 quoted Rose, 'Success', *loc. cit.*, p. 81.
87 Report by A. F. Harvey of TLL, 18 July, 1917, PRO HO 185/227.
88 For his thoughts on this, see Paper on 'Rival Theories of Drunkenness', 27 November, 1918, PRO HO 185/242.
89 CCB, *Carlisle General Manager's Report*, 1918–19, *loc. cit.*, p. 11. Part two of this report was, in effect, a carefully argued manifesto justifying state control, and had been largely written at the CCB headquarters in London.
90 Joseph Rowntree Papers, JR93/V/8.
91 Minutes of W.C., 12, 20 December, 1916, PRO CAB 23/1.
92 Paper G. 107, PRO CAB 24/3, *Memorandum submitted to the Government in December, 1916 . . .*, *PP*, 1917–18, (Cd.8613), xxvi. The paper had been

drawn up by a special committee on 12 December, PRO HO 185/270, PRO HO 185/263.

93 D'Abernon to Lloyd George, 16 December, 1916, Lloyd George Papers, HLRO, LG/F/14/1/1 and PRO HO 185/262.

94 Sir George Younger to Lloyd George, 4 January, 1917, Bonar Law Papers, HLRO, BL/81/2/7.

95 Gourvish and Wilson, *Brewing Industry*, p. 319; Thomas Nixon Carver, *Government Control of the Liquor Traffic in Great Britain and the United States* (New York: Oxford University Press, 1919) pp. 92–5.

96 Carver, *Government Control of the Liquor Traffic*, pp. 53–7.

97 L. Margaret Barnett, *British Food Policy during the First World War* (London: Allen & Unwin, 1985) pp. 94–5, 105–6.

98 Frank A. Coller, *A State Trading Adventure* (Oxford University Press, 1925) pp. 132–203.

99 Appendix II to W.C. 42, 23 January, 1917, PRO CAB 23/1.

100 Secretary of CCB to Secretary Ministry of Munitions, 9 February, 1917, PRO HO 185/265.

101 Cave, *Parliamentary Debates*, (HC), 90, cols. 683–8 (14 February, 1917).

102 Sir George Cave to D'Abernon, 28 February, 1917, D'Abernon to Cave, 1 March, 1917, PRO HO 185/263.

103 Turner, 'State Purchase', *loc. cit.*, pp. 608–9. Also memo on state purchase, May 1916, Brewers' Society Papers, MSS 420/304.

104 Cave to D'Abernon, 14 March, 1917, PRO HO 45/166.

105 Turner, 'State Purchase', *loc. cit.*, p. 609.

106 'Report of Home Office committee appointed to enquire into the position created by the approved restrictions on the output of beer, spirits and wines' 21 March, 1917, paper G.T. 241, PRO CAB 24/8.

107 W.C. 106, 27 March, 1917, PRO CAB 23/2.

108 Turner, 'State Purchase', *loc. cit.*, pp. 609–10.

109 Paper G. T. 643, PRO CAB 24/2.

110 'Memorandum on Lord Milner's Note', 7 May, 1917, (marked 'not sent in'), PRO HO 185/266.

111 W.C. 133–5, 7–9 May, 1917, PRO CAB 23/2. Turner, 'State Purchase', *loc. cit.*, p. 611.

112 W.C. 153, 165, 31 May and 19 June, 1917, PRO CAB 23/2; Memo. by Milner on the 'Necessity for immediate control', 19 June, 1917, G.T.1070, PRO CAB 24/16.

113 John Turner, *Lloyd George's Secretariat* (Cambridge University Press, 1980) pp. 178–9.

114 Gourvish and Wilson, *Brewing Industry*, p. 321.

115 Paper G.T. 1092, PRO CAB 24/16.

116 W.C. 167, 21 June, 1917, PRO CAB 23/3.

117 Turner, 'State Purchase', p. 612.

118 Coller, *State as Trader*, pp. 134–5; Sydney O. Nevile, *Seventy Rolling Years* (London: Faber & Faber, 1958) pp. 112–13.

119 See file in Astor Papers 1060/1.

120 Gourvish and Wilson, *Brewing Industry*, p. 322; Barnett, *British Food Policy*, pp. 163–80.

121 *State Purchase of the Liquor Trade; Reports of the English, Scotch and Irish Committee*, *PP*, 1918 (Cd. 9042), XI.
122 J. Herbert Lewis to Lloyd George, 27 October, 1917, Lloyd George Papers, HLRO, LG/F/32/1/11; Astor to Lloyd George, 1 February, 1918, Astor Papers, 40/767 also Astor to Lloyd George, 20 February, 1918, Lloyd George Papers, HLRO, LG/F 83/1/11; Turner, *Secretariat*, p. 186.
123 W.C. 400, 26 April, 1918, PRO CAB 23/6.
124 G. B. Wilson, *Alcohol and the Nation: a Contribution to the Study of the Liquor Problem in the United Kingdom from 1800 to 1935* (London: Nicholson & Watson, 1940) pp. 335, 432; Gwylmor Prys Williams and George Thompson Brake, *Drink in Great Britain 1900–1979* (London: Edsall, 1980) pp. 59–61; Aldcroft, 'Control of liquor trade', *loc. cit.*, pp. 244–5.
125 Arthur Marwick, *The Deluge: British Society and the First World War* (London: Bodley Head, 1965) pp. 62–8.
126 For Example, Joseph Rowntree and Arthur Sherwell, *State Purchase of the Liquor Trade* (London: Allen & Unwin, [1919]); T. P. Whittaker, *Temperance Reform and State Purchase: Some Lessons of the Past* (London: P. S. King, [1918]).
127 Turner, 'State Purchase', *loc. cit.*, p. 60.
128 Carter, *Control*, esp. pp. 278–81.
129 Memo on beer restrictions, 9 March, 1918, PRO HO 185/265.

7 The Postwar Settlement, 1919–21

1 Arthur Shadwell, *Drink in 1914–1922: a Lesson in Control*, (London: Longman, 1923) pp. 84, 130–1.
2 Ben Tillett to G. H. Roberts, Food Controller, 29 April, 1919, LRC.7, PRO CAB 27/62.
3 War Cabinet Minutes [W.C.], 22 and 29 May, 1919, PRO CAB 23/10, PRO MAF 60/100, PRO CAB 27/62. In November 1919, the continuance of restrictions on spirit sales was also recognised to be 'very unpopular' and bringing 'great odium and unpopularity' upon the Government, PRO MAF 60/100.
4 Sydney O. Nevile, *Seventy Rolling Years*, (London: Faber & Faber, 1958) p. 120.
5 W.C. 573, (29 May, 1919); W.C. 577 (6 June, 1919) & W.C. 580, (16 June, 1919), PRO CAB 23/10, also PRO MAF 60/100.
6 H. A. L. Fisher to Bonar Law, 27 February, 1920, Viscount Davidson Papers, HLRO, DAV/107.
7 Draft memo of D'Abernon circulated 3 February, 1920; memo Austen Chamberlain, 12 February, 1920, PRO MAF 60/100.
8 Memos. Board of Trade 11 July, 1921, Chancellor of the Exchequer 25 July, 1921, PRO MAF 60/100.
9 Minutes 11th Meeting CCB, 6 May, 1919, PRO HO 185/270; D'Abernon, W. C. 573, 29 May, 1919, PRO CAB 23/10.
10 Notes by D'Abernon for H. A. L. Fisher, 25 March, 1919, PRO HO 185/263.
11 Fisher was 'somewhat reluctantly' chosen to chair the Committee on Lloyd George's insistence because of his key role in the Home Affairs Committee

of the Cabinet, Thomas Jones to Hankey, 14 March, 1919, Lloyd George Papers, HLRO, LG/F/23/4/34.

12 Memo by Lord Milner on State Purchase for War Cabinet, 30 April, 1919, GT 7163, PRO CAB 27/62.

13 Minutes, Liquor Restrictions Committee, 9 May, 1919, PRO CAB 27/62.

14 Report and Memo, Liquor Restrictions Committee, 28 May, 1919, G246 and G247, PRO CAB 27/62.

15 *Methodist Times*, 18 March, 1920.

16 B. S. Rowntree to Wardoff Astor, 19 August, 1919, Astor Papers /1061.

17 Memo by Sir John Pedder, 22 April, 1919, PRO HO 185/267.

18 Sir L. Guillmard had the impression that the CCB feared 'that if too onerous controls on beer restrictions were retained the whole system would be endangered including the restrictions on hours of sale'. Minutes of conference at the Treasury 19 June, 1919, Milner Papers, PRO 30/30/14.

19 D'Abernon to Lloyd George 9 July, 1919, enclosing copies of letters to him from Carter of 9 July, and Nevile of 8 July, Lloyd George Papers, HLRO, LG/F/14/1/3,3a,3b.

20 Drafted by J. C. G. Sykes, Secretary of CCB, 23 July, 1919, approved as 'very good I think' by Pedder, PRO HO 185/265 and signed and circulated by D'Abernon, 26 July, 1919, PRO HO 185/267; GT 7822, PRO CAB 24/85.

21 *Parliamentary Debates*, (HC), 117, col. 959, (2 July, 1919).

22 Nevile, *Seventy Rolling Years*, pp. 121–3.

23 *Ibid.*, pp. 126–7.

24 *Ibid.*, p. 126.

25 *Ibid.*, pp. 124–7.

26 PRO HO 45/11019/390339/1.

27 Nevile, *Seventy Rolling Years*, p. 127.

28 Gordon Hewart to Lloyd George, 24 November, 1920, Lloyd George Papers, HLRO, LG/F/27/4/17.

29 Nevile, *Seventy Rolling Years*, p. 128.

30 *The Times*, 18 November, 1920.

31 Memo of meeting Sir John Sykes with Bonar Law, 12 January, 1921, HLRO, DAV/Viscount Davidson Papers, /124. Pedder in a minute of 2 December, 1920 was quite uncertain of the future of his Board, PRO HO 45/11080/422901/3.

32 CPs 2727 and 2728, PRO CAB 27/150; Lloyd George Papers, HLRO, LG/F/96/1/12.

33 Cabinet Minutes, 22 and 24 March, 1921, PRO CAB 23/24/ pp. 161, 218.

34 Memo by Lord D'Abernon for Liquor Restrictions Committee of the Cabinet, 24 March, 1921, circulated 7 April, 1921, PRO CAB 27/150.

35 Cabinet Minutes, 20 April, 1921, PRO CAB 23/25/ pp. 146–49.

36 Nevile, *Seventy Rolling Years*, pp. 132–3.

37 The idea of the 'round table' format may have originated with the Attorney General, Gordon Hewart, who chaired it; he had suggested an attempt to get all-party support the previous November. Hewart to Lloyd George, 24 November, 1920, Lloyd George Papers, HLRO, LG/F/27/4/17.

38 Henry Carter spoke of the changed atmosphere in the Commons following what he inaccurately described as 'the defeat' of Gretton's Bill; the moment was ripe, he believed, 'for reasonable men on both sides to get together and

try to reach agreement on the basis of the CCB's work', Henry Carter to Waldorf Astor, 27 April, 1921, Astor Papers /1064.

39 Astor to Carter, 29 April, 1921, *ibid.* /1064; Astor to T. T. Broad, 28 April, 17 May and 28 July, 1921, *ibid.* /1063.

40 Broad to Astor, reporting progress of the negotiations, 6 May, 11 May, 20 May, 30 May, 18 June, 1921, *ibid.* /1063.

41 Broad to Astor, 30 June, 1921, *ibid.* /1063; Nevile, *Seventy Rolling Years*, pp. 133–4.

42 CP 3139, PRO CAB 24/126/pp. 321–34; Cabinet Minutes 18 July, 1921, PRO CAB 23/26/pp. 127–31.

43 11 and 12 Geo. V, c. 42.

44 For example, speeches in the Commons by Raffan and Nancy Astor, *Parliamentary Debates*, (HC), 144, cols. 2616–24, (22 July, 1921); *ibid.*, 145, col. 1360 (2 August, 1921). Broad's appetite was whetted and he considered he might have further success with a measure to assist the closure of redundant 'on' licences and the better regulation of grocers' licences and clubs, Broad to Astor, 29 September, 1921, Astor Papers /1063.

45 W. Waters Butler to Sir John Baird, Under Secretary of the Home Office, 11 August, 1921, PRO HO 45/11080/422901/20A.

46 H. A. L. Fisher to Lloyd George, 26 May, 1920, 4 June, 1920, Lloyd George Papers, HLRO, LG/F/16/7/57,58.

47 Frank Coller to Arthur Towle, 7 June, 1921, PRO MAF 60/476.

48 For example, the long series of Home Office complaints at the Treasury's parsimony which weakened the financial success of Carlisle, PRO HO 45/11080/422901/21A-48. Treasury and CCB correspondence PRO T 112, see also Heath to D'Abernon, 17 May, 1919, PRO T 147.

49 Memo by Addison, Minister of Health, 24 February, 1920, PRO MAF 60/100.

50 Nevile, *Seventy Rolling Years*, p. 123.

51 *Ibid.*, p. 99.

52 Virginia Berridge, 'The Society for the Study of Addiction 1884–1988', *British Journal of Addiction*, 85, special issue, (1990), pp. 1017–22.

53 Astor to Broad, 28 July, 1921, Astor Papers /1063.

8 Decades of Improvement: The Interwar Years

1 Ernest Selley, *The English Public House as it is* (London: Longman, Green 1927) p. 141.

2 Astor maintained he had been appointed to that body precisely because he had no decided views on the question and no particular knowledge of it *Parliamentary Debates*, (HL), 57, cols. 1115–24 (30 June, 1924). Royal Commission on Liquor Licensing, *Minutes of Evidence* (8th July, 1930), (London: HMSO, 1932), vol. III, p. 1644.

3 Sydney O. Nevile, *Seventy Rolling Years* (London: Faber & Faber, 1958) pp. 107,178–9; D'Abernon to Lady D'Abernon, n.d. [June and August 1917], D'Abernon Papers, Add. MSS, 48936, ff. 18, 21.

4 Bishop of Oxford to Astor, 3 June, 1921, Astor Papers /1067.

5 It was also known as the 'Triple Option Bill' and, after Burge's death, was taken over by Lord Balfour of Burleigh. Astor, however, did all the work for it.

6 Correspondence with the Bishop of Croydon, Sir George Hunter, T. Leif Jones, J. Malins, A. Sherwell, Astor Papers /1064–8.
7 Astor to Miss C. Wilmot, 15 November, 1928, *ibid.*, /1098.
8 Astor to Snowden, 19 September, 1933, *ibid.*, /1127.
9 The prohibitory option would only come into force on a 55 per cent majority, provided this constituted at least 35 per cent of the total electorate. Where no licence failed to carry the day, the prohibitory vote was added to those for limitation.
10 Ed. T. Honeyman, *No Licence!* (Glasgow, [1921]), pp. 9–18.
11 R. B. Weir, 'Obsessed with moderation: The Drink Trades and the Drink Question (1870–1930)', *British Journal of Addiction*, 79 (1984), pp. 104–5.
12 *Return of Voting Areas in Scotland . . . showing . . . the Results of the Polls, . . . PP*, 1921 (Cmd.1264), XXIX; Labour Party, *Labour and the Liquor Trade: Report of the Special Committee Appointed to inquire into the Question of the Liquor Trade* (London: Labour Party, 1923).
13 J. Gillies, *Scotland's No-Licence Areas* (Glasgow, [1926]) p. 6.
14 Typescript report on Kirkintilloch, n.d. but c.1927, in box marked 'Temperance (Scotland) Act' in records of UKA.
15 Gillies, *Scotland's No-Licence Areas*, pp. 6–31.
16 *Scottish Women's Temperance News*, January 1968.
17 A full analysis is provided by Stephen G. Jones, 'Labour, Society and the Drink Question in Britain, 1918–1939', *The Historical Journal*, 30, (1987), pp. 105–22.
18 The Labour campaign for public ownership also received the support of the Conservative magazine, the *Spectator*, *ibid.*, p. 108.
19 B. Seebohm Rowntree to Astor 5 May, 1918, notes of Conference at House of Commons, 5 June, 1918, marked 'confidential', Astor to Rowntree 9 May, 1919, Rowntree to Greenwood 22 May, 1919, Rowntree to Astor 7 June, 1919, Astor Papers/1061.
20 8 November, 1919, conference, PRO HO 190/495.
21 Jones 'Labour and Drink Question', *loc. cit.*, p. 110.
22 Arthur Greenwood, *Public Ownership of the Liquor Trade* (London: Leonard Parsons, 1920); *Record*, November–December 1925.
23 W. Theodore Carr to Sir Edgar Sanders, reporting a House of Commons meeting, 29 July, 1919, PRO HO 190/498.
24 For a full analysis of anti-temperance positions in the labour movement, see Jones 'Labour and Drink Question', *loc. cit.*, pp. 110–3.
25 Astor to H. G. Chancellor, 6 December, 1921, Astor Papers /1064.
26 Mallon to Astor, 3 March, 1926, *ibid.* /1098.
27 Jones, 'Labour and Drink Question', *loc. cit.*, pp. 114–6.
28 Philip Snowden, *Labour and the New World* (London: [Cassell's Social Economic series] 1921) pp. 239–65.
29 *Daily Herald*, 25 June, 1920; Greenwood to Sanders, 3 July, 1920, PRO HO 190/495.
30 Labour Party, *Labour and the Liquor Trade*, p. 10. The report was endorsed at the Party conference, Labour Party, *Annual Conference Report*, 1923, pp. 86, 224. Jones 'Labour and Drink Question', *loc. cit.*, p. 120. See Brewers' Society Papers, MSS 420/390 for proceedings of a meeting between this Committee and the brewers.

31 Accounts were regularly carried in the pages of the *Alliance News* and were aired by sympathetic MPs in Parliament. A particularly vicious attack was launched by Rev. Wilson Stuart, *Drink Nationalization in England and its results. The Carlisle Experiment* (London: J. Clarke [1927]). This was the unauthorised publication of evidence given before a parliamentary inquiry.
32 PRO HO 45/126301/443932/44.
33 J. G. Chisholm of Cromarty Firth State Management, Dingwall District to J. G. Paterson, State Management District Office Scotland, 22 July, 1925, PRO HO 185/124.
34 Selley, *English Public House*, p. 103.
35 G. Bramwell Evens to Home Secretary, 7 April, 1923, PRO HO 45/126301 /443932/4.
36 *Third Report from the Select Committee on National Expenditure, PP*,1920, (138) VII; memo of Sir John Sykes to Sir John Pedder, 11 April, 1922, PRO HO 185/160.
37 J. S. Eagles to Sir John Sykes, 26 October, 1921, PRO HO 190/498.
38 H. A. Rimington, reporting interview with the Home Secretary, Minutes, Carlisle Local Advisory Committee, 18 April, 1923, PRO HO 185/10.
39 Cabinet Paper, 19 March, 1923 C.P.157 (23), PRO CAB 24/159; PRO HO 45/126301/443932/5a.
40 For example: 'Enquiries into licensing questions are always very troublesome', Joynson-Hicks to Lord Desborough, 9 March, 1925, PRO HO 45/126301/443932/32; 'I do not want to stir up Controversy on Liquor Questions during the present Parliament', Joynson-Hicks, 16 July, 1927, PRO HO 45/20416/509542/10.
41 PRO HO 45/126301/443932/17.
42 H. A. Taylor, *Jix. Viscount Brentford: Being the Authoritative and Official Biography of the Rt. Hon. William Joynson-Hicks, First Viscount Brentford of Newick*, (London: Stanley Paul, 1933) p. 22.
43 Draft memo 7 June, 1928, PRO HO 45/13178/522977/3.
44 Memo 11 June, 1928, C.P. 182, PRO CAB 24/195; PRO HO 45/12619/ 522977/3.
45 Royal Commission on Liquor Licensing, *Minutes of Evidence*, vol. I, p. 40, q. 939; Nevile, *Seventy Rolling Years*, pp. 98–9.
46 PRO HO 45/15136/510622/81a.
47 Pedder to Astor, 27 September, 1922, Astor Papers /1067. Pedder, in 1919, did his best to mobilise Whitehall support against the threatened abolition of all wartime restrictions: gloss on draft memo. of J. C. G. Sykes, 23 July, 1919, PRO HO 185/265.
48 Joseph Rowntree and Arthur Sherwell, *British 'Gothenburg' Experiments and Public-House Trusts* (London: Hodder & Stoughton, 1901); Selley, *English Public House*, pp. 69–75.
49 Henry Carter, *The Control of the Drink Trade. A Contribution to National Efficiency, 1915–1917* (London: Longman, Green, 1918) pp. 214–15.
50 For a general analysis of the administrative development of the Carlisle scheme, see R. M. Punnett, 'State Management of the Liquor Trade', *Public Administration*, 44, (1966), pp. 193–211.
51 Selley, *English Public House*, p. 176; H. M. Vernon, *The Alcohol Problem* (London: Baillière, 1928) p. 103 *et seq*.

52 Memo D'Abernon to Cabinet Committee on Liquor Restrictions, 24 March, 1921 (written from Berlin after his resignation as Chairman of the CCB and circulated 7 April, 1921, CAB 27/150. See also his preface to Vernon, *Alcohol Problem*, pp. v–xi.
53 Selley, *English Public House*, pp. 102–3.
54 Rowntree and Sherwell, *British Gothenburg Experiments*, pp. 22–38.
55 Memo J. S. Eagles, December 1925, on Women's bars, also Eagles to Sykes, 18 December, 1925, PRO HO 190/498.
56 Eagles to Sydney Nevile, 20 January, 1927, PRO HO 190/1232.
57 Nevile to Eagles, 15 January, 1927, 1 October, 1927, PRO HO 190/1233. See John R. Greenaway, 'The "Improved" Public House 1850–1950: the Key to Civilised Drinking or the Primrose Path to Drunkenness?', *Addiction*, 93 (1998), pp. 173–81. For history of the "Improved" Public House in an earlier period see David W. Gutzke, 'Gentrifying the British Public House, 1896–1914', *International Labor and Working-Class History*, 45 (1994), pp. 29–43; Robert Thorne, 'The Movement for Public House Reform 1892–1914', in Derek J. Oddy and Derek S. Miller (eds), *Diet and Health in Modern Britain* (Beckenham: Croom Helm, 1985) pp. 231–54.
58 Nevile, *Seventy Rolling Years*, p. 72.
59 *Ibid.*, p. 167.
60 *Ibid.*, p. 171.
61 *Ibid.*, p. 182.
62 *Ibid.*, 169–74; Ernest Edwin Williams, *The New Public House* (London: Chapman & Hall, 1924) pp. 24–9.
63 Williams, *New Public-House*, pp. 84–92.
64 Joynson-Hicks to Lord Desborough 9 March, 1925, memo by Pedder, 8 March, 1925, PRO HO 45/126301/443932/32.
65 Pedder pointed out that statements by Salisbury and Balfour from the Opposition front bench in the Lords during the previous Labour government virtually committed him to setting one up. Memo by Pedder, 8 March, 1925, PRO HO 45/126301/443932/32.
66 Cabinet paper by Lord Salisbury, 10 March, 1925, C.P. 147(25), PRO HO 45/126301/443932/58.
67 *Report of the Committee on the Disinterested Management of Public Houses, PP*, 1927 (Cmnd. 2862), x.
68 Southborough to Joynson-Hicks, 14 October, 1926 and 12 April, 1927, PRO HO 45/12630/443932/100. The view of one official was that Southborough was a weak chairman 'easily bored by finance and . . . letting the other members have their run freely instead of bottling them up', A. E. Mitchell, State Management District Central Office, to Eagles, Carlisle Manager, 10 July, 1925, PRO HO 185/124.
69 See file concerning deputations and letters: PRO HO 45/20416/509542; memo re 'small and informal' deputation of representatives of brewers and retailers on 29 November, 1928, PRO HO 185/126.
70 Deputation of licensing justices to Home Secretary, 29 January, 1929, PRO HO 185/126.
71 Henry Carter had reported to Astor in August 1924 that Pedder had assured him there would be 'no hitch re. Royal Commission', Carter to Astor, 8 August, 1924, also Astor to Carter 10 October, 1924, Astor Papers /1082.

72 Memo by Joynson-Hicks for Cabinet 22 March, 1929, CP 252 (27), PRO HO 45/126301/443932/100; PRO HO 185/126. The actual appointment of the Commission fell to the next Labour Government in July 1929.
73 PRO HO 45/15160/563911/28. There were representatives of the Trade, the clubs, licensing justices, the Home Office, friendly societies, and various social workers and advocates of state purchase: no prohibitionist was included.
74 *Report of the Royal Commission on Licensing (England and Wales), 1929–31*, paras. 28–102, *PP*, 1931–32 (Cmd.3988), XI.
75 *Ibid.*, paras. 361–424.
76 *Ibid.*, paras. 194–238.
77 *Ibid.*, paras. 428–36.
78 Joanne Woiak, '"A Medical Cromwell to Depose King Alcohol": Medical Scientists, Temperance Reformers, and the Alcohol Problem in Britain', *Histoire Sociale/Social History*, 27, (1994), pp. 337–65.
79 Vernon, *Alcohol Problem*; Ernest H. Starling, R. Hutchison, F. W. Mott, and R. Pearl, *The Action of Alcohol on Man* (London: Longman, Green, 1923); Haven Emerson, (ed.), *Alcohol and Man* (New York: Macmillan, 1932).
80 Astor Papers /1106, 1118, 1126. Beveridge, Seebohm Rowntree and Carr-Saunders as well as experts from the realm of medicine, industry and insurance worked for him. But the results of this were disappointing, partly because those involved lacked the time to devote to it, and partly it was difficult to get unanimity among the members of the various 'panels'. Most of the work was not completed by the time the Royal Commission sat.
81 Woiak, '"Medical Cromwell"', *loc. cit.*, p. 363.
82 PRO MH 56/58.
83 *Report of the Royal Commission on Licensing (England and Wales), 1929–31, Majority Report* paras. 730–8, *PP*, 1931–32 (Cmd.3988), XI.
84 Nevile, *Seventy Rolling Years*, pp. 221–2.
85 Sir Edgar had no idea how his remarks had fallen into the hands of the UKA and supposed some brewer had left them lying around, Sir Edgar Saunders to W. R. Nicolson, 20 January, 1934, Brewers' Society Papers, MSS 420/298.
86 *The Times*, 18 November, 1933; *Daily Telegraph*, 18 November, 1933; *Alliance News*, December 1933.
87 *The Times*, 10 November, 1933; PRO HO 45/16239/541004/11; minutes of the Temperance Movement Standing Committee 27 October–1 December, 1933, Methodist Archives, M.A. 250.
88 Nevile, *Seventy Rolling Years*, pp. 22–3.
89 *Parliamentary Debates*, (HL), 96, cols. 410–53 (28 March, 1935), memo. 18 March, 1935, Brewers' Society Papers, MSS 420/298.
90 PRO MH 56/58.
91 *Parliamentary Debates*, (HC), 321, cols. 3182–6 (25 March, 1937).

9 Policy Fragmentation 1945–70: Three case studies

1 The movement, however, could still count on the support of 98 MPs as late as 1960. In many respects, the situation was the reverse of that a century earlier: now the movement had more elite sympathy than popular support.

However, these MPs tended to be backbenchers without much access to Whitehall. Rob Baggott, *Alcohol, Politics and Social Policy* (Aldershot: Gower, 1990) p. 9.

2 *Methodist Recorder*, 13 February, 1941, 26 June, 1941; *Manchester Guardian*, 17 September, 1941.

3 Betsy Thom, *Dealing with Drink: Alcohol and Social Policy from Treatment to Management* (London: Free Association Books, 1999) pp. 20–1.

4 For the New Towns in general, see Mark Clapson, *Invincible Green Suburbs, Brave New Towns* (Manchester University Press, 1998); Frank Schaffer, *The New Town Story* (London: Granada Paladin, 1970).

5 Notes, 18 December, 1948, by Frederic Osborn, for a review of pamphlet G. McAllister 'The Inn and the Garden City', Frederic Osborn Papers, B95. Letchworth had instituted a local option contrary to Howard's inclinations.

6 Ministry of Town and Country Planning / Department of Health for Scotland, *Final Report of the New Towns Committee*, paras. 205–8, pp. 46–7, *PP* (Cmd. 6876), XIV.

7 9 and 10 Geo.VI, c.68.

8 *Report of the Committee on War Damaged Licensed Premises and Reconstruction*, *PP*, 1943–44 (Cmd.6506), IV; Licensing Planning Temporary Provisions Act, 1945, 8 and 9 Geo. VI, c.15. Detailed files concerning the cooperation between the brewers and the government on this matter are to be found at Brewers' Society Papers, MSS 420/320.

9 Memo on liquor licensing and New Towns, 14 March, 1946, PRO HLG 90/15.

10 Memo Country Brewers' Society to MTCP, 17 May, 1946, also P. E. Longmore of Hertfordshire County Council to Sir Granville Ram, Office of Parliamentary Counsel, enclosing letter from Essex and Hertfordshire Brewers' Association, July 1946, PRO HLG 90/15; minutes Reconstruction and Planning Committee, 15 May, 1946, Minute Book 28, Brewers' Society Papers, MSS 420/12; also correspondence May–June 1946, *ibid.*, MSS 420/333.

11 Sir A. Maxwell to R. R. Bannatyne, 18 August, 1941, memo. of meeting, Maxwell and Bannatyne, 5 September, 1941, Bannatyne to Maxwell, 26 September, 1941, memo by Maxwell for Home Secretary, 22 November, 1941, PRO HO 45/24193/806869/67. Maxwell found it 'extraordinary how little interest appears to have been taken in State Management of recent years and how little steam there appears to be behind any policy of extending' it.

12 Papers on extension of Carlisle District, and minute by Chuter Ede, 17 September, 1945, on memo of Sir Alexander Maxwell, 15 September, 1945, PRO HO 185/315. The Brewers' Society quickly became aware of these ideas and urged a proactive response by the local brewers, see correspondence between H. A. Eastwood and Sir Robert Ewbank and subsequent papers, Brewers' Society Papers, MSS 420/304.

13 Memo by J. J. Mallon for Sir Alexander Maxwell, n.d. but sent 30 August, 1946, PRO HO 185/315.

14 Henry Carter to Seebhom Rowntree, 23 September, 1946, Seebohm Rowntree Papers, Borthwick Institute, Temperance/3.

15 Notes of Meeting of Deputation by J. J. Mallon and others, 23 October, 1946, PRO HLG 90/15 also Brewers' Society Papers, MSS 420/323.
16 Newsam (HO) to Miss E. A. Sharp (MTCP), 1 May, 1947 noting a redrafted paragraph reflecting ministerial views which had been 'strongly influenced by an influential deputation led by Mallon'; memo by Maxwell for ministers, 20 December, 1946, PRO HLG 90/15.
17 Carter to Rowntree, 23 September, 1946, Seebohm Rowntree Papers, Borthwick Institute, Temperance/3.
18 F. B. Bell (MTCP) to H. B. Wilson (HO), 12 October, 1946, Wilson to Bell, 18 October, 1946, PRO HLG 90/15.
19 Sir Robert Ewbank (Brewers' Society) to Blake Odgers (HO), Brewers' Society Papers, MSS 420/323.
20 The MTCP had actually sent two officials to reconnoitre conditions at Carlisle, memos D. P. Walsh, 19 and 22 October, 1946, PRO HLG 90/15.
21 Papers and memos between December 1946 and April 1947, PRO HLG 90/15. Despite diligent search, I have been unable to track down the corresponding Home Office files; the Home Office radically reorganised its filing system in 1948–49 and they may have fallen victim to this.
22 Memo by E. A. Sharp, 16 June, 1947, PRO HLG 90/15.
23 General Sir H. Colville Wemyss, newly appointed Director, invited a MTCP civil servant to lunch and a series of memos and position papers were sent, PRO HLG 90/16. See also Minutes Reconstruction and Planning Committee, 16 July, 1947, Minute Book 29, Brewers' Society Papers, MSS 420/12; Wemyss to R. W. McGrath of Cannon Brewery, 25 July, 1947, *ibid.*, MSS 420/323.
24 Notes on deputation from Brewers' Society at the Home Office, 24 October, 1947, PRO HLG 90/16.
25 Minutes Parliamentary Committee, 18 February, 1947, Minute Book 29, Brewers' Society Papers, MSS 420/12.
26 Memo on Licensing Policy in the New Towns by Brewers' Society, 25 November, 1947, PRO HLG 90/16.
27 Minutes 13th and 15th Meeting Standing Ministerial Conference on New Towns, 5 November, 1947 and 4 February, 1948, *ibid.*
28 Reith to Sir Thomas Sheepshanks, 4 and 22 July, 1947, *ibid.*
29 Sharp to Blake Odgers, 13 November, 1947, Sir Frank Newsom to Sharp, 26 November, 1947, *ibid.*
30 Briefing memo for Sharp, 1 December, 1947, see also Sharp to Newsom 3 December, 1947; Silkin himself remained a supporter of state management though willing to report the views of the corporation chairmen, Sheepshanks to Silkin, 11 March, 1948, *ibid.*
31 Minutes, Lord President's Committee, 23 April, 1948, PRO CAB 132/9–10; General Memo on State Management Districts, 8 April, 1948 prepared for meeting with Crawley Development Corporation, 15 April, 1948, PRO HO 185/315.
32 Minutes 22nd Meeting Standing Ministerial Conference on New Towns, 17 November, 1948, PRO HLG 90/17.
33 E. M. King (MTCP) to H. Morrison, 15 December, 1948, memo by Sir Thomas Sheepshanks for Lord President, 14 December, 1948, PRO CAB

124/887; Sheepshanks to Silkin, 15 June, 1948, Beveridge to Silkin, 15 December, 1948, PRO HLG 90/16.

34 M. M. Dobbie (MTCP) to Blake Odgers (HO), 22 November, 1948, memos by Sheepshanks, 15 and 21 December, 1948, PRO HLG 90/18.

35 R. L. Reiss to Frederic Osborn, 17 January, 1949; Osborne to Reiss 18 January, 1949, Frederic Osborn Papers, B122.

36 PRO HLG 90/18–22.

37 Rowntree to Lord Astor, 22 November, 1948, Seebhom Rowntree Papers, Joseph Rowntree Foundation, Temperance/4. See also G. R. Lavers to Mallon, 20 November, 1948, *ibid.*, G. R. Lavers to J. R. Clynes, 10 December, 1948 *ibid.*, Temperance/6.

38 *Morning Advertiser*, 19 November, 1948 and 6 December, 1948; PRO HO 190/1233.

39 E. E. Tetley to Morrison, 12 November, 1948, PRO CAB 124/887; Brewers' Society Papers, MSS 420/330.

40 Minute Books 30 and 31, *ibid.*, MSS 420/13–14.

41 For example, *Daily Graphic*, 10 December, 1948; *Sunday Graphic*, 30 November, 1948.

42 PRO CAB 124/887; *Parliamentary Debates* (HC), 459, col. 1137–8, (14 December, 1948).

43 Lavers to Sir John Mann, 8 May, 1948, Mann to Lavers, 11 May, 1948, Seebhom Rowntree Papers, Joseph Rowntree Foundation, Temperance/1. Also 'many [Labour] members are prepared to accept nationalisation [of Drink] simply because it established a measure that is theoretically desirable to the Socialist mind, namely a state of monopoly. Such people are not in the least interested in nationalisation of the drink trade as a means of achieving disinterested management.' Lavers to Mann, 13 January, 1949, *ibid.* Temperance/8.

44 Sir Hugh Beaver reporting from Executive Committee to the full Council, Minutes Council, 15 December, 1948, Minute Book 30, Brewers' Society Papers, MSS 420/13; minute of meeting with Lord Woolton, *ibid.*, MSS 420/330.

45 Minutes Executive Committee, 1 December, 1948, Minute Book 31, Brewers' Society Papers, MSS 420/14, also minute of this meeting *ibid.*, MSS 420/331.

46 Minutes Executive Committee of NTDA, 9 November, 1949, Minute Book 5, *ibid.*, MSS 420/31.

47 Action Committee/ Executive Committee files re Bing Bill, *ibid.*, MSS 420/331. Minutes Executive Committee of NTDA, 15 March, 1949, Minute Book 5, *ibid.*, MSS 420/31; Minutes Action Committee, 21 and 24 February, 1949, Minute Book 31, *ibid.*, MSS 420/14; see papers in *ibid.*, 420/332. Bing was in touch with Morrison urging the advantages of action, Bing to Morrison, 6 April, 1949, PRO CAB 124/888.

48 Minutes Executive Committee of NTDA, 15 March, 1949, Minute Book 5, Brewers' Society Papers, MSS 420/31; minutes of Reconstruction and Planning sub-Committee on New Towns, 9 January, 1951, minutes of Council, 14 February, 1951, 20 June, 1951, 18 July, 1951, Minute Book 33, *ibid.*, MSS 420/16; notes on Deputation from Brewers' Society and National Retail Liquor Trade organisations, 10 July, 1951, PRO HLG 90/21; note by

Home Office on recommendations from New Town committees on exclusions from state ownership, n.d. but June 1951, PRO HLG 90/22; see also papers in Brewers' Society Papers, MSS 420/323.

49 Memo on ministerial meeting at Home Office, 12 November, 1951, Cabinet Paper 4 December, 1951, PRO HLG 90/26; memo on repeal of provisions of Licensing Act 1949, PRO HLG 90/249; *Parliamentary Debates* (HC), 496, cols. 1151–272, (27 February, 1952); *ibid.*, 505, cols. 33–152 (14 October, 1952).

50 'There is no doubt that the Home Office resented very much the attack on Carlisle. It was that form of our attack that raised their hackles', Brewers' Society Papers, MSS 420/331.

51 For example, 'This is high handed! I feel I ought to enter a mild protest to the [Home Secretary] & say that if the chairmen [of the development corporations] object I shall feel bound to support them.', memo re MTCP conversation with Blake Odgers of Home Office, 27 April, 1949, PRO HLG 90/19.

52 Virginia Berridge, 'The Society for the Study of Addiction', *British Journal of Addiction*, 85 (special issue), (1990), pp. 114, 1031–4, 1044–7.

53 Thom, *Dealing with Drink*, pp. 23–5.

54 R. Elkington to J. C. H. Holden, 28 January, 1957, PRO MH 58/666.

55 A full account is given in Thom, *Dealing with Drink*, p. 28 *et seq.* upon which this draws.

56 Thom, *Dealing with Drink*, pp. 36–9.

57 *Ibid.*, pp. 26–7, 35–6.

58 *Ibid.*, pp. 33, 36–7; also Dr Rees-Thomas to Mr Scott of MH, 12 November, 1953, PRO MH 58/666.

59 Thom, *Dealing with Drink*, p. 34.

60 R. R.Coleman to Hon. Sec. of AA, 24 November, 1953, PRO MH 58/666.

61 Thom, *Dealing with Drink*, pp. 24–5, 32–3; Dr Rees-Thomas to Scott, 12 November, 1953, PRO MH 58/666.

62 D. Parr, 'Alcoholism in General Practice', *British Journal for Addiction*, 54 (1957), pp. 25–39.

63 Memo K. M. Potter, 22 May, 1956, MH to W. E. Wall, 6 June, 1956, PRO MH 58/666.

64 PRO MH 58/666; Thom, *Dealing with Drink*, pp. 41–3.

65 Ministry of Health, *On the State of the Public Health: Report of the Chief Medical Officer* (London: HMSO, 1957) also PRO MH/58/667.

66 Thom, *Dealing with Drink*, pp. 43–5.

67 Minute P. Brenner, 9 September, 1960, PRO MH 58/667, quoted Thom, *Dealing with Drink*, p. 45.

68 Note of Interdepartmental meeting, 14 November, 1960, PRO MH 58/667.

69 Emery to Dodds, 21 November, 1960; Dodds to Emery, 21 November, 1960 PRO MH58/677.

70 Thom, *Dealing with Drink*, p. 47. This was the first time responsibility for alcohol and drugs had been specifically assigned to a medical officer.

71 *Ibid.*, pp. 48–9.

72 Memo by P. Brenner on office meeting to consider paper on alcoholism policy, 22 June, 1961, PRO MH 58/668.

73 Memo HM (62) 43, Ministry of Health, *The Hospital Treatment of Alcoholism* (London, 1962); Thom, *Dealing with Drink*, p. 49.

74 Standing Mental Health Advisory Committee minutes, 18 October, 1961, memo by Dr R. K. Freudenberg, 23 November, 1961, Dr Stevenson to Dr Godber, 24 April, 1962, PRO MH 58/668.
75 Thom, *Dealing with Drink*, p. 59.
76 Dr Griffith Edwards interviewed, Thom, *Dealing with Drink*, pp. 59, 65.
77 Rob Baggott, *Alcohol, Politics and Social Policy* (Aldershot: Gower, 1990), pp. 10–11.
78 Thom, *Dealing with Drink*, p. 49.
79 Full account in letter from Dr Norman Imlah, quoted *ibid.*, pp. 51–6.
80 The Ministry conducted a survey in April 1963 of the progress on the matter, PRO BD 18/1606 and PRO MH 58/668.
81 Memo J. R. Brough, 21 December, 1960, PRO MH 58/667; the relationship of alcoholism to drunkenness was also opaque, M. A. Greenaway to Mr Collins, 5 August, 1960, minute by Collins, 9 August, 1960, PRO MH 58/667.
82 Briefing, 13 May, 1965 for parliamentary question, PRO MH 150/3.
83 P. Brenner to Rev. J. B. Harrison, 8 August, 1962, memo by J. R. Brough, 8 September, 1960, Dr Stevenson to Dr Godber, 24 April, 1962, PRO MH 58/668.
84 Minute G. M. Bebb, 14 May, 1965, PRO MH 150/3.
85 G. M. Bebb to E. Mayston, 27 July, 1965, PRO MH 150/3.
86 Thom, *Dealing with Drink*, pp. 78–83. Baggott is misleading when he describes the Council as simply the child of the temperance movement. The Council's literature took care to distance itself from the temperance position and, in 1965, the Bishop of Croydon resigned as Chairman on the grounds that his presence gave the impression that the Council was a temperance society linked to a denomination. Baggott, *Alcohol, Politics and Social Policy*, p. 9; minute C. Benwell to Mr Perry, 19 March, 1965, PRO MH 150/5.
87 Minutes NAC, Appointments Sub-Committee, 1 June, 1964, PRO MH 150/5.
88 Circular, 27 September, 1962 on NCA, PRO MH 150/5.
89 For example, pamphlet, *Your Alcoholism Information Centre* (London: NAC: 1963).
90 Memos from Chancellor of Duchy of Lancaster's office to Nodder, private secretary to Minister of Health, 1 June, 1965 and 25 November, 1965, PRO MH 150/3.
91 Thom, *Dealing with Drink*, pp. 74–8.
92 PRO MH 154/352.
93 C. Benwell to Perry, 20 October, 1965, R. A. Stein to Minister for Health, 23 February, 1966 and subsequent minutes, PRO MH 150/5.
94 Minute by G. M. Bebb, 14 May, 1965, Bebb to Mayston, 27 July, 1965, memo by Dr Phillipson, 12 August, 1965, Mayston to Dr Phillipson, 9 March, 1966, Benwell to Mayston, 21 April, 1966, PRO MH 150/3.
95 Baggott, *Alcohol, Politics and Social Policy*, pp. 12, 14.
96 J. P. Dodds to Emery, 21 November, 1960, PRO MH 58/667.
97 Memo by Miss Hedley, 4 January, 1966, PRO MH 150/4.
98 For example, memo., G. N. Bebb, 6 January, 1966, PRO MH 150/4.
99 Unsigned memo, 3 January, 1966, PRO MH 150/4.

100 Baggott, *Alcohol, Politics and Social Policy*, pp. 29–34.
101 *Ibid.*, p. 11.
102 *Ibid.*, p. 16.
103 Traffic Sub-Committee Report, 4 August, 1944, memo by Sir H. Alker Tripp, 31 January, 1945, memo by Whitelegge of Home Office, 14 February, 1945, minutes of Road Safety Committee 12–13 July 1945, PRO HO 45/19805 & 19820.
104 William Plowden, *The Motor Car and British Politics* (London: Bodley Head, 1971) p. 332.
105 Memo urging resistance to Mr Graham Page's Road Traffic Bill, 1955, PRO MT 92/36.
106 Plowden, *Motor Car*, pp. 332–3.
107 British Medical Association, *The Relationship of Alcohol to Road Accidents* (London: BMA, 1960).
108 For example, *Daily Express*, 19 April, 1956; *Daily Mirror*, 24 October, 1958; *Daily Telegraph* 24 October, 1958; *Parliamentary Debates* (HC), 591, cols. 24–5, (7 July, 1958); *ibid*. (HC), 599, wr. ans. cols. 149–52, (9 February, 1959); *ibid*. (HL), 217, cols. 178–82, (24 June, 1959); PRO MT 92/109; PRO MT 92/35. Ministers themselves were frustrated at the slow timescale of academic research and publication, PRO CAB 124/1687.
109 For example, article by the Chief Constable of Durham, *Manchester Guardian*, 6 January, 1959.
110 The findings of the Drew researches were not published until 1958, *British Medical Journal*, 25 October, 1958.
111 Lord Chesham, *Parliamentary Debates* (HL), 230, col. 346 (13 April, 1961).
112 Memo D. O'Neill, 27 March, 1956, PRO MT92/36.
113 Harold Watkinson, Minister of Transport, to Lord Hailsham, 27 July, 1959, PRO MT 92/35.
114 Memo D. O'Neill, 20 March, 1956, PRO MT 92/36; D. O'Neill to R. H. L. Cohen, 24 February, 1959, memos by O'Neill on answer to a p. q. from Dr Hastings MP, 6 and 20 February, 1959, PRO MT 92/109.
115 Cohen to O'Neill, 4 March, 1959 and 19 August, 1959, PRO MT 92/109.
116 *Parliamentary Debates* (HL), 217, cols. 178–82 (24 June, 1959); Hailsham to H. Watkinson, 25 June, 1959, PRO MT 92/35; Hailsham to E. Marples, 20 January, 1960, PRO CAB 124/1688.
117 Minute of meeting Home Office and MoT officials, 22 January, 1960, minute of meeting Home Office, MoT and Metropolitan Police, 8 February, 1960, draft paper MoT to Home Affairs Committee of Cabinet, 4 February, 1960, PRO MT 92/122.
118 Papers and reports are in PRO MT 92/122.
119 Minute by Road Safety Division of MoT on draft paper by Home Office, 16 February, 1960, PRO MT 92/122. Legalistic factors weighed heavily with the Home Office, particularly the idea that persons should be obliged to provide evidence of their own guilt.
120 Full papers are to be found in PRO MT 92/122. R. A. Butler, the Home Secretary, did not sit on this Committee but advocated an exceedingly cautious approach, memo by Butler n.d. but March 1959, Butler to Marples, 14 April, 1960, PRO MT 92/122.
121 10 and 11 Eliz. II, c.59.

122 A suspect motorist's refusal to submit to a chemical test was to be made known to the courts, which were to have due regard for it. As officials briefed Macmillan: 'in a sense this takes away some of the voluntary element in the test, but if something on these lines is not done the Government may well be strongly pressed to introduce compulsory testing, as the Scandinavians do.' Briefing for Prime Minister, 1 February, 1961, PRO PREM 11/4032.

123 *Parliamentary Debates* (HC), 654, col. 1384 (28 February, 1962).

124 *Parliamentary Debates* (HL), 230, cols. 339–518 (13 and 17 April, 1961). G. R. Strauss, *Parliamentary Debates* (HC), 654, col. 1377 (28 February, 1962).

125 Memo by Marples (GEN 718/6), 17 October, 1960, PRO MT 92/122.

126 *Safety First*, no. 332, March 1964. RoSPA had always been more cautious than the PA and relations between the two bodies were not always good.

127 J. R. Coates to Miss Hall, 20 March, 1964, PRO MT 92/285. For MoT influence on wording in *Safety First*, see PRO MT 92/284.

128 Memo on Law on Drink and Driving by Road Safety Division of MoT, reporting the Minister's personal position, 21 January, 1965, PRO HO 310/14; *This Week*, ITV 17 December, 1964.

129 *Daily Telegraph*, 4 January, 1964; minutes Working Party on Breath Testing Motorists, PRO HO 310/15 and PRO MEPO 2/10378.

130 MoT and Home Office joint advice on ministerial line to be taken on Graham Page's bill, 16 February, 1965, Home Affairs Committee of Cabinet, 19 February, 1965, note of a meeting between George Thomas and Graham Page, 24 February, 1965, PRO HO 310/14.

131 The range in the rest of Europe in those countries where limits had been introduced was between 30 and 150 mg.

132 Notes of meeting MoT officials and representatives of the motoring organisations, 20 December, 1965, PRO MT 92/947.

133 Interdepartmental Meeting between Home Office and MoT, 9 September, 1965, PRO HO 310/28 and PRO MT 92/347.

134 Final Report of Working Party on Breath Testing of Motorists, August 1965, PRO HO/310/11 and PRO MEPO 2/10378; cf. report that the police 'are likely to object very strongly' to random checks, K. A. L. Parker, Home Office, to J. S. Orme, MoT, 13 August, 1965, PRO MT 92/347.

135 Sir Thomas Padmore to Sir Charles Cunningham, 2 September, 1965, and Minutes Interdepartmental Meeting Home Office and MoT, 9 September, 1965, PRO HO 310/28 and PRO MT 92/347; minute by F. Graham-Harrison to Home Secretary, 5 October, 1965, PRO HO 310/26; 'I continue to be surprised at the line taken by the Home Office on random checks. The more I consider the position the more worried I am that random checks will be unacceptable', memo by Fraser, 4 October, 1965, PRO MT 92/347.

136 Memo, George Thomas, 10 August, 1965, PRO HO 310/25; note by private secretary of George Thomas's views, note of interdepartmental ministerial meeting, 6 October, 1965, PRO HO 310/26. Sir Frank Soskice, the Home Secretary, was also reported to be 'firmly convinced' of the need for random checks, minute L. E. Dale of MoT, 20 August, 1965, PRO MT 92/347.

137 Fraser 'said that his officials shared the Home Secretary's view, but he regarded the matter as a political one and thought that, although spot checks would be a considerable deterrent to drunken driving, it would be

very difficult to get such a provision through Parliament', note of interdepartmental ministerial meeting, 6 October, 1965, PRO HO 310/26.

138 Memo by George Thomas, 10 August, 1965, PRO HO 310/25; Douglas Houghton, Chancellor of Duchy of Lancaster to Harold Wilson, 14 October, 1965, PRO PREM 13/2149. He had to be satisfied with a White paper published before Christmas, *Road Safety Legislation, PP*, 1965–66 (Cmnd. 2859), XIII.

139 Transport issues in general had now become high profile. Harold Wilson insisted that drink/driving be discussed at the Cabinet, and had to be dissuaded from referring it as an ideal topic for some new parliamentary select committee system he was toying with introducing as a way of reforming Parliament, Douglas Houghton to Wilson, 14 October, 1965, PRO PREM 13/2149; minute of Cabinet meeting, 21 October, 1965 and memo. by W. W. Scott of minister's private office MoT, 21 October, 1965, PRO MT 92/347.

140 Note of interdepartmental meeting at the Home Office, 13 January, 1966, PRO MT 92/348.

141 Submission to Minister, R. S. Bell, 10 October, 1966, PRO MT 92/347.

142 Baggott, *Alcohol, Politics and Social Policy*, pp. 137–8.

143 *Parliamentary Debates* (HC), 735, col. 985 (7 November, 1966).

144 15 and 16 Eliz. II, c.30.

145 Barbara Castle, *Fighting all the Way* (London: Macmillan, 1993) pp. 375–7.

146 Barbara Castle, *The Castle Diaries 1964–70* (London: Weidenfeld & Nicolson, 1984) pp. 307, 371.

147 Interestingly, Graham Page had never seen it as crucial. Minutes of meeting with Pedestrians' Association, 12 November, 1965, PRO MT 92/352; *Parliamentary Debates* (HC), 724, cols. 736–9 (10 February, 1966).

148 Baggott, *Alcohol, Politics and Social Policy*, pp. 142–3. For papers on the enforcement problems, see PRO HO 310/119.

149 Richard Marsh had succeeded Barbara Castle as Minister of Transport in April 1968. Kaufman to Wilson, 4 September, 1968, Marsh to Wilson, 30 September, 1968, Callaghan to Marsh, 19 November, 1968, PRO PREM 13/2149.

150 Baggott, *Alcohol, Politics and Social Policy*, p. 133.

151 *Ibid.*, pp. 43–9.

152 Minutes Executive Committee of NTDA, Minute Book 1950–56, 1 November, 1951, Brewers' Society Papers, MSS 420/32.

153 *Ibid.*, MSS 420/296.

10 Epilogue: A brief sketch of the period after 1970

1 The body had close links with the Christian Economic and Social Research Centre.

2 Both directors of the Institute of Alcohol Studies, Derek Rutherford and Andrew McNeill, had links with the NCA.

3 A full analysis can be found in Rob Baggott, 'Alcohol, Politics and Social Policy', *Journal of Social Policy*, 1986, 15 (1986), pp. 467–88. See also pertinent remarks, Andrew Barr, *Drink: a Social History* (London: Pimlico, 1998) pp. 314–17.

4 Royal College of Psychiatrists, *Alcohol and Alcoholism* (London: Tavistock, 1979). The consumption model was enthusiastically endorsed by the WHO.
5 From the mid-1980s health ministers happened to be more sceptical about alcohol control policies, for example, Kenneth Clarke.
6 John Henderson and David Cohen, 'No strategy for Prevention', in A. Harrison and J. Gretton (eds), *Health Care UK* (London: Chartered Institute of Public Finance and Accountancy, 1984) p. 66.
7 Central Policy Review Staff, *Alcohol Policies in United Kingdom* (Stockholm: Sociologiska Institutionen Stockholm Universitet, 1982).
8 Rob Baggott, *Alcohol, Politics and Social Policy* (Aldershot: Gower, 1990) pp. 41–5.
9 David Robinson, 'The Erroll Report: Key Proposals and Public Reaction', *British Journal of Addiction*, 69 (1974), p. 101; Derek Rutherford in a Review of Thom's book posted on Alcohol and Temperance History Group website, http://listserv.muohio.edu/SCRIPTS/WA.EXE?A2=ind0206&L=athg&F=&S=&P=1
10 The three were the National Council on Alcoholism, the Federation of Alcoholic Residential Establishments and the Alcohol Education Centre. Baggott, 'Alcohol, Politics and Social Policy', *loc. cit.*, p. 485.
11 Betsy Thom, *Dealing with Drink: Alcohol and Social Policy: from Treatment to Prevention* (London: Free Association Books, 1999), pp. 198–202. See also interesting remarks in Derek Rutherford's Review of Thom's book posted on Alcohol and Temperance History Group website, *loc. cit.*
12 Baggott, *Alcohol, Politics and Social Policy*, pp. 74–94.
13 Barr, *Drink*, pp. 320–2.
14 The overall recommended weekly limit was thereby raised. The point was that some drinkers were binge drinking on one or two days of the week but remaining under the old safe limits, *Guardian*, 13 December, 1995; *Independent*, 13 December, 1995.
15 Brewers' Society Papers, MSS 420/296–8.
16 For example, Baggott, *Alcohol, Politics and Social Policy*; Alan Maynard and Philip Tether (eds), *Preventing Alcohol and Tobacco Problems*, vol. 1 (Aldershot: Avebury, 1990); Derek Rutherford, 'The Drinks Cabinet: UK Alcohol Policy', *Contemporary Record*, 5 (1991), pp. 450–67.
17 A good account is given in *Independent*, 18 July, 1989. See also *Independent*, 9 June, 1989, 11 July, 1989. On implementation see *Guardian*, 26 October, 1992. See also John Greenaway, 'The Drink Problem back on the Political Agenda', *Political Quarterly*, 61 (1990), pp. 87–8.
18 Baggott, *Alcohol, Politics and Social Policy*, pp. 114–32; Barr, *Drink*, pp. 144–6.
19 Liberalisation of Sunday hours followed in 1995, following complications over the general question of Sunday trading.
20 *Guardian*, 3 May, 2001.
21 Barr, *Drink*, p. 186.
22 Greenaway, 'Drink Problem', *loc. cit.*, 90.
23 *Guardian*, 14 December, 2002.
24 *Observer*, 2 February, 2003.
25 Rob Baggott, 'Licensing Law Reform and the Return of the Drink Question', *Parliamentary Affairs*, 40 (1987), p. 515.

26 The foremost parliamentary spokesman of the alcohol control lobby in the 1970s and 1980s was Sir Bernard Braine, an influential Conservative backbencher.

11 Drink, the Political Process and Policy-Making in Britain

1 Paul Smith has shown the limited way in which either major party in the 1870s could be said to have developed coherent social policies. Paul Smith, *Disraelian Conservatism and Social Reform* (London: Routledge & Kegan Paul, 1967).
2 M. Ostrogorski, *Democracy and the Organization of Political Parties* (London: Macmillan, 1902); A. V. Dicey, *Introduction to the Study of the Law of the Constitution*, 5th edn (London: Macmillan 1897).
3 J. Chamberlain, 'A New Political Organization', *Fortnightly Review*, New series 22 (1877), p. 133.
4 Samuel H. Beer, *Modern British Politics: a Study of Parties and Pressure Groups* (London: Faber & Faber, 1965) pp. 52–61.
5 Jon Lawrence, *Speaking for the People: Party, Language and Popular Politics in England, 1867–1914* (Cambridge University Press, 1998) esp. pp. 13–21, 164–83. H. V. Emy has also pointed to the importance of such quasi-organised groupings on social issues, H. V. Emy, *Liberals, Radicals and Social Politics, 1892–1914* (London: Cambridge University Press, 1973) pp. 45–53.
6 See analysis in David W. Gutzke, *Protecting the Pub: Brewers and Publicans Against Temperance* (Woodbridge: Boydell Press, 1989) pp. 225–6.
7 Lawson to Whyte, 26 November, 1889, UKA Minutes.
8 See analysis, D. A. Hamer, *The Politics of Electoral Pressure: a Study in the History of Victorian Agitations* (Hassocks: Harvester, 1977) chs 11–13.
9 F. W. Newman, *The Permissive Bill more Urgent than any Extension of the Franchise* (Manchester: UKA, 1865) p. 11.
10 *Alliance News*, 11 June, 1864, p. 189.
11 UKA, *Annual Report*, 1859, p. 2.
12 Paul McHugh, *Prostitution and Victorian Social Reform* (London: Croom Helm, 1980) p. 240.
13 *The Times*, 22 October, 1879, p. 10.
14 *Alliance News*, 16 February, 1884, p. 99.
15 Lawson to James Whyte, 28 July, 1900, UKA Minutes.
16 Lawson to Canon Hicks, 30 April, 1906, quoted J.H. Fowler, *The Life and Letters of Edward Lee Hicks, Bishop of Lincoln 1910–1919* (London: Christophers, 1922) p. 197; Lawson to Whyte, 3 January, 1901, UKA Minutes.
17 David Dixon, *From Prohibition to Regulation: Bookmaking, Anti-Gambling and the Law* (Oxford University Press, 1991) p. 6.
18 Edward Bristol, 'The Liberty and Property Defence League and Individualism', *Historical Journal*, 18, (1975), pp. 761–89.
19 Brian Harrison, *Drink and the Victorians: The Temperance Question in England 1815–1872* (London: Faber & Faber, 1971) pp. 387–405.

20 W. H. Greenleaf, *The British Political Tradition*, 3 vols (London: Routledge, 1983, 1987).
21 G. R. Searle, *Morality and the Market in Victorian Britain* (Oxford University Press, 1998) esp. pp. 240–52.
22 Maurice Cowling, *1867: Disraeli, Gladstone and Revolution* (Cambridge University Press, 1967), p. 340.
23 Andrew Jones, *The Politics of Reform, 1884* (Cambridge University Press, 1972), p. 11.
24 A. B. Cooke and John Vincent, *The Governing Passion: Cabinet Government and Party Politics in Britain 1885–86* (Brighton: Harvester, 1974) pp. 21–2.
25 Maurice Cowling, *The Impact of Labour 1920–1924. The Beginnings of Modern British Politics* (Cambridge University Press, 1971) pp. 6–7.
26 L. V. Harcourt (Harcourt's son and secretary) to Chamberlain, 15 April, 1893, John Wilson (Chamberlain's secretary) to Harcourt, 17 April, 1893, J. Chamberlain Papers, JC5/38/99, 212.
27 This is true even of such a cynical manoeuvrer as Lord Randolph Churchill, whose papers reveal him to have spent a good deal of time and effort to investigating the issue, Lord Randolph Churchill Papers, 1/26.
28 Chamberlain, however, remained a consistent supporter of municipal or disinterested control, for example, in 1894 going on a platform to support the Bishop of Chester's approach.
29 Oliver MacDonagh, *A Pattern of Government Growth 1800–1860: the Passenger Acts and their Enforcement* (London: MacGibbon & Kee, 1961); Oliver MacDonagh, *Early Victorian Government 1830–1870* (London: Weidenfeld & Nicolson, 1977).
30 Dixon, *From Prohibition to Regulation*, esp. ch. 6.
31 Jill Pellow, *The Home Office 1848–1914: from Clerks to Bureaucrats* (London: Heinemann, 1982); R. Davidson and R. Lowe, 'Bureaucracy and Innovation in British Welfare Policy 1870–1945', in W. J. Mommsen (ed.), *The Emergence of the Welfare State in Britain and Germany* (London: Croom Helm, 1981) pp. 263–95.
32 Viscount Gladstone Papers, Add. MSS, 46092, ff. 1–2.
33 Arthur Marwick used the wartime liquor restrictions as an example of his thesis that the First World War had brought about a major social change in Britain. However, this claim ignores the evidence of declining consumption before 1914, as well as the fact that the proactive restrictionist approach ended with the demise of the CCB, Arthur Marwick, *The Deluge: British Society and the First World War* (London: Bodley Head, 1965) p. 68.
34 Keith Middlemas, *Politics in Industrial Society: the Experience of the British System since 1911* (London: Deutsch, 1979).
35 Brewers' Society Papers, MSS 420/296.
36 J. J. Richardson and A. G. Jordan, *Governing under Pressure: the Policy Process in a Post-Parliamentary Democracy* (Oxford: Martin Robertson, 1979).
37 James S. Roberts, *Drink, Temperance and the Working Class in Nineteenth-Century Germany* (London: Allen & Unwin, 1994) pp. 128–32.
38 Steve Olson and Dean Gerstein, *Alcohol in America: taking Action to Prevent Abuse* (Washington, DC: National Academy Press, 1985), pp. 8–11; Joseph R. Gusfield, *Symbolic Crusade. Status Politics and the American Temperance Movement* (Urbana: University of Illinois Press, 1972). Interest in a public

health perspective aimed at discouraging consumption in general has emerged in more recent years.

39 David M. Fahey, 'The Politics of Drink in Britain: Anglo-American Perspectives', *Proceedings of the Ohio Academy of History* (Ohio, 2000) pp. 2–4.

40 Matthew Hilton, *Smoking in British Popular Culture 1800–2000: Perfect Pleasures* (Manchester University Press, 2000).

41 Dixon, *From Prohibition to Regulation.*

42 Judith R. Walkowitz, *Prostitution and Victorian Society: Women, Class and the State* (Cambridge University Press,1980); McHugh, *Prostitution and Victorian Social Reform*; Paula Bartley, *Prostitution: Prevention and Reform in England 1860–1914* (London: Routledge, 2000).

43 Virginia Berridge, *Opium and the People: Opiate Use and Drug Control Policy in Nineteenth and Early Twentieth Century England* (London: Free Association, 1999).

44 *Ibid.*, p.xxix.

45 John Greenaway, Steve Smith and John Street, *Deciding Factors in British Politics: a Case-studies Approach* (London: Routledge, 1992) pp. 15–21; Martin Burch and Bruce Wood, *Public Policy in Britain* (Oxford: Martin Robertson, 1983), pp. 21–5.

46 H. Simon, *Administrative Behaviour*, 2nd edn (New York: Free Press, 1958).

47 Noel Buxton and Walter Hoare, 'Temperance Reform' in C. F. G. Masterman (ed.), *The Heart of the Empire*, [1st publ. 1901] Bentley B. Gilbert (ed.) (Brighton: Harvester Press, 1973), p. 171.

48 James Kneale, 'The Place of Drink: Temperance and the Public, 1856–1914', *Social and Cultural Geography*, 2, no.1 (2001), pp. 47–8.

49 For example, first William Hoyle, and then the Rev. Dawson Burns published an annual account of the Nation's 'Drink Bill' in *The Times*. Later in the twentieth century the tradition was maintained by G. B. Wilson, *Alcohol and the Nation* (London: Nicholson & Watson, 1940) and G. P. Williams and G. T. Brake, *Drink in Britain 1900 to 1979* (London: Edsall, 1980).

50 *First Report of the Select Committee of the House of Lords on Intemperance* evidence qs. 2356–62, *PP*, 1877 (171), XI, quoted Martin J.Wiener, *Reconstructing the Criminal: Culture, Law, and Policy in England, 1830–1914* (Cambridge University Press, 1990) p. 298, see also p. 155.

51 Joanne Woiak, '"A Medical Cromwell"', *Histoire Sociale/Social History*, 27 (1994), p. 364.

52 Brewers' Society Papers, MSS 420/297.

53 D. Braybrooke and C. Lindblom, *A Strategy of Decision* (New York: Free Press, 1963); C. Lindblom, 'The Science of Muddling Through', *Public Administration Review*, 19, (1959), pp. 79–88; Greenaway, Smith and Street, *Deciding Factors*, pp. 24–9; Burch and Wood, *Public Policy*, pp. 25–31.

54 Graham T. Allison, *Essence of a Decision: Explaining the Cuban Missile Crisis* (Boston: Little, Brown, 1971). Allison originally produced two separate models, organisational process and bureaucratic politics models, but later merged the two.

55 Peter John, *Analysing Public Policy* (London: Pinter 1998) p. 45.

56 B. Jenkins and A. Gray, 'Bureaucratic Politics and Power: Developments in the Study of Bureaucracy', *Political Studies*, 31, (1983), pp. 177–93.

57 P. A. Hall, 'The Movement from Keynesianism to Monetarism: Institutional Analysis and British Economic Policy', in S. Steinmo, S. K. Thelen and F. Longstreth (eds), *Structuring Politics* (Cambridge University Press, 1992).
58 Giandomenico Majone, *Evidence, Argument and Persuasion in the Policy Process* (New Haven: Yale University Press, 1989) p. 2.
59 Hugh Heclo, *Modern Social Politics in Britain and Sweden: from Relief to Income Maintenance* (New Haven: Yale University Press, 1974).
60 H. C. Jenkins-Smith and P. Sabatier, 'Evaluating the Advocacy Coalition Framework', *Journal of Public Policy*, 14 (1994), pp. 175–203.
61 P. A. Hall, 'Policy Paradigms, Social Learning, and the State: the Case of Economic Policymaking in Britain', *Comparative Politics*, 25 (1993), pp. 275–96.
62 For fuller analysis of the applicability of Hall and Sabatier's models see John Greenaway, 'Policy Learning and the Drink Question in Britain, 1850–1950', *Political Studies*, 46 (1998), pp. 903–18.
63 John, *Analysing Public Policy*, p. 172.
64 John W. Kingdon, *Agendas, Alternatives, and Public Policies*, 2nd edn (New York: Longman, 1995).
65 *Ibid.*, p. 194.
66 Frank R. Baumgartner and Bryan D. Jones, *Agendas and Instability in American Politics* (Chicago: University of Chicago Press, 1993).
67 *Ibid.*, p. 16.
68 Steven Lukes, *Power: a Radical View* (London: Macmillan, 1974).

Bibliography and Location of Unpublished Sources

Viscount Astor Papers, Reading University Library, Reading.
Arthur Balfour Papers, British Library.
Andrew Bonar Law Papers, House of Lords Record Office.
Lord Brabourne Papers, Kent County Record Office.
Brewers' Society Papers, Modern Records Centre, University of Warwick Library, Coventry.
John Bright Papers, British Library.
John Burns Papers, British Library.
Sir Henry Campbell-Bannerman Papers, British Library.
Cairns Papers, Public Record Office, Kew.
Joseph Chamberlain Papers, University of Birmingham Library, Birmingham.
CETS Papers, Lambeth Palace Library.
Randolph Churchill Papers, Churchill College, Cambridge.
Joseph Cowen Papers, Newcastle Central Library.
Randall Davidson Papers, Lambeth Palace Library.
Viscount Davidson Papers, House of Lords Record Office.
Viscount Gladstone Papers, British Library .
W. E. Gladstone Papers, British Library.
Hambleden (W. H. Smith) Papers, W. H. Smith & sons, Swindon.
Sir Edward Hamilton Papers, British Library.
Sir William Harcourt Papers, Bodleian Library, Oxford.
David Lloyd George Papers, House of Lords Record Office.
Liberal Party Election Addresses, National Liberal Club, London.
Methodist Church Archives, John Rylands Library, University of Manchester.
Viscount Milner Papers, Public Record Office, Kew, London.
Sir Frederic Osborn Papers, Welwyn Garden City Central Library.
Public Record Office, classes: BD, CAB, HLG, HO, MAF, MEPO, MH, MT, PREM, PO, Kew, London.
William Rathbone Papers, University of Liverpool Library, Liverpool.
Joseph Rowntree Papers, The Joseph Rowntree Foundation, York.
Seebohm Rowntree Papers, The Joseph Rowntree Foundation, York.
Seebohm Rowntree Papers, The Borthwick Institute, York.
Third Marquess of Salisbury Papers, Hatfield House, Hatfield, Herts.
UKA Minute Books and Papers, Alliance House, London.

Index